Studies in Philosophy

and the

History of Philosophy

Founded in 1960 by John K. Ryan

/ 2, 95~

Studies in Philosophy and the History of Philosophy

Volume 5

ANCIENTS AND MODERNS

Edited by

John K. Ryan

THE CATHOLIC UNIVERSITY OF AMERICA PRESS

Washington, D. C.

1970

TABLE OF CONTENTS

A GLOSS ON *REPUBLIC* 487 C

by

GREGORY DESJARDINS

In the *Republic* Adeimantus complains that dialetic is just another game of πεττεία, with λόγοι instead of pebbles. This image epitomizes rather than depreciates dialectic, since it serves to summarize and clarify the place of definition in dialectical method. For πεττεία proceeds, like dialectic, through reciprocal moves to exhibit the ὅροι of a field.

Aristotle says that Socrates first fixed thought on definitions (*Metaphysics* 987ᵇ3) for he inquired into what is (τί ἔστι), and in this way he was trying to syllogize because the starting-point of syllogisms is what is (1078ᵇ24-29). A statement (λόγος) of what[1] a thing is is often, at Socrates' request, the starting-point in a Platonic dialogue, for the speakers often formulate and examine definitions (ὅροι). Yet many of these dialogues appear to be inconclusive just because the opening statement was wrong either as a whole or in part. Euthyphro, for example, commits both errors since he first identifies piety with what the gods love and then, after Socrates suggests that piety should rather fall under justice, and not pleasure, Euthyphro runs awry at a subordinate division by mixing sacrifice with pleasure. The syllogism, on the other hand, cannot demonstrate unless its premises are true;[2] the first demonstrations of a science must begin with definitions[3] and science advances through new syllogisms (*Posterior Analytics* 78ª13). But the method of division cannot demonstrate being and what is (*Prior Analytics* 46ª37) or

---

[1] Cf., e.g., *Euthyphro* 5 D7, *Charmides* 159 A10, *Laches* 185 B6, *Protagoras* 311 D6 & 312 C4, *Meno* 71 B4, *Theaetetus* 145 E9 & 146 C3, *Philebus* 13 E5, etc.

[2] *Post. An.* i.2.

[3] *Ibid.* ii.3.

indeed demonstrate at all[4] inasmuch as it must rather beg the definition (46ᵇ5) when trying, for example, to establish that man is mortal by premissing that animal is mortal or immortal and that man is animal. Division, then, is at best a feeble syllogism (46ᵃ33), for the major should include the middle term and not conversely, but animal includes man.[5] And Aristotle found the method to be useless in natural science, since it yields unnatural divisions.[6]

To the contrary, Plato thought that dialectic, unlike other methods, does not "butcher" things (*Phaedrus* 265 E3) but divides by forms (κατ' εἴδη) at the natural joints, and only dialectic can define what each thing is (*Republic* 532 A6-7, 533 B2-3). Moreover, with Platonic definitions, demonstration is unnecessary since, as Speusippus said, "it is impossible for anyone to define any of the things that are unless he knows all the things that are."[7]

I

With the comment that the method is easier to describe than to use, Socrates explains the origin of dialectic in the *Philebus* (16); it was given by the gods to men, and has come down by way of this saying:

> All things that are ever said to be consist of a one and a many, and have in their nature a conjunction of limit and unlimitedness. This being the ordering of things we ought, whatever we are dealing with, to assume a single idea and search for it, for we shall find it there contained; then, if we have laid hold of that, we must go on from one to look for two, if the case admits of two, otherwise for three or some other number. And we must do the same again with each of the ones thus reached, until we come to see not merely that the one that we started with is a one and an unlimited many, but also just how many it is. But we are not to apply the character of un-

[4] *Ibid.* ii.5 & 13.

[5] *Pr. An.* i.31.

[6] *Parts of Animals* i.2-3.

[7] P. Lang, *De Speusippi Academici Scriptis* (Frankfurt, 1964), Fr. 31b. Compare *Post. An.* ii.13.97a6ff: "To define and divide one need not know the whole of existence. Yet some hold it impossible to know the differentiae distinguishing each thing from every single other thing without knowing every single other thing; and one cannot, they say, know each thing without knowing its differentiae, since everything is identical with that from which it does not differ, and other than that from which it differs."

limitedness to our plurality until we have discerned the total number of ideas the thing in question has intermediate between its one and its unlimited number. It is only then, when we have done that, that we may let each one of all these intermediates pass away into the unlimited and cease bothering about them.

Socrates observes finally that to go too quickly or too slowly from many to one or one to many is to lose the track of the intermediaries, and yet "it is the recognition of those intermediaries that makes all the difference between dialectical and eristic discussion."

According to the Seventh Letter (342), dialectic uses words, statements, and images (εἴδωλα, examples, things) to achieve knowledge of the things that are. That is, dialectic is the most complete method since it utilizes the whole all at once—and not only words or only things—in the pursuit of knowledge, because examples, words, and statements exhaust the full resources of discourse. Further, because dialectic employs the whole, it is able, as other methods are not, to improve as a whole; for dialectic serves simultaneously to clarify terms, to instruct, and to discover truths about things.

Plato shows what dialectic is by dividing it off from other methods with which it may be confused; it is especially because it proceeds κατ᾿ εἴδη that dialectic is to be differentiated from the others, for forms are surely not to be found only in words and statements or in images and things. (1) By the abuse of statement, eristic neglects things and therefore follows words[8] rather than truth.[9] When, as in the *Euthydemus*, contentious speakers ignore qualifications, they are missing the intermediates, because qualifications mark parts in the whole; but division is by forms instead of words, and an interlocutor is praised if he can supply a name once a division has been found (*Theaetetus* 147) for sometimes, indeed, there is a shortage of names (*Sophist* 267 D). Other positions are even more dogmatic than eristic because they neglect discourse altogether;

---

8 *Republic* 454 A4-9: ". . . many fall into it even unwillingly and suppose they are not quarreling (ἐρίζειν) but discussing (διαλέγεσθαι), because they are unable to consider what's said by separating it out into its forms. They pursue contradiction in the mere name of what's spoken about, using eristic, not dialectic, with one another."

9 *Republic* 499 A4-9: "Nor, you blessed man, have they given an adequate hearing to fair and free speeches of the sort that strain with every nerve in quest of the truth for the sake of knowing and that 'nod a distant greeting' to the subtleties and contentious quibbles (ἐριστικά) that strain toward nothing but opinion and contention (ἔρις) in trials as well as in private groups."

they are what today might be called idealist and materialist, and they battle as gods and giants (*Sophist* 246). (2) On one hand, there are the "friends of forms" who cannot account for concreteness and change; so Aristotle accused Plato in *Metaphysics* i.9 and xiii.4-5. (3) And on the other, there are those who break up what is into small parts, saying that there is only body.[10] None of these partial methods defines natural parts, and so inevitably they "mix everything together" (*Phaedo* 101 E5).

The dialogues themselves often begin with a name or word[11] or an example[12] or both (e.g. *Republic*), and Socrates asks what this thing is. Sometimes a speaker will rejoin with examples instead of a statement or formula (λόγος) and in that case he is induced to collect the examples into a whole. For example, Euthyphro receives explicit instruction on how to offer a trial λόγος (5 D), just as in many places throughout the dialogues speakers are asked to gather the point of an analogy into a statement (*ibid.* 10 B-C). Sometimes, again, a statement offered as a definition will be immediately countered with an example to show that the λόγος is too narrow or too wide, that it collects an improper whole. Socrates presents Cephalus with the counter example of returning a weapon to a man gone berserk, and concludes (331 D2) "Then this is not the ὅρος of justice, to tell the truth and give back what one has received."

The initial statement sets up one whole to be resolved into many parts; that is to say, the statement is tested by dividing down to see what it contains and especially to see whether it contains the thing in question. The division interprets the statement, for a λόγος

---

10 But a μέρος need not be an εἶδος, cf. *Statesman* 263 A-B.

11 *Sophist* 218 B-C: "What now concerns us both is our joint inquiry. We had better, I think, begin by studying the sophist and try to bring his nature to light in a clear formula. At present, you see, all that you and I possess in common is the name. The thing to which each of us gives that name we may perhaps have privately before our minds, but it is always desirable to have reached an agreement about the thing itself by means of explicit statements, rather than be content to use the same word without formulating what it means."

12 Socrates tells Polus, "No one is asking what kind of art (ποία τις τέχνη) Gorgias has, but what (τίς) it is and what we should call Gorgias" (448 E6-7); when Socrates finally works out a rough statement of what rhetoric is from Gorgias' admissions, Gorgias replies that Socrates has defined (ὁρίζεσθαι, 453 A7) it sufficiently well.

is itself composed of "unstable" words [13] that purport to express a judgment on the part of one who might know, but only when that judgment is fully expressed can its truth be determined. Socrates therefore tries to understand the statement (cf. *Republic* 338 C) or at least wants to learn what its proposer has in mind (*Gorgias* 453 C, 454 C). Sometimes the speaker admittedly has nothing in mind and his statement is hearsay (*Charmides* 161 B), but words attached to no speaker cannot discourse (*Phaedrus* 275). The youngest is often selected because he is least pretentious and most likely to speak his mind (*Parmenides* 137 B). Sometimes division exposes parts such that the speaker could have had nothing in mind, and the man may come rather to know his own ignorance. Euthyphro did not know at the first whether his statement was in fact a definition of the thing in question, and he is led to reject his statement once the division has laid open its parts. No dialogue is for that reason a failure, for the way of division is to separate what is not the thing from what it is, and so when a λόγος is rejected the man has learned at least what the thing is not. Positively, this provides a lesson concerning the λόγος that is the ὅρος, namely, that one must have the proper whole and know its many parts; and since fully to know a part as a part one should be able to say what wholes include it, and since every whole short of an all-inclusive whole is part of that whole, therefore to have the proper whole is evidently possible only to one who knows this whole as a part of the whole that is not also a part, namely, everything.

The dialectical moments of collecting the many into one and dividing a whole into parts are termed συναγωγή and διαίρεσις, respectively; they are described by Socrates in the *Phaedrus*. Collection, literally translated, is "things in many ways separated to lead to be seen together in one idea so that one defining (ὁριζόμενος) makes clear each thing about which he wants to explain" (265 D3-5). Division is the "reverse" of this: "to be able to cut again by forms, by the joints, as it is by nature, and not to try to break any part, dealing in the way of a bad butcher" (265 E1-3). In order to collect many things under one idea one must see how they are the same; analogous examples often serve the purpose of leading one to perceive the similarity involved, though usually with the caution that he should admit only so much as he thinks (e.g. *Gorgias* 453). This

---

13 Cf. Seventh Letter 343 B.

collection may be required at any stage, not only at the beginning of an inquiry, but at stages both higher and lower, more or less inclusive, than the initial stage as well. So, for example, Socrates draws an analogy with the arts to determine what Euthyphro meant by care of the gods (13), and in the *Sophist* (222 C) two groups are collected to make a distinction between persuasion and violence. Διαίρεσις or division, on the other hand, relies on differences. Examples may be presented in helping another to discern the primary difference to be divided, for instance, when Gorgias is brought to distinguish knowledge from belief (454). These ways of treating kinds according to whole and part, same and different, many and one, are said to be characteristic of the dialectician, when he is accidentally discovered in the *Sophist:*

> Dividing by kinds, not taking the same form for a different one, or a different one for the same—is not that the business of the science of dialectic? And the man who can do that discerns clearly one form everywhere extended throughout many, where each one lies apart, and many forms, different from one another, embraced from without by one form, and again one form connected in a unity through many wholes, and many forms, entirely marked off apart. That means knowing how to distinguish, kind by kind, in what ways the several kinds can or cannot combine. (253 D)

In the *Republic,* Socrates mentions two unique abilities of the διαλεκτικός; he is "the one who grasps the account (λόγος) of the being (οὐσία) of each thing" (534 B3) and he alone is συνοπτικός (537 C7). If the synoptic view is necessary in order to define any thing properly, then to define something is to relate it to and to distinguish it within the whole of things. Similarly, if definition of a thing is seeing it together with all things, one cannot define anything until he can define everything. Dialectical ascent from the Cave or up the Divided Line is inseparable from the ability to define, since by going up one can see more; the higher one is, the broader is the field in view. And one who contemplates the whole in σύνοψις will be highest. If it is true that definition is collecting the thing as part of a whole and then that the best definition is to collect as a part of the widest whole, definition is ideally the marking out of a thing as part of the whole of things. There is no knowledge apart from the good, the goal of dialectic (τέλος, *Republic* 506 D3), which means at least that no knowledge of a thing, nor any definition, can be apart from knowledge of the whole because the good (although, or perhaps because, it is beyond οὐσία) is the first principle or highest point of what is. Definition is just the widest application of dialetical method, or διαίρεσις of the last συναγωγή, locating any one within every many taken as one.[14]

II

Definition is therefore a *sur-vey* in both senses of marking out the field and of grasping the field as a whole. Plato's use of ὅρος so ranges over sensible and intellectual vision that we can find an analogy between the view of the bodily eye and of the mind's eye. In other words, Plato exploits the spatial sense of ὅρος in behalf of the intellectual survey of the field of forms.

Originally ὅρος was the stone or pillar placed to mark a border or boundary, and then came to stand for the boundary itself. Of the forty-odd occurrences of the term in the dialogues, only in six places is ὅρος used in this sense: *Timaeus* 25 C5, *Critias* 110 D6, *Laws* 778 E5, 843 C7, 849 E5, 855 A2. With Plato, the term's application tends to spread. Timaeus uses it twice in explaining the plan for construction of the human body, first when he refers to the neck as an isthmus and rough boundary between the mortal and immortal parts of the soul (69 E1) and then in reference to the navel as an upper bound of the lowest part of the soul (70 E2).

---

[14] J. S. Mill, *On Bentham and Coleridge* (New York, 1962), pp. 56-57. "Bentham's method of laying out his subject is admirable as a preservative against one kind of narrow and partial views. He begins by placing before himself the whole of the field of inquiry to which the particular question belongs, and divides down until he arrives at the thing he is in search of; and thus by successively rejecting all which is *not* the thing, he gradually works out a definition of what it *is*. This, which he calls the exhaustive method, is as old as philosophy itself. Plato owes everything to it, and does everything by it; and the use made of it by that great man in his Dialogues, Bacon, in one of those pregnant logical hints scattered through his writings, and so much neglected by most of his pretended followers, pronounces to be the nearest approach to a true inductive method in the ancient philosophy. Bentham was probably not aware that Plato had anticipated him in the process to which he too declared that he owed everything. By the practice of it, his speculations are rendered eminently systematic and consistent; no question, with him, is ever an insulated one; he sees every subject in connexion with all the other subjects with which in his view it is related, and from which it requires to be distinguished. . . ."

Ὅρος is used of other than spatial limits; in the *Laws*, legislators must decide time limits for disputing property titles (954 C3), age limits for marriage and public service (785 B2), upper and lower bounds for personal wealth (744 D7), limits on the proper form of public ritual (772 B4). In the *Philebus,* Socrates refers to the boundaries of musical intervals, which produce musical scales (17 D1). In the *Republic* (373 D10) necessary wants set themselves a natural limit.

As a ὅρος is the limit of a thing, so any limit of a thing may be a ὅρος. That is, anything which serves to delimit another thing can be said to be its limit; and so the ὅρος can be a mark or criterion, even a test, to distinguish or mark off that thing from other things. Speaking in behalf of the earth-born giants, the Eleatic stranger proposes δύναμις as the ὅρος of the things that are (247 E3, 248 C4). The Athenian stranger disputes Clinias' ὅρος of a well-constituted city, that it be so equipped as to be victorious over its rivals in warfare (626 B7), for as he later attempts to show, victory in the field is a dubious ὅρος for the praiseworthiness of a practice (638 A5). The *Sophist* opens with Socrates' question to the stranger whether people in Elea think the terms sophist, statesman, and philosopher apply to the same or different things; the *Sophist* and *Statesman* are hunts for definitions. The dividing by forms in these dialogues is presented as a search upon a large field. Of several occurrences of ὅρος in them, the most striking is at *Sophist* 231 A9. Theaetetus said that the stranger's description of the purifier of souls has some resemblance to the sophist. The stranger replied, "so has the dog to the wolf—the fiercest of animals to the tamest. But a cautious man should above all be on his guard against resemblances; they are a very slippery sort of thing. However, be it so, for should they ever set up an adequate defense of their confines, the boundary in dispute will be of no small importance."

The dialogues are boundary disputes over terms, for they aim to define (ὁρίζειν, διορίζειν) terms by dividing them off from, and by means of, other terms. The slippery resemblances of which the stranger spoke play a critical role in such a hunt, for as sameness and likenesses lead to collection, so differences and unlikeness require divisions. That is why the dialogues criticize analogies as well as use them. "As if this were like that," says Thrasymachus (337 C2). "Perhaps," Socrates says, "it is somehow unlike what I am comparing it to" (*Phaedo* 99 E6). "I somehow think that this is no longer like these others" (*Meno* 73 A4). Critias complains, "This kind of knowledge is not like these others, nor are they like each other. But you proceed as if they were alike" (*Charmides* 165 E4); and later (166 B) when Socrates has offered another analogy, "That is what I was saying, Socrates. Your inquiry has now arrived at the very point in which temperance differs from all the kinds of knowledge; but you are looking for some likeness between it and the others." Socrates objects, "You have taken up an unlike thing with the same λόγος" (*Republic* 408 D7). "I am like the electric ray if it benumbs others because it is numb itself; but otherwise not" (*Meno* 80 C6-7).

Similarity and difference among terms help to clarify and interpret those and other terms once some proportion is introduced by way of the host of dialectical distinctions (knowledge/opinion, being/becoming, action/passion, internal/external, mind/body, good/pleasing, city/individual, ruler/ruled, etc.)—distinctions which can produce a dialectical "net" (*Theaetetus* 165 E, *Sophist* 235 B) to order whatever terms are involved and to define each of them by means of the others. For a term is defined by telling where it lies in the field of terms, that is, it is defined only in relation to other terms. Because the field is made from distinctions, the definition reads like a proportion; for example, rhetoric is a form of flattery, or rhetoric is to cookery as justice is to medicine.[15] The "net" of analogies may be exhibited in matrices, as ordered arrays of elements in two, and sometimes three, dimensions. These matrices serve to spatialize the relations of terms determined in dialogue, and in this way they are images of the field of forms just as each term occurring in discourse is an image of form. (Indeed, possibly the forms would not be thought to constitute a "field" but for such spacing of *termini*.) Or they can be used, as they are in mathematics, to solve problems, such as the degree of the tyrant's misery in the *Republic*. Unlike mathematics, however, the whole cannot be constructed or described independently of its parts; Plato's matrices cannot be vacant spaces waiting to be filled since what the matrix is depends on how which terms come to be compared in discourse. Finally, not

---

[15] Aristotle tends rather to contrast definition (he uses both ὅρος and ὁρισμός) and analogy or proportion (ἀναλογία); cf. especially 1048a37 and 1016b34. On the protracted war between logic and dialectic, see R. P. McKeon, "Dialectic and Political Thought and Action," *Ethics*, 65 (1954), 1-33.

least important is the use of verbal matrices to give a rational account, a ratio, of irrational or incommensurable parts. This is doubtless the function of his best known matrix, the Divided Line,[16] where as Brumbaugh says, "the incommensurables, instead of presenting a problem, have been added to produce a rational result; with the theory of ideas in the background, the dissimilarity of knowledge and opinion (symbolized as an incommensurability) is presented in a context which recognizes the possibility of presenting their exact relation in an analogical statement. The problem arises when the attempt is made to find some element or unit which can serve as the least common measure."[17]

III

According to the story of the old Egyptian god Theuth, which is retold in *Phaedrus* 274 D, the same person who invented arithmetic and calculation (λογισμός), geometry and astronomy, also invented πεττεία and κυβεία or dice, and γράμματα. Theuth is mentioned again at *Philebus* 18 Bff, where Socrates describes his application of method to the discovery of letters.[18] Plato occasionally compares πεττεία with arithmetic, geometry, and calculation.[19] Against Gorgias' claim that only the art of rhetoric has to do with words (λόγοι), Socrates says (450 D) "But there are other arts that secure their result entirely through speech (διὰ λόγου) and have practically no need, or very little need, of action—arithmetic, for instance, and calculation (λογιστική) and geometry and πεττευτική and many other arts, some of which involve almost as many words as actions, and many of them far more, their whole achievement and effect in general being due to speech." In the seventh book of the *Laws* the Athenian stranger maintains that all people should, like the children in Egypt, be taught mathematics along with

---

[16] Cf. Euclid VI.30 and II.11 on division according to mean and extreme ratio.

[17] *Plato's Mathematical Imagination* (Bloomington, 1954), p. 271.

[18] Cf. the recurrent analogy of γράμματα and εἴδη: *Cratylus* 393 D, *Republic* 402 A-C, *Theaetetus* 206 A-B, *Sophist* 253 A-C, *Statesman* 278 A-C.

[19] On the differences among these, and Plato's opinion of them, see R. S. Brumbaugh, *The Role of Mathematics in Plato's Dialectic* (Chicago, 1942) and *Plato's Mathematical Imagination* (Bloomington, 1954), as well as Jacob Klein, *Greek Mathematical Thought and the Origin of Algebra* (Cambridge, Mass., 1968), Pt. I.

their letters and become sensitive to problems of commensurability and incommensurability; for, as he says, "a man must be able to distinguish them on examination, or else must be a very poor creature. We should often propound such problems to each other— a much more elegant pastime for the elderly than πεττεία—and give our passion for victory an outlet in amusement worthy of us" (820 C). But Clinias replies that there is none the less not much difference between these studies and the game of πεττεία. Considerable skill and practice are necessary to becoming expert in πεττεία (Republic 374 C5) and only a few become really good (Statesman 292 E7).

It is true that we do not know very much about πεττεία,[20] but it is also true, and indeed decisive, that most of what we know reinforces the analogy between it and dialectic. For example, the playing pebbles were also called ὅροι and the playing board could be called a field (χώρα), although more often the spaces on the board were called χῶραι.[21] Of course, the analogy does not turn simply on these names, and yet it is surely the more apt because of them. More vital to the analogy are the facts that the game is completed by reciprocal moves which affect the position of ὅροι on the field and that the final result depends entirely on what each player contributes. There is also the obvious priority of the rules of the game to any of the game's results, to which we may compare the stranger's advice in the Statesman that "we must prize first and foremost the μέθοδος itself of dividing by forms what can be" (286 D8-9), that is, we should value the way before any λόγος that stands or falls by the way.

A field theory of definition seems to be a natural consequence of the position that, pace Aristotle, no signs are univocal, but that instead meaning varies with context, so that the meanings of any sign in different contexts are at best related only analogically. Plato's use of πεττεία to illustrate the place of definitions in dialectic would then appear to be no mere curiosity of his imagination, but rather an epitome of his philosophy, as well as a basis for comparing and contrasting him with more recent philosophers.

The Catholic University of America

---

[20] Cf. lusoria tabula in Pauly-Wissowa, Realencyclopaedie.
[21] John Burnet, Early Greek Philosophy (London, 1930), #49.

QUID ARISTOTELES

DE LOCO SENSERIT

THESIM

FACULTATI LITTERARUM PARISIENSI

PROPONEBAT

H. BERGSON

SCHOLAE NORMALIS OLIM ALUMNUS

LUTETIAE PARISIORUM

EDEBAT F. ALCAN, BIBLIOPOLA

M DCCC LXXXIX

2

ARISTOTLE'S CONCEPT OF PLACE

by Henri Bergson

A Translation with an Introduction *by*

John K. Ryan of *Quid Aristoteles de loco senserit*

TRANSLATOR'S INTRODUCTION

During the years from 1883 to 1888 when he was teaching philosophy in the Lycée Blaise Pascal in Clermont-Ferrand Bergson wrote both his principal doctoral dissertation, *Les Données immédiates de la conscience,* and his Latin dissertation, *Quid Aristoteles de loco senserit.* His interest in the problems of space, including those proposed and answered so strikingly by various pre-Socratic philosophers—Pythagoreans, Eleatics, Heraclitus, Leucippus, and Democritus—began early in life and both dissertations are expressions of it. Aristotle too, as physicist, philosopher, and historian of philosophy, has his part in the record of these problems, and in *Quid Aristoteles de loco senserit* Bergson gives a compact synthesis and criticism of one aspect of Aristotle's contribution to the general discussion.

For the most part Bergson restricts himself to what Aristotle has written in the fourth book of his *Physics,* and he makes only a few citations from other parts of the *Physics.* Certain other books by Aristotle are used. There are 25 quotations from or references to *On the Heavens,* seven from *On Generation and Corruption* and six from the *Metaphysics.* Other works used are *On the Soul, Categories, Meteorologics, On the Generation of Animals,* and *On the Movement of Animals.*[1] The treatise *De lineis insecabilibus*[2] is also quoted.

---

[1] While Bergson states that *On the Movement of Animals* was not written by Aristotle himself, W. D. Ross writes in *Aristotle* (London: Methuen, 1953), p. 12, "The *De Motione Animalium* has by many writers been regarded as spurious . . . but recent opinion is in its favour."

[2] Cf. Harold H. Joachim, *De Lineis Insecabilibus* (Oxford: Clarendon Press, 1908) which gives both the Greek text and an English translation, as does

Little use is made of ancient commentators on the *Physics*. Simplicius is quoted seven times and Philoponus four times. Alexander of Aphrodisias is twice quoted from Simplicius, as is Theophrastus once. There are two references to Plato, one to Diogenes Laertius, and one to Cicero. Some use is made of Leibniz and Kant and Bergson shows that in his earlier years he accepted Kant's theory of space as an a priori form.

Certain nineteenth-century writers are noted as having discussed Aristotle's doctrine on place: F. Ravaisson briefly in his *Métaphysique d'Aristote* and Eduard Zeller even more briefly in his *Philosophie der Griechen*. Three other works are named in a very limited bibliography. He writes disparagingly of what C. A. Brandis has on place in his *Aristoteles,* and still more disparagingly in criticism of a Latin dissertation by G. A. Wolter and of a German work by Otto Ule.

Apparently Bergson was unaware of the work done by medieval and renaissance commentators on the *Physics*. The names of some such writers may be listed: Averroes, Robert Grosseteste, Albertus Magnus, Thomas Aquinas, Roger Bacon, Egidio Colonna, Walter Burley, John Buridan, Albert of Saxony, Marsilius of Inghem, Agostino Nifo, Dominicus Soto, and Silvester Maurus. The list could go on and on, and perhaps all such authors have not yet been accounted for by students of medieval and renaissance thought. If Bergson lacked knowledge of even the greatest of the medieval commentators on the *Physics,* it is an indication of the handicap under which a serious student of philosophy labored less than a hundred years ago. Of the 25 centuries of western thought ten or more were largely ignored as if they had not been, and gross misrepresentations were accepted as established facts. Happily, as far as scholarship is concerned there has been a vast change, and ignorance as to what was done in physical science as well as in other areas during those ten centuries is gradually being displaced by detailed knowledge. Unfortunately, some of the old obstacles of indifference or hostility to the past still persist and operate against the diffusion and acceptance of such knowledge.

In Bergson's case there could have been nothing like culpable

W. S. Hett in the Loeb Classical Library volume of Aristotle's *Minor Works* (London: Heinemann, 1955). The author of the work was a member of the peripatetic school. Both Theophrastus and Strato have been suggested as possible authors.

indifference to what had been done between the days of the Greek commentators on Aristotle and the few nineteenth-century writers that he names. In this regard he was no doubt merely the victim of the lycée and university of his time. If he had been led to the *Commentarium in* VIII *libros De physico auditu* by St. Thomas Aquinas he perhaps would not have found much to his purpose there. Still he might have said, as he did later in life, that although not familiar with St. Thomas, yet when he had come across one of his texts he had agreed with him.[3] Even so the inadequacy of Bergson's bibliography must be marked against him.

In his prefatory note Bergson states that it is his purpose to analyze the doctrine on place presented in *Physics* IV, extract from it Aristotle's definition of place, and establish the supporting line of argument. In this way, Bergson claims, he will show why Aristotle substitutes place for space, and why, as a consequence, he evades rather than answers the problems of space. Of the nine chapters that make up the dissertation, the first six are expository. In chapter VII Bergson states certain problems arising from Aristotle's doctrine. "Unless you examine it deeply and interpret it carefully, this description of place does not seem to be wholly consistent either with the rest of Aristotle's teaching or with itself." Place is described as immobile and the place par excellence is the immobile heaven. Again, the elements are immobile, since each acts as a place, and yet the elements are also mobile. The third difficulty is found in the doctrine of primary place, i.e., the place of a particular body at a given time, which seems to be both mobile and immobile. Bergson's answers to the problems are given in chapter VIII.

In the concluding chapter Bergson sums up his findings, stresses the concern of contemporary thinkers with space rather than place, states his assent to a Kantian view of space as a mental form, compares Aristotle's approach to that of Leibniz, finds that the crux of the Aristotelian theory is the distinction between act and potency, and separates place from extension. Aristotle, he concedes, was not unaware of the problems raised by the conception of infinite empty space but thought them to be insuperable. Hence Bergson holds that he has established his thesis that Aristotle "eliminated rather

---

[3] Cf. the writer's "Henri Bergson: Heraclitus Redivivus" in John K. Ryan, ed., *Twentieth-Century Thinkers* (Staten Island, N.Y.: Alba House, 1965), pp. 29 and 33. Raissa Maritain is the authority for Bergson's commendation of St. Thomas Aquinas.

than settled the problem," and "buried, if the phrase is permissible, not only space in bodies but the question itself."

Aristotle's review and criticism of various ancient theories of place and his statement of his own doctrine are an impressive example of his scientific and philosophical method. Handicapped by the inadequate physics of his time, particularly by his own view of lightness and heaviness as natural properties of bodies, and lacking the aid of the advanced mathematics of our era, he nevertheless keeps rigorously to the problems at hand. He finds that each thing in nature has its place and that its place is real. His problem is to isolate, so to speak, place and define its reality, and he solves it by a process of elimination. Place is not something alien to a body and its parts; it is not an element; it is not a cause; it is neither matter nor form; it is neither the body itself nor a bodily quality; it is not the empty interval that remains after an object has been moved from the place where it was. Distinction is made between potential place and actual place and between common place and primary place. The last is found to be the inner surface of the surrounding body.

Aristotle takes note of how a thing is located relatively to an observer. If we walk around a statue, let us say, it is now in front of us and now behind us, or it is now at our right and now at our left hand. So also if a stranger standing in the center of Athens asked where Aristotle's Lyceum was located he would be given directions: "Go straight ahead, turn left outside the walls and you will find it near the Ilyssus." But the final question is just what is the place of the statue or of the Lyceum when one gets to it. Aristotle, the cautious investigator and philosopher of things as they are, cannot rightly be charged with evading the problem of space and failure to solve it in Kantian or analogous terms. He examines the physical universe and finds no space as such, and certainly no unlimited empty space, but rather, we may say, that there is a sum total of places and that the universe itself, which provides a place for each thing in it, has no place.

Bergson's main criticism of Aristotle, that he evades rather than solves the problem of space, therefore seems to be unjustified. His observation that Aristotle is sometimes obscure is a minor charge, and it may be that Bergson does not take sufficiently into account the fact that the *Physics* is a record of lectures and subject to the limitations both of lectures and of records of them. The criticism that Aristotle misinterprets Plato—"He even criticizes Plato who 'thought that matter and the receptacle (of ideas) are identical,' "— leads us to reflect that Aristotle was closer to Plato than we are, that he usually knew whereof he spoke, and that on most points it is rash to differ from him. It has well been said, "Beware of the mace of the mighty Stagirite!"[4]

It is not to be expected that Bergson would write Latin with the ease and fluency of such medieval thinkers as Anselm, Aquinas, and Bonaventure, for whom Latin was a living language. His Latin is correct but stiff and stilted. If one looks for parallels to the French style for which he was famous, certain striking phrases and various effective similes and metaphors will be noted. Thus he states that in Aristotle matter and form are "comrades and sharers in the fortunes of a body," whereas place is an impassive witness to those fortunes. At one point Aristotle is described as not pleading his own case but merely calling common sense to the witness stand. An object is held in place "like a jewel in its setting." Plato's receptacle of ideas is said to be blood brother to the empty space of modern thinkers rather than to Aristotelian matter. Movement in a straight line produces and, so to speak, "spins off circular movement." Questions as to place and the void are joined by Aristotle "in the closest bonds of kinship." Particles of earth seek the companionship and embrace of water. The lower elements continuously change into each other and are "reborn from their own offspring." A basic principle "contains and nourishes the relation of place to matter and form." Bodily parts are said to delegate to the body as a whole that power to occupy a place which they claim for themselves when set free from the body, and there is reference to "the emancipation of place." Certain comparisons are based on the theatre and place is said to play the role of effect rather than cause. Such phrases and analogies are usually introduced by words like "ut ita dicam" by which Bergson modestly indicates that they are his own.

Quid Aristoteles de loco senserit possesses substantial merit. Because it is so clear and compact a synthesis of what *Physics* IV says about place, it illustrates not only Aristotle's mind at work but Bergson's as well. It shows Bergson's early interest in some of the dominant themes of his mature thought—the reader will note the

---

[4] Cf. Joseph Rickaby, *Studies on God and His Creatures* (London: 1924), p. 35.

references to Aristotle's dynamic universe—and it gives evidence of some of the modern thinkers who influenced him, particularly Kant. This dissertation has as well another kind of historical merit as an illustration of the high character and great value of a culture and a form of education that have almost disappeared. Bergson's *petite thèse* shows clearly his knowledge of Latin and Greek and it reveals the intellectual standards and discipline that had resulted in no small part from youthful study of the two languages and their literatures. Not the least of the gifts that came to him was the humanistic education that made writing *Quid Aristoteles de loco senserit* and *Les Données immédiates de la conscience* possible before he was thirty and in later years *Matière et mémoire, L'Evolution créatrice, Les Deux sources de la morale et de la religion,* and the other works.

Quid Aristoteles de loco senserit has not, as far as the writer knows, been previously translated into English. The translation closely adheres to the Latin and grace of style has been sacrificed to fidelity to the text. It may be noted that the Latin "animal" as descriptive of Aristotle's universe is translated as "living thing," and that "mundus" is rendered as "world" and "universum" as "universe." Bergson's use of a dash to break up a long paragraph has been retained, as has his style of references.

The translation of Bergson's Latin text and notes is complete. In accordance with the best usage Bergson gives in footnotes the complete Greek text of the passages from Aristotle and others which he quotes or refers to. In this English rendition of the work only the references to such passages are given and the corresponding Greek texts have been reluctantly omitted.[5] Bergson's other foot-

---

[5] To do so would have been to fulfill a counsel of perfection, against which both the expense and the difficulty of getting so many Greek texts set up correctly have been deterring factors. In this connection one is tempted to ask, "Ut quid perditio haec?" When St. Francis de Sales was urged to add certain references to the second (1609) edition of his *Introduction to the Devout Life,* he wrote that "the learned do not need such things and the others do not bother about them." In the present case the learned have the Greek text of the *Physics* in the critical edition of W. D. Ross (Oxford: 1950) and along with the other works of Aristotle quoted by Bergson it is also available in the Berlin edition and in the Loeb Classical Library. The Diels edition of Simplicius and the Vitelli edition of Philoponus are likewise accessible to the learned. Presumably the others will not be disturbed by the absence of the Greek texts.

notes, in which he comments in Latin on points in Aristotle or on other subjects, are given in full.

A French translation of *Quid Aristoteles de loco senserit* by Robert Mossé-Bastide which appeared in 1949 under the title *L'Idée de lieu chez Aristote* [6] has been helpful in making this English translation. The Mossé-Bastide work cannot be called complete since it omits the Latin footnotes. The most important of these are the note to the Preface that contains Bergson's bibliography, and two extensive notes in chapter VI, one of which contains a severe criticism of G. A. Wolter's *De spatio et tempore quam praecipua Aristotelis ratione habita,* while the other has important matter on Aristotle's doctrine.

JOHN K. RYAN

The Catholic University of America

---

[6] In *Les Études Bergsoniennes,* II (1949), 27-104. The French translation by Robert Mossé-Bastide is preceded by an introduction (pp. 9-25) by Rose-Marie Mossé-Bastide.

ARISTOTLE'S CONCEPT OF PLACE

by

HENRI BERGSON

Preface

In Book IV of his *Physics* Aristotle discusses certain rather obscure problems regarding place but he nowhere speaks clearly and in detail of what we mean by space. Hence it will be worth the effort to give a literal exposition, if we can do so, of the very difficult doctrine contained in that book. In this way we may extract from it a definition of place in order to reveal the hidden thought and series of arguments that led Aristotle to a doctrine in which, by substituting place for space, he seemingly avoids rather than settles disputes which, in our opinion, refer above all to space. However, our principal task is to ascertain what is Aristotle's true thought with regard to place. If we succeed in bringing this to light, the rest will become clear.[1]

---

[1] Brandis (*Aristoteles*, II,[2] p. 739-751) discusses Aristotle's definition of place but only in such fashion that he seems to enumerate and summarize the Aristotelian arguments rather than interpret them. Ed. Zeller states the question effectively, but only touches lightly on it so as to concentrate on the particular difficulties of the subject (*Philosophie der Griechen*, 3rd ed., II,[2] p. 398). F. Ravaisson (*Métaphysique d'Aristote*, vol. 1, pp. 565, 566) has written a few but valuable things on the same subject.—Wolter (*De Spatio et Tempore, quam praecipua Aristotelis ratione habita*, Bonn, 1848) in an orderly way describes certain parts of Book IV. However, since he wished to harmonize Aristotle's definition of place with modern philosophy, he was led to assert that Aristotle discusses not only place but space as well, which error our whole argument will refute. Ule (*Untersuchung ueber den Raum und die Raumtheorie des Aristoteles und Kant*, Halle, 1850) has compared the Aristotelian with the Kantian doctrine. To summarize briefly his opuscule: Ule holds that Aristotelian space is a kind of substance placed between the world and God. We have found nothing farther removed from Aristotle's teaching than this.

I

Arguments by which Aristotle establishes that place really exists.

Aristotle first establishes that place is a definite reality by many arguments, certain of which are at variance with the rest of his doctrine and somewhat obscure. However, this difficulty is resolved if we remember that here Aristotle is discussing not so much his own as the common opinion. He will examine the nature of place elsewhere. For the present he is concerned only with the fact that no one thinks and no one speaks—not even one who says or thinks what is false—without by that very fact admitting that place is real.

We say therefore that all things whatsoever are somewhere. Next, while we know from experience that there are various kinds of movement or change, we truly and properly give the name of movement to that which pertains to place.[1] Again, the fact that bodies succeed to other bodies is sufficient evidence that there is near at hand a kind of immobile scene onto which they advance one after the other.[2] Where water was, there is found first air, for example, and later something else. This would be impossible if place were confused with the things enclosed. You will fully understand this argumentation, which is frequently used by Aristotle, if you consider water enclosed in a vessel. As long as it remains there it seems to cohere with the vessel in such wise that you think that a solid whole can be made out of the vessel and the water. But if air in turn succeeds to the water, then, since the vessel can be identified neither with the water nor with the air, it is necessarily distinct from each of them.—However, someone may say, what is precisely at issue is whether place can be compared to a vessel or to any other thing existing apart by itself. When Aristotle employs such a comparison as a proof, does he not seriously prejudge the point at issue?—Aristotle would in fact be open to this charge if he were pleading his own case. However, he now does nothing but call as witness common opinion which, whenever it states that air has entered a vessel where water had previously been, means by those very words there is a certain similarity of place to a vessel.

We will put a like interpretation on the argument that Aristotle

[1] *Physics* IV, 208, a, 29.—Cf. *Physics* VIII, 260, a, 25.—*Physics* VIII, 261, a, 27.
[2] *Physics* IV, 208, b, 1.

deduces from the movement of natural simple bodies. "Since fiery
bodies tend upward and earthy bodies tend downward, so long as
nothing obstructs them, it necessarily follows that place is not only
real but also that it apparently possesses a certain power."[3] However, Aristotle both eliminates place from the number of causes[4]
and a little later gives a reason why elements are borne toward
their proper places without being impelled or drawn by any force.[5]
We therefore continue to assume that here it is a matter not so
much of Aristotle's as of the common opinion.

Nature itself has defined by fixed laws not only high and low
but also other opposites, such as right and left and before and
behind.[6] Although such opposites apparently adapt their character
to our will, as happens whenever we turn our body around and
things that were behind us now face us, or things are changed from
right to left or from above to beneath us, yet since fiery and light
things fly upward into a certain region that stands highest in the
world, and contrariwise earthy and heavy things are shifted about
by a contrary movement, it must be that opposites do not depend
solely on our bodily position but exist by themselves and maintain
a fixed and stable order in the world.[7]—All this becomes clear if we
refer to Book II of *On the Heavens*[8] and Book I of *On the Generation of Animals*,[9] or even to passages in *On the Motion of Animals*
which, although not written by Aristotle himself, yet provides us
with Aristotelian doctrine.[10] From these books we gather that
there is no right or left, no above or beneath, no before or behind
for anything except a living thing, which, because it possesses a
definite center to which it refers other things, has these fixed and
definite opposites. Since the Aristotelian world is a living thing,
these opposites are especially found in the world. There will therefore be a certain right part of the world where the stars take their
rise and a left where they set. There will be a highest region to
which light objects soar and a lowest region to which they descend.
Now if we reflect that man too is a living thing in which the center

[3] *Physics* IV, 208, b, 8.
[4] *Physics* IV, 209, a, 20.
[5] *Physics* IV, 215, a.
[6] *On the Heavens*, I, 271, a, 26.
[7] *Physics* IV, 208, b, 14.
[8] *On the Heavens*, II, 284, b, 30.
[9] *On the Generation of Animals*, I, 12, 15. Cf. *History of Animals*, I, 12, 12.
[10] *On the Motion of Animals*, 702, b, 17.

does not remain immobile, as it does in the world, but is borne about in every direction, you can understand how it is possible for the same opposites to be unchanging for the world but changing for man.—But let us now return to our subject. We say that place is real since it is defined in the world by determinate opposites.

We will now explain the argumentation relating to geometrical figures. "Although mathematical objects are not themselves in place, still in relation to our position they have a right and left which are not derived from nature but so named solely from our position." [11] We will recognize that these opposites are not derived from nature if we reflect that geometrical figures are not living things and that they do not exist at all unless formed by our minds.[12] Still, some of them appear to be on our right and others on the left, and from this it follows that we transfer such opposites from our body to those figures according to the position that we conceived for each of them. Finally, you will understand the content of the argument if you grasp what Aristotle wishes to prove, namely, that an image of place is so firmly fixed in our minds that we assign place and opposites pertaining to place even to things that have no place.

Two arguments remain, one of which concludes in this fashion: "Those who say that there is a void also think that place exists, since a void would be a place deprived of body."[13]—Even though empty space extends nowhere (which Aristotle demonstrates a little later), it follows from what most people say of a void that an image of place has been formed within their minds.—We may say that the force and meaning of another argument, one taken from Hesiod, are similar. Hesiod writes that Chaos was the first of all things, a place as it were for all things to come. "Wonderful, therefore, would be the power of place, first of all things. That without which no other things exist but itself exists apart from them is necessarily the first existent being. While things that are in place pass away, place itself does not perish."[14]—Aristotle will confirm by many arguments the thesis that place exists neither before

[11] *Physics* IV, 208, b, 22. In Simplicius (Diels ed., p. 525, 526, 1. 16 sqq.) we read ὡς τὰ μόνον λεγόμενα διὰ θέσιν. A completely unnecessary emendation made by Alexander (ὥστε μόνον αὐτῶν νοεῖσθαι τὴν θέσιν) has been received into the codices. (See Simplicius, Diels ed., p. 526, 1. 16 sqq.)

[12] Cf. *Metaphysics* XIII, 1092, a, 17.

[13] *Physics* IV, 208, b, 25.

[14] *Physics* IV, 208, b, 29.

things nor apart from things. Since this is so, the Aristotelian argumentation clearly regards the following single point: so absurd is it to hold that place is nonexistent that in contrast common opinion greatly exaggerates the power of place.—Sufficient has now been said of common opinion. Let us next investigate the nature of place considered as an accepted reality.

II

Difficulties which, according to Aristotle, confront those who discuss place.

Before proceeding to a description of place, Aristotle, as is his custom, shows how much obscurity the subject holds and perhaps adds to it by his discussion. To those asking what genus place belongs to Aristotle points out the many contrasting but equally insoluble difficulties that they will meet, whether they reduce place to a corporeal mass or prefer some other nature.[1] First, then, the three things common to both place and body, viz., length, width, and depth, seemingly show that a body's mass and its place are the same thing.[2] However, we are brought to a contrary opinion if we consider that two bodies cannot be fused into one,[3] which would clearly be the case if we held the place where a body rests to be itself a body. If the body departs, the place remains. From this it must follow either that place is contrary to the nature of body or that two bodies appear to be simultaneously within one another.

It will then be demonstrated not only that place is not contrary to the nature of body but also that it especially participates in such a nature. Just as there must be a fixed and definite space for the body itself, so also for the surface and other limits of a body. Thus where a surface, a line, or a point of water has been perceived, precisely there we also find a surface, line, and point of air. But since there is no difference between a point and the place of a

[1] *Physics* IV, 209, a, 4.
[2] *Physics* IV, 209, a, 5.
[3] *Physics* IV, 209, a, 6.

point, we must in like manner identify the place of a surface with the surface itself and the place of a body with that body.[4]

A further problem arises as to why there is no difference between a point and the place of a point. Philoponus and Simplicius, in different ways but each acutely, attempt to explain this very obscure argument of Aristotle. If we distinguish the indivisible point from the place of the point we introduce into this indivisible point two realities, viz., the point and the place of the point.[5] Such is Simplicius's explanation. Philoponus argues in a different way, and, in my opinion, more in keeping with Aristotle's doctrine. He discusses the problem thus: if you ascribe to a point its own proper place, you picture the natural place of that point as being, for example, either higher or lower. Since bodies that by nature occupy a lower place are called heavy, while contrariwise those that rise to a higher place are called light, you necessarily attribute either heaviness or lightness to a point, which is completely unintelligible.[6] We will add a third interpretation drawn from Aristotle's definition of place. Aristotle will later establish by proofs and arguments that no body has a place unless it is both put within another body and moves about within it. But an indivisible point can in no way be contained or surrounded since it cannot be touched by anything without immediately being absorbed into that thing.[7] Moreover, it cannot even be moved since, as Aristotle will demonstrate in Book V of the *Physics,* the movement of an indivisible point can neither be nor be conceived. From this it is concluded that a point lacks place.

What remains to be said? By the first argument Aristotle confirms that if we consider the individual parts, we do not obtain a place separate and distinct from body, but if all the parts are considered together place is obtained. Hence it is self-contradictory for you to ascribe place both to the parts of a body and to the entire body. He offers a neat solution to this difficulty by showing that the parts of a body potentially occupy place whereas a body actually does so. We will consider this subject elsewhere. For the time being, he makes the darkness thicker before dispersing it.

Let us proceed to another disputed question. Since place differs

---

4 *Physics* IV, 209, a, 8. Cf. *On the Soul,* I, 409, a, 21.

5 Simplicius, *On the Physics,* Diels edition, p. 531, 1. 24.

6 Philoponus, *On the Physics,* Vitelli edition, p. 507, 1. 35 sqq.

7 Cf. *De lineis insecabilibus,* 971, b, 7.

from body, should it not be listed in the number of elements, either corporeal or incorporeal? Yet what is inconsistent with the nature of body can have no likeness to a corporeal element, nor can a thing displaying length, breadth, and depth be termed incorporeal.[8]— When Aristotle speaks of corporeal elements we must understand that he means earth, water, air, fire, and ether. As Philoponus states, incorporeal elements are those from which syllogisms or words, for example, are made, such as propositions and syllables.[9] It is quite obvious that neither kind can be affirmed of place. Simplicius raises a question as to why Aristotle thinks that corporeal elements must necessarily be present in a body, since, as Aristotle himself states, every body is made up of matter and form, both of which are incorporeal.[10] If place is either matter or form, is it not an incorporeal element of a body? We have an answer at hand, provided by Simplicius himself.[11] Aristotle undoubtedly eliminates matter and form, since he will later discuss each of them more fully. The question here is with regard to the other elements.

A third question presents itself. Should place be included among the causes?[12] Aristotle establishes four causes: that out of which, that in which, that by which, and that for which, or better, matter, form, efficient cause, and lastly end or purpose, as we usually name them. Why, someone asks, does he eliminate place from the number of causes without giving any reason for doing so? Actually, he will discuss at length the difference between place and matter and between place and form. No one will assert that place is an efficient cause, since place in fact lies inert and ready to receive anything whatsoever. It remains then for us to investigate why Aristotle is unwilling to number place among the causes he calls ends or purposes, since each and every body is held by him to tend spontaneously, as if by its own will, to some abode proper and natural to it. This is a rather difficult question and neither Simplicius nor Philoponus gives an adequate explanation of it. Philoponus notes [13] that the cause rightly called an end is already situated in the very

8 *Physics* IV, 209, a, 13.

9 Philoponus, *On the Physics,* Vitelli edition, p. 508, 1. 10 sqq.

10 Simplicius, *On the Physics,* Diels edition, p. 532, 1. 18.

11 *Ibid.,* 1. 26.

12 *Physics* IV, 209, a, 18, sqq.

13 Philoponus, *On the Physics,* Vitelli edition, p. 509, 1. 29.

thing that seeks that end, so that each and every thing potentially contains its own end and shares in its nature and even in its name. For example, one who strives for the good as an end can already be called a good man. But in fact a moving thing can in no wise be said to share in the place where it will come to rest. Hence there is nothing common to both place and end. In Simplicius we find the same interpretation expressed in different words: End is proper to each thing, whereas place is public, if I may so put it.[14]—For our part, we say that neither reply has much to do with the Aristotelian doctrine. In Aristotle's opinion, a certain region in the world is assigned to each element, and similarly its own end is assigned to each movement. But there is this difference between place and end: an end is given *before* the thing that tends to that end, whereas place is given *after* the things making up the universe have been arranged and put in order. Manifestly, air tends to the place for air, lying between the moist and the fiery regions, not because it is drawn by that place as though by some end, but because air is so constituted that it comes to rest between water and fire and moves within the other elements. From this rest arises the natural place of air. Therefore, since it is not an end but a result and product as it were of natural movement, we state that natural place plays the role of effect rather than of cause.

There remain two trifling arguments, the first of which is formulated as follows: If place is a thing, then since all things are in place there will be the place of a place, so that you would proceed into infinity.[15] The second is stated thus: Since every body occupies a place, it is necessary that every place be filled by a body. But if this is so, increase on the part of bodies is unintelligible, since it seems to require empty space within which bodies can increase.[16]

It is now necessary to think through to a definition of place which will bring all controversies to an end.—If you extract the principle and cause of them all you find one and the same hypothesis underlying the discussions concerning space: place is something separate that stands by itself. Aristotle will elsewhere demolish this hypothesis and openly attack it, but for the present he puts off dealing with it. To oppose the emancipation of place, if I may so put it, and again

14 Simplicius, *On the Physics,* Diels edition, p. 533, 1. 29.
15 *Physics* IV, 209, a, 23.
16 *Physics* IV, 209, a, 26.

enclose space within the bodies from which it has unseasonably departed, such is Aristotle's purpose, such is the goal of his whole discussion.—But let us proceed in a clear and orderly manner.

III

The order Aristotle observes in his reflections on the nature of place.

It is difficult to discern what order Aristotle keeps in his thoughts on this subject. To be more clearly understood he speaks first of place and next of the void, but he proposes the two problems in such a way that each one seems to merge with the other. Hence we will disengage if we can Aristotle's abstruse meaning so as to reveal the order he holds to in his reflections.

First, therefore, he considers a given body situated in a fixed and definite place. He asks what this place is: Is it the body itself or a quality of the body? Obviously, it is neither one. Since this is the case and neither the body nor qualities of the body have provided any help, he eliminates body, and next proceeds to investigate what remains. What remains, so it seems to most men, is an empty interval. Led on therefore to a new investigation, namely, that place should be defined as though it were an empty interval, Aristotle has established by many proofs and arguments that a void can neither exist by itself nor be conceived by the mind. Once it has been made certain that place is neither a body nor a quality of a body, and not even the interval that apparently remains after a body has been removed, Aristotle necessarily turns to the only thing that remains: namely a surrounding body in which the thing is held enclosed like a jewel in its setting.—We now have the series and connection of images by which Aristotle has been led to conclude that a place is the interior surface of the surrounding thing.[1]

Let us explain item by item why place is neither a body nor any quality of an enclosed body, and not even the empty interval itself which apparently remains after the body has been removed.

[1] *Physics* IV, 211, b, 6.

IV

*How Aristotle distinguishes place from the matter and the form of
the body.*

Because of the evident similarity of place to matter and form,
for certain thinkers place is something proper to an enclosed body,
namely, either its matter or its form. Like form, place coincides
with a body; like form, it follows upon and delimits the outward
contour of a body.[1] But still closer is the relation of place to matter,
for like matter place is as it were the common theatre of various
changes, e.g., where white succeeds to black or soft to hard.[2] Aristotle
expresses this thought in a rather obscure statement which we
here closely translate into Latin in these words: "In so far as
place appears to be an interval of magnitude, it is more likely to be
matter. Yet magnitude and an interval of magnitude are not the
same thing. We apply the name interval to what is enclosed and
defined by a form as by a surface and limit. Matter belongs to
this class, and so also the indeterminate. When a sphere's limit is
removed and also the sphere's attributes, nothing remains but
matter."[3] As far as we can make out, Aristotle calls that which
limits magnitude and that which is limited an interval of magnitude.
Hence, if you say that form is a limit, it necessarily follows that
what receives a limit and attribute from form, but of itself lacks
the limit and attribute, is matter. Therefore, in as much as some
hold that place is an interval of magnitude, they signify matter.—
Someone will ask: Does not an interval signify two realities, whether
you call an interval that which merely receives a limit or that which
also receives an attribute? If you admit the second meaning of the
term, an interval indeed means nothing but matter to you, namely,
something that is about to receive attributes or qualities and already
potentially contains them. But the first meaning of the word, that
an interval may receive any limits whatsoever and may be shaped
into a sphere, a cylinder, or any other geometrical figure, completely
rejects what I may call physical attributes. If you so conceive an
interval, it will not be matter but a void. Does not Aristotle, when
he calls an interval that which receives both limit and attribute, as

[1] *Physics* IV, 211, b, 11.
[2] *Physics* IV, 211, b, 29.
[3] *Physics* IV, 209, b, 6.

if geometrical and physical qualities could not be separated, prejudge the very thing at issue with the result that while apparently
defining it, he denies absolutely that an empty interval can exist by
itself?—Aristotle would in fact incur this charge if he was not later
on to speak against the void. For the time being he silently passes
over the first meaning of the term; he concerns himself only with
the opinion of those who think that place is, if I may so put it, a
material interval. He even criticizes Plato who "thought that matter
and the receptacle are identical." [4] But in our opinion, if Aristotle
attributes the Aristotelian meaning to the word matter, this seems
scarcely a Platonic interpretation of the *Timaeus*. From the *Timaeus*
one concludes that place is that receptacle of ideas which admits all
modifications whatsoever but is by nature indeterminate. We would
say that this principle, which is destitute of potency, is blood brother
to our empty space rather than to Aristotelian matter.—Whatever
the case may be, some say that place is form while others, among
whom Aristotle incorrectly includes Plato, say that it is matter.

That both groups err gravely Aristotle establishes chiefly by four
arguments.

The first argument runs: Neither matter nor form can be
separated from the thing that occupies a place, but place can be so
separated. Where air was, there water or fire has more likely suc-
ceeded. In the same way we recognize that place is neither a part,
nor a quality, nor a condition of a body. [5]

Let us proceed to the second argument. If place is either matter
or form, how is it that every body whatsoever tends to its own
proper natural place? "A thing that has no movement within itself
and does not admit the contraries we call high and low cannot be a
place." [6] Let us speak plainly, place is necessarily that in which and
to which a body moves. But a body cannot move within itself nor
can it seek the high or the low by a natural movement if it possesses such contraries within itself. It is therefore necessary that you
establish both these contraries and the theatre of movement outside
the body. Therefore place is outside matter and form.

The third of the four arguments is stated as follows: If you posit
place within a body, then place will be moved about with that body;
therefore place will change place. However, place could not change

[4] *Physics* IV, 209, b, 10.
[5] *Physics* IV, 211, b, 35.
[6] *Physics* IV, 210, a, 2.

place unless it had already occupied a place. Aristotle concludes that it is completely absurd for a place to be in place.[7]

Finally, since the fourth argument is somewhat obscure we will translate it word for word into Latin. "When water comes from air, its place ceases to be, since the body that has been made does not possess the same place. But what is this destruction of a place?"[8] Simplicius's interpretation is at least probable: The magnitude of the air decreases when water is produced out of air; therefore a part of its place is destroyed if place is matter or form.[9] However, it is impossible to conceive in any manner the destruction of place. Alexander[10] and Philoponus[11] think that the argument refers to form rather than to matter, and that in his reasoning Aristotle therefore came closer to the following opinion. When water is made out of air, the form of the air ceases to be; therefore the place also perishes if you hold that place is form. This is a more acute interpretation and I think that it is confirmed by certain words of Aristotle himself. In the book entitled *On Generation and Corruption* we read that air cannot be changed into water unless the prior form perishes root and all and another form is begotten.[12] Therefore it is in conformity with reason that form rather than magnitude is meant by our fourth argument. Nevertheless, the first interpretation can be reduced to the second, since magnitude, although not a form, is still something belonging to the form.

Let us draw up a brief summary of the entire discussion. Place is neither matter nor form, since matter and form show themselves to be companions and sharers in the fortunes of a body, if I may so express it, whereas place is an impassive witness of those fortunes. If we penetrate deeper into Aristotle's innermost thoughts, we find that a definite and very subtle principle underlies all his arguments, namely, that there is such a reciprocal connection and continuation of matter and form that you cannot say where form begins and where matter ends. Place, however, is something fixed and definite and it cannot be reduced to form without being immediately joined

7 *Physics* IV, 210, a, 5.
8 *Physics* IV, 210, a, 9.
9 Simplicius, Diels ed., p. 549, 1. 12.
10 Alexander in Simplicius, Diels ed., p. 549, 1. 26.
11 Philoponus, Vitelli ed., p. 526, 1. 1.
12 *On Generation and Corruption*, I, 319, b, 14.

to matter and therefore to body itself.[13] You will perceive that the entire line of reasoning is contained in this inadequately stated conception and, I may say, inwardly sustained by it.

V

Reasons why Aristotle thinks that place cannot be an empty interval and that empty space cannot be conceived in any way.

Now once the enclosed body, which apparently does not belong to the place, has been removed, it is probable that if any empty interval remains then it alone is the place.

Although Aristotle does not discuss the void until after completing his description of place, he joins both questions in the closest bonds of kinship, as is evident at the very beginning.[1] "Just as with regard to place so also with regard to the void, it is the task of the natural philosopher to inquire as to whether it exists or not, how it exists, and what it is. In fact, from opinions on them, one concludes to similar reasons for belief or doubt on the two subjects. Those who say that the void exists make it a kind of place and receptacle which is full when containing a mass such as it is capable of holding and empty when deprived of it, as if place and the void are the same reality but differ from one another in their mode of existence." —As far as we can understand it, they believe that place presents itself in different ways according to whether it is full or empty but they speak of place in itself as an empty receptacle.

Aristotle returns to the same idea in his conclusion: "Some think that the void exists separately and by itself . . . ; which amounts to saying that place is a separate reality." [2] He states the same thing in other words but a little more fully: "It is believed that the void is something real because place appears to be such, and for the same reasons. It is because of local movement that some say that place is something apart from the bodies that occupy it, while others assert the same of the void. They think that the void, as that in which

---

[13] *Physics* IV, 209, b, 17.

[1] *Physics* IV, 213, a, 12.
[2] *Physics* IV, 216, a, 23.

motion takes place, is the cause of motion, and this is just what certain others assert of place."[3] To solve the difficulty in a few words: some believe that movement cannot be conceived except in a place open to movement or even in a void where movement is unimpeded by any obstacle. They therefore think that since place and the void have the same power to receive movement, they differ from one another in name rather than in fact.

Since this is so and since place seems to be an empty interval, if we prove that the void does not exist in any way, then another definition of place must be sought. It is for this reason that Aristotle attacks the void so forcefully and fully. But since Aristotle considers that all the arguments, whether they affirm or deny that the void exists, are not at all probable, he first weighs the latter and then the others. Finally he reveals his own personal view which he bases on various arguments.

Those who have argued against the void have erred gravely not because they attacked the void itself but rather because of a fallacious way of speaking about it. He writes: "They have shown that air is a reality and that it has a certain power by inflating bladders and by keeping air enclosed in water clocks. But men believe that the void is an interval in which there is no sensible body, since those who hold that all things whatsoever are corporeal say that the void is that in which there is absolutely nothing. From this it follows that what is filled with air is not a void. Hence what must be proved is not that air is real but that there does not exist a difference or separate interval which penetrates through every body in such wise as to interrupt its continuity . . . or even, the continuity of the body being admitted, that it is something apart from the body."[4] Since the first part of this doctrine refers to Democritus, Leucippus, and certain others who introduced the void between the atoms themselves, as Aristotle himself states, and in so doing broke the continuous character of the body, the second part seems to refer to the Pythagoreans who located the void outside the bodies. However it may be, Aristotle thinks that natural philosophers who argue against the void do not really meet the issue. Those who have defended the void have come closer to it. Let us now examine their arguments.

The thesis that movement is completely inconceivable unless there are empty intervals they support principally by three arguments.

[3] *Physics* IV, 214, a, 21.
[4] *Physics* IV, 213, a, 22.

First, they assert that nothing can be received into an interval that is already filled. If this were done, then there would be two bodies, one within the other. Not only this, but, since no reason or distinction can be advanced why a third and a fourth body could not occupy the same interval, there could be not merely two things but any number of bodies brought together in a single place. You fashion a large object out of many small things by joining them together, and within your interval, even if very small, you have simultaneously located any number of bodies. You must therefore admit that the greatest thing can be contained in the smallest and you must include within those limits not only many things equal in size but also many unequal in size. This seems to be completely absurd.[5]—Although Aristotle does not identify the authors of this argument, a little later on he assigns it to Melissus[6] who, although denying that there is a void, makes use of this argument to demonstrate that bodies can move only in a void. From this he concludes that there is no movement whatsoever.

They derive a second argument from the fact that when certain bodies come together they apparently contract, as happens when a cask filled with wine also takes in the skins in which the wine was contained. They therefore maintain that there are present empty spaces into which the compressed parts are transferred.[7]

The third argument is derived from the growth of living things, which can be brought about only if food is diffused throughout empty spaces, or even from a mixture of ashes and water: if a vessel is filled with ashes, it still takes in as much water as would fill the empty vessel.[8]

Lastly, Aristotle recalls the opinion of the Pythagoreans who hold that an infinite void, a sort of very thin breath, extends beyond the heaven in such wise as to be drawn in by the breathing heaven. Hence arose the distinction of diverse natures, hence that of continuous things, and hence first of all that of numbers.[9] If Aristotle had gotten to the heart of this rather Pythagorean doctrine, he might perhaps have departed a little from his own opinion. He would have understood that although empty space cannot be defined in the man-

[5] *Physics* IV, 213, b, 2.
[6] *Physics* IV, 213, b, 12.
[7] *Physics* IV, 213, b, 14.
[8] *Physics* IV, 213, b, 18.
[9] *Physics* IV, 213, b, 22.

ner of the physicists, it is nevertheless necessary for our own thought so that we may distinguish things from things and even concepts from concepts. Although the Pythagoreans presented this idea only in a confused way, yet in my opinion they wonderfully surpassed the others on this point. However, Aristotle touched only lightly on the Pythagoreans. He was concerned solely with the arguments by which the physicists defended the case for empty space. Before refuting such arguments he tries to extract a precise definition of empty space from the opinions of its advocates.

Therefore they call the void that in which there is nothing. Since all things, no matter what they are, appear to be corporeal, and what lacks body is said to be empty, it follows that where no body is contained there is absolutely nothing.[10] You may ask, "What shall we call a body or a corporeal thing?" Aristotle answers that a body is that which can be touched and therefore has either heaviness or lightness.[11] If you wish to explore the reason why Aristotle thinks that all things which are touched are also heavy or light, you will perhaps find that Aristotle attributes to bodies a certain inner force by which they resist you when you touch them and move upwards or downwards. The principle of each property is therefore the same. However it is, in effect the void is that which nothing heavy and nothing light occupies. If you think that a point fulfills this definition, you are seriously mistaken. The void is of necessity a place or interval in which a body can be contained, and therefore it possesses magnitude.[12] A second and more subtle question arises. If the interval had color or sound, would it be empty or not? Aristotle responds, "It will certainly be empty if it can receive a tangible body; if it cannot, it will not be empty."[13] Let us briefly sum up the discussion: If there were empty space, it would have to be defined as entirely lacking in body and yet open to a body that would occupy it.

Having defined what they call the void, Aristotle is now ready to criticize those who think that bodies can be moved only in empty space. First, therefore, since there are various kinds of movement, it is clear enough that even in the full at least what is called qualitative change can be effected, a fact that escaped Melissus.[14] Moreover, even

10 *Physics* IV, 213, b, 30.
11 *Physics* IV, 213, b, 35.
12 *Physics* IV, 214, a, 4.
13 *Physics* IV, 214, a, 9.
14 *Physics* IV, 214, a, 25.

for a movement that occurs in place we state that empty space is in no way necessary. "Moving bodies can succeed to other moving bodies where there is no separate interval in addition to themselves. This is manifest in the whirling motion of continuous things such as liquids."[15] To grasp Aristotle's meaning draw a ring in a solid continuous substance. If the ring revolves so that parts succeed to the place of parts, it is possible for it to be moved although there is no empty interval. A fish moves in the water in the same way: since the water is full inside and presents an unmoved surface, it must be that coherent with the fish, if I may put it so, there is a circle of water which moves around within itself. Since the same can be said of any element that contains a mobile object, there is no reason to postulate an empty interval to explain movement.

Nor are the arguments taken from the increase and compression of bodies any stronger. A body may be compressed, for example, if it ejects air enclosed within it, even though it contains no vacuum at all within itself. "Again a body increases in size not only when another body enters it but also by transmutation, for instance, when air is produced out of water."[16] The meaning of this statement is that bodies increase in size not only by taking in food, as of course occurs in animals, but also by undergoing a conversion which changes them qualitatively and increases them in size. It even seems to Aristotle that the argument based on food taken in is hardly consistent. "Either any and every part is not increased, or it is not increased by a body, or two bodies can be in the same place, . . . or the whole body must be void, if it is increased in every part and is increased by means of the void."[17] We must realize that a body cannot increase unless its particular parts increase. Aristotle holds that within themselves the parts are continuous, for he did not foresee the doctrine of modern physicists and could in no way represent to himself particles separated by intervals and held in equilibrium by equal charges. Since this is the case, it must be either that each part increases in itself, and two bodies may be contained one within the other, or that we say that an entire body is a void since it increases by the accretion of single parts and all the parts are continuous among themselves.

[15] *Physics* IV, 214, a, 28.
[16] *Physics* IV, 214, a, 33.
[17] *Physics* IV, 214, b, 5.

Having refuted the arguments advanced by his opponents, Aristotle next takes up his own doctrine. That there is absolutely no void he establishes by other arguments, especially by that relating to natural movement.[18]

Bodies are set in motion or kept at rest by determinate causes, and the void has no quality or difference whereby one object in it may be said to be above and another below. Hence you will find no cause why a body placed in the void would be carried here rather than there or even why it would prefer to rest in one spot rather than in other. Therefore in the void bodies can neither stand still nor move about.[19] All this becomes clear if we recall the Aristotelian theory of movement. Aristotle has concluded that all things that are moved are moved by force or by nature. Those moved by nature are borne upwards by their lightness or downwards by their heaviness, whereas motion caused by force arises from an external thrust. Since Aristotle establishes two kinds of motion, we will therefore first discuss that brought about by nature.

To the various elements constituting the universe Aristotle assigns a fixed and definite order rising not from fortuitous chance but from the very nature of things. Since this is so and since the elements have their proper place in the world just as parts do in an animal, it must be that earth is borne to the region of earth and air to air not by any impulsive or attractive force but by a certain inward desire. Therefore they strive towards their proper place as to fulfillment of their form, as if different regions of the world were distinguished by different functions and also by different qualities. But there is no quality in the void and no limit in the infinite by which any region may be enclosed or defined. Therefore in the void bodies are carried neither to this place nor to that, nor do they naturally remain at rest here rather than there. But since one and the same body can neither simultaneously be borne about every which way nor simultaneously rest everywhere, and since there is no reason why it should choose any motion or rest, it necessarily follows that in empty space they can neither be impelled by natural motion nor possess natural rest.[20]

Nor can a body be moved in the void contrary to nature "except

---

[18] We omit here a more difficult passage (*Physics* IV, 214, b, 24) which we will explain later. See p. 48.

[19] Cf. Leibniz's third letter to Clarke, Erdmann edition, 752, a.

[20] *Physics* IV, 215, a, 1. Cf. *Physics* VIII, 4; *On the Heavens* III, 2.

as something that is carried."[21] There is this difference between Aristotle and modern physicists: our physicists assert that once impelled a body endlessly continues in its motion, whereas Aristotle concludes that a motion once begun can continue only by perpetual maintenance of the impulsive force. We will not be surprised at this opinion if we note that for natural motion, which Aristotle holds to be completely free, there is continually present an active cause, like an inward desire, which endlessly renews its effect. But if the cause of natural motion is continuously at work, so too things moved contrary to nature continuously resist outside pressure. From this it follows that a continual renewal of the impulse is necessary. This being so, we understand that movement contrary to nature can be continued in the air or in any other corporeal element. When air, divided and compressed by a body thrown into it, is reflected back on itself, it then restores to the body the motion thus received, so that its motion is continuously renewed by an impulse sent from one side to another. It could also be that a body cast into the air or any other element propels certain particles of matter by which still other particles are next propelled until, the circuit being completed, the body receives the motion sent on before it now restored to it from behind, and is endlessly moved as it were by a new impulse.[22] Whichever explanation you choose, you come back to the same thing: an impulsive force cannot be maintained in the void.

To the physical proofs are added mathematical arguments by which it is established that in a void the speed of movement would be infinite and that it could not be compared with any other.

Let a certain weight A be borne through medium B in time Γ, and also through medium Δ, which we suppose to be thinner but equal in length, in time E. The thinner the body traversed is, the more rapid is the speed of the traversing body. Therefore time E will have the same proportion to time Γ as density Δ has to density B. But if B is air and Δ is the void, then Δ will have no proportion to B and consequently E will have none to Γ.[23] This involved argument advanced by Aristotle would, I think, be explained by modern mathematicians something like this: Let us suppose v to be the speed of the traversing body, and let us denote the density of the traversed

21 *Physics* IV, 215, a, 17.
22 *Physics* IV, 215, a, 14. Cf. *On the Heavens*, III, 311, b, 22.
23 *Physics* IV, 215, a, 25.

body by the letter d. Lastly, let there be a certain constant number, m. Since Aristotle supposes that the speed of the traversing body increases in the same proportion as the density of the traversed body decreases, we have $v = \dfrac{m}{d}$. But in this formula if we make $d = 0$, then it would necessarily follow that $v = \infty$. From this we conclude that in the void speed would be infinite.

Aristotle attempts to establish the same conclusion by a more subtle argument, which we will attempt to interpret rather than express in so many words.

Let there be a certain space Z equal to length B, and hence equal to length Δ. If weight A could pass through this interval in a certain time H, then, since time H would necessarily be shorter than time E— if Δ is filled with air, for example, while Z is a vacuum—it would follow that in that same time H the same weight would pass through only part of length Δ in body Δ. We will designate this part by letter Θ. This being posited, let us suppose another body, whose density has the same proportion to the density of body Δ as time H has to time E. This body, which Aristotle has not named, we will designate by the letter I. Since the speed of weight Δ in body I has the same proportion to the speed in body Δ as the density of body Δ has to the density of body I, and this proportion is the same as the proportion of time E to time H, weight A would cover the length of body I, equal to length Z, in the same time as it covers part Θ of body Δ. Therefore the speed in body I has the same proportion to the speed in Δ as the speed in Z has to the speed in Δ. From this we conclude that the speed in Z is equal to the speed in I, and that weight A will cover length I in time H. But we have designated by the letter H the time in which the same interval will be traversed in the void. It therefore follows that equal intervals of the void and of body I will be traversed in the same time. But since we have arbitrarily defined the density of body Δ, and therefore of body I, the final conclusion will be that in a given time weight A will traverse an empty space equal to any length whatsoever. This, we say, is completely absurd.[24]

All this will become clear if we translate Aristotle's words into the language of modern mathematicians. Aristotle assumes that in

---

[24] *Physics* IV, 215, b, 19.

the void the speed of a certain weight A is equal to a finite magnitude v, so that it would there cover a certain interval Z in time t. He then selects a certain body Δ through which weight A will pass. If v' is the speed of the weight in body Δ, and t' the time in which it passes through length $\Delta = Z$ in body Δ, we necessarily have $v' < v$, and hence $t' > t$. From this it results that in time t, weight A, placed in body Δ, covers only part Θ of length Δ. This being posited, let us denote the density of body Δ by the sign d', and let us select density d'' of some new body in the same way, so that we have $\dfrac{d''}{d'} = \dfrac{t}{t'}$. Since Aristotle thinks—and this is completely false—that the speed of the traversing body increases in the same ratio as the density of the traversed body decreases, we could write, if we denote by sign v'' the speed of the same weight in this new body:

$$\frac{v''}{v'} = \frac{d'}{d''}.$$

But since we have posited

$$\frac{d'}{d''} = \frac{t'}{t},$$

it necessarily follows that

$$\frac{v''}{v'} = \frac{t'}{t}.$$

Since the relations of speeds and times are inverse, from this it follows that

$$\frac{t'}{t} = \frac{v}{v'}.$$

From this it is concluded that $v = v''$.

But if you now recall that we have arbitrarily defined body Δ, and hence speed v', as equal to any magnitude, you can affirm the same of speed v''. Since speed v is equal to it, it necessarily follows that in the void speed is equal to any number whatsoever and that the same weight will traverse in the same time both great and small distances of the void. Nothing seems more absurd than this.

If you compare this second conclusion with the first one, you find that Aristotle's argument is self-contradictory. According to the first argument speed in a void is infinite, whereas in the second it is made indefinite, that is, equal to any number whatsoever. Therefore it is probable that Aristotle has committed not only an error in physics but also one in mathematics.

The whole source of the mathematical error lies in this, that a finite part of the void can be traversed in a finite time H. We would say that this is completely contrary to Aristotle's physical doctrine. Since the speed of the traversing weight is assumed to increase at the same rate as the density of the traversed body decreases, speed in the void will be infinite. But if a weight is carried through the void at an infinite speed, the finite interval Z will be traversed not in any finite time but in no time whatever. Since Aristotle did not understand this mathematical consequence, and designated by a fixed number H the time in which interval Z was traversed in the void, he necessarily finds that in the same time H the same distance Z of a certain body Δ will be traversed—and that therefore the speed will be the same in both the void and the full. To solve the problem in a few words, modern mathematicians have distinguished between the infinite and the indefinite. By the indefinite they mean that which equals any magnitude whatsoever, and by the infinite that which is greater than any magnitude.—To these two things so different from one another, Aristotle incorrectly, I believe, has given the same name and the same meaning.

What Aristotle has written on the proportion of zero to number especially displays this confusion: "The void has no proportion by which it is exceeded by a body, just as zero has no proportion to a number. For while four exceed three by one and two by a greater number, and one by still more than two, there is no proportion by which they exceed zero. Of necessity, that which exceeds is divided into the excess and that which is exceeded. That is why four will be that by which they exceed and nothing."[25] Aristotle has apparently confused the two concepts which our mathematicians call proportion and difference. He has perceived that the proportion between zero and a finite number cannot be compared to any other proportion, but he has not sufficiently grasped why and how this is so.

Nor is the argument taken from the nature of a transported body any firmer. "We perceive that bodies having a greater power, either of heaviness or of lightness, but otherwise having the same configuration, traverse more quickly an equal space in the propor-

[25] *Physics* IV, 215, b, 12.

tion which their magnitudes have to one another. Hence they will be carried through the void in the same way. But this is impossible. For what reason will they be moved more quickly? In plena this happens of necessity, for they are divided more quickly by the force of the larger body. In fact what is carried or propelled divides the traversed body according to its shape or force. Therefore [in the void] all things will move with the same speed. But this is impossible."[26]— This is a strange argument and, I think, unworthy of Aristotle. He first assumes that speeds are unequal in the void because they are unequal in every traversed body. He then notes that in the void there is no cause why different bodies should move with different speeds. Since he would have to conclude from this that speeds are equal in the void, he prefers to establish that the void has absolutely no existence.

Let us now pass from physical and mathematical arguments to those which can in some sense be called metaphysical. Aristotle cautiously and gradually approaches his own thesis: what we call a void is simply an interval inserted between the limits of a body and it is incorrectly abstracted from the thing itself. At least it is in this fashion that we interpret the statement in which Aristotle attaches an ambiguous meaning to the word void. "What they call a void will be seen to be a true and proper void if considered in itself."[27] Aristotle means that if the void existed apart by itself, it would truly and properly be worthy of that name since no body whatsoever could be contained in it. Let us see by what proofs he confirms this assertion.

If we place a cube, for example, in water or in the air, an amount of water or air equivalent to the cube will be displaced. But since nothing can give way in the void, it must be that the same interval which previously existed by itself in the empty now permeates the cube. But the cube has a certain magnitude equal to that interval, and although this magnitude cannot be separated, it still differs from all qualities. Therefore, as long as an empty interval is occupied by the magnitude of the cube, it must be either that two things are each one within the other—than which nothing seems more absurd—or else that what we call an empty interval is simply the magnitude of the cube wrongly separated from the cube.[28]

[26] *Physics* IV, 216, a, 13.
[27] *Physics* IV, 216, a, 26.
[28] *Physics* IV, 216, a, 33. We omit an extremely difficult passage Simplicius

Aristotle continues to discuss this problem more rigorously as he refutes arguments relating to density. Some think that the rare is what contains more of the void, whereas the dense is that in which less of the void is included: things that are rare are likewise lighter and rise upwards because they are borne aloft by their emptiness. However, if emptiness is the cause why light objects ascend, it is necessary to explain why heavier objects descend. Still more, if a body is lighter and faster in so far as it contains more of the void, then the void itself moves with infinite velocity. This can in no wise take place, for just as bodies would not move in the void, so also if the void itself existed, it would remain immobile.[29] Yet Aristotle concedes that certain things become rarer and others denser, for unless he conceded this, no movement would now be intelligible.[30] Yet they err grievously who think that in things there is some sort of empty interval which becomes lesser or greater as density increases or diminishes. They distinguish between the elements in a body and the void, placing the elements on this side and the void on that. The reality is far different. The nature of matter is so arranged that it keeps enclosed, as I may say, its two powers of now expanding and now contracting. These powers are not in such and such particles but in solid and continuous matter: if you consider even its least part you will there find potential magnitude and parvity. "If the convexity of a larger circle is made that of a smaller circle, no part becomes curved which previously was not curved but straight. Increase or decrease does not result from a loss."[31] We grasp the diffi-

---

and other interpreters pass over without comment, and apparently it should not be attributed to Aristotle. Cf. *Physics* IV, 216, b, 17 and following.

[29] *Physics* IV, 217, a, 5.

[30] *Physics* IV, 217, a, 10. We will interpret this argument somewhat as follows. Since we deny that there is a void a question arises as to how things can move when condensation and rarefaction have been eliminated. If there is no condensation or rarefaction, it follows that even the least motion when it hits something as it goes on its course finally strikes on the farthest part of the heaven. It also follows that there remains the same mass of water passing off into the air and of air turned into water. Since this is not the case, and the mass of water changed into air is clearly increased, it must be that either the farthest heaven expands (which is completely absurd), or when water changes into air, an equivalent mass of air is somewhere converted into water. However, this does not always occur, since not all movement is circular. (See p. 66.) From this one concludes either that there is absolutely no movement or that bodies condense and rarefy.—Cf. *On the Heavens* 111, 7.

[31] *Physics* IV, 217, b, 2.

culty. Aristotle believes that increase takes place not by the insertion of longer or shorter intervals, but by greater or lesser stretching, if I may so speak, of all the parts. Since bodies are seen now to grow greater and now to lessen, philosophers have thought to separate from matter this power to increase and decrease, as if it were existent in itself. They have called this power the void. This power must be restored to inmost matter and united to the body itself. Therefore, let us say that the void is either absolutely nonexistent or, if it exists, it is simply matter itself in so far as it potentially contains the rare and the dense, which are the principles of lightness and heaviness.[32]

VI

How Aristotle sums up place in a dialectical definition.

Three of the four definitions within which we thought place could be enclosed have been discussed and rejected.[1] Place is neither matter

---

[32] *Physics* IV, 217, a, 21—217, b, 27, and *On Generation and Corruption* I, 321, b, 14.

[1] At this point Aristotle introduces certain extremely obscure opinions (210, a, 24, - 210, b, 27) which we will attempt to explain although they scarcely seem to pertain to the subject. There are eight ways in which a thing can be in another thing: as a part in a whole, as a whole in its parts, as species in genus or as genus in species (a genus is contained in the definition of a species as τὸ μέρος τοῦ εἴδους ἐν τῷ τοῦ εἴδους λόγῳ, as form in matter, and as a thing to be done in a moving cause (ὡς ἐν βασιλεῖ τὰ τῶν Ἑλλήνων), as movement in an end, and lastly as a thing enclosed in a vessel or in a place.—Someone may ask if a thing can be in itself?—Since the question is twofold, according as you mean whether a thing is in itself *per se* or *per aliud*, Aristotle will prove that a thing can be in itself *per aliud* (that is, by its own parts) but in no wise *per se*.

"A whole may be said to be in itself because its parts are both that which it contains and that which is contained (μόρια τοῦ ὅλου τὸ ἐν ᾧ καί τὸ ἐν τουτῷ). Certain descriptions of a whole object are drawn from consideration of its parts (λέγεται κατὰ μέρη): for example, a thing whose surface is white is called a white object and a man whose mind is learned is called learned. Hence the jar will not be in itself, nor will the wine be in itself, but the jar of wine will be in itself. For both, namely, that which is in a thing and that which it is (ὁ τε γὰρ καὶ ἐν ᾧ) are parts of the same whole. The jar will be in the jar of wine in the same way as whiteness or learning is in a man." (We believe that lines 210, a, 33-34 should read as follows: οὕτω μὲν οὖν ἐνδέχεται αὐτό τι ἐν ἑαυτῷ εἶναι (πρώτως δ' οὐκ ἐνδέχεται) οἷον τὸ λευκὸν ἐν σώματι. For unless

nor form, nor is it an empty interval which apparently remains after a body has been removed. It remains that a body's place is that by which that body is surrounded: I mean air, for example, if the body

the words πρώτως δ'ουκ ἐνδέχεται are placed in parenthesis the statement will be completely different from the others). Aristotle therefore means that in this way the wine is enclosed in the jar so that out of the jar and the wine there is made a complete entity which we call jar of wine. Therefore the jar of wine, inasmuch as it is wine, is contained in the jar, but inasmuch as it is a jar, it contains the wine. From this it follows that in some sense the jar of wine contains itself. Therefore it is by its parts, namely, the wine and the jar, and not by itself (πρώτως), that the jar of wine is in itself. The same thing happens when we say that a man is white or learned. Whiteness, for example, is not in the man but in the man's body, and not even in his whole body but in the surface of his body. (However, it is still not contained in the surface as a part in a whole because these two, surface and whiteness, differ from one another by both sense and nature.) Therefore, as long as the jar and the the wine remain separate, there is no reason to say that the jar and the wine are parts. They become parts if we have a jar of wine and this is in itself, just as whiteness is in a man.—What we arrive at inductively (ἐπακτικῶς) —for even though you recognize the eight kinds of inclusion you find that a thing can in no wise be in itself—we confirm by the same line of reasoning. If the jar of wine were in itself *per se* (and not just through its parts), it would follow that the jar is both the jar and the wine and that the wine is both the wine and the jar. But such is not the case: the amphora does not receive the wine because the amphora is wine but because the wine is such, and the wine is not contained in the amphora because it is the amphora but because the amphora is such. So if you consider the definition itself (τὸ εἶναι), you find that the meaning of the container differs from that of the thing contained. But if we set aside the definition and reflect on a consequence or accident (τὸ συμβεβηκός), we come around to the same result. If the amphora were in itself then, since it is not only itself but also contains the wine, it would follow that each of the two things is in the other (ἅμα δύο ἐν ταυτῷ ἔσται), —than which nothing is more absurd. From these various arguments it follows that a thing cannot be in itself.—To Zeno's question as to whether a place may occupy a place, Aristotle answers that it is possible for "a primary place to be in another thing, not as in a place but as a determination or affection."

If you now wish to know how Aristotle finally regards these very minor arguments, it seems to me that the matter must be put somewhat as follows.

Since all things, no matter what they may be, are said to be somewhere and thus to occupy a definite place, Aristotle is concerned lest we think that a place must be assigned its place itself, so that the same question concerning place would be raised without end. He now takes precautions so that this will not occur. Therefore before he establishes that above all there are two places, on the one hand *primary* place (namely, the interior surface of the container) and on the other *common* place or the entire heaven, he is concerned to show how each of them lacks a place. *Primary* place is in something, not as a thing placed in a place but as a limit in a thing limited (οὐδὲν γὰρ κωλύει ἐν ἄλλῳ

is in the air.[2] But is it the entire air or a part of the air? In fact, when we say that a body is situated in the air, we do not mean the entire air but that nearest portion of it which touches and encloses the body. If this were not so, the place would not be uniform with the body.[3] But the place of which we commonly speak, which Aristotle calls primary (that is, proximate) place, cannot be said to be either larger or smaller than the body contained in it.[4] From this it follows that place is the inner surface of the containing reality.

The steps by which Aristotle arrives at this definition are clear and evident. He first rejects anything in the enclosed body that would be foreign to the nature of place, namely, matter, form, and interval. He next rejects anything in the container that did not seem to belong to the proper place of the enclosed body. By the first series of eliminations he is brought to the exterior form or limit of the enclosed body, and by the second to the interior surface of the container. But since the body's limit moves along with the body itself, and since place cannot change into place, he finally eliminates the limit of the enclosed body, so that there remains nothing except the limit of the thing by which the enclosed body is touched. Therefore, having pursued, so to speak, two series of eliminations verging to a mid point, he stops at this mid point and in the same way defines place as the interior limit and surface of the container.

By this first definition of place many things blocking the way have been removed. For if you so define place it necessarily follows that the primary place encloses the thing there situated, but nevertheless is not a part, nor a condition, nor an interval, nor anything else of that thing. Moreover, it will follow that the place can be separated from the thing enclosed, and that it will be neither greater nor smaller than the enclosed body.[5]

Perhaps you will ask, "What is this thing we call the container?" It is a just question, since there is found nothing that does not contain its own parts. Accordingly, if you examine the matter further,

---

μὲν εἶναι τὸν πρῶτον τόπον, μὴ μέντοι ὡς ἐν τόπῳ ἐκείνῳ, ἀλλ' ὥσπερ ἡ μὲν ὑγίεια ἐν θερμοῖς ὡς ἕξις, τὸ δὲ θερμὸν ἐν σώματι ὡς πάθος). Not only is *common* place in no place but it even is in no thing: it is contained in itself by its own parts, as we will see later.

2 *Physics* IV, 212, a, 2.
3 *Physics* IV, 211, a, 24.
4 *Physics* IV, 211, a, 27.
5 *Physics* IV, 210, b, 35.

you will conclude that each and every body is the place of those parts which it holds enclosed. However, Aristotle has determined that the inclusion of a thing placed in its place is of one kind and the inclusion of a part in a whole is of another.[6] If the container and the contained are *continuous*, you have the inclusion of part in whole; if they are *contiguous*, it is the inclusion of a thing placed in place. What we may term contiguous and continuous must be defined. Aristotle discusses this distinction chiefly in three places, two of which you will find in the *Physics* and the third in the *Metaphysics*.[7] "Things whose extremities are simultaneous are said to be contiguous; the continuous are those whose extremes are identical." Let us substitute one word for another: things whose mutually touching extremities are either separate, or at least can be separated in thought, are called contiguous, while the continuous are those whose extremities neither begin to be nor cease to be but are so blended together that they appear to be one and the same thing.

But if we postulate that the parts of some given body are continuous with one another, while the body itself is necessarily contiguous to another body in which it is contained, do we not assign a place to the body but deny it to its parts? Aristotle replies that a thing may have place in two ways: actually and potentially. The body itself actually occupies a place, since it is in contact with the container. Moreover, that part which is so contained in a whole that it is contiguous to rather than continuous with other parts actually has a place: for example, a grain in a heap, since it in fact touches other grains and exists apart from them. But parts properly so called, which are not contiguous to but continuous with one another, possess place not actually but potentially. If you break up a body and release its enclosed parts, each part will immediately occupy a place: it was therefore already prepared for the place, and in that way had the place potentially.[8] But as long as its parts enclosed within the body are continuous and cohesive with one

---

[6] *Physics* IV, 211, a, 29. "When it is separate and contiguous it uses the surface of the container ($\tau\hat{\omega}$ $\dot{\epsilon}\sigma\chi\acute{a}\tau\omega$ $\tauο\hat{υ}$ $\pi\epsilon\rho\iota\acute{\epsilon}\chi ο\nu\tau ο s$) as a primary place ($\dot{\epsilon}\nu$ $\pi\rho\acute{\omega}\tau\omega$) which surface is neither greater than the enclosed body nor less than it in size ($\tauο\hat{υ}$ $\delta\iota\alpha\sigma\tau\acute{η}\mu\alpha\tau ο s$) but equal to it."

[7] *Physics* VI, 231, a, 22.—*Metaphysics*, X, 1068, b, 27; 1069, a, 6.—*Physics* V, 227, a, 11, sq.

[8] *Physics* IV, 212, b, 3.

another, each of them remains there in the manner of a part in a whole, not as a thing placed in place. Meanwhile, as I may put it, they delegate to the whole body that power to acquire a place which they claim for themselves when set free.[9]

The question now arises: In what way can we in practice distinguish the continuous from the contiguous and the part from the whole? It is of little value to confine the contiguous and the continuous in a dialectical definition; it is necessary to search further in order to know by what signs the second cohere with one another whereas the first merely touch one another. If you examine the matter in depth you find that there is no note whereby the contiguous can be distinguished from the continuous if the world is so constituted that all things in it remain immobile. But since some things move about and some things remain immobile, we call those continuous which cannot be moved except conjointly but those contiguous which have such association with one another that while one remains at rest the other can be moved, or even when both are set in motion each one may be moved independently, one to this place and the other to that. We now grasp the meaning of Aristotle's remark, "There would be no dispute about place, if there were no movement."[10] We also grasp why Aristotle has contracted into the following words the first part of his whole argument about place: "Place is necessarily the limit of the surrounding body. By surrounded body I mean that which is mobile."[11]

We will clarify the following obscure argument of Aristotle in

---

[9] We may perhaps now understand a certain statement pertaining to both the void and place which Bekker and others by what is in my opinion a textual error have made very obscure: καὶ πῶς ἐνέσται ἢ ἐν τῷ τόπῳ ἢ ἐν τῷ κενῷ· οὐ γὰρ συμβαίνει, ὅταν ὅλον τεθῇ ἐν κεχωριομένῳ τόπῳ καὶ ὑπομένοντι σώματι (*Physics* IV, 214, b, 24). If we substitute σῶμά τι for σώματι it immediately becomes clear. It is concerned with the fact that neither space nor void can exist as something separate. Aristotle argues thus: A thing can be neither in a place existing by itself nor in a vacuum. If an interval would exist separate and by itself it would be close to the body placed there, or it would permeate, so to speak, all the parts of that body. Therefore, the parts of the body would possess a place in the same way as the entire body. But in fact as long as the body's parts remain in the body (ἂν μὴ χωρὶς τιθῆται), they possess place only in potency; actually they are not in place but in the whole. Place cannot permeate throughout the parts: from this it is gathered that place is not an interval.

[10] *Physics* IV, 211, a, 12.

[11] *Physics* IV, 212, a, 6.

almost the same way, but first, at the risk of speaking in a barbaric way, we will translate it literally into Latin.[12]

> Because what is contained and separate is often changed, while the container remains unchanged—as, for instance, water flowing out of a vessel—for that reason the interval between the limits seems to be something, something as it were over and above the displaced body. This is not the case, but one of the bodies which are interchanged, and have the power of contact with one another, falls into place. If the interval existed apart by itself and could remain in itself, there would be infinite places. When air is exchanged for the water, all its parts do the same in the whole as all the water did in the vessel. Therefore, if the place were simultaneously transferred, there would be the place of a place, and simultaneously there would be many places. But in fact when the entire vessel is moved—in which vessel the part too is moved—there is not a different place for a part but the same place. For the air and the water, and also the parts of the water, succeed one another in the container where they are and not in that place where they are, namely, where the whole of which they are parts is, which is part of that place which is the place of the whole world.

We interpret Aristotle's meaning in the following way. If you consider water and air enclosed within a vessel and alternately moving to and fro, you say that the place of each of them is the vessel itself, or rather that immobile reality, whatever it is, by which the mobile vessel is surrounded. If you carry this vessel about, the parts of the air or water will not change place, for in fact they do not as yet possess a place. They were contained within the mobile vessel and were moved about as parts in a whole, not as something placed in a place: what does not have a place cannot change place. Therefore, while the vessel changes its place, nevertheless the parts exist and are moved in that same vessel, not locally, since they do not have a place, but totally. Indeed, if you thought the interval lying between the sides of a vessel to be something real in itself, you would necessarily think the same concerning the interval that extends between any two parts of the water since it is certainly a part of the whole interval. Therefore, the same relation that all the water had to the containing vessel, each part will likewise have to the parts by which it is surrounded. Just as the vessel can change place in the air, so also each part of the water can change place within the vessel. This being posited, let the vessel

12 *Physics* IV, 211, b, 14.

be transferred to another place: it follows that the part of the
water moved within it will then occupy two places at the same time;
first, the place to which it transferred itself within the vessel, and
second, the place which the vessel occupies in the air, or if you prefer, in the whole world. But that there are two places, each one within the other, or, as Aristotle says, that there is a place of a place, is
altogether absurd. From this we conclude that both those who think
that the interval is something real in itself and those who think
that mobile things are moved inside a mobile body in the same way
as mobile things within the immobile are caught in the same error.
Our definition must therefore be corrected or rather completed. Let
us say that place is that reality which contains within itself the
movement of other things but is itself unmoved.

Aristotle states briefly and concisely: "Just as a vessel is a place
that can be moved about, so also place is an immobile vessel.... To
be a place is to be immobile."[13] Therefore as often as that in which
an enclosed object moves also moves, we may say that the enclosed
object is moved as in a vessel and not as in a place. "When anything
is moved in a mobile object, and what is in it is transferred, such as
a ship on a river, it uses the containing object as a vessel rather than
as a place. To be a place is to be immobile . . . Hence it is
rather the entire river that is a place, because it is immobile."[14] We
will interpret this passage somewhat as follows: Picture a ship
borne down stream on a river and men moving from one spot to
another on the ship. We may say that the place of these men is
neither the moving ship nor even the inner moving boundary of
the water surrounding the ship, but the whole river which is in fact
forever restricted within its unmoved banks. Therefore, we may say
that the men and the ship are in the river's moving current like
water and air within a vessel, while current, ship, and men are in
the whole river as in a place. Hence from these things—current, ship,
and men—there has been fashioned a certain whole, parts of which,
although not continuous among themselves, possess place only potentially. Their sum total possesses place in actuality. We now at
long last understand Aristotle's statement, "Place is the primary
immobile limit of a container."[15] If a mobile object within a mobile

---

[13] *Physics* IV, 212, a, 14.—*Physics* V, 224, b, 5.—Cf. *Metaphysics* X, 1067, b, 9.
[14] *Physics* IV, 212, a, 16.
[15] *Physics* IV, 212, a, 20.

object is moved and this second is contained within a third, we have mobile limits of mobile things. But if we advance progressively through these, then we will conclude that the primary immobile limit that we find on our path is truly a place.

It remains for us to inquire which are the absolutely primary immobile limits. We have said that whatever is moved is moved either by force or by nature. Things moved by nature are borne either downward by heaviness or upward by lightness. Things which are moved contrary to nature are those set in motion by an external thrust. Thus it results that by their own will and weight earthy things are borne towards earth and humid things towards water, while airy and igneous things fly up toward the air or fire as though their very nature strives toward those higher regions.[16]— Aristotle has expressed the same thought in many different ways either in his *Physics* or in other works:[17] the proper act of heaviness is to tend downward and that of lightness to be borne aloft. How important this distinction is for his other doctrines may be gathered from Book IV of *On the Heavens*. There Aristotle seems to pride himself on the fact that while many other philosophers had previously explained how certain objects are heavier or lighter than others, he stands out as the first to discover the causes of heaviness and lightness and to show clearly why certain objects tend downward and others move aloft.[18] We have already spoken of these causes, but we find in the latter book a fuller explanation.[19] In it Aristotle establishes that there are three kinds of movement, the first of which pertains to magnitude, the second to form or quality, and the third and last to place. Just as the connection between increase and the cause of increase or that between change and the cause of change is not due to chance but comes from the very nature of the things that increase and of the things that have been changed, so also with regard to place. We see that what moves and what is moved are most frequently conjoined not by a chance event but by nature itself and an eternal principle. Consequently, a body of whatever kind is moved by a certain internal appetite to its proper

[16] We borrow these words from Cicero who expresses Aristotle's thought in Latin. Cf. *Tusculan Questions*, 1, 17, and *On the Nature of the Gods*, II, 16.

[17] *Physics* IV, 215, a, 2; *Ibid.* VIII, 255, a, 2; *On the Heavens* IV, 1-5; *Physics* V, 230, b, 12; *On the Heavens*, II, 296, b, 27.

[18] *On the Heavens* IV, 308, a, 34.

[19] *On the Heavens* IV, 310, a, 23.

place as to the fulfillment of its form.[20] For this very reason Aristotle criticizes[21] the Pythagoreans who, when they reflected on the pre-eminent dignity of fire, thought that fire must therefore be situated at the middle point of the world, as if what is most important in life would necessarily be central in place. But the case is far different, for place does not have power to act but only to complete an act.[22] For example, you find that water changed into air immediately rises or aspires toward the region of air. This is not because air is drawn toward the natural place of air as if by an active force, but because within the airy form, which the changed water has taken on, there is contained a desire for a certain new place. So true is this that what has become air does not gain possession of its own nature as long as it is away from its natural region. But since among themselves the elements form a continuum from the middle to their extremities, and water therefore embraces earth, air embraces water, fire embraces air, and finally the ethereal body embraces fire, we must divide the universal sphere into rings, each of which will be assigned to a natural element as its natural place. As a result those are truly and properly the primary immobile limits by which the natural elements, disposed according to a natural order, are limited. With regard to any other limits whatsoever, they have an uncertain rest, if I may so put it, which seems to be maintained by force or chance and not by nature and right.

Someone may say that if the nature of the elements is so constituted that they desire to occupy a fixed and definite interval in the world, how is it that you now assert the interval to be something real in itself after having already denied it. What is in itself nothing can in no way be desired. Moreover, in the book entitled *On the Heavens*, does not Aristotle himself recognize that the interval is something in itself, since he speaks as follows? "If someone would transport the earth to the place where the moon now is, each and every particle of earth would be borne not toward the earth but to that same place where it is now located,"[23]—as if particles of earth tend not to the earth itself but rather to that interval, situated within the water, which is usually filled by the earth. We will respond that the particles of earth are attracted neither by the earth

[20] *On the Heavens* IV, 310, a, 34; *Meteorologics* II, 363, a, 30.
[21] *On the Heavens* II, 293, b, 1.
[22] *On the Heavens* II, 293, b, 11.
[23] *On the Heavens* IV, 310, b, 3.

itself nor by the interval. Aristotle denies that like things are attracted to like as if by an active force, and he also denies that the interval exists by itself. But the nature of the earth is so constituted that it comes to rest within water and is moved about among the other elements. Therefore each and every particle of the earth seeks neither the earth nor the empty interval but, so to say, the embrace and companionship of water. In Book I of *On the Generation of Animals*[24] we read that a fixed and definite place is assigned to the parts of a living thing for fulfillment of their functions. Since Aristotle holds that the world is like a living thing, it is of necessity that any particle of matter, without being drawn or constrained, and, no empty interval being posited, yet desires the companionship of those parts and is borne towards them. Among them it fulfills its proper function, and so contributes as much as possible to the universal body.

If this is the case and if we define natural place by this close conjunction whereby the elements are held together throughout the entire world, as in a living thing, it necessariy follows that just as the whole living thing is the place of its own parts, in like manner that is truly and properly a place which contains and conserves within its embrace the arrangement and order of all things, namely, the entire heaven. Hence, after Aristotle has said that every immobile limit is a primary, meaning proximate, place, he adds that the place that is common, and preeminently deserving to be called place, is the heaven. Or rather, to speak plainly, it is that which is especially immobile in the heaven, viz., on one side the middle and on another the surface: "The middle of the heaven, and the surface of the rotating system which is turned toward us, properly and preeminently seem to all men to be 'up' and 'down,' since the middle always remains at rest whereas the surface of the circle always maintains itself in the same manner."[25]—How it is that what Aristotle calls the "surface of the rotating system" is immobile, will be explained elsewhere. For the present it will be sufficient for us to note that all things are placed within the heaven but the heaven

24 *On the Generation of Animals,* I, 12.

25 *Physics* IV, 209, a, 31; 212, a, 26; 212, a, 21. Cf. *On the Heavens* IV, 310, b, 7.

itself does not possess a place.[26] Since certain things are said to
possess place of themselves while others, as Aristotle states, possess
place because of their parts, we will state that the parts of the
heaven, among which one part embraces another, are collocated in
the heaven, while the heaven itself, since it is not contained within
anything else, lacks place.[27] From this it follows that the extreme
surface of the heaven must be deemed supremely worthy of the
name place, not only because it contains all things but also because
it is itself contained nowhere.

That beyond the heaven there is nothing—no body, no void, not
even space[28]—Aristotle confirms by many arguments. Some of these,
those pertaining to the void, have already been examined by us, and
the others, those drawn from the fact that matter cannot extend into
infinity, now require our consideration. Since many different arguments are found in the *Physics* and *Metaphysics* and also in the
work entitled *On the Heavens*,[29] showing why the world cannot extend into infinity, we will select only those by which the Aristotelian
doctrine of place can be clarified.

First, then, Aristotle again and again urges the following argument. If the world were infinite, a proper place in it could not be
assigned by nature to each element. In Book I of *On the Heavens* he
writes: "If things have heaviness or lightness, there will be either
some furthest place in the universe or a middle one; but this cannot
be if the universe is infinite. Where there is neither a middle nor an
extremity, where there is no up and no down, there is also no place
for movement by bodies. Take away place and you take away movement. It is necessary that things move either according to nature
or against nature, and these movements are determined by the
difference between a proper and an alien place."[30]—He repeats the
same argument but more concisely in Book II of *On the Heavens*:
"In an infinite world there could be neither an upper nor a lower
place: it is by this difference that heavy and light are deter-

---

[26] *Physics* IV, 212, b, 18; 212, a, 31; 212, b, 8.

[27] *Physics* IV, 212, b, 12.

[28] *On the Heavens* I, 279, a, 11.—*On the Heavens* II, 287, a, 12. Cf. Leibniz's
fourth letter to Clarke, 7 (Erdmann edition, 756, a).

[29] *Metaphysics* X; *Physics* III; *On the Heavens* I.

[30] *On the Heavens* I, 276, a, 6. Cf. *Metaphysics* X, xi, 14.

mined."[31]—Someone may ask why it is impossible for things that rise to go on rising into infinity. We have the answer in Book I: "Since contrary places are sought by contrary movements, if one of the contraries is determined then the other is also determined. The middle is in fact determined, for from no matter what point that which sinks starts down, it cannot go beyond the center. It is therefore necessary that the higher place also be determined."[32] This is a strange answer and it is a good illustration of Aristotle's astonishing confusion of physics and logic.

Nevertheless it is clear that we must inquire why other worlds, and therefore other places, cannot exist beyond this world of ours. Aristotle concludes that this is completely impossible. If another world were to exist somewhere beyond our own, it would necessarily be made up of the same elements, since it is out of earth, water, air, fire, and ether that whatever was potentially contained in matter has been brought to actuality. You must attribute the same power and the same mode of operation to the same elements: if this were not so they would be the same elements only in name and not in fact. Therefore whatever particles of earth or of fire you assign to that other world, it must be that they, like particles of our earth and particles of our fire, will strive by their own proper movement to the middle or to the limits of our world. In fact since a particle of earth which is borne toward the middle of our heaven necessarily moves away from the extremity of that other world, and since that particle of fire which strives toward the limits of our world gets closer to the middle of its heaven, it necessarily follows that we must either say that there the same body moves to the middle but here to the extreme, which seems completely absurd to Aristotle, or admit that that other world and our heaven are one and the same.[33]

A little later on we find a quite similar argument which we condense somewhat as follows. If you assume any body whatsoever to exist beyond the heaven, you will say that it occupies either its own or another's place. But if it occupies another's place, it must be that some other body, for which that was the proper and natural place, has been expelled from it. Therefore, whether you state that that place is the proper place of the enclosed body or of some other body, you must in each case posit a natural place outside our world. But

31 *On the Heavens* II, 295, b, 8.—Cf. *On the Heavens* I, 7 (274, b 7; 275, b, 29 sqq.)

32 *On the Heavens* I, 273, a, 8.   33 *On the Heavens* I, 8.

this is absurd since the natural places of the elements are all contained within our heaven.[34] If you compare these arguments and others bearing on the same subject in Books III and IV of the *Physics*,[35] where it is demonstrated that movement into infinity can neither be nor be conceived, you will have a continuous series of arguments by which Aristotle passes first from natural movement to natural place and then from an image of natural place to a denial of infinite space. We sum up these arguments as follows.

Since it is by their own impulse that certain bodies are borne downwards and certain others upwards, and since movement can strive only to a natural place, it necessarily follows that by each and every element—earth, water, air, fire, and ether—a fixed and proper place in the world will be occupied. Now since bodies placed in another element, for example, particles of earth in the air, keep to a fixed and definite path in that element so as to return as it were to their own proper region, and whereas just as in an infinite element we find no difference by which diverse movements may be defined and no reason why the displaced bodies may be borne here rather than there in that element, it necessarily follows that the elements are finite and that finite places are occupied by finite elements in a finite world. This established, whatsoever body you conceive as placed outside the world will necessarily be composed of the same elements, since it is from our elements that whatever potentiality was embedded in matter has been evolved. In fact, since the same elements have the same natural movements, and the natural places of the elements are contained within our heaven, any body you posit outside it will immediately fall into our world, and it was therefore improperly assigned a place elsewhere. Therefore from a consideration of natural movement it follows that the world is a kind of living thing, and that the simple elements, like the parts of a living thing, exercise their proper functions in certain proper places which they desire when lost and cling to when found again. It also follows that a foreign body uses the element it traverses as a *primary* place, the element itself uses a surrounding element as a *proper* place, and finally all the elements use the heaven as a *common* place. Therefore each part of the heaven, in so far as it is surrounded by other parts, occupies a place, but the entire heaven, outside of which there is

[34] *On the Heavens* I, 9. Cf. *Physics* III, 5.
[35] *Physics* III, 5; IV, 8.

nothing void and nothing corporeal in which it could be contained, lacks place.[36]

36 Wolter (*De Spatio et Tempore*, Bonn, 1848; pp. 23-25) tries to show that Aristotle not only discusses place but also considers "absolute" space, which "penetrates through all bodies in world from the farthest surface of the heaven down to the center of the earth." Our entire explanation of Aristotle's doctrine refutes such an interpretation of it. If space of such kind existed it would be reduced either to the void or to a sort of interval conceived by our minds. Each of these is completely at odds with Aristotle's doctrine. However the arguments offered for this position must be considered.

Aristotle writes place "διαστήματα ἔχειν τρία" (209, a, 4) in the part of his discussion where he states the conflict of opposing opinions and shows and amplifies the difficulties of the subject, as we have already seen (p. 24). After he has rejected the other opinions he then states his own.

Nor is the argument that Wolter derives from the fourth book of *On the Heavens* any stronger: Ἔστι δὲ δή τι καὶ τὸ μεταξὺ τούτων, ὃ πρὸς ἑκάτερον αὐτῶν λέγεται θάτερον· ἔστι γὰρ ὡς ἔσχατον καί μέσον ἀμφοτέρων τὸ μεταξύ. Διὰ τοῦτο ἔστι τι καὶ ἄλλο βαρὺ καὶ κοῦφον, οἷον ὕδωρ καὶ ἀήρ. (On the Heavens IV, 4). We have seen that by the words τὸ μεταξὺ τούτων he does not mean any intermediate space but corporeal elements arranged in a natural order, which are called light or heavy, so that each of them lies nearer either to the limits or to the center of the world.

In fact from the words τὸ κενὸν ἀνάγκη τόπον εἶναι εἰ ἔστιν ἐστερημένον σώματος (*Physics* IV, 214, a, 16) Wolter concludes that "space is a reality spread throughout the whole expanse of the world and filled with bodies." In my opinion nothing is farther from Aristotle's thought than this. The words ἐστερημένον σώματος must be referred not to τὸ κενόν, since they would then be useless, but to τόπον. We therefore translate Aristotle's statement into Latin thus: "If there were a void it would be a place deprived of a body." But Aristotle holds that a place deprived of a body cannot possibly exist.

I would say that a more acute argument is that taken from two passages in the *Physics:* ἐν ᾧ γάρ ἐστιν, ἀντιμεθίσταται ὁ ἀήρ καὶ τὸ ὕδωρ ἢ τὰ μόρια τοῦ ὕδατος, ἀλλ᾽ οὐκ ἐν ᾧ γίνονται τόπῳ, ὅς μέρος ἐστὶ τοῦ τόπου ὅς μέρος ἐστὶ τόπος ὅλου τοῦ οὐρανοῦ. (*Physics* IV, 211, b, 27) καὶ μένει δὴ φύσει πᾶν ἐν τῷ οἰκείῳ τόπῳ ἕκαστον οὐκ ἀλόγως· καὶ γὰρ τὸ μέρος τόδε ἐν τῷ τόπῳ ὡς διαιρετὸν μέρος πρὸς ὅλον ἐστιν, οἷον ὅταν ὕδατος κινήσῃ τις μόριον ἢ ἀέρος. (*Physics* IV, 212, b, 32). From these passages Wolter concludes that each and every place is like a part of a certain space terminated by the entire heaven. However, Wolter apparently has no understanding whatever of the meaning of the words τόπος ὅλου τοῦ οὐρανοῦ. Aristotle confirms over and over that the entire heaven lacks a place, whereas the parts of the heaven, since some parts are included in other parts, occupy place. Hence it is clear that by the words ὅλου τοῦ οὐρανοῦ it is not the entire heaven, which in fact lacks a place, but all the parts of the heaven that are meant. Therefore, what Aristotle calls τόπον ὅλου τοῦ οὐρανοῦ is simply the whole corporeal mass of the world, which, since it has parts that are enclosed within other parts, is the place of its parts. Therefore, we may say that any natural place—earth, water,

VII

Difficulties into which Aristotle's definition of place falls.

Practically nothing further concerning place is to be found in Book IV of the *Physics*. However, if you were satisfied with these doctrines you would confine yourself to Aristotle's exoteric teaching and not get down into his deeper thought. Unless you examine it deeply and interpret it carefully, this description of place does not seem to be wholly consistent either with the rest of Aristotle's teaching or with itself. As we see it, there is a threefold problem. Let us first indicate what it is, and then solve it if we can.

After Aristotle has defined place in such wise that it will necessarily be immobile, he states that the supreme place, that especially deserving of the name, is the heaven. Yet Aristotle thinks that not only is the heaven not immobile but that among all things it alone moves with an eternal movement. Hence it results both that place is immobile and that the heaven, which is truly and properly called place, moves eternally. We would say that this difficulty, one

---

air, fire, and ether—are parts of the whole world, and in this way μέρη εἶναι τοῦ τόπου ὅς ἐστι τόπος ὅλου τοῦ οὐρανοῦ, or even ὡς διαιρετὰ μέρη εἶναι πρὸς ὅλον. Therefore, what is here at issue is the whole heaven or world and not any space put in between the middle and the limits of the heaven.

There remains an argument taken from the *Categories* which Wolter thinks is the weightiest of all: πάλιν ὁ τόπος τῶν συνεχῶν ἐστί. τόπον γάρ τινα τὰ τοῦ σώματος μόρια κατέχει ἅ πρός τινα κοινὸν ὅρον συνάπτει. Οὐκοῦν καὶ τὰ τοῦ τόπου μόρια, ἅ κατέχει ἕκαστον τῶν τοῦ σώματος μορίων, πρὸς τὸν αὐτὸν ὅρον συνάπτει, πρὸς ὅν καὶ τὰ τοῦ σώματος μόρια. Ὥστε συνεχὴς ἄν εἴη καὶ ὁ τόπος. πρὸς γὰρ ἕνα κοινὸν ὅρον αὐτοῦ τὰ μόρια συνάπτει. (*Categories* 6.) From this Wolter wishes to conclude that "space so much belongs to all things that not even the parts of continuous bodies lack it." But if you examine Aristotle's words carefully, you perceive that here he is concerned not with all the parts of a body but only with those that occupy a place. Aristotle therefore argues as follows: "Since a place is that which contains within itself a corporeal thing, there cannot be continuous parts of a body unless there is a continuous place." In the *Categories* he is not concerned with which of a body's parts a place must be assigned to and which must be denied a place. Since he there says, τὰ τοῦ τόπου μόρια ἅ κατέχει ἕκαστον τῶν τοῦ σώματος μορίων, you must understand ἕκαστον τῶν τοῦ σώματος μορίων ἅ ἐστιν ἐν τόπῳ. But in the *Physics* he establishes that actual place is not to be attributed to all parts of a body but only to those which occupy the surface of the body. Therefore the passages taken from the *Categories* do not refer to the whole body but to the surface of the body.

already recognized by Theophrastus,[1] is increased rather than lessened by words Aristotle inserts into Book IV of the *Physics* itself: "It is because the heaven is always in motion that we judge it especially to be in place," [2] as though he were not to state a little later that the heaven lacks a place.

Let us proceed to a second difficulty. We have shown that any element is the place of an inferior element which is contained in the first like a ring enclosed within another ring. Aristotle's doctrine on proper places can be understood in no other way. We have therefore made those elements immobile, since, as Aristotle states, "Place means to be immobile." But note how Aristotle emphasizes that the elements move, are changed about, and cannot remain in the same places. In Book II of *On Generation and Corruption* we read that "If each of them remained in its own place . . . they would no longer be separate and distinct . . . It is impossible for any of them to remain in a fixed place." [3] From this it is concluded that even though place means to be immobile, yet the elements set within the heaven both function as natural places and move about.

Finally, the third difficulty arises from what Aristotle calls *primary* and we name *proximate* place. Primary place is the inner surface of the containing object. For example, we say that the surface of the air touching and surrounding a particle of earth put into the air is a primary place. Since certain bodies occupy place in actuality and others in potency, those alone have place in actuality which are separate from the contacting thing, and for that reason can be called contiguous and not continuous with it. But as long as the thing enclosed remains immobile, there is no reason to say that the container and the contained are separate. It can be that from these objects, which seem to be two, one solid body is fashioned, and that the thing you call the enclosed—since the things you believed to be contiguous are continuous—does not occupy a place in actuality but only in potency. As we have said, it acquires an actual place for itself when it moves about as a separate thing. It is therefore by motion that the conjunction of bodies and by motion that our difficulty are destroyed. This being established, see how something marvelous and almost unbelievable results: a body has a place on

[1] Theophrastus in Simplicius, Diels edition, p. 604, 1. 5 sqq.
[2] *Physics* IV, 211, a, 13.
[3] *On Generation and Corruption* II, 337, a, 11.

condition that it exists apart from its place. An enclosed object, then, in the strictest sense uses a contacting and containing surface as its place at the moment when by its departure it destroys the association, and it is then no longer either touched by that surface or contained in it. You must therefore say that a body possesses its place when it leaves its place, which seems to be completely absurd, or hold that there is a mobile place, the limit of the container, which follows the body. But if you hold to this opinion you abandon Aristotle's definition which states that primary place is an immobile limit.

To sum up, we have said that a mobile body is contained within the immobile limit of the containing thing as in its primary place, that a simple element is contained within the immobile element by which it is surrounded as in its proper place, and finally that all things are contained within the unmoved surface of the heaven as in their common place. But note that the heaven moves, that the elements move, and that the surface of each containing thing moves. Therefore, we have not entirely grasped Aristotle's meaning, since to examine these matters more easily we have commanded many things that were necessarily in motion to stand still. Now, if we are to restore interrupted movement to the Aristotelian world, it will be worth the effort to inquire as to what will become of place.

VIII

How the problem can be solved.

We can deduce from Book II of *On the Heavens* how it is that the heaven can be called both mobile and immobile. To those asking why the heaven is globe-shaped Aristotle responds: "If we ascribe any other form whatsoever to the heaven, it will change place as long as it revolves." [1] In Book VIII of the *Physics* he makes the same statements with regard to the properties of a sphere. "A globe both moves and remains at rest since it occupies the same place." [2] He arrives at a similar conclusion in the following words: "For a revolving body the place in which it begins and the place where it

[1] *On the Heavens* II, 287, a, 11.
[2] *Physics* VIII, 265, b, 1.

ends are identical." [3] But nowhere has he more clearly and nowhere more elegantly explained the matter than in Book I of *On Generation and Corruption,* where he writes that "the parts of a sphere change place but the whole sphere remains in the same identical place." [4]

However, a question arises: In what sense of the word can we say that the sphere retains the same place? Aristotle has denied that place is an interval inserted between the limits of the thing in place. Now, however, when he says that a revolving sphere always retains the same place, does he not seem to define place in such wise that it is an immobile interval occupied by the mobile sphere?

In my opinion,. if Aristotle were questioned he would answer somewhat as follows. The heaven, of which we are speaking, is that limit which sustains the fixed stars in their determinate seats. Because it is neither enclosed within nor touched by any other thing, it does not have a place and therefore it cannot move. But the parts of the heaven, of which one encloses another, occupy a place; therefore they must change place as long as the heaven revolves. If you wish to understand how the parts change place, it must be taken thus: If a straight line is drawn upwards from above our head, it intersects the most remote surface of the heaven at a certain point Z. Since this point is sited at the extreme end of an immobile line drawn from the immobile earth, it is itself immobile. But if you stand at this point, then for you the parts of the heaven will change place, since you will see different stars passing by at different moments. Therefore, although the fixed stars keep the same order among themselves, still for you standing at point Z and seeing on your left things that were on your right and things close at hand which were far distant, the arrangement of parts will appear to be changed. Hence it comes about that the parts of the heavenly sphere, which itself lacks place, have place and change place.[5] But if you consider some other sphere, interpretation of Aristotle's doctrine will be even easier for you. When it is enclosed by some surrounding body, and its place is the inner limit of that surrounding body, then as the sphere rotates it keeps the same place since it is contained within that same limit. However, its parts change

3 *On the Heavens* I, 279, b, 3.
4 *On Generation and Corruption,* I, 320, a, 22.
5 *Physics* IV, 212, a, 31.

place, since at different moments they touch different parts of that limit.

To sum up, Aristotle means that circular movement is of one kind and movement in a straight line is of another. As far as we can understand it, a thing whose parts change place because of the complete thing moves in a straight movement, where a thing that moves because of its parts moves with a circular movement. A thing that is borne straight forward changes place, but since the parts enclosed within it occupy a place only potentially they change place only potentially. But circular movement is engendered by the law that it must always keep the same place; therefore the parts of the globe's surface change place, but the globe itself does not. We may therefore draw up the Aristotelian doctrine, as we see it, as briefly as possible in these words: In movement in a straight line the parts are moved by the whole; in circular movement the whole is moved by the parts.

This being established, two rather obscure statements become clear. One of them, taken from Book IV of the *Physics*, we have already expressed in Latin in the following way: "The extremity of the rotating system properly and especially seems to all men to be 'up' . . . because the surface extremity of the circle always maintains itself in the same manner."[6] What Aristotle calls "the extremity of the circle" we have termed "point Z." Although many parts of the revolving heaven pass in turn through this point, yet each one of these parts, when it is at point Z, presents itself to us in the same way. We find another much more obscure statement in Book VI on the *Physics*: "First, the parts of the globe never remain in the same place; then the whole globe itself is always in motion, for it is not the same circuit that is taken from point A, and from B, and from C, and from the other distinct points, except as one who is a musician and a man, that is, *per accidens*."[7]—We will interpret this text very easily if we ascend to our point Z. When the different points A, B, and C of the revolving heaven pass through the immobile point Z, then for you as you stand at point Z the circumference of the heaven which will be taken from A, B, and C and the other individual points passing one by one through this immobile point Z, will not be the same. Therefore, for you the image of the heaven will change, even though the entire heaven

6 *Physics* IV, 212, a, 21. See p. 53.
7 *Physics* VI, 240, a, 34.

does not have a place and does not change. You affirm that all these numerically infinite images are yet one and the same heaven, just as a man who practices music and the other arts, and thus assumes many roles, is still a man.

We will reply in much the same way to Simplicius and other critics who wonder why Aristotle sometimes says that circular movement occurs as to place and sometimes denies that the heaven moves in place.[8] The parts of any revolving globe move as to place. On the other hand since the whole globe is always contained within the same limits, and even though it cannot be said to be immobile it neither changes place nor moves as to place. But what we say of any globe applies much more to the heaven. As Aristotle himself says, its several parts occupy place and change place, but its whole surface cannot change place for the reason that it has no place.

Let us now descend from the heaven to the lower elements, and from the first question that was advanced to the second. We may wish to know how each element can be called a natural place even though it moves, as Aristotle himself asserts.

First of all, Aristotle has explained again and again how the elements are united by a bond of proximity. Just as there is a certain power in matter out of which many forms are evolved, so also the other elements are already potentially contained in each element.[9] Elements are therefore born out of elements—out of water air, and out of air fire—so that whatever elements are contiguous can also be said to be cognate, and are bound to one another not only by proximity but also by affinity. For this reason fire has a resemblance to air and air to water, as if neighboring elements show a sort of family likeness.[10] This relationship is marvelous and, if I may so put it, reciprocal. In Book I of the *Meteorologics* we read that water drawn out by the rays of the sun is changed into air and flies upward. Then, because of lack of heat, water is again made out of the air and turns back down.[11] The same thing is stated in Book IV of the *Physics*: "Water is potentially air, and in another way air is potentially water."[12]

[8] Simplicius, ed. cit., p. 602, 1. 23.
[9] *Physics* IV, 213, a, 1. Cf. *Meteorologics* I, 2, 3, 4.
[10] *On the Heavens* IV, 310, a, 33. *Physics*, IV, 212, b, 29. Cf. *On the Heavens* IV, 4.
[11] *Meteorologics* I, 346, b, 24.
[12] *Physics* IV, 213, a, 2.

Since this is so and alternately water turns into air and air into water, it must be that changes among the elements turn as it were in a circle, and, if the expression may be permitted, move within a sort of circle of qualities reborn from their own offspring. Out of continuous and kindred elements, such as air and fire, something whole is produced, the parts of which change place with one another while the universe itself always occupies the same place. Therefore, like the heaven, it is by reason of their parts rather than by themselves that the elements move. Just as the fixed stars in the ultimate heaven maintain among themselves the same order as they circle about, so in like manner the same order, the same continuum of elements arranged in plan from earth to heaven, is maintained, although among themselves the single parts of each element change form and place.

We not only arrive at this conclusion by reason but we confirm it by Aristotle's own words. In Book I of the *Meteorologics* we read that the mutual change of water into air and air into water imitates the circular movement of the sun: out of water and air there results a certain river as it were which moves both upward and downward.[13] In Book II of *On Generation and Corruption* he writes—I am not sure whether it is a recollection of a statement by Heraclitus[14]— that all things that interchange among themselves show a similarity to circular movement. The change of water into air and of air into water, although made in a straight line directed both upwards and downwards, still imitates circular movement by its continuity.[15] Moreover, he explains the causes of this imitation in the same book: the circular movement of the heaven is transmitted to each of the nearby elements, from the extreme to the middle; from that movement arises the revolution of the sun; from the sun's revolution the changes of the year result; finally, from the circle of yearly changes the circular change of water and air proceeds.[16] From this we can conclude that it is for the same reason that the heaven is called the common place and the elements natural places. Since the elements move after the pattern of the heaven, they also imitate within the same boundaries the circular movement of the heaven. However there is this difference between them: the heaven entirely lacks

13 *Meteorologics* I, 346, b, 35.
14 Diogenes Laertius, IX, 8.
15 *On Generation and Corruption,* II, 337, a, 1.
16 *On Generation and Corruption* II, 338, a, 17.

place, and is therefore a place in the highest degree, while the simple elements, enclosed in the heaven, function as places not of themselves, but, as I may say, by a kind of delegation from the heaven and in imitation of it.

It remains for us to pass from these problems to those we were led into by the definition of primary place. We find that primary place is a slippery and elusive thing which seems to vanish almost as soon as it appears. Primary place is defined as the limit of the containing reality, and we say that this containing reality although itself immobile yet surrounds a mobile body. It must necessarily follow that the containing reality particularly wins for itself the function and title of place at the moment when, with the departure of the enclosed body, it makes manifest its own stability. But then it is no longer a place. Therefore the question arises of how a body most precisely possesses a primary place at the very moment it gives up its primary place. To this question, raised perhaps by a kind of excessive curiosity or scrupulosity on our part, we will answer by a conjecture rather than a firm argument taken from Aristotle.

Since the heaven by its circular movement contains within unmoving limits the common place of all things, while the lower elements, imitating the circular movement by a similar revolution, maintain among themselves the unmoving arrangement and order of natural places, it is according to reason that there be some third kind of natural circular movement by which our third problem about the mobility of place may be solved. In Book IV of the *Physics* we read that a body may be moved even in complete space as long as other bodies in turn succeed to it, and that an unbroken series so to speak of things turning about like a whirlwind is kept up. This arrangement had already been expressed by Plato,[17] and for that reason Aristotle merely indicates it rather than develops it.[18] Since in the Aristotelian world all things are plena and all can move, it is probable that from the movement of any body placed in a different element a sort of spinning movement that imitates the circular revolution of the heaven will be born. Therefore, if a particle of earth passes through the air, since it propels particles of air by which other particles are propelled, the movement sent before itself

[17] Plato, *Timaeus*, 58E, 59A.
[18] *Physics* IV, 215, a, 14.

it receives again, restored to it from behind. The result is that even if the particle of earth follows a straight line, it fashions a globe of things congealed together like a mobile ring. But since this ring is moved by its parts rather than by itself, and is therefore contained within unmoving limits, like a river in its bed, this ring keeps to the same place as it is whirled around. Therefore, if you determine that the primary place is that surface within which the mobile ring turns, it will be possible for the primary place to be an immobile surface and for the enclosed thing to move. It is not because of the departure of the thing enclosed but rather because of the presence of the ring revolving within the same limits that primary place wins the honors of place.[19]

IX

The origin and meaning of Aristotle's theory of place and its relation to his metaphysical and physical doctrines. Why most philosophers have discussed space whereas Aristotle has discussed place.

We are now at last in a position to explain in a few words why Aristotle substitutes place for space, the difficulties into which he has fallen because of this, and by what hidden thought and then by what chain of explicit arguments he has led to a theory by which, as it seems to us, he evades rather than answers the chief question concerning space.

Aristotle thinks, just as do most philosophers of our own time, that space is in some way a container in which corporeal things have been placed and move. However, since like Kant we divide cognition into two elements, namely, matter and form, and hence conclude that in themselves the qualities of things lack space, we therefore assert not only that bodies are in space but that space is in bodies. It follows that it is impossible to discuss the place of a whole body without discussing the place of its parts, and it therefore seems

---

[19] Aristotle not only does not maintain that all motion is circular but he explicitly denies it: οὐκ ἀεὶ δ'εἰς τὸ κύκλῳ ἡ φορὰ, ἀλλὰ καὶ εἰς εὐθύ. (*Physics* IV, 217, a, 19.) Here the point at issue is qualitative motion. Although such motion in some way imitates circular movement, it is made in a straight line running from the middle to the extremity of the heaven. Local motion, even if in a straight line, still produces and, if I may so put it, spins out circular movement after itself.

that extension itself must be discussed. Extension having been thus separated from physical qualities, it has been necessary to investigate not only with regard to bodies the place they occupy but also with regard to qualities the place through which they acquire extension. From this we conclude that for us it is a question not of place but of space.

Moreover, from our distinction between matter and form it follows that even if all things in a finite world are plena, our space can yet be said to be both empty and infinite. While holding that all qualitative changes revolve in a finite cycle and that beyond definite limits nothing perceptible to the senses can be found, nevertheless we progress in thought beyond this and we do not permit ourselves to be enclosed in any space, no matter how vast, without immediately desiring to fly beyond it. Therefore, since our philosophers have determined that there are two modes of existence —one of concrete reality composed of matter and form, the other of free and independent form—we understand how it is possible for every concrete object made up of matter and form to be finite, while the form extends into infinity.

To us it does not appear in any way contradictory either that empty space exists somewhere or that it is at least mentally conceivable. Since we define place and extension in such wise that the extension of a body arises from a relation of its parts and place from a relation of bodies, we call space that through which the relation is made and movement takes place, namely, the condition of extension and movement. Therefore, if we imagine two bodies so placed in the world that they are not separated by any other thing perceptible to the senses or defined by some quality, and if you cannot pass from one to the other without moving yourself—since movement consists in change of relation and what has no existence of any kind cannot be moved—we are forced to admit that relation, change of relation, and the condition for change of relation have real existence. Now that which effects the change of relation, or at least receives and undergoes it, we call empty space. Therefore, to those asking how can that exist which is devoid of quality and power and thus completely inactive, we reply that there are two modes of existence: one we call physical, that of an object composed of matter and form, the other mathematical, yet no less real, that of form separated from matter. We thus understand how our space is both empty and boundless.

Aristotle is unable to concede this to us, nor would he wish to do so even if he could.

If empty space existed it would be wholly inactive, and Aristotle holds that a thing that is wholly inactive is totally nonexistent. Hence since he conceives no type of existence except that which is contained either in act or in the power to act, and since empty space lacks both of these, he concludes that empty space cannot exist in any way. For this reason he rebukes Leucippus and Democritus who postulate empty space for their atoms as a theatre of movement, as if that which is nothing could exist in any way.[1] But since in Aristotle's vocabulary the two terms "to be" and "to be determinate" mean the same thing, it necessarily follows that all real beings whatsoever are defined not only by a fixed quality but also by finite magnitude. Therefore we have a metaphysical principle from which Aristotle proceeds to arrive at a denial of space as we describe it. His whole discussion of place is comprised within this principle as its inner spirit. But there remains the series of physical arguments by which Aristotle, even if he were not obligated to do so by the rest of his doctrine, was brought to substitute place for space. We describe these arguments as follows.

For our part when we mentally conceive space as unlimited and completely devoid of qualities and differences, we think of bodies as equally adapted to rest and movement and as indifferent to whether they are borne here or there. Hence we think that motion is not inseparably joined to the nature of body but is something extrinsic and to be added to the body. From this it follows that for us the different kinds of movement seem to differ from one another not by physical character, so to speak, but rather by a mathematical principle. Therefore we associate our boundless space with a kind of geometrical concept of movement. We assign motion to the geometricians to be studied mathematically, just as we do shape. But since Aristotle makes a physical rather than a mathematical distinction between the different kinds of movement and believes that there is one character or appetite that tends downwards and another that moves upwards, for this reason he was led to reject completely our boundless space and to discuss place. He holds that movement coheres with body and flowers forth from its inmost nature. For

---

[1] *Metaphysics* I, 985, b, 4; *Metaphysics* III, 1009, a, 25.—Cf. *On Generation and Corruption* I, 317, b, 8.

instance, fire moves upwards as though to attain its proper form, while open running water comes to rest only at the moment when it finds a bed prepared for it, as it were, between earth and air. Therefore it is by qualities differing from one another, and by a different spirit, that the motion which indicates gravity and that set off by lightness are inwardly penetrated. But if natural movements differ from one another in quality, so also their limits, that is, natural places, differ in quality. But what is discussed here is not space as we conceive it, the parts of which are indicated only by geometrical differences. Instead of empty boundless space, we will now have places which are not only limited in size but also definite in quality. Therefore, the world, like a living thing, will consist of fixed elements that maintain a fixed order. What conserves this order, namely this complex of each and every containing element, and therefore the heavens, in which all things are contained, is what we will truly and properly call place. From this we conclude that Aristotelian place does not exist before bodies but arises from bodies, or rather from the order and arrangement of bodies.

Among more recent philosophers we find certain things relevant to this subject. Leibniz, for example, has thought to derive space in much the same way from the order and arrangement of elements. It is therefore worth our effort to ask why Leibniz went on to a study of space, whereas Aristotle lingered, if I may put it so, in place.

Like Aristotle, Leibniz thought that there is no empty space in which bodies dwell like fish in water. Since space arises from the composition and conjuncture of things, and bodily parts are themselves bodies, we must either proceed into infinity or come to incorporeal elements, whose multiplicity expands into a confused image of extension, just as unseen drops merge together to form a colored cloud. Thus what Leibniz holds as to the relation of one body to other bodies he also asserts of the relation of one part to other parts. Just as place arises from a conjuncture of bodies, so also extension arises from a conjuncture of parts. From this it follows that every element in bodies, considered apart from the others, lacks not only place but extension as well and that it appears to be the task of philosophers to discuss not merely place but first of all extension and space.

I believe Aristotle would have stated a very similar opinion if he had studied body and the parts of body in the same manner. But since he thinks that a body actually occupies a place while bodily parts do so only potentially, he considers separately these two things, place and extension, which modern philosophers have joined so closely together, and believes that what he has said concerning a body's place must in no wise be transferred to the place of its parts. Let us set aside, as far as it pertains to place, the Aristotelian distinction between act and potency. The affinity of place and extension will immediately appear, and for us the matter at issue will no longer be between us and Aristotle but between us and Leibniz.

Let us consider a certain part of a body placed within that body. Just as the entire body uses the surface of the containing reality as its place, in like manner this part will possess its place, namely, the surface by which it is enclosed and confined within the body. But since the same can be said of a part of a part, the sum total of the body will be resolved into a series of limits, each of which will be at surface embracing another surface. Now the surface itself will be divided into lines and the line into parts of lines, each of them included in others. Since this division will go on into infinity, as Aristotle himself states, and since a bodily mass is resolved into inclusions of inclusions, if I may so put it, it is less according to reason that corporeal extension should arise from such unstable and fleeting parts than from a conjuncture of parts. Therefore, just as place results from an arrangement of bodies, so also corporeal extension issues from the interconnection of parts, and we will not depart far from Leibniz, who holds that the parts lack extension and that the image of an unbroken but infinitely divisible extension, since it is a confused image, dissolves into a manifold of undivided and incorporeal elements.

If all this is granted, then the coherence of the Aristotelian world will be shattered and instead of a single living being there will be an infinite multitude of incorporeal elements lacking all power to contact and impel one another. Not at all alarmed at this consequence, Leibniz conceives each element to be a separate living thing that corresponds to the others, not by any means of communication but by a certain preestablished harmony. Now Aristotle has conceived no such agreement, and even if he had conceived it he would have thought it neither necessary nor even useful. Therefore, he has settled on the body's surface and has assigned an actual place to the whole body and a merely potential place to its parts. Because of this distinction it is permissible for Aristotle to maintain intact the continuity of corporeal parts among themselves, and to discuss space in such manner that it apparently has no relation to extension. Therefore, in this distinction between act and potency we find the crux of Aristotle's theory in so far as he separates place from extension.

To resolve the problem in a few words, we may say that place has a twofold affinity, one with the unlimited and the other with extension, and that modern philosophers have struggled hard to elucidate it. Aristotle, however, so describes *common* place and *primary* place as to distinguish the one from extension and the other from the unlimited. The twofold problem that has given such trouble to later thinkers he seems to have eliminated rather than settled.

Aristotle would deserve criticism for this if he had been unaware of the question that he had set aside. But he was not ignorant of Democritus's doctrine of unlimited empty space and he even gave especial praise to Plato for being the first to discuss place.[2] Therefore he foresaw the difficulties arising from our free and unlimited space but in fact judged them to be insuperable. In doing so he hardly seems to be culpable if we remember that the problem is recent, indeed almost of yesterday, since it concerns cognition itself rather than things known, namely, the distinction between form and matter. Therefore, he wishes space, which had been prematurely liberated by Leucippus and Democritus, to be brought back again into bodies in such a way that instead of space there would be substituted place, and instead of an infinite theatre of movement the enclosure of finite things within finite things. By this device he buried, if the phrase is permissible, not only space in bodies but the question itself.

Seen and read through, at the Sorbonne, Paris, June 29, 1889.

A. Himly, Dean of the Faculty of Letters, the University of Paris.

Permission to publish is granted.

Gréard, Rector of the University of Paris.

[2] *Physics* IV, 209, b, 16.

INDEX OF CHAPTERS

3

ARISTOTELIAN THEMES

by

Thomas Prufer

Does Aristotle specify or repudiate the work of Plato? The nuanced answer depends on the many meanings of the terms, and these meanings in turn depend on answers to questions concerning the unwritten teaching of Plato, conflicts within the Academy, the reconstruction of lost works of Aristotle from doxographies and plagiarism, the authenticity and chronology of collections and interpolations of lecture notes, memoranda, and polished pieces. Competent opinions are not always in agreement. For example, W. Jaeger understands "we" to mean in several places "we Platonists," but see E. Frank, "The Fundamental Opposition of Plato and Aristotle," *American Journal of Philology* 61 (1940) 183-185; analysis of place names in the *Historia Animalium* (D'Arcy Thompson and H. D. P. Lee) indicates that scientific organization of the *apeiron* of appearances concerned Aristotle during his stay at Assos, Mytilene, and the Macedonian court.

The need to reconcile texts has led to hasty use of the principle of genetic strata or to declarations of spuriousness, a need sometimes increased by unquestioned or anachronistic presuppositions of the philologian. On the other hand, philosophers, Aquinas and Leibniz, for example, have found a consistency and clarity which disregard the aporetic character of many texts.

The popular opposition between Plato and Aristotle in terms of transcendence and immanence must be reformulated in the light of *Metaphysics* 997a34ff and 1040b27ff, from which it is clear that Aristotle is concerned to work out a sense of separate being, i.e., being neither cosmological nor anthropological, rejecting any sense which impugns separateness by doubling the beings with which we are familiar (Plato, *Parmenides* 130-135; Aquinas, *De substantiis separatis* #61).

We do not know our way about in the most radical question, "What is being?", a theme of endless inquiry. Justification of answers to this question is the science being sought; found, this science would be first philosophy, free and exact, or theology. Answers to the question will be complex: being is said in many irreducible senses, but being is also said with reference to one primary and fundamental sense. Biological and astronomical processes, on the one hand, and speech, art, and virtue, on the other, are the context within which answers to the question are sought. Because what it means to be a being is not separable from beings, the term *ousia* (beingness) is accurately translated "entity" (not "substance").

In his inquiries Aristotle is concerned to leave undisturbed or to restore what is at first and usually manifest and said. Entity is not only what is said of something; it is also that of which something is said but which itself is not said of anything. Entity is not only being able to see, for example, but also seeing, and entity as activity is more fundamentally that activity which is not subordinate to a result and which is not over with because it is complete. (Shipbuilding is for the sake of the ship being built; healing ceases when it is achieved.) Entity is what it always means to be of a kind, what it means to be a sphere, for example; being in this sense is manifest against a background (192b34 without comma) and neither comes to be nor ceases to be. Entity is also that which comes to be and ceases to be; this lump of bronze becomes a brazen sphere. Entity is use or importance; being an axe is not so much being of iron as being for cutting. Structure is subordinate to function and picturing to narrating. A stone flute and a dead hand *are* not flute and hand because they do not function as flute and hand; feathers, fur, and scales *are* the same insofar as they have the same function. That entity is more fundamental which is more of an actuality for its own sake and therefore not self-cessating and which is not the actuality of . . . (not *ti kata tinos*, not *eidos to enon*).

The most primary and fundamental sense of entity is beyond the accesses to it both through the cyclic processes of the visible non-human order, especially the generation of animals and the locomotion of the heavens, and through art and virtue, the excellences of production and action. Insofar as soul spans the difference between body (414a20-21) and the form of forms (432a2), it mediates between these accesses and quiescent mind. Separate entity is both unmoved mover beyond the otherness of a completeness anticipated or lost, and contemplation of what is most excellent, contemplation itself, beyond the otherness of scene, use, passion, friends, and deliberation about what will either come to be or not come to be, depending upon choice. Cosmic process and human production and action are underived from and irreducible to, yet overarched by the necessary and eternal actuality which they imitate in their difference from it, an actuality beyond instrumentality and futurity: separate mind (*nous*) unmindful of human affairs. The divinely self-sufficient life of contemplation is better than life with others in action and passion (403a25). The anachoretic life *par excellence* is God, beyond courage and moderation, justice and generosity. No one would seem to wish for his friend the good of being God, for then friendship would cease. God does not order by commanding; the well-being of the best is without action. God and the cosmos have no foreign affairs. Take away from the living not only production but action as well; what is left but contemplation? Such is the joyful actuality of the divine (1154b26-28, cf. 431a6-7).

Aristotelian cosmos has as its principle neither artificer nor soul, yet nature orders means as if it foreknew ends. The form of what comes to be by art is in the soul, but the forms of the cosmos are not in a factive soul. Natural forms are unmoved movers, neither coming to be nor ceasing to be, and natural motion (*entelecheia ateles*) is the recapitulation of indwelling form. The fully developed offspring is prior to the seed from which it develops and prior to both is the generator whose form is the end of the generated. The making of nature is the cycle: reconciliation in eidetic identity of the priority of eternally anterior actuality with the priority of the eternally to be actual end; that which is to be or anticipated completeness is the anterior activity of the complete from which the seed proceeds (Siger of Brabant, *De aeternitate mundi* III, 42 Dwyer; Pomponazzi, *De naturalium effectuum causis seu de incantationibus* XII ad 8, Basel 1556, 298-317).

What is the relation between separate contemplation of contemplation and quiescent cosmic forms? How are the several senses of mind-which-makes related to perfective and unplurified mind without exemplary *logoi* (Proclus, *In Timaeum*, I 266.28-267.1 Diehl)? Pletho's polemic (*De platonica et aristotelica philosophia* XVII, PG 160, 909ff) accuses Aristotle of falling into the impiety of Anaxagoras by denying nonhuman providential mind, and

Aquinas' repetition of *Nicomachean Ethics* 1179a24-25 (#2133) is a correction (*In libros Physicorum* #974; *In libros Metaphysicorum* #2535). Lack of nonhuman providential mind is supplied by human art and virtue, yet this art and virtue imitate the teleology of nature. Nature does not imitate art, but art nature; art is for aiding nature and for completing what nature leaves undone. Insofar as nonhuman order is craftsmanlike, the naturalness of human activities which order present affairs to anticipated excellences is saved without impugning the priority of eternal and impassible mind.

Logos spans the cosmological and anthropological accesses to silent mind (*nous*) (252a11-14, 639b15-17, 1253a9-10. 1332a38ff, 1334b15). The irreducible actuality of speaking together is the context of the art of drawing out implications of opinions, the art of giving reasons for facts (for saying that . . .), and the thematization of the presuppositions operative in any speech, a thematization mediated by the use of speech to destroy speech (1006a25-26, 1007a19-20, 1008a31, 1025b28-30, 1041a14-15, b2-4). Although there can be no veridical speech about future chance and choice, poetic speech imitating action fills this space by limiting the indefinite context of preceding and succeeding actions (beginning and end) and by tightening the syntax of episodic actions to a likeness of organic necessity. This limiting and tightening fit action for contemplation, but for the sake of delight in constructed form, not for the sake of science or of action (1460b13-14). The character of the speaker and the passion of the hearer are powerful vectors in speech which moves to decision. Contemplative friendship or the sharing of speech in the knowledge of what is primary and fundamental (1141a20-22, 1170b10-13) is the highest form of the specifically human imitation of separate entity: science is of the necessary and eternal, and because the friend is another self, contemplation of a friend's contemplation is self-contemplation (Michael of Ephesus, *Commentaria in Aristotelem graeca* XX, 518-519).

The question of the relation between mind and teleological nature lies behind the question of the relation between the contemplative life of science insofar as it is an imitation of the necessary and eternal, and the political life of action insofar as it has a foundation in nonhuman order. Behind the question of the relation between contemplation and the city is a cosmological question: are the circlings of the heavens willed by star-souls with a sense of the sublunar or are they the natural movements of first body (Alfarabi, *The Philosophy of Aristotle*, 59.5ff Mahdi)?

Does first unmoved mover mean mover of the first sphere? Are the many unmoved movers considered one principle, separate entity? Can nonbodily movers be many, not many instances of one kind, but numbered by the priority and posteriority of moved spheres one to another? The relation of separate minds one to another is understood in a cosmological, not an emanationist context.

Cosmic *erōs* for the actuality of mind is an Aristotelian crux: "if moved by desire, then besouled" (Theophrastus, *Metaphysics* 5a28ff Ross-Fobes). Human excellence or the life of the city longs for godlike deathless act, not as first body, imitating in cyclic motion the rest and joy of self-contemplation, swings the constellations, nor as sublunar nature, which works like a workman, works without the mind of a workman, but as speech with others longs for the perfecting silence of solitary *nous*. Nature is suspended from mind, and human excellences of word and deed are lived between them: nature teleological without anticipatory mind, mind contemplative without argumentative speech.

Another crux is the sense in which there is one science of entity, a science of the beingness both of any being and of that being which *is* in the most primary and fundamental sense. Either the science of being as being is simply the science of the most primary sense of being, or the unity of the science is the unity of many senses of being said with reference to the one most primary sense which as loved and imitated is the principle of unity, or the failure to achieve a science of separate entity forces radical inquiry back toward cosmology and anthropology, which are nevertheless known not to be concerned with the only or the most primary senses of being. Some have even said that creation *ex nihilo* is the *sensus plenior* of the crucial text: "universal because first" (1026a30-31).

To say that deathless mind is caused with the generation of each human body, although that generation is not its adequate cause, cuts across the Aristotelian distinction between that which cannot cease to be because, being always, it has not come to be, and that which must cease to be because it has come to be (Theophrastus apud Themistium, *Commentaria in Aristotelem graeca* V/3, 102.24-29, 108.22-28). Creation, undermining the position that the union of generated body and ungenerated mind is less than essential, blurs the clear line between eternal mind and the imitation of that eternity by eternal coming to be and ceasing to be.

The subordination of nature to will, a reversal of Aristotle's deepest presuppositions and conclusions, began with the theological exploitation of his analysis of choice (H. Langerbeck, *Aufsätze zur Gnosis* (1967) 146-166; Philoponus on natural place and on the eternity of the world, *Commentaria in Aristotelem graeca* XVII, 581.18-21; X, 1333.23-27) and continued in Aquinas' use of his analysis of friendship for a theology of charity (*Summa theologiae* I-II, 65, 5) .

Philosophers and Jewish, Christian, and Muslim interpreters of Scripture struggled over the anthropology of *nous,* God's liberality, his knowledge of matter and possibility, and his providence of chance and choice. Aristotle supplied theology with instruments of exposition, analysis, and polemic, but to the degree that these instruments were used for new ends this new use changed the sense they had in the hands of their forger and called forth restorations whose theological sense is to be indices of the gratuity of grace (Scotus, Prologue to the *Ordinatio* #12).

The Catholic University of America

4

JUSTICE IN GENERAL AND GENERAL JUSTICE IN ARISTOTLE

BY

JOHN E. PATTANTYUS

Aristotle formulated his notion of justice in view of the Greek cultural and philosophical tradition concerning the meaning of justice. While it is impossible even to sketch here the broad spectrum of meanings that δίκη, justice, possessed in pre-Aristotelian Greek thought, a few introductory remarks should suffice in order to have a readier understanding of Aristotle's contributions in this subject.

The notion of δίκη developed from the original meaning of "the traditional way of the community," and this designation of "the customary" in time acquired a juridically coercive and normative force. Thus δίκη became associated with the concepts of a suit at law, right, justice, truth, legal judgment, and retribution or recompensation.

The word δίκη also had mythological roots as naming the goddess daughter of Themis, and it is in this form that it appeared in the poets and tragic writers. The early Greek philosophers demythologized δίκη and projected into the heavens its role within the polis in order to explain the movement and order of celestial bodies. In this sense, δίκη appears as cosmic justice.

Democritus brought δίκη down from the heavens and back into the polis, and established a naturalistic ethics of which the basis, origin, and sanctions no longer derived from the gods but from human nature itself. This loss of a transhuman perspective for justice led to complete ethical relativism at the hands of some sophists who advanced the pleasure principle, in the form of the advantage of the stronger, as the ultimate moral standard.

Plato opposed the ethical nihilism and relativism of the sophists by securing morality both within the heavens and within the nature of man. In this way, man is not the ultimate and only judge of his moral actions, yet the moral thrust of his life wells up from the inner depths of his soul. Thus Platonic justice is both transcendental and immanentistic.

Aristotle's theory of justice was designed as a way to the political and ethical advancement of the polis as he knew it. His doctrine had therefore an actual political context as its historical frame of reference and for its background earlier philosophical thought about justice. He thus formulated his notion of justice with full knowledge of the actual condition and previous history of the polis and of the demands it made on him and he also did so as part of the Greek cultural and philosophical tradition with regard to the meaning and value of justice. Since justice (δίκη) is the customary way of doing things in the community, i.e., the tradition, the δίκη of the polis, it was natural for Aristotle to build upon the Greek tradition of justice—δίκη of δίκη—in raising the structure of his own doctrine. He could not disregard the Greek philosophical past, of which he was an heir, in proposing an ethical theory for his present but also for the future.

Since Aristotle was Plato's student in the Academy from 368/7 to 348/7 B.C.,[1] it is not surprising that the Platonic theory of justice had its influence on him. A line of development can be detected in the evolution of his own theory of justice stretching from the Platonic period of his younger years to his mature thought. Plato envisioned the virtue of justice as a rope stretching between the radical poles of the transcendent and the immanent, between the realm of the divine and that of the human soul. This notion of justice is at the same time transcendentalized and interiorized. The psychological aspect of justice sees it as the harmony of the three parts of the soul, according to Plato. So the virtue of justice originates in the just soul, emerges from it, enters the political agora, orders the polis by making everybody do his own business, and finally ascends to the transcendental realm.

It is interesting to note that Aristotle's anthropology indicates three periods according to the three-stage development of his psychology: 1) the Platonic tripartite conception of the soul in Aristotle's dialogues and early treatises written as still a member

[1] Cf. Werner Jaeger, *Aristotle—Fundamentals of the History of His Development,* trans. Richard Robinson (Oxford: Oxford University Press, 1962), p. 11.

of Plato's Academy; 2) the instrumental psychology of his middle period, which underlies his *Magna Moralia, Eudemian Ethics* and *Nicomachean Ethics* (presupposing that all three of these works are authentic[2]); and 3) the distinctively original hylomorphic psychology of his mature years, as presented in his *De Anima*.[3] The profound influence of Plato's psychologized ethics on Aristotle is clearly seen in his ethical works: his ethical remarks in his Platonic period are made against the background of Platonic psychology; his middle period shows a departure from Plato and the development of his own instrumental psychology, on which his ethical treatises are based; and his final period of hylomorphic psychology does not have its ethical implications worked out.[4] In other words, except for the hylomorphic period, each of the two previous stages of the development of Aristotle's psychological doctrines has its corresponding ethical phase. In this development of Aristotelian ethics as reflecting the first two stages in the evolution of his psychology, the development of Aristotle's notion of justice can be traced.

Of the exoteric works of the younger Aristotle only fragments survive, which makes it difficult, if not impossible, to give a satisfactory account of their contents. The *Protrepticus*, fragment 5, asserts that the end of ethical knowledge is proper discrimination between what is just and unjust, and that the soul is more valuable than the body; therefore, the care of the soul, in striving for its excellence (ἀρετή), is man's primary duty. These are clear echoes of Plato. Although Aristotle says in this same fragment that "a good man is more defined and ordered than a bad man"—and being ordered is a synonym for being just—the problem of justice

2 Although controversy surrounded the question of the authenticity of the *Eudemian Ethics* (subsequently cited as EE) and of the *Magna Moralia* (to be referred to as MM), it seems that the authenticity of these ethical writings alongside the *Nicomachean Ethics* (cited as NE) has been proved. Cf. Hans von Arnim, *Die drei aristotelischen Ethiken* (Wien-Leipzig, 1924); Max Hamburger, *Morals and Law* (New Haven: Yale University Press, 1951), pp. 1-6; Emmanuel M. Michelakis, *Aristotle's Theory of Practical Principles* (Athens: Cleisiounis Press, 1961), pp. 2-3, No. 5; Franz Dirlmeier (ed.), *Aristoteles Nikomachische Ethik* (Berlin: Akademie-Verlag, 1964), pp. 438, 443-44; Ingemar Düring, *Aristoteles* (Heidelberg: Carl Winter Universitätsverlag, 1966).

3 Cf. R. A. Gauthier, *La Morale d'Aristote* (Paris: Presses Universitaires de France, 1958), pp. 1-16, especially p. 3.

4 *Ibid*. The development of Aristotle's psychology is the subject of François Nuyens, *L'évolution de la psychologie d'Aristote* (Louvain: Editions de l'Institut Supérieur de Philosophie, 1948).

is not explicitly discussed in this or any other surviving fragment of the *Protrepticus*. For this reason, it is a gross exaggeration to say, as Mary Clark does, that "Aristotle's early views on Justice can be found in Fragment 52[5] of the *Protrepticus*."[6] Unfortunately, there is no shred of evidence in the text to substantiate this statement.

It is most unfortunate that only a few short fragments came down to us from the Aristotelian dialogue entitled *On Justice*. Evidently, among the exoteric works of Aristotle, it was in this work, and not in the *Protrepticus,* that he explicitly dealt with the question of justice. This dialogue was probably "the most extensive and . . . one of the most popular of his early works."[7] Ever since 1863, when J. Bernays published his *Die Dialoge des Aristoteles* in which he suggests that the exoteric works had been alluded to or even quoted by Aristotle in his esoteric treatises,[8] attempts have been made to reconstruct the lost exoteric works by ferreting out these references.[9] Efforts have been made in reconstructing also the dialogue *On Justice,* of which the crowning result was P. Moraux's book.[10] His main thesis is that there are references to *On Justice* in the surviving esoteric works of Aristotle, especially those dealing with ethical and political matters. He also searched in Cicero, Plutarch, Stobaeus, and other ancient writers for traces of the dialogue. The main objection to Moraux's thesis is that there is no assurance that passages in Aristotle's esoteric works dealing with the question of justice refer to or are quoted from *On Justice,*

[5] Following Walzer, Ross changed Rose's numbering of the fragments and his fragment 5 is Rose's 52. W. D. Ross (ed.), *The Works of Aristotle,* Vol. XII: *Select Fragments* (Oxford: At the Clarendon Press, 1952), pp. 30-34.

[6] Mary Clark, "Platonic Justice in Aristotle and Augustine," *The Downside Review,* 82 (1964), 25.

[7] Anton-Hermann Chroust, "Aristotle's 'On Justice': A Lost Dialogue," *The Modern Schoolman,* 43 (1966), 249. The author acknowledges his indebtedness to this excellent article.

[8] Paul Moraux, *A la recherche de l'Aristote perdu—Le dialogue "Sur la Justice"* (Louvain: Publications Universitaires de Louvain, 1957), p. 14, No. 1; also Chroust, *ibid.*

[9] Besides the work of Bernays in this field, E. Heitz, *Die verlorenen Schriften des Aristotles* (Leipzig, 1865) and Jaeger's book—first published in 1923— already referred to, are the other noteworthy attempts to determine the content of the lost dialogue *On Justice.* Cf. Moraux, *ibid.,* pp. 14 ff., Chroust, *ibid.,* pp. 249-55.

[10] Cf. No. 8 above.

as these passages either may not refer to his exoteric works at all—
and if they do, it would be no more than guesswork to state which
passages are such references and which ones are not—or if it could
be proved without any shadow of a doubt that they echo his
exoteric works—a difficult it not impossible thing to do—even
then it would have to be shown that the passages refer specifically
to *On Justice* and not to other lost exoteric works of the younger
Aristotle, which also discuss ethico-political problems.[11] This twofold objection is formidable and underlines the difficulties inherent
in the task of trying to reconstruct a lost work by any author and
the amount of free interpretation and mere conjecture that necessarily goes into it. On the other hand, Moraux's basic contention,
that Aristotle's longest exoteric work on justice would be used by
him in dealing with the same topic in his esoteric works, would
seem to be correct. The problem is to translate this abstract statement into the concrete task of identifying these references in practice.

Another objection to Moraux's attempt to reconstruct the Aristotelian dialogue *On Justice* can be formulated on the basis of
Gauthier's theory that the first two stages of the evolution of
Aristotle's psychology identify the two-stage development of his
ethics. Therefore, Aristotle's psychology is the ground in which
his ethical theories germinate; once the psychological foundation
is changed, there is a corresponding shift in his ethics. Thus the
heavily psychologized and psychologically based ethics of Aristotle
would make problematic an attempt to translate any ethical statement from its proper stage of psychological development into the
other of this same development. Aristotelian ethics, according to
Gauthier's interpretation, is not a strictly ethical matter, since it
presupposes a definite psychology of man which is blended with it.

11 Chroust, *ibid.*, p. 254, No. 31, lists the following critical reviews of Moraux's
work: G. Verbeke, "Bulletin de litterature aristotélicienne," *Revue philosophique
de Louvain*, 58 (1958), 606-14; G. R. Morrow, *Gnomon*, 30 (1958), 441-43;
A. Kern, *Scholastik*, 35 (1960), 117-18; R. Weil, *Revue philosophique de la France
et de l'étranger*, 87 (1962), 401-12; A. Jannone, "I logoi essoterici di Aristotele."
Atti dell' Istituto di Scienze, Lettere ed Arti, 113 (1954/55), 249-79; A. Jannone,
"Les oeuvres de jeunesse d'Aristote et les 'Logoi Exōterikoi,'" *Rivista di cultura
e medioevale*, 1 (1959), 197-207. Jannone's first article is not a response to
Moraux's book, but rejects even the possibility of reconstruction on the basis
that Aristotle's lost works are not the same as his exoteric works. Chroust holds
this contention untenable.

If one were to separate Aristotle's ethics from psychology as its base, and thus transpose it to a different stage in the evolution of his thought, falsification would likely result, since it is not merely a question of a different stage in the development of his ethics, but also in that of his psychology. The ethical superstructure of Aristotle's anthropology would be imposed on the alien substructure of a different stage of his psychology.

This psychologically immanentized, interiorized, i.e., psychologically based, ethics is clearly a direct heritage from Plato, for whom the interiorized notion of the virtue of justice is the order and harmony of the three parts of the soul. In accepting Gauthier's views concerning the psychological basis of Aristotle's ethics, we shall briefly indicate the development of the Aristotelian concept of justice. Again, it should be stressed that Aristotle accepted the Platonic position that the human soul is one of the radical poles of the virtue of justice, the immanent source of its origin.

For these reasons, the writer does not look with favor on Moraux's attempt to reconstruct the dialogue *On Justice*. But before dismissing this whole problem—an important one, since the work was the most extensive and direct treatment of justice by Aristotle among his lost exoteric works—it should be pointed out that Moraux, in view of Gauthier's position, mistakenly attributes the psychological instrumentalism of the second stage in the evolution of Aristotle's psychology to his first ethical, i.e., psychological, stage. Moraux explicitly says[12] that psychological instrumentalism is the basis of the ethical doctrine concerning justice in Aristotle's *On Justice*, which was written during the first and not second period of the evolution of his psychology.

Nuyens maintains that instrumentalism, which views the body and soul as two substances that are not merely fortuitously united, so that there is a cooperation between them in the sense that the soul uses the body as its instrument and the soul is localized in the

---

[12] Moraux, *ibid.*, p. 155, takes cognizance of the Platonic tripartite division of the soul and then says that Aristotle differed from it by subscribing to a double division of the soul as rational and irrational (cf. pp. 57, 151, 160), not noticing that Plato also held the same bipartite division in announcing the supremacy of the rational part over the two irrational parts of the soul, i.e., the irascible and the appetitive parts. Cf. Plato, *Republic*, 441 e, 440a-441a; *Phaedrus*, 246a-248b. In other words, the rational-irrational division of the soul is also Platonic and does not necessarily conflict with its tripartite division.

heart,[13] belongs to the middle, transitional stage of Aristotle's psychology and underlies his esoteric ethical treatises and the *Politics*.[14] With regard to the first stage, when the young Aristotle wrote all of his exoteric works, including *On Justice*,[15] and also the *Organon*,[16] Nuyens asserts that with certain modifications it closely copies Plato's psychology. Thus in the *Eudemus*, or *On the Soul*, Aristotle understands the soul as a substance in the Platonic sense.[17] Like Plato, the younger Aristotle sees the body as the prison of the soul, the soul as existing before the body, a definite antagonistic dualism of body and soul, and the soul as having independent existence apart from the body, that is, the soul is immortal and separable from the body.[18] All these Platonic ideas are upheld by Aristotle in the *Protrepticus*,[19] but certain new features appear. These last are not irreconcilable with the Platonic position, yet adumbrate the direction in which Aristotle's theory of the soul was to evolve. A teleological principle is introduced,[20] and although the body's subjection to the soul is acknowledged, a certain interdependence of body and soul is recognized.[21] This mitigated Platonism of cooperation between body and soul is also expressed in *On Philosophy*.[22] Since *On Justice* was written at approximately the same time as the *Protrepticus*,[23] the same Platonic psychology must have constituted the foundation of its teachings concerning justice.

Nuyens attends only to the twofold character of Aristotelian psychology under the body-soul problematic and the noetic problem. He leaves unexamined the question of the division of the soul as such, although its tripartite division is characteristically Platonic. Jaeger is of more help at this point, since he at least notes the

---

13 Nuyens, *ibid.*, pp. 161-63.

14 *Ibid.*, pp. 185-97.

15 Moraux remarks, *ibid.*, p. x, that *On Justice* was written when Aristotle was 35 years old and at approximately the same time as the *Protrepticus*.

16 Cf. Nuyens, *ibid.*, pp. 106-18.

17 *Ibid.*, p. 83.

18 *Ibid.*, pp. 84-88.

19 *Ibid.*, p. 93.

20 *Ibid.*

21 *Ibid.*, p. 95.

22 *Ibid.*, p. 97.

23 Cf. footnote 15 above.

bipartition of the soul as the basis of Aristotle's ethics, and states that

> [Aristotle's] ethics . . . is built on a very primitive theory of the soul, namely the division of it into a rational and an irrational part. This venerable doctrine, appearing in Aristotle as early as the *Protrepticus*, is simply Plato's. For practical reasons he left it undisturbed in later days, although his psychology had advanced a long way in the meantime and he no longer recognized parts of the soul at all. In ethics it remained convenient to work with the old ideas, and no errors followed serious enough to vitiate the ethical results.[24]

In this crucial passage Jaeger not only holds that the Platonic conception of the soul found in Aristotle's psychology persists in the twofold division of the soul, but also clearly proposes the view that Gauthier was to champion more than thirty years later, namely, that Aristotle's ethics is based on his psychology.

All these remarks concerning the Platonic character of Aristotelian psychology in its initial phase are much too general to be of help in seeing how it relates to the specific ethical problem of justice. For light on this particular point, Aristotle's early esoteric writings must be examined.

It has already been noted that the logical works of Aristotle belong to the same early Platonic period as the exoteric writings. Among the logical works of interest in this respect, the *Categories* and especially the *Topics* should be mentioned. Both of them are considered early works that were written while Aristotle was still a member of Plato's Academy,[25, 26] and it is not surprising to find in them indisputable evidence of the profound influence that Plato exerted on his pupil. Fortunately, passages in both of these logical works indicate a psychologized, psychologically interiorized concept of the virtue of justice. While the *Categories* has only the significant statement that "justice and injustice require as their subject the human soul,"[27] the *Topics*, which is considered *"platonicien fort accentué"*[28] and is placed at the very beginning of Aristotle's literary activities[29] as reporting the results of discoveries in logic made in

24 Jaeger, *ibid.*, pp. 332-3.

25, 26 *Ibid.*, pp. 369, 47 in footnote; Nuyens, *ibid.*, pp. 106 ff.

27 *Categories*, 14 a 18: δικαιοσύνη δὲ καὶ ἀδικία ἐν ψυχῇ ἀνθρώπου.

28 Nuyens, *ibid.*, p. 115.

29 *Ibid.*, p. 133.

the Academy,[30] contains a number of passages which, alone in the whole Aristotelian corpus, report the Platonic tripartite division of the soul with the concomitant virtues.[31] These passages are so Platonic that they could well have been written by Plato himself, had they not been found in the *Topics.*

The younger Aristotle terms it a "commonplace" that man as man and man as mortal possesses a tripartite soul as his distinctive property.[32] The relation existing among these three parts of the soul is also exactly the same as Plato envisioned it: the distinctive property of the reasoning faculty is to command the appetitive and irascible faculties, while the latter two are supposed to obey the reasoning faculty.[33] Like Plato, Aristotle also assigns the virtue of prudence (φρόνησις) or "primary wisdom" to the reasoning part, and the virtue of temperance or "primary temperance" to the appetitive part of the human soul.[34] He does not expressly assign the cardinal virtue of fortitude to the irascible part of the soul, but this is clearly implied when he states that fear, the opposite of courage, resides in the irascible part.[35] In this same place, he again lists all three parts of the soul and specifies the proper sensations that take hold of them when their distinctive virtues are absent. Thus shame, resulting from foolishness, exists in the reasoning part, and pain, resulting from the absence of pleasure, invades the appetitive faculty. It is understandable that Aristotle fails to give a complete ethical exposition in the *Topics,* since it is a work on logic and not on ethics, and he merely uses these psychologico-ethical references as examples to illustrate points in logic. It is not surprising therefore that he does not specifically indicate in the *Topics* the relationship between the virtue of justice and the soul. There is only one place where he lists all four cardinal virtues (justice, fortitude, wisdom, and temperance), and remarks that they all belong to the same genus.[36] He does not correlate the cardinal

30 Jaeger, *ibid.,* p. 47.

31 Cf. Dirlmeier, *ibid.,* p. 278. Dirlmeier *(ibid.)* calls attention also to Hans von Arnim's *Das Ethische in Aristoteles Topik* (Wien-Leipzig, 1927), wherein the ethical doctrine in the *Topics* is fully explored, but the present writer did not have access to this work.

32 *Topics,* 133 a 31-3.

33 *Ibid.,* 129 a 13-4.

34 *Ibid.,* 136 b 12-14; 138 b 2-5.

35 *Ibid.,* 126 a 7-9.

36 *Ibid.,* 108 a 2-3.

virtues with the soul. Nevertheless, keeping in mind the passage in the *Categories* stating that the human soul is the subject of justice,[37] the distinctively Platonic tenor of the above remarks in the *Topics* permits one to presume that Aristotle also held the Platonic idea that the virtue of justice is the order and harmony of the three parts of the soul. There seems to be no convincing reason to suppose that Aristotle closely follows Plato in his psychologically immanentized ethics only concerning the three cardinal virtues of wisdom, fortitude, and temperance, and not with regard to the virtue of justice. Rather it would seem that he had no opportunity or need to use the virtue of justice and its relationship to the soul as an example in logic.[38]

[37] Cf. note 27 above.

[38] A most instructive passage according to the Platonic pattern of psychologized justice is found in the short Aristotelian treatise *On Virtues and Vices* (VV). This also corroborates the contention that all the four cardinal virtues, justice included, are connected with specific parts of the soul or with their order among themselves, as Plato taught. Since controversy surrounds the authenticity of VV—although Paul Gohlke, *Die Entstehung der aristotelischen Ethik, Politik und Rhetorik*, 1944, seems to have established that Aristotle himself is its author —it is best to present the evidence from VV in a footnote and not in the main body of the text. The passage in question runs as follows (VV 1249 a 31-1250 a 3):

> "If in accordance with Plato, the soul is taken as having three parts, prudence is virtue of the rational part, gentleness and courage of the irascible, of the appetitive temperance and self-control, and of the soul as a whole (ὅλης δὲ τῆς ψυχῆς) justice (ἡ δικαιοσύνη), liberality and great-spiritedness; while vice of the rational part is folly, of the irascible ill-temper and cowardice, of the appetitive profligacy and weakness of the will, and of the soul as a whole injustice (ἡ . . . ἀδικία)·

Again, in VV 1250 a 12 and 25, Aristotle affirms that justice is the virtue of the soul and injustice is its vice.

Virtue (ἀρετή) denotes a specific excellence, ability, fitness, the maximum in efficiency, the optimum capacity which an animate or an inanimate being has for accomplishing most successfully and in the most excellent way the essential function for which it exists (cf. Aram M. Frenkian, "La notion d'*aretē* et l'éthique d'Aristote," *Helikon*, 1, 1961, 440; Bruno Snell, *The Discovery of the Mind*, New York, Harper Torchbooks, 1960, p. 158). Aristotle refers to virtue as "a certain excellence of perfection" (*Metaphysics*, 1021 b 20; NE 1106 a 15), and from this it may be concluded that this virtue or excellence of the tripartite soul as tripartite is that its three parts do not interfere with each other's specific virtue, but that the three faculties work in complete order and harmony among themselves. In other words, the virtue of the whole soul is jusice. Thus through the mediation of the notion of virtue, justice in the soul is identified with the harmony of its three parts. So indeed, in his early Platonic period, Aristotle did hold the identical same view as Plato concerning the meaning and function of the virtue of justice in the human soul.

Since the *Topics* was written at the same time as the Aristotelian dialogues,[39] the Platonic tripartite theory of the soul must have been the psychological background against which Aristotle developed his theory of justice in *On Justice,* and not the bipartite concept of the soul, which is characteristic of the next stage of his theory.

In moving from the first stage of Aristotle's psychology to its second stage, we pass to the mature expression of his ethical views as expressed in the *Magna Moralia, Eudemian Ethics, Nicomachean Ethics,* and the *Politics.* Psychologically speaking, this is the period of mechanical instrumentalism. In this middle period of Aristotelian psychology, the heavily accentuated Platonic conception of the soul is shed, antagonism between body and soul disappears, and the soul is considered to be dependent on the body for its existence.[40] These are already definite indications of the way that Aristotelian psychology was to evolve into its next stage within the framework of the hylomorphic theory in which dependence of soul on body and vice versa gained formulation in a context of form and matter.[41]

But there was not only a change in Aristotle's assessment of the relationship between the soul and the body but also in his view of the soul and its parts. Plato has a double division of the soul: according to its three parts and according to a twofold division whereby he ranges the two irrational parts against the rational part, which latter is to rule the other two.[42] As has been already noted, Aristotle's first stage of psychological and ethical development is

---

39 E. S. Forster, in the introduction to his translation of the *Topics* in the Loeb Classical Library series, p. 267, refers to the work of H. Maier (*Die Syllogistik des Aristoteles,* Tübingen, 1900) in substantiating that the *Topics* was definitely written during Aristotle's stay in the Academy of Plato when he also wrote his dialogues.

40 Cf. Nuyens, *ibid.,* p. 163. This mutual dependence of soul and body on each other precludes the possibility of both the preexistence and the immortality of the soul, at least to a great extent. Anyhow, this was definitely the case in the final, hylomorphic stage in the evolution of Aristotle's psychology: the soul simply cannot exist without the body, just as form cannot exist without matter.

41 *De Anima,* 412 a 27-8: "The soul is the first grade of actuality of a natural body having life potentially in it."

42 Plato, *Republic,* 439 e. Cf. also footnote 12 above.

characterized by a stress on the Platonic tripartite division of the human soul. On the other hand, the second stage in Aristotle's development moves on from Plato's tripartite division to his understanding of it as consisting of a rational and an irrational part. This is still Platonic inasmuch as it distinguishes two parts, but it is gravitating toward the novel and distinctively Aristotelian hylomorphic conception of the soul as an undivided whole that vivifies the body as its form and actuality.

An examination of the Aristotelian psychology underlying the ethical doctrines in the *Magna Moralia, Eudemian Ethics, Nicomachean Ethics,* and *Politics* unmistakably exhibits the above characteristics of Aristotle's instrumentalist psychology.

The psychological instrumentalism of Aristotle's ethico-political treatises is consequent upon the earlier development of the same doctrine in his biological works.[43] The soul-body relationship of instrumentalism in terms of the body's subordination to the soul is clearly stated in the *Eudemian Ethics:*

> The relations of soul and body, craftsman and tool, and master and slave are similar, between them there is no partnership /properly speaking/; for in these relations there are not two terms associated, but the former constitutes one unity, while the latter forms part of the former without constituting a unity by itself[44] . . . For the body, in effect, is the soul's tool born with it.[45]

The same sentiment is expressed also in the *Nicomachean Ethics:*

> For where there is nothing in common between ruler and ruled, there is no friendship either, since there is no justice. It is like the relation between a craftsman and his tool, between soul and body, or between a master and his slave; the latter are all benefited by their users.[46]

The *Politics* denies that soul and body are a single substantial unity.[47] On the one hand, it maintains that the body is prior in its development to the soul,[48] and on the other, that of the two factors

43 Cf. Nuyens, *ibid.,* pp. 147-61.

44 This sentence in the Greek original is rather condensed (EE 1241 b 20-1):
οὐ γὰρ δύ' ἐστίν, ἀλλὰ τὸ μὲν ἕν, τὸ δὲ τοῦ ἑνὸς οὐδ' ἕν.

45 EE 1241 b 17-23.

46 NE 1161 a 33-1161 b 1.

47 P 1334 b 18. Cf. NE 1178 a 20; Plato, *Phaedo,* 78 b-c.

48 *Ibid.,* b 21.

constituting an animal, the soul is by nature the ruling part and the body obeys it.[49]

Proceeding from the instrumentalism of the body-soul relationship[50] in the psychology of Aristotle's ethico-political esoteric works,

[49] *Ibid.*, 1254 a 34-6.

[50] Before departing from the problem of instrumentalism in Aristotle's psychology, some remarks are in order concerning fragment 6 of the *Protrepticus* which treats of the soul and its parts. It has already been noted that Nuyens places the *Protrepticus*, along with the other dialogues of Aristotle, *On Justice* included, and also his treatise *Organon*, in the first stage of Aristotelian psychology, i.e., that prior to the instrumentalist stage. Contrary to this, Gauthier, (*ibid.*, pp. 18, 22) says that the passages of *Protrepticus*, fragment 6, are parallel to those of NE setting forth mechanical instrumentalism. This would imply that the psychology of the *Protrepticus* belongs not to the first, but the second period, and, therefore Moraux would be vindicated in assigning the instrumental psychology of the second period to *On Justice*. The passages from fragment 6 that Gauthier cites are as follows (here for clarity's sake larger segments will be quoted from the fragment, but they include those which Gauthier cites):

> Part of us is soul, part body; the one rules, the other is ruled; the one uses, the other is present as its instrument. Therefore the use of the subject, i.e. of the instrument, is always directed to that which rules and judges of our own interest; the other element follows and its nature is to be ruled. . . . That which is by nature more originative and authoritative is the better, as man is in relation to the other animals; therefore soul is better than body (being more authoritative), and of soul, that which has reason and thought; for such is that which commands and forbids, and says what we ought to do or not to do. (Ross, *Select Fragments, ibid.*, pp. 34-35).

In a cursory reading this passage seems to parallel the instrumentalism and bipartite soul theory of the NE of a later period. However, if this passage is not read in isolation, but is compared with other fragments of the *Protrepticus,* it appears immediately that Aristotle's instrumentalism here differs from that of the NE, MM, EE, and P *(Politics)*. In fragments 10 b and 15 of the *Protrepticus*, Aristotle regards the relationship between soul and body in terms of antagonism: the soul is chained to the body as to a cadaver. Plato also has a theory of psychological instrumentalism (cf. *Phaedo*, 79 e-80 b, 94 b, 94 d; *Timaeus*, 34 c; *Laws*, 896 c), but it is in terms of this antagonism between soul and body. It is clear from fragments 10 b and 15 of the *Protrepticus* that it is this Platonic instrumentalism that we encounter also in fragment 6. In other words, the *Protrepticus* belongs to the initial period of Aristotle's psychology, as Nuyens says.

Curiously enough, Gauthier not only disagrees with Nuyens on this point, but also contradicts himself. He has a section (*ibid.*, pp. 3-8) which he entitles *La phase idéaliste: Le "Protreptique."* This means that he assigns the *Protrepticus* not only to the second, but also to the first phase of Aristotle's evolution of psychology. On p. 5 he says that this work of Aristotle rests on the late Platonic idealism of the *Timaeus* and the *Laws*. Now if he acknowledges this, it is

the question of the parts of the soul itself is to be examined. He introduces this topic by noting that the student of political[51] matters must study the nature of the soul[52] since happiness through the exercise of virtue is the proper end of the polis,[53] and the distinctive virtue of man[54] is "the active exercise of the soul's faculties in conformity with (the) rational principle."[55] In short, an expert in the nature and function of the polis must also be well versed in psychology. This is an unambiguous statement attesting to the vital relationship between psychology and political ethics in the classical practice of including ethics within the science of politics.[56]

The Platonic bipartite division of the soul[57] into a rational part and an irrational part has many illustrations in Aristotle's ethical treatises[58] and in the *Politics*.[59] While this Aristotelian concept of instrumentalistic cooperation between the soul and body regards it

---

difficult to see how he could confuse this type of Platonic instrumentalism with the instrumentalism of Aristotle's middle period, when the Stagirite considered the body not the mortal enemy of the soul, but its co-worker. Interestingly enough, Nuyens (*ibid.*, p. 94) also cites the first lines of *Protrepticus*, fragment 6, but simply bypasses the instrumentalism clearly expressed in it, as though it would not fit the schemata of the three stage-development of Aristotle's psychology. In summary, the solution to this uncertainty concerning the instrumentalism of the *Protrepticus* and of the ethical and political treatises of the second period lies in the important distinction between the Platonic instrumentalism accepted by the younger Aristotle in the first stage of his development and the distinctively Aristotelian instrumentalism of the second stage. Neither kind of instrumentalism would seem to be in necessary conflict with the tripartite division of the soul and both of them are, in fact, alongside with its bipartite division. It may be stressed again that the bipartite division does not necessarily exclude, but may very well include, the tripartite division of the soul as it clearly does in Plato.

51 By political the all-inclusive classical sense of the word is meant.

52 NE 1102 a 24.

53 Cf. P 1280 b 7-8.

54 NE 1102 a 16.

55 NE 1098 a 7.

56 Cf. MM 1181 a 23-26; NE 1094 a 28, b 11, 1130 b 26-29; *Rhetoric*, 1356 a 25-27; Plato, *Gorgias*, 517 d; *Euthydemus*, 291 b-c.

57 Plato, *Republic*, 588 b ff.: *Phaedrus*, 246 a ff.; *Timaeus*, 41 c-44 c; 69 c-70 b.

58 NE 1097 b 33-1098 a 5, 1102 a 26-1103 a 3, 1119 b 15, 1138 b 8, 1168 b 19-21, 1172 b 10; EE 1219 b 28-1220 a 4; MM 1182 a 24-28, 1185 b 5. Interestingly enough, MM 1185 a 22 has the Platonic tripartite division of the soul along with the bipartite division referred to in MM in this footnote. Apparently, the MM is a transitional work.

59 P 1254 a 28-b 5, 1260 a 4-8, 1277 a 5-10, 1333 a 16-25, 1334 b 17-21.

as advantageous to both—a definitely un-Platonic notion—,[60] Aristitle still keeps to the Platonic vision of the soul by distinguishing two parts in it.[61] The main characteristic of this bipartite division of the soul is that the priority of the rational part over the irrational is stressed in all the Aristotelian passages referred to above. The rational part is considered as the ruling principle to which the irrational part is to be subject. This governance of the rational over the irrational part is termed virtue ($\dot{a}\rho\epsilon\tau\acute{\eta}$)[62]: the state of excellence providing the possibility of most effective functioning.

Corresponding to Plato's threefold division of goods for man— external goods, goods of the soul, and those of the body[63]—, Aristotle lists the same classes and remarks that a man cannot be happy unless he possesses all three.[64] But true to his Platonic heritage, he affirms the supremacy of the soul over the body by saying that man's distinctively human good is the activity of the soul in accordance with the best and most perfect virtue.[65] This same spiritualistic view is even more clearly expressed when he says that "by human virtue we mean not that of the body, but that of the soul; and happiness also we call an activity of soul."[66] Aristotle acknowledges the need for the possession of all three classes of goods, spiritual as well as bodily and external. Hence in his procla-

---

60 Platonic instrumentalism, which was accepted by the younger Aristotle during his days in the Academy, envisions a perpetual hostility between the soul and the body, regarding the latter as the tomb of the soul. Cf. also the end of footnote 50.

61 This is not merely a logical but a real distinction between the parts of the soul. Such a distinction was vehemently rejected by Aristotle in the third and last stage of his psychology as set forth in the hylomorphic theory of the *De Anima*. Cf. *De Anima*, 411 b 5-13:

"Some hold that the soul is divisible, and that one part thinks, another desires. If, then, its nature admits of its being divided, what can it be that holds the parts together? Surely not the body; on the contrary it seems rather to be the soul that holds the body together; at any rate when the soul departs the body disintegrates and decays. If, then, there is something else which makes the soul one, this unifying agency would have the best right to the name of soul, and we shall have to repeat for it the question: Is *it* one or multipartite? If it is one, why not at once admit that 'the soul' is one? If it has parts, once more the question must be put: What holds *its* parts together, and so *ad infinitum?*"

Cf. *ibid.*, 432 a 24-b 7; 433 b 1 ff. See also Dirlmeier, *ibid.*, pp. 292-3.

62 NE 1102 b 13-1103 a 10.

63 *Euthydemus*, 279 a-b; *Philebus*, 48 e; *Laws*, 743 e.

64 NE 1098 b 12-5; P 1323 a 24-7, 1332 a 39-42, 1332 b 16-23, 1333 a 16-8, 37-9.

65 NE 1098 a 15-7.

66 NE 1102 a 16-8.

mation of the goods of the soul over the two other kinds he intends no Plotinian or Manichean contempt for nonspiritual realities but merely recognizes a hierarchy of values.

Gauthier finds this Platonic [67] spiritualistic character of Aristotle's anthropology to be so pronounced that he entitles one of his chapters *L'homme, c'est l'esprit*.[68] In this chapter, under an identical subtitle,[69] he cites a number of passages from the *Nicomachean Ethics*[70] and one from the *Protrepticus*[71] in order to corroborate his contention. This is another facet of the essentially psychological character of Aristotle's ethical doctrine.

How did Aristotle conceive this psychologically immanentized, interiorized virtue of justice in the soul (again a Platonic doctrine)? Plato's notion of the spiritually interiorized virtue of justice as the order and harmony of the parts of the soul is connected with his tripartite division of it.[72] He does not expressly repeat the same doctrine with regard to the bipartite division of the soul, namely, that justice is also the order and harmony of the rational and irrational parts. If all three parts are in harmony, this clearly implies that the two parts—constituted out of these same three parts—are also in harmony. That this reasoning is not incorrect, appears from Aristotle's remarks on the subject.

Aristotle notes that in all composite things there is a plurality of parts. In living beings especially there is always found a ruling and a ruled principle combined in a common unity, which is likened to a harmony.[73] That the reference to harmony is a veiled allusion to justice is clear from another passage, where different constitutions, justice, and harmony are mentioned in one breath.[74] An explicit statement of the virtue of justice as the order and harmony of the parts of the soul is presented at the very end of Chapter V of the *Nicomachean Ethics*:

> In a metaphorical and analogical sense . . . there is such thing as justice (δίκαιον) . . . between different parts of one's nature,

67 Plato, *Laws*, 959 a-b; *First Alcibiades*, 130 a-b.
68 Gauthier, *ibid.*, Chapter II, pp. 17-45.
69 *Ibid.*, p. 43.
70 NE 1166 a 16-7, 22-3; 1168 b 31-3; 1178 a 2-7.
71 *Protrepticus*, fragment 6.
72 Cf. Plato, *Apology*, 29 d-e, 30 a-b; *Gorgias*, 464 c, 477 c, 526 d; *Republic*, 439 d-e, 440 a-441 a, 441 e, 443 d-444 a, 444 b, 612 b; *Phaedrus*, 246 a-248 b.
73 P 1254 a 29-33.
74 EE 1241 b 28-33.

not, it is true, justice in the full sense of the term, but such justice as subsists between master and slave, or between the head of a household and his wife and children. For in the discourses on this question a distinction is set up between the rational and irrational parts of the soul.[75]

In this passage, note should be taken of Aristotle's designation of the proper order between the rational and irrational parts of the soul as justice only in a metaphorical or analogical sense, that this order or justice means the subjection of the irrational part to the rule of the rational one, and that this metaphorical manner of speaking of justice in the soul is something which is to be found in certain writings. In the opinion of various commentators this is a reference to Plato's *Republic,* especially to such passages as 441 a, 443 d, and 432 a.[76] This would mean that Aristotle does not make such an interpretation of justice his own, but merely attributes it to someone else. This indicates an important and definite shift from the original Platonic position.

The same conclusion is gained if the contrary of the virtue of justice, the vice of injustice, is examined as presented by Aristotle. If justice is order and harmony, then injustice would be its opposite, disorder and disharmony. Morally inferior persons[77] have a civil war raging in their souls, one part dragging them in this way and the other in that, as if to tear them asunder.[78] But again, this is only a figurative way of speaking, because no one can commit injustice against himself voluntarily, and the acts of justice and injustice are voluntary.[79] If the irrational part, under the onslaught of passion, overpowers momentarily the rational part, this is not voluntary. Strictly speaking, therefore, one cannot commit injustice against oneself,[80] i.e., the distinction between justice and injustice

---

[75] NE 1138 b 6-9. This is Rackham's translation in the Loeb Classical Library edition of NE.

[76] Cf. Rackham's note in the Loeb edition, p. 323. See also J. A. Stewart, *Notes on the Nicomachean Ethics,* Vol. I (Oxford: At the Clarendon Press, 1892), p. 538; Alexander Grant, *The Ethics of Aristotle,* Vol. II (London: Longmans, Green & Co., 1866), p. 143.

[77] NE 1166 b 7.

[78] NE 1166 b 20-23.

[79] NE 1134 b 12, 1136 b 1 ff., 1138 a 4-28, 1138 b 5-13.

[80] MM 1196 a 26-8.

does not properly describe the relationship between the rational and irrational parts of the soul.

The reason for this shift of interpretation in the psychologized concept of justice is found in Aristotle's novel idea of assigning specific virtues to the two parts of the soul: intellectual virtues to the rational part and moral virtues to the irrational part.[81] Since the rational is superior to the irrational, the intellectual virtues are also superior to the moral virtues. As a result, not even justice, the highest kind of moral virtue, may or can command and supervise the relationship between the two parts of the soul. In other words, this novel view is rooted in the fundamental rationalism of Aristotle's ethics. Interiorized justice still retains its meaning as order and harmony in the soul, but its scope is limited to the irrational part.[82] The larger harmony of the soul as a whole, that is,

---

[81] EE 1220 a 4: "Virtue has two forms: moral and intellectual" ($\dot{\alpha}\rho\epsilon\tau\hat{\eta}s$ $\delta'\epsilon\ddot{\iota}\delta\eta$ $\delta\acute{v}o$, $\dot{\eta}$ $\mu\grave{\epsilon}\nu$ $\dot{\eta}\theta\iota\kappa\grave{\eta}$ $\dot{\eta}$ $\delta\grave{\epsilon}$ $\delta\iota\alpha\nu o\eta\tau\iota\kappa\acute{\eta}$). See also EE 1220 a 8-11: "Since the intellectual virtues involve reason, these forms of virtue belong to the rational part, which as having reason is in command of the soul; whereas the moral virtues belong to the part that is irrational but by nature capable of following the rational part of the soul." MM 1185 b 4-7: "The constituent parts (of the soul) have been ranged under two headings, namely the rational and irrational. In the rational part arise prudence, shrewdness, wisdom, aptitude, memory, and the like; while in the irrational part arise these (moral) virtues: namely temperance, justice, courage, and all other states of character which are considered praiseworthy." NE 1103 a 4-7: "Virtue also is differentiated in correspondence with this (bipartite) division of the soul. Some forms of virtue are called intellectual virtues, others moral virtues: wisdom or intelligence and prudence are intellectual, liberality and temperance are moral virtues."

John Burnet, in his *The Ethics of Aristotle,* London, 1900, p. 63, denies that MM 1182 a 24 is correct in assigning to Plato the bipartite division of the soul with appropriate virtues to each part. Commenting on this assertion, Jackson remarks that by "admitting . . . that Plato assigns appropriate virtues to irrational parts of the soul, I do not admit that Plato thereby anticipates Aristotle's distinction of $\dot{\eta}\theta\iota\kappa\acute{\eta}$ from $\delta\iota\alpha\nu o\eta\tau\iota\kappa\grave{\eta}$ $\dot{\alpha}\rho\epsilon\tau\acute{\eta}$. For, granted that Plato does not insist that all $\dot{\alpha}\rho\epsilon\tau\acute{\eta}$ is $\dot{\epsilon}\pi\iota\sigma\tau\acute{\eta}\mu\eta$, he does insist that such $\dot{\alpha}\rho\epsilon\tau\acute{\eta}$ is not $\dot{\epsilon}\pi\iota\sigma\tau\acute{\eta}\mu\eta$ is $\delta\acute{o}\xi\alpha$." See Reginald Jackson, "Rationalism and Intellectualism in the Ethics of Aristotle," *Mind* 51 (1942), 344, note 2.

[82] EE 1223 b 11-14: "The self-controlled man will act justly ($\delta\iota\kappa\alpha\iota o\pi\rho\alpha\gamma\acute{\eta}\sigma\epsilon\iota$) and more so than the man who lacks self-control; for self-control is moral virtue, and moral virtue makes men more just. And a man exercises self-control when he acts against his desire in conformity with rational calculation ($\kappa\alpha\tau\grave{\alpha}$ $\tau\grave{o}\nu$ $\lambda o\gamma\iota\sigma\mu\acute{o}\nu$)." So justice and self-control have to do with man's appetitive self and both of them are under the rule of the rational principle.

The reverse side of the coin is seen in EE 1223 a 37-b 1:

the harmony of its two parts with one another, is no longer a question of a moral, but of a rational principle.[83]

This rationalism of Aristotle's ethics is a feature of his conception of man. In the *Protrepticus*, he remarks concerning the rational part of man that "this part is, either alone or above all other things, ourselves."[84] The rational character of man, indeed this direct and unqualified identification of man's reason with his ruling, true, and distinctive self, is forcefully stated in the *Nicomachean Ethics*.[85]

"All moral degradation makes a man more unjust, and lack of self-control seems to be moral degradation; and the uncontrolled man is the sort of man to act in conformity with (irrational) desire contrary to rational calculation, and he shows his lack of self-control when his conduct is guided by (irrational) desire; so that the uncontrolled man will act unjustly by acting in conformity with (irrational) desire."

As the just man acts under the guidance of reason, the unjust man functions by the "light" of unreason. In either case, justice is a moral virtue subject to the rule of reason, and as moral virtue it has to do with the non-rational part of man.

83 NE 1102 b 12-18: "There also appears to be another element in the soul which, though irrational, yet in a manner participates in rational principle. In self-controlled (continent, self-restrained) and uncontrolled (incontinent, unrestrained) people we approve their principle, or the rational part of their soul, because it urges them in the right (moral) way and exhorts them to follow the best (moral) course; but their nature seems also to contain another element beside that of the rational principle (or: 'another element which is against the rational principle'), which combats and resists that principle." This passage clearly affirms the supremacy of reason over both parts of the soul and its supervision of man's moral life. The same sentiment is expressed also in *ibid.*, 26-29, and 1145 b 11-13.

84 *Protrepticus*, fragment 6. Cf. P. 1253 a 10; *Topics*, 103 a 28, 130 b 8, 132 a 20, 133 a 22, 134 a 15, 140 a 36.

85 Reflecting on the terms "self-controlled" and "uncontrol", as both denoting a relationship with reason, Aristotle remarks that "the intellect is the man himself" (NE 1168 b 34-1169 a 1). At another place (*ibid.*, 1166a 15-17), he says that "it is a mark of a good man to exert himself actively for the good; and he does so for his own sake, for he does it on account of the intellectual part of himself, and this appears to be a man's real self." Finally, he emphatically notes (*ibid.*, 1178 a 5-8): "that which is best and most pleasant for each creature is that which is proper to the nature of each; accordingly, the life of the intellect is the best and the pleasantest life for man, inasmuch as the intellect more than anything else is man."

In all these passages, a single thing is stressed: the rationality of the human animal is his specific, distinctive mark separating him from all other animals. Indeed, reason is so characteristic of human nature that he does not hesitate to identify man with his reason or intellect.

Aristotle's ethics is psychological in tenor and his psychology is rational; his instrumentalism upholds the supremacy of the soul *vis-à-vis* the body, and within the soul itself he proclaims the superiority of the rational part over the irrational part. Because his psychology is rational, his ethics also becomes rational through being psychological. Aristotle's ethics is a statement of the practical consequences of man's rational nature: it is a rational examination of man's moral life that prescribes rules of conduct based on man's nature precisely as rational. Man's moral behavior should follow the dictates of reason so that the good man would be, at the same time, the wise man also. There is no separation possible between genuine moral and intellectual virtues,[86] just as the two parts of the human soul and the soul and the body—in the conception of Aristotelian instrumentalism in the transitional period of his psychological development—cannot be separated from each other without unfortunate consequences. Aristotle's ethics is based on a fruitful psychological synergism of the intellectual and moral virtues under the rule of reason.

The rationalism of Aristotle's ethics[87] presupposes a distinction within the rational part of the soul.[88] In accordance with the different aspects under which they view their common object, truth, Aristotle distinguishes theoretical reason from practical reason. While practical reason aims at truth from the practical viewpoint of directing action, issuing in right desire, theoretical reason disregards utilitarian action and production and is concerned solely

[86] Cf. Henry B. Veatch, *Rational Man—A Modern Interpretation of Aristotelian Ethics* (Bloomington, Ind.: Indiana University Press, 1966), pp. 110-12.

[87] Jackson (*ibid.*, p. 343) defines ethical rationalism in terms of an identification of moral right and wrong with truth and falsity. This is a practical application of reason to moral conduct.

[88] Jackson maintains (*ibids.*, pp. 358-9) that Aristotle fails to make this necessary distinction in man's rational part of the soul, so that instead of making a distinction between practical and theoretical reason, he merely distinguishes between practical and theoretical knowledge. In this way, in Jackson's opinion, Aristotle cannot provide an adequate basis for an ethical rationalism and slips into ethical intellectualism, which is a term of abuse for Jackson, indicating the elevation of "the intellect at the expense of the will" (p. 344, note 1) so that the intellect does not have any practical orientation, but remains a purely contemplative faculty. Jackson's position is judged untenable by the present author for the simple reason that Aristotle does in fact make a distinction between practical and speculative reason, not merely between practical and speculative knowledge. Cf. following note.

with the contemplation of truth as such.[89] Theoretical reason, which is also called the scientific faculty, contemplates those first principles which are invariable, whereas practical reason, the calculative faculty, deals with principles subject to variation.[90] The intellectual virtue of the contemplative intellect is wisdom and that of the practical intellect is prudence.[91]

Prudence (φρόνησις) is clearly distinguished from the practical intellect, a faculty,[92] and is said to be a virtue,[93] concerned with

89 NE 1139 a 21-32. Some lines further down (ibid., b 12), Aristotle simply declares that "the work of both intellectual parts of the soul is the attainment of truth." In the Politics (1333 a 25) he also mentions that the rational part is subdivided into two: practical and theoretical reason. The Magna Moralia also attests to this bipartition of reason (1196 b 14-17): "We have already sketched in outline the nature of the soul, distinguishing its rational part from its irrational. And this rational part is again divisible into two: the property of one being to deliberate on action and that of the other to acquire knowledge."

90 NE 1139 a 6-12. Concerning practical reason, the Magna Moralia states: "The deliberative and purposive faculty is concerned with sensible objects and with things in motion, and, to speak comprehensively, with whatever is liable to growth and decay. We deliberate on what is in our power to do or not to do by purposive action; on matters which admit of deliberation and of purpose whether positive or negative; such matters being perceptible by sense, and subject to the movement of change. So that, according to our reasoning, the purposive faculty of the soul is concerned with perceptible things" (MM 1196 b 27-33). Armstrong, in the Loeb Classical Library edition of MM, translates μόριον (part) as faculty, thus instead of "purposive part of the soul" we have "purposive faculty of the soul" in the preceding translated passage.

91 NE 1145 a 7-11; MM 1197 a 11-6.

92 There is an instructive summary of the relationship of practical reason and practical wisdom or prudence in terms of their nature and function as presented in Michelakis, ibid., p. 61: "In many passages of the Nicomachean Ethics, Phronēsis is considered to be right reason. This right reason of Phronēsis knows, but does not find the good end, which is a universal and a cause of action in prakta. Nous praktikos is that which finds the good end, from the particulars, and which are first principles of ta prakta. Phronēsis then proceeds from the universals by practical syllogisms. Nous praktikos does not posit the end as the aim of action, but only thinks that. Phronēsis knowing the end posits it as the aim of action, inasmuch as the positing of the aim of action is a rational function. In other words, Phronēsis judges about what ought to be done, taking a function of nous praktikos, for it is the function of thinking. Nous praktikos provides Phronēsis with first principles, and Phronēsis from them proceeds further as reason."

The only objection that the present writer has to this interpretation of prudence is that it fails to give any stress to its character as a virtue, albeit an intellectual virtue. In reading the passage one has the impression that

action.[94] Aristotle defines it as "a truth attaining rational habit, concerned with action in relation to the things that are good for human beings."[95] It is important to note in this definition that like the faculty from which it proceeds prudence is directed toward the acquisition of truth. In other words, $\phi\rho\acute{o}\nu\eta\sigma\iota\varsigma$ directs moral action toward the good inasmuch as it has truth value, i.e., inasmuch as the good and the true coincide. The intellectual virtue of prudence is intimately connected with the moral virtues and determines the right standard for them in the idea of truth.[96] This again highlights the rationalism of Aristotle's ethics: the rightness of moral action is determined by its relationship with rational truth.

Prudence as an intellectual virtue is a habit of the mind whereby man facilitates the attainment of truth concerning practical matters, which also include the field of ethical conduct. Since the moral virtues are subject to the intellectual virtues in general, they are also under the rule of prudence, and since justice is a moral virtue, it submits to prudence.

The dependency of justice on prudence throws new light on that connection between justice and truth, which had not escaped the notice of pre-Aristotelian thinkers.[96a] Aristotle uses the phrases true things ($\tau\acute{a}\lambda\eta\theta\eta$) and just things ($\tau\grave{a}\ \delta\acute{\iota}\kappa\alpha\iota\alpha$) as synonyms.[97] In another passage, he simply declares that "the just is true . . . but not that which merely seems so."[98] In other words, justice is truth,

---

$\phi\rho\acute{o}\nu\eta\sigma\iota\varsigma$ is also a kind of practical reason, an intellectual faculty—dealing with means—located within the larger practical reason—which treats of ends. In other words, Michelakis seems to confuse a faculty with its excellence or at least he does not make the proper distinctions between them. $\Phi\rho\acute{o}\nu\eta\sigma\iota\varsigma$ should be clearly understood not as a faculty, but as a virtue, the proper perfection and excellence of practical reason. Cf. next note.

93 MM 1197 a 19-20, 1198 a 22-32; P 1253 a 34, 1281 b 4.

94 MM 1197 a 2-3: $\mathring{\eta}\ \phi\rho\acute{o}\nu\eta\sigma\iota\varsigma\ \pi\epsilon\rho\grave{\iota}\ \tau\grave{a}\ \pi\rho\alpha\kappa\tau\acute{a}$.

95 NE 1140 b 20-2.

96 NE 1178 a 17-9.

96a Cf. *Iliad*, XII, 433 ff. Pindar also sees justice in terms of truth and truth in terms of justice (cf. *Pyth.*, IV, 180). Plato (*Republic*, 331 c) defines justice as truth-telling. See also Hesiod, *Theogony*, 233-38; Aeschylus, *Agamemnon*, 752-3; Euripides, *The Phoenician Maidens*, 469-72.

97 *Rhetoric*, 1355 a 22.

98 *Ibid.*, 1375 b 3-4. Aristotle (MM 1196 b 2-3), in commenting on the judgment of a judge in an athletic contest, says that the judge "so far as he failed to give a decision which is just in truth and in fact, he is guilty of injustice." Alfarabi formulated the relationship between truth and justice in terms of

and injustice is falsity. This is an eloquent and persuasive statement of the rationalism inherent in the psychologically interiorized
virtue of justice. Under direction of the truth-seeking intellectual
virtue of prudence and in harmony with it, the politico-moral virtue of justice attains the ethical good inherent in whatever is just.
This ethical good will be a "true" good to the extent that the
quality of justice approximates the truth which practical reason
perceives in the situation. Truth is the standard against which
justice is measured and perfect justice coincides with truth itself.

Since prudence aims at truth in directing the moral virtues, including justice, toward the good in actual action and deals with
things preceptible, mobile, subject to sensible growth and decay,[99]
under the guidance of φρόνησις the moral virtues ascend from the
interior recesses of the irrational part of the soul to the broad day-
light of the external world. Thus justice does not remain merely
an internal principle, ordering the movements of the irrational part
of the soul but, propelled and directed outward by the truth-
oriented impulse of practical reason, it enters the extramental realm
of the polis. Just as within the soul the irrational part and its moral
virtues are to be subject to the rational part, so also the externalized
virtue of justice is to remain always subject to the dictates of reason
in the realm of the public agora.

A comparison between Plato's and Aristotle's notions of justice
could perhaps be made most conveniently in terms of the general
tenor of their philosophical conception of reality. Over against
Plato's artistic orientation, Aristotle's scientific bent is readily recognized as a basic difference between the two.[100] Plato's idealism,
transcendentalism, universalism, mysticism, and religious outlook
may be contrasted with Aristotle's realism, immanentism, seeing the
universal in the entelechy of the particular, rationalism, empiricism,
and naturalism. Plato's philosophy is characterized by a politico-
ethical search for the realization of the morally good in the polis,
thus lifting the polis out of the abyss of moral disintegration. For
Aristotle the morally good is not the supreme concept; his ration-

---

prudence and justice: "The most powerful deliberative virtue and the most
powerful moral virtue are inseparable from each other." Alfarabi, *The Attainment of Happiness*, xxvi, 10 in Alfarabi's *Philosophy of Plato and Aristotle*,
trans. Muhsin Mahdi (New York: The Free Press of Glencoe, 1962), p. 32.

99 Cf. footnote 90 above.

100 Cf. Jaeger, *ibid.*, pp. 14-5.

alism is basically metaphysical, man's rational self is lauded as the
superior of his moral being, and the morally good stands under the
judgment of the metaphysically and intellectually true.[101] These
are very general and perhaps over-simplified statements which cannot capture or even intimate the depth and complexity of these
two systems of philosophy, but may indicate their broad characteristics.

In ethics, Aristotle discovers the norms of human actions not in a
transcendental, super-sensible, religious realm, but in the immanent
nature of man as a rational political animal. He affirms the autonomy of an ethics, which is to know and deal with man in the polis
in this life. This naturalistic morality does not need divine sanctions or extramoral motives to assure its validity or justification
and survival. The essence of morality is to be gained from the
analysis of human nature. In this naturalistic context the ultimate
judge of conduct is not the divine, but human reason itself. Finite
reason provides the ultimate criteria of moral behavior in the
ethical rationalism of Aristotle. This is a humanistic ethics that
secularizes and demythologizes the heteronomous ethics of Plato.
The truth discovered by the light of human reason alone is also
the morally good, and it is always man's mind which has the final
word in ethical matters without recourse to divine laws. In following and greatly enlarging the naturalistic autonomous ethical
views of Democritus, Aristotle brought down the ethical norms
from the transcendental Platonic heaven and placed them in man's
rational nature as rational. In proclaiming the autonomy of ethics
as capable of dealing with the this-worldly transactions and life of
men in the polis, Aristotle announces the emancipation of man
from divine tutelage. Man has come of age, to use a contemporary
formula. This humanistic naturalism in ethics is made possible by
his confidence in the power of human reason.

The basic question which faced Aristotle was the very possibility
of a naturalistic ethics that would attempt to deal with this-worldly
ethical realities in this-worldly terms and without reference to religion. This is, of course, the most fundamental question of ethics
as a philosophical discipline. Plato's heteronomy in ethics solves
this problem by sacrificing the autonomy of morality to the gods.

101 *Ibid.*, pp. 44-45, 188, 200, 210-12, 379; Frederick Copleston, *A History of Philosophy*, Vol. I, Part II (Garden City, N. Y.: Doubleday & Co., 1962), pp. 113-20.

He formulates his fundamental ethical norms and their justification in relationship to the transcendental realm. Motivation for good moral conduct is also provided by the hope of the immortality of the soul and rewards after death. Aristotle abridges this Platonic vision of reality to the empirically sensible "real" world. Once the religious foundation is removed from under morality, the stable, universally valid, objective ethical norms are shattered, and to escape the ensuing moral anarchy and subjectivism, some other stable, universally valid, and objective basis must be found for morality. The sophists demonstrate the danger of an inadequately based naturalistic ethics, and Plato therefore must secure his ethics in the "heavens." Unwilling to yield the autonomy of philosophical ethics, Aristotle saves it by basing it on the stable, universally valid, and objective foundation of man's rational nature. Thus human acts are not measured against a divine standard, but against the rule of natural reason as manifested in the dictates and demands of man's rational nature.

This divergence between Plato and Aristotle is clearly illustrated in their notions of justice. For Plato, justice has a cosmic significance, not merely a role in the community of men. This transcendental character of justice is further stressed by his insistence that internal justice in the soul is externalized in the polis with a view to divine judgment after death. Human justice has cosmic significance and, in being just, man acts in accordance with the will of the gods. Thus the virtue of justice is based on divine command: human virtue has a religious dimension since it extends in significance, sanctions, and motivations beyond the naturalistic, this-worldly dimension of reality. The human virtue of justice is a consequence and image of divine and cosmic justice from which it receives its vindication and ultimate foundation. Through the faithful practice of the virtue of justice, man becomes divinized: for man the path of morality leads to the attainment of the ultimate perfection.[102]

Aristotle agrees with Plato that there is an internal, psychologized aspect to the virtue of justice. But while he accepts a modified view of the position and role of justice in the soul, in accordance with his bipartite division of the soul and the supremacy of reason, he does not seek a transcendental, religious foundation on which to base his human morality. The ultimate reasons for the human vir-

---

102 Cf. *Theaetetus*, 176 b, c; *Cratylus*, 412 d, e, 413 a; *Gorgias*, 508 a, 523 a-b; *Republic*, 612 c, 613 a, 613 e-614 a, 614 b-621 b; *Phaedo*, 107 c-108 c.

tue of justice do not follow from a divine command, but from the demands of man's rational nature. For him, there is no need to refer to extramoral, superhuman norms since man's reason is able to discern them in the exigencies of human nature. The ultimate court of appeal is not divinity but natural reason. Thus Aristotle makes immanent in man's rational nature Plato's transcendental, stable, universally valid, and objective norms.

There is a way to become like the divine, but this is not the way of the pursuit of the moral virtue of justice, as in Plato. Aristotelian rationalism asserts the superiority of the intellectual over the moral virtues and of the theoretical over the practical life.[103] Happiness is the teleological end of human activity and it is gained through the exercise of virtue. Virtue is activity according to one's nature, which in man is a rational nature. Since for man virtue is activity in accordance with reason, happiness is gained through the exercise of intellectual virtue.[104] But since in terms of its object the speculative intellect is higher in rank than the practical intellect, its intellectual virtue, wisdom, is superior to that of the practical intellect.[105] This means that for man the most perfect type of happiness is activity according to the highest kind of virtue, i.e., according to the intellectual virtue of wisdom, which activity is the contemplation of the invariable first principles.[106] Since ethics, under the guidance of the practical intellectual virtue of prudence, has as its object mobile being, the perfect kind of happiness for man in intellectual contemplation is superethical: the happiness produced by the exercise of moral virtue falls short of the happiness of contemplation. The logical consequence of Aristotle's rationalism is that man becomes divinized not by practicing the moral virtue of justice, as in Plato, but by exercising the superethical intellectual virtue of wisdom.[107]

Although the moral virtues and the happiness they produce are inferior to the intellectual virtues and subject to them, and the happiness they produce is exactly in proportion to the relationship

---

[103] NE 1102 a 23-1103 a 10, 1103 a 14-8, 1108 b 9, 10, 1117 b 24, 1139 a 1, 1178 b 7-32; EE 1220 a 4-13, 1221 b 29-34; P 1260 a 6.
[104] Cf. NE 1097 b 21 and 28, 1098 a 7, 14, and 17 in conjunction with NE 1139 b 17.
[105] NE 1141 a 17, 1141 b 3.
[106] NE 1139 a 7-8.
[107] NE 1178 b 7-32.

existing between the irrational and rational part of the soul, still there is no irreconcilable conflict between them nor is their separation possible. It is impossible to be practically wise without being good.[108] Therefore in Aristotelian anthropology the irrational part of the soul and morality are indirectly connected with the divine through subjection to reason and its divinizing activity of contemplation. Whereas for Plato, morality is immediately joined with the transcendental and the divine, Aristotle's rationalism interposes the mediation of reason. In this sense, even if indirectly, the latter's naturalistic ethics is connected with the divine. In Aristotle's self-contemplating godhead[109] there is found neither any ethical quality nor any transcendental ethical norm for mortal men to follow. Therefore, his rigorously logical self-consistency of ethical rationalism fixes a rational, nonmoral, transcendental heaven over the field of morality, so that the sovereignty of the human intellect over morality is absolute. For him only man's mind superintends ethics without any divinely based transcendental ethical norms. In consequence, the virtue of justice always remains subject to the dictates of reason. Whereas in Plato the virtue of justice stretches between the two poles of the human soul and the transcendent, for Aristotle the direct connection between justice in the soul and the supersensible is severed and human reason takes the place of the ethical transcendental realm as the secure Archimedean point of guidance.

It is within this perspective of the psychologically based and reason-directed "laicized"[110] virtue of justice that Aristotle's theory of the politically externalized virtue of justice is to be seen. Although divested of religious dimensions within a naturalistic and autonomous morality, the external virtue of justice in the polis still retains a radically pervasive meaning and function, especially as general justice.

*   *   *

108 NE 1144 a 37.

109 *Metaphysics*, 1074 b 34; NE 1178 b 10-8. In contradistinction to Aristotle's super-moral godhead, Plato's divinity possesses ethical qualities, among them the virtue of justice. Cf. Plato, *Seventh Letter*, 342 d.

110 Cf. René Antoine Gauthier & Jean Yves Jolif (eds.), *L'Ethique à Nicomaque*, Tome II, Partie I-e (Louvain: Publications Universitaires de Louvain, 1959), p. 325.

The fifth book of the *Nicomachean Ethics* is devoted to the treatment of the concept of justice. Gauthier and Jolif offer the following division of the book:[111] the first portion, chapters one to seven, discusses justice from the objective point of view: that which a just man must do. Under this heading, justice is considered abstractly, as general and particular justice, followed by a concrete application of these principles in the life of the polis. The remaining chapters, eight to eleven, take up the concept of justice from the subjective point of view: the manner in which just actions are to be done in order to make the person, who posits them, just. In what is to follow an attempt will be made to investigate Aristotle's theory of general justice from the abstract and objective point of view. The foregoing discussion concerning the psychological basis of justice has already touched upon important points of justice from a subjective point of view. On the other hand, St. Thomas Aquinas considers the externality of justice, that is, that it is concerned primarily with what a man does externally, as the virtue's chief and distinctive characteristic, so that he judges as secondary the way just acts internally and subjectively influence the just man.[112]

Aristotle opens his discussion of justice in the *Nicomachean Ethics* by defining it as "that moral habit which makes people disposed to do what is just and causes them to act justly (δικαιοπραγοῦσι) and to wish for what is just (τὰ δίκαια)."[113]

In an analysis of this definition of justice, it is seen that its genus is given as a moral habit or disposition (ἕξις): justice is a moral virtue. Aristotle insists that virtue is the essence and genus of justice,[114] and in his ethical writings justice is always mentioned as

111 Gauthier-Jolif (cited subsequently as GJ), *ibid.*, pp. 328-29.

112 S. Thomae Aquinatis, *In decem libros Ethicorum Aristotelis ad Nicomachum expositio*, cura et studio Raymondi M. Spiazzi (Romae: Marietti, 1949), 886: "Circa iustitiam et iniustitiam praecipue attenditur quid homo *exterius* operatur. Qualiter autem afficiatur interius non consideratur nisi ex consequenti." The translation of this work used in this study is St. Thomas Aquinas, *Commentary on the Nicomachean Ethics*, trans. C. I. Litzinger (Chicago: Henry Regnery Co., 1964).

113 NE 1129 a 7-9.

114 *Topics*, 143 a 15-9: "You must see whether in his description he passes over the genera, for example, when he defines justice as 'a state productive of equality,' or 'distributive of what is equal'; for by such a definition he passes over virtue, and so by omitting the genus of justice he fails to state its essence; for the essence of a thing involves its genus."

a virtue.[115] Since happiness is the result of exercising or following virtue, man will gain happiness by practicing the virtue of justice. However, this will not be that supreme happiness which belongs to the exercise of the intellectual virtue of wisdom in the contemplative life. Yet within the active life of the polis, where man strives for excellence, immortal fame, and happiness in the agora by "speaking great words and doing great deeds,"[116] the moral virtue of justice will produce a true and satisfying happiness that is proper not to the sphere of solitary intellectual contemplation but to the politico-moral sphere of action in the polis. The measure of happiness attainable through any virtue is dependent on the excellence of the virtue in question in addition to the subjective efforts of the individual practicing it. Therefore, justice, the most perfect—if we are permitted to anticipate—of moral virtues, seems to afford the greatest possible ethico-political happiness.

This definition also specifies justice in the abstract, the principle[117] or object of justice:[118] what is just (τὸ δίκαιον), ius in Latin,[119] and "right" in English.[120] In this highly abstract sense

·115 Cf. NE 1108 b 7, 1129 a 3 ff.; MM 1193 a 39 ff., 1193 b 6; VV 1249 b 26 ff.

116 Homer, Iliad, IX, 442-43.

117 Stewart, ibid., p. 374. He states that δικαιοσύνη, the virtue of justice, is the moral habit of acting in accordance with this abstract principle.

118 Divi Thomae Aquinatis, Summa theologica, Tomus tertius (Paris: Apud J.-P. Migne editorem, 1864), II-II a. 57, a. 1: "iustum est obiectum iustitiae." This work will be referred to as ST.

119 The words ius, iustum, iustitia are given two etymological derivations: 1) either they derive from the Sanskrit root ju (yu), meaning "to bind" (cf. jugum, jungere), or 2) they come from yos in the Vedas or yaos in the Avesta. These latter two words have no specific meaning, which can be very clearly defined, but have to do with the worship of deities, their propitiation, and submission to the divine will. Thus, ius is related to the names Zeus, Iovis, and Jupiter. Cf. Giorgio del Vecchio, Justice, trans. Lady Guthrie (New York: Philosophical Library, 1953), pp. 3-4.

120 P. N. Zammit, "The Concept of Rights according to Aristotle and St. Thomas," Angelicum 16 (1939) 248:
"Etymologically the word 'Right' is derived from the Anglo Saxon riht or ryth, German recht, Latin rectus (from regere, to rule or to guide). In its root it is connected with the word 'Rich', which is derived from the Anglo Saxon rice, meaning rule (as in bishopric), related with the German Reich which means empire, Latin rex (also from regere, to rule or to guide), Sanskrit rajàn (to rule)." Skeat gives the etymology of "right" as a derivative participle form from the base Rak, to rule or answer to, originating from the root Rag, to rule, direct, from which the Latin rectus (reg-tus), the past participle of regere—to rule—comes.

of justice as that which the just man does,[121] the object or end which his just deeds aim at,[122] "right" is recognized as the very reason for positing just acts.[123] "Right" is a conformity, a congruence, a principle of co-ordinating persons,[124] "of adjusting, joining or fitting the different political values."[125] This abstract concept of "right" may be defined as "a measure (equality) due to somebody" (*aequalitas alteri debita*).[126] It is constituted by three elements: equality, due, and the other.[127] The notions of equality and otherness will be treated at some length in what is to follow. Suffice it to say at this point that equality is the measure, rule, or congruence, the "right" measure that is due to someone even before justice comes on the scene, usually in order to correct the damage suffered by a wronged, i.e., unequally treated, right. Thus right belongs only to persons, responsible agents, who are capable of respecting the rights of others—the reverse of right being duty. The force of obligation in rendering others their proper, equal rights is involved in the notion of "due." This "due" denotes mutuality: one person is obliged to respect the rights of others so that his rights may also be respected by them. The virtue of justice orders, coordinates the rights of men, not of a single man. This otherness is the important quality of the object of justice: the rights of any man are always considered *vis-à-vis* those of others. The right

---

Walter W. Skeat, *An Etymological Dictionary of the English Language* (Oxford: At the Clarendon Press, 1898), p. 510. Cf. Ernest Klein, *A Comprehensive Etymological Dictionary of the English Language*, Vol. II (Amsterdam: Elsevier Publishing Company, 1967), p. 1348.

[121] Plato, *Gorgias*, 460 b: ὁδὲ δίκαιος δίκαιά πράττει.

[122] ST II-II, q. 57, a. 1, ad 1: "Hoc nomen 'ius' primo impositum est ad significandum ipsam rem iustam."

[123] ST II-II, q. 80, a. 1: "Ratio iustitiae consistit in hoc, quod alteri reddatur quod ei debetur secundum aequalitatem."

[124] Vecchio, *ibid.*, pp. 1-2.

[125] Ernest Barker, *Principles of Social and Political Theory* (Oxford: At the Clarendon Press, 1951), p. 102.

[126] Zammit, *ibid.*, p. 262, gives a more complete definition of "right" on p. 250: " 'Right' strictly speaking is not what is materially just or exact, but that measure that has served as a rule or criterion to make things or actions just or correct."

[127] Cf. Zammit, *ibid.*, pp. 262-66. On p. 266, Zammit notes that the essence of right is equality: "A right is a sort of equality due to somebody. It is due because it is equal; and similarly it is due to somebody else, precisely because it is equal."

of one man is regarded as the duty of another: right is always other-related.[128]

While the object of the virtue of justice is right, its matter is relatedness toward another, πρὸς ἕτερον or *alteritas*.[129] By its very essence the virtue of justice denotes a relation to another.[130] The reason for this is that "justice can never be attained so long as each person is solely preoccupied with what is due to him, with his rights, and not with what he himself owes to others."[131]

This relatedness toward another, this otherness, is a characteristic feature of the virtue of justice and distinguishes it from all the other virtues: justice is essentially a social virtue.[132] Although Aristotle specifies two distinct meanings of justice,[133] and also of injustice,[134] both kinds contain in themselves the idea of relationship to another person.[135] Man can practice many virtues without re-

128 Cf. Josef Pieper, *Justice*, trans. L. E. Lynch (New York: Pantheon Books, 1955), pp. 12-15, 20-21; Robert O. Johann, "Love and Justice", in Richard T. De George (ed.), *Ethics and Society*, (Garden City, N. Y.: Doubleday Anchor Books, 1966), pp. 40-45.

129 ST II-II, q. 58, a 1: "Est autem iustitia proprie circa ea quae ad alterum sunt, sicut circa propriam materiam." The Greek preposition πρός with accusative as in the phrase πρὸς ἕτερον signifies a movement or direction toward something. Cf. Henry George Liddell and Robert Scott, *A Greek-English Lexicon* (Oxford: At the Clarendon Press, the 1966 reprint of the 1940 9th edition), p. 1497. Thus, πρός is used in expressions denoting (1) a place toward which movement occurs (cf. *Iliad*, XII, 239; *Odyssey*, XIV, 381; Aeschylus, *Prometheus Bound*, 830); (2) various kinds of reciprocal action (cf. Thucydides, V, 22); and (3) a relationship between two entities (cf. Aeschylus, *ibid.*, 489; Sophocles, *Philoctetes*, 1441; Euripides, *Orestes*, 427). In all these uses of πρός with the accusative case, dynamic movement is stressed in a context of interrelatedness.

130 ST II-II, q. 58 a 2: "Cum nomen iustitiae aequalitatem importet, ex sua ratione iustitiae habet quod sit ad alterum; nihil enim est sibi aequale, sed alteri."

131 Johann, *ibid.*, p. 45.

132 ST II-II, q. 57, a 1: "Iustitiae proprium est inter alias virtutes ut ordinet hominem in his quae sunt ad alterum."

133 NE 1108 b i, 1129 a 32 ff.; MM 1139 b 2.

134 NE 1130 a 32 ff.

135 NE 1130 b 1: "The significance of both (kinds of injustice, i.e., of general and particular injustice) consists in a relation to one's neighbor" (πρὸς ἕτερον)· Although the preceding passage refers to other-relatedness or πρὸς ἕτερον as characteristic of both kinds of injustice, a valid inference may be made to general and particular justice that they also would be characterized by other-relatedness, since Aristotle notes that there are certain basic characteristics in contrary states whereby they are recognized as contraries of the same state. Cf. NE 1129 a 18-25.

lationship to other people, e.g., a man alone in a forest may be brave in the face of natural dangers, and another may be temperate even if he is a hermit. On the contrary, the virtue of justice always requires as a *conditio sine qua non* the presence of other human beings in the sense of a reciprocal other-relatedness or πρὸς ἕτερον.[136] Right, the object of justice, inevitably and inseparably involves this reciprocal availability or otherness, the presence in some way of other persons, as the matter of the virtue of justice. Strictly speaking, one can be just only toward another.

Man is other-related in a twofold sense as a political or social being: 1) he is other-related in himself in the polarity of the most basic of communal situations when only two persons are present. In this instance, he is related to the other in respecting the rights of the other. 2) But the other person can also be related to him in respecting his rights and then the direction of other-relatedness is from the other toward him. The social selfhood of man is formed by the perpetual two-way movement of reciprocal relatedness where right, the object of justice, is aimed at in giving and receiving what is the due share of each in equality at both ends of the community-constituted polarity. (Of course, this polarity may take on three distinct configurations: 1) one to one; 2) one to many; and 3) many to one.)[137]

Since man is defined by Aristotle as a political animal, this entails that man is by nature other-related. And since other-relatedness is the distinctive mark of the virtue of justice, this in turn means that man is by nature a just animal, i.e., justice is imbedded in human nature as political. The same conclusion follows if man is considered as a person. A person possesses rights, and rights are the object of justice. The object of any virtue signifies the basic rootedness of the virtue in it. Hence inasmuch as man as a person possesses rights, he is also characterized by the virtue of justice, since one cannot speak of the virtue of justice in connection with a "rightless" subperson. Finally, if in the human person the virtue of justice and politicality are both present, it clearly indicates that

---

[136] Cf. Giovanni Drago, *La giustizia e le giustizie—Lettura del libro quinto dell 'Etica a Nicomaco* (Milano: Marzorati, 1963), p. 63.

[137] The polarity of relatedness in the virtue of justice indicated by the phrase πρὸς ἕτερον stresses that justice is concerned with external things, using them when dealing with other men. Cf. ST. II-II, q. 58, a. 3, ad 3: "Iustitia . . . consistit circa exteriores res quantum ad hoc quod utitur eis ad alterum."

these two qualities are vitally connected with each other: whatever is genuinely political, in the full classical sense of the term, is also just; and whatever is just is also political. Justice is essentially a political virtue and the excellence of politicality is simply justice.

Aristotle distinguishes general or universal justice from particular justice by calling the first legal (τὸ νόμιμον) and the second equal justice (τὸ ἴσον).[138] This divison of justice rests on the consideration of whether justice concerns the whole community in a one to many other-relatedness or it governs only the relationship between individuals.[139]

Inasmuch as it is justice, general justice also falls under the genus of virtue.[140] In determining the precise meaning of general justice, Aristotle uses the method of ascertaining the meaning of its contrary, injustice in general, from the notion of the lawless man (ὁ παράνομος). He opposes the notion of general justice as perfect virtue,[141] or as the totality of virtues, literally "whole virtue" (ὅλη ἀρετή),[142] with that of the totality of injustice.[143]

With regard to this methodological approach in Aristotle, Stewart cautions that it has only logical value. It is only the just man who knows in fact what the virtue of justice is in its essence and also knows what injustice, the privation of justice, is. The unjust man knows only what justice is not and sees it only as the opposite of injustice, and such opposition is an accidental, not an essential note of justice.[144] In knowing the essence of a being, one can go from the positive principle to its privation, but the reverse epistemological process does not yield the knowledge of the essence of the positive principle in itself.

---

138 NE 1108 b 7-9, 1129 a 34, 1130 b 6-7; MM 1193 b 2 ff.

139 *Rhetoric,* 1373 b 20-4:
"The actions that we ought to do or not to do have been divided into two classes as affecting either the whole community (πρὸς τὸ κοινόν) or some one of its members. From this point of view we can act justly (δικαιοπραγεῖν) or unjustly in either of two ways: towards one definite person or towards the community (πρὸς τὸ κοινόν). The man who is guilty of adultery or assault is doing wrong to some definite person; the man who avoids service in the army is doing wrong to the community."

140 NE 1129 b 26.

141 *Ibid.*

142 NE 1130 a 9.

143 *Ibid.,* a 23.

144 Stewart, *ibid.,* p. 380.

It is highly significant that Aristotle approaches the meaning of
general justice in connection with the notion of law (νόμος). That
man is unjust who is lawless, grasping, and unfair, or literally unequal (ἄνισος), whereas the just man is law-abiding (νόμιμος) and
fair, or literally equal (ἴσος). He concludes by saying that "the just
is the lawful and the fair (equal), and the unjust the unlawful and
the unfair (unequal)."[145] From this it is clear that the concept of
"just" corresponds to the notions of legal and fair or equal, and
that of "unjust" to those of illegal and unfair or unequal. The two
distinct acceptations of the notion of justice indicated here identify
general justice (ἡ καθόλου δικαιοσύνη) and particular justice (ἡ κατὰ
μέρος δικαιοσύνη). The moral law kind of legality is characteristic of
general justice and equality of particular justice. Thus the odd
phrase "equal justice" identifies equality as the distinctive trait of
particular justice.

These distinctions are crucial. When introducing them, Aristotle
speaks of the danger of equivocation, since there are distinct notions
referred to under the terms justice or injustice, and if the necessary
distinctions are not made in these abstract notions, error easily slips
in on account of their similarities.[146] It is precisely such distinctions
that Aristotle makes when breaking down the unjust into its sub-
classes of unlawful, grasping, and unequal. All three are kinds of
injustice and they should not be confused one with the other.
Similarly, justice can be divided into two kinds: that which has to
do with legality and that which has to do with equality. Injustice
in general is opposed to justice in general, but their subdivisions
correspond in a specific sense: lawless injustice is the opposite of

---

[145] NE 1129 a 32-4. The fair or equal man (ἴσος) is a man of particular
justice, whereas the equitable man (ἐπιεικής), also called fair, is one who
exercises the virtue of equity (ἐπιείκεια). Aristotle defines the equitable man as
"he who is inclined to take less than his legally just rights" (MM 1198 b 26; cf.
MM 1198 b 26-28, 33-1199 a 3; NE 1137 b 13-1138 a 2, 1143 a 19-35; Rhetoric,
1374 a 26-b 23). This is not the place to discuss the relationship of equity
with the notion of justice, therefore it should suffice to say that the truly just or
fair man is the equitable person, not the equal (or fair in the sense of equal)
man, since the equitable man is just according to the spirit of justice, whereas
an equal (ἴσος) man satisfies justice according to the letter of law. So fair
in the sense of equitable is more perfect than fair in the sense of equal. These
two distinct senses of fair should be kept separate. In this article fair is used in
the sense of equal and not of equitable.

[146] Ibid., a 26-30.

law-abiding justice, and unequal injustice is the opposite of equal justice. These lines of comparison between the kinds of justice and injustice should not be confused. Aristotle's bipartition of the notion of justice in general is a truly new and original contribution since as late as Euripides[147] law-abiding and equal were identified.

The symmetry in the corresponding subdivisions of justice and injustice is disturbed by the fact that whereas justice has two subkinds, three subkinds are listed for injustice: lawlessness, covetousness and inequality. As the first and the third kinds of injustice have corresponding opposite kinds of justice, covetousness seems to be somewhat out of place. It is this kind of vice which is blamed by Thucydides as the root-cause of the moral degradation of the polis.[148] It is regarded as the opposite of justice and if it were eliminated, peace and justice would once more descend on the polis. The question, of course, is to which kind of justice is covetousness opposed? An examination of passages from Greek literature would indicate that covetousness is opposed to equality, that is, particular justice.[149] In other words, it is another name for the inequality of injustice.[150]

This line of reasoning is confirmed by Aristotle's observations that the covetously unjust man is concerned with obtaining more than his fair (equal) share of external goods, which are not the end but only the means to the good life[151] and have to do with material prosperity (εὐτυχία) or adversity (ἀτυχία),[152] and not with the internal beauty of the soul.[153]

Aristotle proceeds to identify general justice with legality[154] and for this reason, general or universal justice is also called legal

---

147 *The Phoenician Maidens*, 583: τὸ γὰρ ἴσον νόμιμον ἀνθρώποις ἔφυ.

148 Thucydides, III, 82: "The cause of all these evils was the lust for power arising from greed (πλεονεξία) and ambition."

149 Cf. Plato, *Gorgias*, 483 b-484 b, 508 a. See also GJ, pp. 335-6.

150 GJ say (p. 337) that ὁ πλεονέκτης was the traditional way of saying ὁ ἄνισος. By reversing this customary way of speaking, i.e., by saying "unequal" instead of "grasping" ("covetous"), the specific kind of injustice that is covetousness is clearly indicated. That is, this is merely a question of terminology, and, for the sake of clarity, Aristotle decided to denote an old vice by a new name.

151 NE 1099 b 27.

152 NE 1129 b 1-5.

153 See the prayer of Socrates to Pan in Plato's *Phaedrus*, 279 b-c.

154 NE 1129 b 12: "All lawful things are just in a certain sense" (πῶς). Stewart (*ibid.*, p. 389) calls attention to the adverb πῶς. This modifier shows that laws in their widest acceptation as moral customs and usages—and not in their technical sense, which has to do also with particular justice, as in

justice.[155] Already in the *Topics,* he associates the notions of justice
and law and calls justice the preservative of laws.[156] In this, he follows Plato, who also identifies νόμιμον with δίκαιον.[157]

   The important thing to note here is that this traditional identification of general justice with law is a specifically, Greek concept
flowing from the omnicompetence and fundamentally moral nature
of the polis.[158] Therefore by the terms law and law-abiding, Aris-

---

penal law, corrective justice, commercial justice, etc.—are identical with general
justice. Cf. NE 1130 b 23: "The actions that spring from virtue in general
(i.e., from general justice) are in the main identical with the actions that are
according to law."

   [155] St. Thomas Aquinas in the ST uses the terms *iustitia generalis* and
iustitia legalis interchangeably (e.g., ST II-II, q. 58 *passim*). But in his commentary on the NE (numbers 900-12), he refers to general justice exclusively
as legal justice. Such legal justice (νόμιμον) is not to be confused with legal
justice, a kind of particular justice, which appears as νομικὸν δίκαιον in
Aristotle as a subdivision of political justice (πολιτικὸν δίκαιον) (NE 1134 b 18)
and appears in St. Thomas' commentary as *iustum legale* (*Expositio*, numbers
1020-23). It is this legal justice, the concrete appearance of the abstract notion of
justice in the polis, which is also known as conventional justice, the opposite
of natural justice. Aristotle's identification of general justice with law in the
broad sense has nothing to do with this legal or conventional justice.
   Cf. Allan H. Gilbert, *Dante's Conception of Justice* (Durham, N. C.: Duke University Press, 1925), p. 39:
"The term 'legal justice' as St. Thomas employs it in his comment seems not
to mean the same thing as 'legal justice' of Lectio 2 (which, under sections
900-912, considers law in the broad sense of moral law or ethos of the community). Here it means what is enacted by law, without respect to the justice of
the enactment; there it meant what was in accord with the end of law—to bring
men felicity." Evidently, general justice cannot be identified with law in the
narrow technical sense of positive law, since there could well be distinctly
unjust and viciously immoral laws enacted by corrupt governments. Such laws
would be far from just.

   [156] *Topics,* 149 b 33.

   [157] In *Theaetetus,* 172 a and *Republic,* 339 b, 359 a, Plato describes the
genesis and essential nature of justice in connection with legislation and notes
that men "name the commandment of the law the lawful and just" (νόμμόν
τε καὶ δίκαιον)·

   [158] Cf. W. L. Newman, *The Politics of Aristotle* (Oxford: Clarendon Press,
1887), I, 209-10: "The Greeks ascribed to the constitution a far-reaching ethical
influence. . . . In the vaster states of today opinion and manners are slower to
reflect the tendency of the constitution: in the small city-states of ancient
Greece they readily took its color. It was thus that in the view of the Greeks
every constitution had an accompanying ἦθος, which made itself felt in all the
relations of life. Each constitutional form exercised a moulding influence on

totle understands something quite distinct from the modern concept of law, which, in its specifically restrictive juridical sense and without the strong ethical overtones it had in the polis, takes its origin from Roman jurisprudence.[159]

In the traditional Greek acceptation of law, it is something much wider than mere positive or conventional law, and it includes both written and unwritten law. It should be noted here that νόμος is also used by the Greeks in as wide a sense as the custom, usage of the community, the ethos.[160] In other words, νόμος is identified with

---

virtue. . . . Each constitution embodied a scheme of life, and tended, consciously or not, to bring the lives of those living under it into harmony with its particular scheme." Thus the picture of the polis emerges as essentially a moral community, "the executive authority of an ethical society" (Roger Chance, *Until Philosophers are Kings*, London, 1928, p. 160), that "by nature (is) the moral legislator for all its citizens" (Werner Jaeger, *Paideia*, New York, 1943, Vol. II, 157). For the Greeks the polis is "a moral agent, a person" (Newman, p. 285) and "like Calvin's Church it exercises a 'holy discipline' " (Earnest Barker, ed., *The Politics of Aristotle*, New York, 1962, li).

159 Cf. Anton-Hermann Chroust, "The Function of Law and Justice in the Ancient World and the Middle Ages," *Journal of the History of Ideas* 7 (1946), 301.

160 Grant, *ibid.*, pp. 101-102:
"The view given here of law, which is expressed still more strongly below, ch. xi. par. 1, is quite different from modern views. Law is here represented as a positive system . . . aiming at the regulation of the whole of life, sometimes, however, with a bias of class-interests, and sometimes only roughly executed (ἀπεσχεδιασμένος). This educational and dogmatic character of the law was really exemplified to the greatest extent in the Spartan institutions. Athens rather prided herself (according to the wise remarks which Thucydides puts into the mouth of Pericles) on leaving greater liberty to the individual. But Plato and Aristotle both made the mistake of wishing for an entire state-control over individual life." One could argue the point with Grant whether within the church-like moral institution of the polis it was a mistake for Plato and Aristotle to make the power of the polis omnipresent or whether this was the natural, acceptable and expectable way of life for the men of antiquity. Cf. John Leofric Stocks, *Aristotelianism* (Boston: Marshall Jones Co., 1925), p. 104; George H. Sabine, *A History of Political Theory* (New York: Holt, Rinehart & Winston, 1961), pp. 96, 100; C. Delisle Burns, *Greek Ideals* (London: G. Bell & Sons, 1917), pp. 64, 84; H. D. F. Kitto, *The Greeks* (London: Penguin Books, 1951), pp. 11, 75; Chance, *ibid.*, pp. 7-8; Jaeger, *Paideia*, I, 74-5. All these authors take up a position opposite Grant's and argue for the omnicompetence of the polis as something desirable and willingly accepted by the ancients since the primary care of the polis was the happiness of all its citizens through the practice of virtue. Therefore the polis is radically different from the modern political organization, the state, which does not have this pervasive moral character.

δίκη, understood in its broad meaning as the traditional way of the community. The present identification simply indicates the close relationship between the broad traditional Greek acceptations of law and justice.

As a result of confusion concerning the ancient broad and morally charged meaning of νόμος, some misunderstandings resulted from the identification of universal justice with the law. At the end of the last century, D. G. Ritchie[161] defined Aristotle's general justice as "Righteousness or Rightness of conduct; it is the fulfilling of the whole law, written and unwritten." Twenty-four years later, Ernest Barker,[162] basing himself on the syllogism: law=reason; but reason=the moral obligation; therefore, law=the moral obligations, stated the classical Greek meaning of law in the broad sense as follows:

> The law enjoins courage, and continence, and consideration: it speaks about every virtue and vice, commanding and forbidding. Its rules are laid down by political science, as the standard of what men should do, and what they should forbear to do. As the moral code of a community, law sets forth the end, the Final Good, which that community pursues. The content of the law being thus identical with that of morality, it follows that action in accordance with that content, or justice, is equivalent to action in accordance with the content of morality, or virtue.

Four years after the publication of Barker's book, Vinogradoff, writing on the history of jurisprudence, attributed a narrowly juridical concept to the classical understanding of νόμος in the wide sense, and, consequently, injected a restrictively legalistic notion into the Aristotelian concept of general justice.[163] Since he was a jurist, Vinogradoff's mind was preconditioned for such an interpretation.

His error did not pass unnoticed. Paul Shorey called attention to this distortion in Vinogradoff's work, and noted that "Aristotle's Universal Justice seems to me an ethical, rather than a legal, con-

---

[161] "Aristotle's Subdivisions of 'Particular Justice,'" *The Classical Review* 8 (1894), 185.

[162] Ernest Barker, *The Political Thought of Plato and Aristotle* (New York: Dover Publications, 1959), pp. 321-2. The first version of this work was published in 1918, under the title *Greek Political Theory: Plato and His Predecessors*.

[163] Paul Vinogradoff, *Outlines of Historical Jurisprudence*, Vol. II (Oxford: At the Clarendon Press, 1922), pp. 57-9.

ception and what legal reference there may be is brought in only in subordination to, and in illustration of, the ethical idea."[164]

In answer Vinogradoff explained that he consciously interpreted Aristotle's identification of general justice with law in a legalistic sense, because he felt that otherwise no standard of justice would apply to "such juridical categories as crime and punishment, property and possession, relations between the city and the citizen" . . . as "neither distributive nor corrective justice supply such standards, but justice in general does supply them from the point of view of *compulsory morality.*"[165]

This interpretation seems to take no account of Aristotle's discussion of legal justice, in the strict sense, which applies to the concrete juridical exigencies of the polis the abstract principles of justice as general and particular.[166] Vinogradoff seems to have been misled by the common scholastic designation of general or universal justice as legal justice and failed to notice that legal justice is of two totally different kinds: 1) an abstract principle as general justice; 2) a species of political justice, a result of legal enactments.

The erroneous juridical understanding of general justice found a new supporter in H. H. Joachim in his posthumously published commentary on the *Nicomachean Ethics*,[167] the latest such commentary to appear in English, where he assumes that Aristotle's work is a direct reflection of Athenian legal structures. This view was challenged by A. R. W. Harrison,[168] who emphasizes that general justice is before all else a moral habit, a ἕξις, and not a science (ἐπιστήμη) or faculty (δύναμις), a crucial distinction which Aristotle made.[169] Harrison denies that Aristotle had more than a mere academic "interest in the actual legal institutions of the Athens of his day," and consequently that his politico-ethical works are not based "on the substantive law of Athens."

To show that it is incorrect to identify νόμος, as used in con-

---

164 Paul Shorey, "Universal Justice in Aristotle's Ethics," *Classical Philology* 19 (1924), 279-80.

165 Paul Vinogradoff, an untitled rejoinder to the above, *ibid.*, p. 281.

166 NE 1134 b 18 ff.

167 H. H. Joachim (ed. & commentator), *Aristotle, The Nicomachean Ethics*, edited by D. A. Rees (Oxford: At the Clarendon Press, 1951).

168 A. R. W. Harrison, "Aristotle's Nicomachean Ethics, Book V, and the Law of Athens," *Journal of Hellenic Studies* 77 (1957), 42, 46.

169 NE 1129 a 12-4. Cf. Stewart on this problem: *ibid.*, pp. 376-8.

nection with general justice, with law in the contemporary juridical
sense, a brief look at some passages in Aristotle will suffice. Even
in his younger days Aristotle had associated the virtue of justice
with the preservation of ancestral customs and usages as well as
of enacted laws.[170] It is important to notice that "ancestral usages"
(τὰ πάτρια . . . νόμιμα) are precisely νόμοι in the broad sense. In
this same vein, he says that for general justice the name legal justice
(τὸ δίκαιον . . . κατὰ νόμον) is not an inappropriate designation,
"for men say that what the law [in the broad sense] enjoins is just.
Now the law [in the broad sense] commands brave and temperate
action; and, in a word, all action which we recognize as inspired
by the virtues."[171] This passage also reflects on the relationship of
general justice and law in the wide sense as far as their genesis is
concerned: δίκη, as the traditional way of the community, seems to
precede laws as customs and to serve as their inspiration. Thus we
would have three developmental stages in the organization of Greek
community life: θέμις was the most remote and mythically grounded beginning of tribal customs. A transitional stage is provided by
δίκη, which was more concrete and less superhuman in connotation
than θέμις.[172] Finally, νόμος channels clan morality into a more
formalized and humanized direction. The mythological roots of
these three concepts are the goddess Θέμις as the mother of Δίκη, the
goddess Justice, and of 'Εὐνομία, the goddess Law.[173] Thus Justice
and Law are sisters in the Olympian realm. At any rate, the idea
of law in this broad sense is merely the diffuse expression of the
ethos of the community and cannot be simply identified with its
later restricted notion as legal enactment.

The morally charged meaning of law is used in the *Nicomachean
Ethics,* for Aristotle says that law commands man to practice the

---

170 VV 1250 b 17-8. The reverse side of the coin is visible when Aristotle speaks
of unjust men who transgress ancestral customs and usages and disobey (enacted)
laws and the rulers. Cf. *ibid.,* 1251 a 37-8.

171 MM 1193 b 3-5.

172 Cf. R. C. Jebb, *Homer: An Introduction to the Iliad and Odyssey* (Boston:
Ginn & Co., 1894), p. 48; Jane Ellen Harrison, *Themis* (Cleveland: Meridian
Books, 1962 reprint of the work originally published in 1912), pp. 483, 485, 516,
517; Hartvig Frisch, *Might and Right in Antiquity,* trans. C. C. Martindale
(Kφbenhavn: Gyldendalske Boghandle, 1949), pp. 49, 58-60; Henri van Effenterre
et Hélène Trocmé, "Autorité, justice et liberté aux origines de la cité antique,"
Revue philosophique de la France et de l'étranger, 154 (1964), 428, 429-30.

173 Hesiod, *Theogony,* 901-03.

virtues of courage, temperance, gentleness, and all the other virtues, and at the same time, forbids acts of moral weakness.[174] This law resembles moral laws or church laws which prescribe ethical conduct. In the concept of the common good he sees a link between the virtue of general justice and law. The law aims at the common welfare, the happiness of the community.[175] Similarly, "in one of its senses the term 'just' is applied to anything that produces and preserves the happiness, or the component parts of the happiness, of the political community."[176]

Inasmuch as happiness is the final end both of the polis and of general justice, the notions of the polis and of general justice are most intimately associated in their common objective. Thus general justice becomes the political virtue *par excellence,* the moral quality that the teleologically oriented polis must have precisely as teleologically oriented. If "the meaning and nature of everything . . . is to be looked for in the end of its being,"[177] and if the attainment of this end presupposes a certain quality as its *conditio sine qua non,* then this indispensable quality is inseparably bound up with the meaning of that being whose end it serves. In this sense, the virtue of general justice appertains to the very being of the polis as the means of achieving the political end of happiness.[178]

---

174 NE 1129 b 20-5.

175 *Ibid.,* 14-5.

176 *Ibid.,* 17-9.

177 W. D. Ross, *Aristotle* (New York: Meridian Books, 1961), p. 230.

178 Anton-Hermann Chroust (*Function of Law and Justice,* p. 299) notes that for the ancients "justice . . . was looked upon mainly as the preservation of the social *status quo;* for the maintenance of the social *status quo* constituted the ultimate end and significance of law in the ancient world." In a note to this statement, he characterizes this *status quo*-minded concern of ancient justice and law as corresponding to the Greeks' static conception of reality and to their rationalistic and ontological outlook. Certainly, if one's vision of history is not rectilinear but circular, the uncertainties and the intellectually unpenetrable perplexities of the historical flux are eliminated to a great extent in the intelligible patterns of eternal recurrence. The conservatism inherent in this tradition-ridden ancient community, where the traditional ways (δίκαι) and usages (νόμιμα) of the ancestors held complete sway in all aspects of community and private life, was truly inevitable and in accord with the profound influence that Parmenides' monistic immobilism exercised on the Greek mind. Thus general justice, as the accepted way of the ancients and their customs, served a double purpose of not merely reminding the contemporary generation of the usages of the ancestors, it not merely looked backwards to see what was before, but

The essentially political nature of the virtue of general justice may be approached from another angle. After joining the notions of general justice and of law, Aristotle proceeds to focus attention on the relationship between general justice and moral virtues. The immense moral value of general justice as a virtue is effectively conveyed by the pronouncement that general justice is a perfect [i.e., complete][179] virtue[180] or the totality of virtue [entire virtue] and not merely a part of virtue.[181]

In addition to the three uses of the phrase "perfect [i.e., complete] virtue" (τελεία ἀρετή) in the *Nicomachean Ethics*,[182] it appears only twice elsewhere in the entire Aristotelian corpus, both times in the *Magna Moralia*.[183] The first two uses in the *Nicomachean Ethics*[184] differ from all other occurrences of the phrase inasmuch as they appear in the discussion concerning happiness, while the others are the definition of general justice. Thus a syllogism can be set up: happiness is perfect virtue; but perfect virtue is general justice; therefore, happiness is general justice. And because the happiness in question is political happiness, which is the end of the polis, general justice is identified with political happiness. Since political happiness is the end of the polis, the virtue of justice is essentially connected with the end of the polis, that is with the polis as such. This again leads to the conclusion that the virtue of general justice is political virtue *par excellence*.

---

it also had the perpetuation of these same traditions as its end in looking forward toward the future. Thus happiness in the political community was to be achieved in the same traditional way as it has always been in the past. Justice and law, in the broad sense, were the rails on which the polis could move safely, rapidly and in perfect uniformity from the past into the unknown stretches of the future. This is not simply a desire for a healthy continuity with the past, but, in a sense, a wishful yearning to re-enter the past.

179 The adjective τελεία suggests totality, wholeness, completeness, something which includes everything within itself so that nothing remains outside it. Cf. GJ, p. 341 ad 1129 b 26. This idea is conveyed by Aristotle in his use of the modifier τελεία in *Metaphysics*, 1021 b 21 and also in *Physics*, 207 a 13.

180 NE 1129 b 26. Cf. *ibid.*, 30, 31. In P 1260 a 17, Aristotle says that the ruler must have the complete or perfect intellectual virtue. This is the only instance where τελεία is used to modify not moral but intellectual virtues.

181 NE 1130 a 10.

182 NE 1129 b 26, 30, 31.

183 MM 1193 b 6, 10.

184 NE 1100 a 4, 1102 a 6.

In the expression "justice is a political virtue" the adjective "political" is most important. Virtue is the genus of justice and is not justice without any qualification. Under the genus of virtue, political is the specific difference of justice, which distinguishes it from all other virtues.

Immediately after the assertion that justice is perfect or entire virtue, Aristotle hastens to add the crucial qualifying phrase, "but not absolutely, but (only) in relation to others" ($\pi\rho\grave{o}s$ $\H{\epsilon}\tau\epsilon\rho o\nu$).[185] That general justice is complete or perfect virtue in a certain sense is also indicated in the *Magna Moralia*, where it is said that "justice is a certain kind of complete virtue."[186] This "certain kind" ($\tau\acute{\iota}s$) is a vague allusion to the $\pi\rho\grave{o}s$ $\H{\epsilon}\tau\epsilon\rho o\nu$ of the first statement. This relatedness to others, this political dimension of plurality, distinguishes general justice from all other virtues.[187] In other words, general justice is the totality of all virtues, but only in a certain sense and for a specific reason. This sense and this reason are the matter of justice, the relatedness toward another. General justice is not merely a quantitative aggregate of all possible virtues put together: there is also an important qualitative difference involved. General justice is perfect virtue not in its possessor's acts toward himself but toward others.[188] For this reason Aristotle affirms that one cannot commit injustice against himself in the strict sense, since an actual duality of other-relatedness is missing.[189]

This qualitative difference between general justice and the totality of all the other virtues simply and absolutely taken is sharpened by Aristotle's statement that inasmuch as the totality of all virtues is considered as a moral disposition or habit in itself, intrasubjectively considered, it is not the virtue of justice, but it becomes such only when this sum of all virtues is displayed toward

---

185 NE 1129 b 26.

186 MM 193 b 6; cf. *ibid.*, 10.

187 ST II-II, q. 57, a. 1: "Iustitiae proprium est inter alias virtutes ut ordinet hominem in his quae sunt ad alterum."

188 NE 1177 a 31-2: "The just man needs people towards whom and with whom he shall act justly" ($\delta\iota\kappa\alpha\iota o\pi\rho\alpha\gamma\acute{\eta}\sigma\epsilon\iota$).

189 NE 1134 b 12. Cf. ST II-II, q. 58, a. 2: "Secundum similitudinem accipiuntur in uno et eodem homine diversa principia actionum, quasi diversa agentia; sicut ratio, et irascibilis, et concupiscibilis; et ideo metaphorice in uno et eodem homine dicitur esse iustitia, secundum quod ratio imperat irascibili et concupiscibili, et secundum quod haec obediunt rationi, et universaliter secundum quod unicuique parti hominis attribuitur quod ei convenit."

others when the virtues become transsubjective and other-oriented.[190] As St. Thomas says, "legal justice is essentially the same as all virtue, but differs therefrom logically."[191] Virtue is a habitual state of character, and justice as a virtue is certainly that. But within this genus of virtue, its specific difference is πρὸς ἕτερον, relatedness toward others.

This analysis is borne out by Aristotle's logic. In the *Categories*, Aristotle classifies habit (ἕξις) under two distinct categories: on the one hand, habit is a quality (ποιότης),[192] and, on the other, it is a relation (πρὸς τί).[193] Moral virtue simply taken is a habit and belongs to the category of quality, but when this virtue or moral habit is a quality that places the person possessing it in relationship to something outside himself, then it belongs to the category of relation. The moral habit is then both a quality and a relation at the same time. Aristotle also gives as examples knowledge and attitude, which also are simultaneously both qualities and relations: on the one hand, knowledge is a quality of the knower and attitude a quality of its possessor, but, on the other hand, one is knowledge of something and the other is an attitude toward something. But just as virtues simply speaking, i.e., virtues that are only qualities, are not relative to something external, so also the individual branches of knowledge—as examples Aristotle gives grammar and music—are not relative to something else. Thus grammar is the knowledge of grammar, and music is the knowledge of music.[194]

When this analysis is applied to virtue and justice, it is seen that virtue as a habit simply or absolutely taken (ἀρετὴ ἁπλῶς) is merely a quality, but the virtue of justice as a moral habit belongs to the two categories of quality and relation at the same time, since its specific difference as a moral habit is that it is a quality toward other (s) (ποιότης πρὸς ἕτερον).

Since both (numerically) complete virtue absolutely speaking (τελεία ἀρετὴ ἁπλῶς) and general justice, as perfect virtue toward another (τελεία ἀρετὴ πρὸς ἕτερον), are moral habits, they belong to

---

190 NE 1130 a 12-4.

191 ST II-II, q. 58, a. 6: "Iustitia legalis est idem in essentia cum omni virtute; differt autem ratione." The translation of the ST is from *The "Summa Theologica" of St. Thomas Aquinas*, trans. Fathers of the English Dominican Province (London: Burns Oates & Washbourne Ltd., 1929), volume 10.

192 *Categories*, 8 b 27.

193 *Ibid.*, 6 b 4, 11 a 22.

194 *Ibid.*

the category of quality, and are therefore only logically distinct, inasmuch as general justice places its possessor in a relationship with the community, whereas when the virtues are privately practiced for the benefit of the subject alone, they are merely an immanent quality. It is relatedness to others which makes justice not simply another virtue, but perfect virtue.[195] This is an authentically and characteristically Greek idea. Just as man, the political animal, becomes perfect in the polis, in constant relationship with his peers in the leisured freedom of the agora, so also, virtue becomes perfect not when practiced in isolation from others, but when virtue is other-oriented. The quality of perfection is bestowed both on men and on virtues through politicality.

Since the ancient Greeks were so very politically minded, it is only to be expected that Aristotle recognizes in other-relatedness that additional but crucial quality which confers perfection on justice as a virtue. Precisely because justice is a virtue that pre-supposes the existence of a community, it implies all other virtues[196] in a political context. "This is why justice is often thought to be the most excellent of the virtues, and more wonderful than 'the evening or morning star'; and we have the proverb 'in justice are all the virtues comprehended.' "[197]

Justice is an immanent quality but it is not therefore passive; it is an active dynamic attribute of an act directed toward another person. The very relatedness of political man to others through the virtue of justice involves this functional notion, because these politi-

---

195 For the ideas expressed in this analysis see Stewart, *ibid.*, pp. 394, 401-02.

196 P 1283 a 39.

197 NE 1129 b 26-30. The statement that "in justice are all the virtues comprehended" is from Theognis' *Elegies*, fragment 147. Although he does not mention it by name, it is clearly of general justice that Alfarabi talks about when he discusses the moral virtue which "is the perfect and most powerful virtue," such that it "turns out to have a power equal to that of all the virtues together. . . . This virtue is such that when a man decides to fulfill its functions, he cannot do so without making use of the functions of all the other virtues. If he himself does not happen to possess all of these virtues—in which case he cannot make use of the functions of particular virtues present in him when he decides to fulfill the functions of that virtue—that virtue of his will be a moral virtue in the exercise of which he exploits the acts of the virtues possessed by all others, whether they are nations, cities within a nation, groups within a city or parts within each group. This, then, is the leading virtue that is not surpassed by any other in authority." Alfarabi, *ibid.*, xxiv, 10-19, p. 31.

cal relationships are interactions. Justice, according to Aristotle, is "perfect virtue, because it is the practice of perfect virtue."[198] But it is not solely the exercise or practice of perfect virtue as virtue that confers the special note of perfection on general justice so that it includes all virtues in itself, but the fact that this actual exercise of it is directed toward others. As Aristotle notes, justice "is perfect (virtue), because he who possesses it can exercise his virtue toward others and not merely in himself; for there are many who can practice virtue in their own private affairs, but cannot do so in their relations with another."[199] In his commentary on these passages, St. Thomas says that "justice itself is a certain perfect virtue not simply in itself but in relation to another. Since it is better to be perfect not only in oneself but also in relation to another, it is therefore often said that this [general] justice is the most excellent among all virtues."[200] He goes on to say that "legal justice is a perfect virtue because a man who has this virtue can employ it in relation to another and not to himself only—something not characteristic of all virtuous people. Many can practice virtue in things pertaining to themselves, but not in the things pertaining to others."[201] Thus, the virtue of general justice, by incorporating in itself all virtues, through its own other-centeredness rescues the other virtues from a morbid self-concern and imparts altruism to all virtues.

It is this other-regarding aspect of justice which will expose a man's true self and will show whether he is concerned only about his own selfish good or is able to overcome the centripetal forces of the apolitical virtues. For this reason Aristotle cites the saying of Bias that " 'Public office will show the man,' for in public office one is necessarily in relation to others ($\pi\rho\grave{o}s$ $\H{\epsilon}\tau\epsilon\rho\text{o}\nu$) and in a com-

---

198 NE 1129 b 31.

199 NE 1129 b 32-1130 a 1.

200 *Expositio*, 906: "Ipsa iustitia est quaedam virtus perfecta non simpliciter, sed in comparatione ad alterum. Et quia esse perfectum non solum secundum se, sed in comparatione ad alterum potius est, propter hoc multoties dicitur, quod haec iustitia sit praeclarissima inter omnes virtutes."

201 *Ibid.*, 908: "Iustitia legalis est perfecta virtus, quia ille qui habet hanc virtutem, potest uti virtute ad alterum, et non solum ad seipsum; quod quidem non convenit omnibus virtuosis. Multi enim possunt uti virtute in propriis, qui non possunt ea uti in his quae sunt ad alterum."

munity."[202] Indeed, public office by its very name indicates that its holder is not an isolated person, but oriented toward the many under his care. As a public figure, he is not concerned with his own private affairs but with the things which pertain to the community, and is faced with the polis at the other end of the πρὸς ἕτερον polarity.

All the other virtues aim at the good of the subject but the virtue of justice, because it points outside the subject toward another, aims at the good of another.[203] It is for the attainment of this good of the other that the virtue of justice is exercised. This good of the other as the end of the virtue of justice can be conceived in a twofold way, depending on whether the just man is directed in his just act toward the community at large or toward particular individuals. If the act of justice aims at the community as a whole, then it is an act of general justice and it seeks to secure the common good. On the other hand, if the act of justice is posited for the good of certain individuals, then it is an act of particular justice.[204] It is the common concern of general justice, which seeks

202 NE 1130 a 2-3. Similar sentiments are expressed also in Sophocles, *Antigone*, 175-77: "No man can be fully known, in soul and spirit and mind, until he has been versed in rule and lawgiving."

203 NE 1130 a 3-5. Euripides divides men into two classes: those who are just and are concerned with the good of their neighbor, and those who are concerned solely with their own gain and advancement, always seeking only what is best for their own selves without regard for others. Cf. *Heracleidae*, 1-5. In *Republic*, 343 c, Plato also defines the virtue of justice as the good of the other.

204 Fragment 3 of Aristotle's dialogue *On Justice* states that "a great number of philosophers, but principally Plato and Aristotle, said much about justice defending it and bestowing the highest praise on it because it assigns each man what is his own and preserves equity in all things, and maintained that while the other virtues are, so to speak, silent and inward, it is justice alone that is not so self-contained and hidden, but stands forth boldly in readiness to act well for the general good." Ross, *Select Fragments*, p. 101. Aristotle stresses that general justice is the cause of good to the community at large. Cf. *Rhetoric*, 1362 b 28.

St. Thomas is very helpful in explaining the terse statement of Aristotle concerning the good of the other and how this is the distinguishing matter for separating general from particular justice. ST II-II, q. 58, a. 5:

Iustitia . . . ordinat hominem in comparatione ad alium; quod potest esse dupliciter: uno modo ad alium singulariter consideratum; alio modo ad alium in communi, secundum scilicet quod ille qui servit alicui communitati, servit omnibus hominibus qui sub communitate illa continentur. Ad utrumque ergo se potest habere iustitia secundum propriam rationem. Manifestum est autem quod omnes qui sub communitate aliqua continentur, comparantur ad communitatem sicut partes ad totum; pars autem id quod est,

directly the good of the whole community—and through it indirectly, the good of its constitutive parts—that distinguishes it both
from particular justice and from all the other virtues.[205] Thus
general justice does not render the rest of the virtues superfluous,
since it is only indirectly that it concerns particular goods, inasmuch as they are parts of the common good. In distinction, the
particular virtues are immediately directed either to the good of
individuals other than the subject, as in the case of particular justice,
or to the good of the subject himself, as are all the other particular
virtues.[206]

In accordance with the teleological principle that the end of a
being specifies its nature and is in accordance with it, the transcendent moral value and importance of general justice are indicated by its end, the common good. General justice is related to the
particular virtues exactly according to the proportion that the
common good is related to the particular goods within it. Just as
general justice is not a mere quantitative aggregate of all the virtues without any qualitative difference, so also the common good
is not only a numerical accumulation of individual goods but is
qualitatively different from them. Thus, the adjective τελεία is applied to general justice in a double sense: both as a quantitatively
inclusive totality of all other virtues and as the qualitatively distinct

---

totius est; unde quodlibet bonum partis est ordinabile in bonum totius.
Secundum hoc ergo bonum cuiuslibet virtutis, sive ordinantis aliquem
hominem ad seipsum, sive ordinantis ipsum ad aliquas alias personas singu-
lares, est referibile ad bonum commune, ad quod ordinat iustitia. Et
secundum hoc actus omnium virtutum possunt ad iustitiam pertinere,
secundum quod ordinat hominem ad bonum commune. Et quantum ad
hoc iustitia dicitur virtus generalis.

[205] ST II-II, q. 58, a. 7:

Iustitia legalis non est essentialiter omnis virtus; sed oportet praeter iustitiam
legalem, quae ordinat hominem immediate ad bonum commune, esse alias
virtutes quae immediate ordinant hominem circa particularia bona; quae
quidem possunt esse vel ad seipsum, vel ad alteram singularem personam.
Sicut ergo praeter iustitiam legalem oportet esse aliquas virtutes par-
ticulares, quae ordinent hominem in seipso, puta temperantiam et forti-
tudinem, ita etiam praeter iustitiam legalem oportet esse particularem
quamdam iustitiam, quae ordinet hominem circa ea quae sunt ad
alteram singularem personam.

Ibid., ad 1-m:

Iustitia legalis sufficienter quidem ordinat hominem in his quae sunt
ad alterum; quantum ad commune quidem bonum, immediate; quantum
autem ad bonum unius singularis personae, mediate. Et ideo oportet esse
aliquam particularem iustitiam, quae immediate ordinet hominem ad
bonum alterius singularis personae.

[206] Cf. *ibid.*, as above.

perfection of virtue directed to the common good of the whole polis as such.[207]

Although Aristotle does not formally treat of the relationship existing between general justice and the particular virtues which it contains or of that obtaining between their ends, the common and particular goods, the correctness of the foregoing analysis can be supported from his discussion of the connection of the whole with its parts.

It is true that the whole is in its parts, since there can be no whole if there are no parts,[208] yet the whole and its parts cannot simply be said to be the same. The whole is in its parts in a manner different from the way that the parts are in a whole. The mere presence of parts does not necessarily mean the existence of the whole, because the whole is not merely the quantitative sum total of all its parts; there is also a qualitative difference.[209] Although the parts of a whole may be said to be prior to it in time, absolutely speaking the whole is still prior to the parts, since the parts are elements of the whole and are explained by reference to it.[210] Therefore, the whole is naturally superior to its parts:[211] there is a certain perfection which is proper only to the whole precisely as the whole, whereby it transcends the manifold plurality of the parts and gives them unity and new meaning.[212]

Transferring these findings to the ethico-political order, Aristotle asserts that, since the whole is of necessity prior to the part, the polis is by nature clearly prior to the household and to the particular individuals.[213] There is not merely a difference of quantity or size, but a difference of kind between the polis as the whole and the household as its part.[214] The community as the whole is superior to the household and individuals constituting it. In terms of this superiority, the common good of the whole polis, which con-

---

207 *Ibid.*, ad 2-am:

Bonum commune civitatis et bonum singulare unius personae non differunt solum secundum multum et paucum, sed secundum formalem differentiam. Alia enim est ratio boni communis et boni singularis, sicut alia est ratio totius et partis.

208 *Physics*, 210 a 16.

209 *Topics*, 150 a 16, 18-21; *Metaphysics*, 1035 a 1-3.

210 *Metaphysics*, 1034 b 27-33.

211 P 1288 a 27.

212 *Metaphysics*, 1023 b 26-7.

213 P 1253 a 19-20.

214 P 1252 a 10, 13.

sists in the total complex of those conditions of a leisured and free
political life that provides the citizens with the possibility of
achieving their own perfection in a certain fullness of measure and
also with some relative ease,[215] this common good is also superior
to the individual good of the members of the polis. Therefore, the
aspirations, virtues, and good of the individuals should always
have a regard for the aspirations, virtues and good of the whole
polis.[216] On the other hand, the interests of the part and the whole
are in a sense the same.[217] There is a reciprocal relationship between the common good and the individual good: each is impossible of perfect realization without the other.[218] Happiness is
the ultimate end of both the whole polis and of the individual
citizens, but "the whole cannot be happy unless most, or all, or
some of its parts enjoy happiness."[219] Since happiness is the result
of the practice of virtue, [220] the polis must be virtuous, so that its
virtue may redound to the citizens' virtue. Thus the question of
the relationship between common good and individual good leads
to the question of general justice and its relationship with particular
virtues.

The transcendent superiority of the political virtue of general
justice, as whole and perfect virtue, over the particular virtues is
seen, then, not only as something quantitative but also qualitative,
involving as it does the natural priority of the whole over its parts.
This preeminence of general justice is to be understood also in the
sense that it imparts unity and a new political meaning to all the
particular virtues, by directing them toward the one common good

215 Cf. the definition of "the common welfare" in the "Declaration on Religious Freedom" of the Second Vatican Council, Article 6 in Walter M.
Abbott (ed.), *The Documents of Vatican II* (New York: An Angelus Book,
1966), p. 683.

216 P 1260 b 14-5.

217 P 1255 b 10.

218 ST II-II, q. 47, a. 10, ad 2: "Ille qui quaerit bonum commune multitudinis, ex consequenti etiam quaerit bonum suum, propter duo: primo quidem
quia bonum proprium non potest esse sine bono communi vel familiae, vel
civitatis aut regni. Inde et Valerius Maximus dicit de antiquis Romanis quod
'malebat esse pauperes in divite imperio, quam divites in paupero imperio.'
Secundo quia cum homo sit pars domus vel civitatis, oportet quod homo con-
sideret quid sit sibi bonum ex hoc quod est prudens circa bonum multitudinis.
Bona enim dispositio partium accipitur secundum habitudinem."

219 P 1264 b 18-9.

220 P 1329 a 23.

of the whole community. By its other-centered orientation, general justice coordinates and orders all the acts of the particular virtues. Thus, as contained within the act of general justice as parts in a whole, the acts of particular virtues cease to be merely private and concerned only with the good of the subject, but take on a new, a political meaning, and aim at the transubjective good of the "great other," the polis.[221] Just as man is given his properly human perfection and meaning only within the polis, to which he is related as a part to the whole, so also, particular virtues are imparted their fullest perfection and meaning within the other-oriented act of general justice. The many subjects themselves and the acts of each subject's particular virtues are all united by general justice and, as the supreme political virtue,[222] it directs everything and everybody in one powerful thrust toward the transcendent common good of political happiness.

By directing the acts of all particular virtues to the common end of the polis, general justice imparts a political dimension to every particular virtue and thus establishes the sphere of political or community, that is, social, morality. In this way, the acts of particular virtues function on two distinct levels: they remain the perfection of the subject and aim at his good, but at the same time, if these particular virtues are considered as parts of general justice as the whole virtue, they point beyond the subject to the political common good.[223] By directly enhancing the good of the

221 ST II-II, q. 58, a. 6: "Iustitia legalis dicitur esse virtus generalis, in quantum scilicet ordinat actus aliarum virtutum ad suum finem, quod est movere per imperium omnes alias virtutes; sicut enim charitas potest dici virtus generalis, in quantum ordinat actus omnium virtutum ad bonum divinum, ita etiam iustitia legalis, in quantum ordinat actus omnium virtutum ad bonum commune." Ioannes B. Schuster (ed.), *De Iustitia: Aristotelis Ethicorum ad Nicomachum Liber V,* Cum commentariis Silvestri Mauri (Romae: Apud Aedes Pont. Universitatis Gregorianae, 1938), p. 14, No. 15: "Iustum legale continet actus omnium virtutum, in quantum per leges praecipiuntur in ordine ad utilitatem communem; ergo iustitia legalis est, per quam exercemus actus omnium virtutum in ordine ad bonum commune; ergo iustitia legalis est virtus quaedam perfecta, non absoluta ac respiciens solum nos ipsos, sed ad alterum ac respiciens bonum commune." Cf. *ibid.,* p. 15, No. 16: "Per iustitiam legalem utimur omnibus virtutibus et exercemus actus earum in bonum aliorum."

222 P 1253 a 38.

223 ST II-II, q. 58, a. 6: "Potest tamen quaelibet virtus, secundum quod a praedicta virtute (speciali quidem in essentia, generali autem secundum virtutem), ordinatur ad bonum commune, dici iustitia legalis."

subject, particular virtues indirectly contribute to the common good, since the subject is a part of the community and his good a part of the common good. Flowing from man's nature, which is political, his every act, at least indirectly, becomes political. Therefore, every act of a particular virtue not only is in accord with that virtue, but also with virtue entire, general justice. Conversely, by offending against a particular virtue a man will transgress against the dictates of general justice, that is, against all morality. For example, an honest policeman not only practices the virtue of honesty, but is also a good citizen and is just toward the public at large; on the other hand, a dishonest policeman not only offends against the particular virtue of honesty, but also against general justice and the common good and is a criminal. Aristotle gives the example of a man, who in anger voluntarily kills himself. He commits an act of injustice not against himself, since no one submits voluntarily to injustice, but against the polis.[224]

It is the crucial quality of other-directedness that in terms of politicality confers the name of whole and perfect virtue on general justice and transforms the individual morality of particular virtues into political morality. Hence, this relational quality is the characteristic of general justice to such an extent that equality, the other constitutive element of justice, is not mentioned by Aristotle at all. This presumably signifies that general justice does not have a special mean or is not in a special mean[225] and that its mean is the whole mean of all particular virtues together, just as general justice is all virtue. In other words, the mean for general justice is implied in the idea of general justice as the entirety of all virtues, and the mean for general justice will be the manifold mean of all the particular virtues taken together.

There is no mention made of a mean in the religious idea of justice as the totality of all virtues and as expressive of the whole of morality. It is as descriptive of fundamental and all-inclusive moral goodness that in the Judeo-Christian biblical tradition [gen-

---

224 NE 1138 a 9-13.

225 It is to be clearly understood that virtue is not a mean, but rather it has a mean or is in a mean. Aristotle defines moral virtue as "a state of character concerned with choice, lying *in a mean*" ($\grave{\epsilon}\nu\ \mu\epsilon\sigma\acute{o}\tau\eta\tau\iota$). Cf. NE 1106 b 36. Oates is most emphatic against the confusion which simply identifies virtue as a mean, instead of virtue being in a mean. See Whitney J. Oates, "The Doctrine of the Mean," *Philosophical Review*, 45 (1936), 390.

eral] justice as such is attributed to God and to the upright man. This is the righteousness of God and of the elect.[226] Thus general justice covers the whole length and breadth of morality and includes all the other virtues with their particular means. Strictly speaking, because justice is so profoundly other-oriented, it addresses itself to the need, the good, of the other and adjusts to this other according to his changing needs. General justice, as a radical openness to the other, cannot be reduced to a mathematical, a quantitative, equality. It is not a question of equality, that is, quantity, but of the quality of unswerving loyalty to the totality of the tradition of the community and to its vision of the good life.

The Greeks envisioned the good life in the polis as a leisured, free practice of virtue in the agora, aiming at the fullness of happiness possible within the active life of the polis. Since this virtue is to be practiced in the polis, it is naturally political by definition. This somewhat vacuous formal concept of political virtue is now given a full substantive content when it is identified as the virtue of general justice. General justice, as perfect general other-related virtue, contains two distinguishable elements: 1) a passive element: the tradition of the ancients, a complex of customs and usages, something inherited from the past; and 2) an active element: a virtue, the perfection and totality of all virtues, an active habit of loyalty to the "vision splendid" of the good life as seen by the ancestors and now to be actualized and kept alive.[227] Thus when it is said that the polis is a moral community aiming at the common good through the exercise of virtue, the statement can be rendered more precise by adding "through the exercise of the virtue of general justice." General justice, therefore, as the traditional concept of the good life practiced today, is truly expressive of the whole ethos of the polis in the most concise way possible.

In the concept of the virtue of general justice the ancient Greeks reached the highest peak in their morality. This is not the height found in the Christian ethics of other-centered love, yet the other-

226 Cf. John L. McKenzie, *Dictionary of the Bible* (Milwaukee: Bruce, 1965), pp. 739-43. Cf. especially Deut., 32, 4; Pss. vii, 11; ix, 8; cxix, 137, 138, 142; cxlv, 17; Romans 1:17; 2:2; 3:21-6; II Timothy 4:8.

227 This is another way of stating the conception of $\delta \iota \kappa \eta$ as both a descriptive and a normative or prescriptive idea at the same time. It is the same virtue of justice, but these are two distinguishable sides of the same coin. In other words, general justice as a moral fact both describes and prescribes the traditional way of the good life.

regarding aspect of justice is certainly a movement away from a merely egoistic and self-centered ethic. This is not to say that the Greek who possessed the virtue of general justice was a man who had a wholly disinterested love and regard for others. The pagan just man was ultimately selfish as Aristotle pictures him.[228] But the good pagan at least wished to attain his own good mediately, through the other-directed virtue of justice, so that by aiming directly at the good of another, the common good, it might redound to his own good. This a more honorable and noble way of self-love than the self-centered greed of the unjust man who only regards himself and nobody else.[229] If this is selfishness, it is at least enlightened selfishness: it seeks the good of the self through that of another person, and, in the process of securing happiness for the self, it first brings happiness to the other.

When the virtue of justice is proposed as the most perfect virtue precisely because it is other-directed, there is recognition that man can increase his own worth only by going outside himself. The man who is concerned with his own self in such a way that he closes himself off from the outer world in unenlightened selfishness and concentrates solely on his own good actually defeats his purpose. In such self-imprisonment he cannot augment his own worth, just as a sum of money carefully hidden so as not to be lost cannot increase. It is only from the outside that additional quantities of goodness can enter the individual, and it is through the political virtue of justice that one of the most enlightened of ancient pagans

---

[228] Cf. W. F. R. Hardie, "The Final Good in Aristotle's Ethics," *Philosophy* 40 (1965), 287, 290, 292-3.

[229] Cf. NE 1168 b 12-33. Aristotle knows that all men are "lovers of themselves" (*Rhetoric*, 1371 b 20), that they want to become rich, honored, have bodily pleasures (*Rhetoric*, 1371 b 1; P 1271 a 17; NE 1159 a 16-9, 1168 b 16-7), and that they are attached to their own habits (*Rhetoric*, 1369 b 16, 1370 a 6), but he offers a rationally thought-out, sensible way of acquiring these goods, since the seeming short-cut of self-enclosed, intellectually unenlightened selfishness is self-defeating. Aristotle's ideal man is selfish, self-regarding, but, at least, in an intelligent way. He knows that the direct method of gaining increase in self-worth does not succeed, so he proposes an indirect way by first assisting someone else in an other-directed act of justice. This is the *do ut des* principle consciously applied in Aristotle's ethical rationalism in the form of the virtue of justice. There are some interesting remarks along these lines in E. Weil, "L'Anthropologie d'Aristote," *Revue de métaphysique et de morale* 51 (1946), 11.

saw an effective way to contact others and secure a desired growth in personal happiness.

The other-relatedness of the virtue of justice, and especially of general justice as the whole complex of all virtues and morality, is essential for the formation and maturation of the self. The subject becomes aware of himself by seeing himself against the background of the other as the nonself. At first, the nonself is an object, simply that which is not the subject. But, within a human political context, there comes the recognition that "the other" is not merely an object, but is also a subject. Therefore, the original subject-object relationship is transformed into intersubjectivity. The self's fully developed self-consciousness envisions the mutuality of this intersubjective relationship in the sense that just as it regards the other subjects as standing over against it as "other," so also, the same polarity makes it available to others as the "other" *vis-à-vis* their own selves. By measuring the self against this transubjective standard in the other-relatedness of the virtue of justice the self comes to full self-understanding. Through it, the self can, in a sense, stand outside of itself, put itself in the place of the nonself subjects and through their eyes see its own subject as an "other." Thus the subject attains a mature degree of self-identity by understanding himself not only as the self for its own self, but that it is at the same time an "other," and is also for others.

This intersubjective correlation through otherness, that is, through the other-relatedness of the virtue of justice, recognizes the fundamental equality of all the subjects involved, self as well as other selves. The reciprocity of rights and duties rests on this basis as the self understands itself not only *sub specie identitatis,* but also *sub specie alteritatis.* The virtue of justice is called upon to minister to the needs of intersubjective intercourse, by always calling attention to the otherness inherent in the self. In this way, it limits the excessive claims of the self in the name of the "other" and perpetuates fluidity and proper balance in intersubjective relationships. Since general justice includes all the reflexively self-oriented particular virtues, it gives voice not only to the self, but, through other-relatedness, also gives an ear to the other: *Audiatur et altera pars.*[230] Therefore, the Aristotelian just man has a certain nobility

---

[230] Aristophanes cites a similar proverb in connection with justice. Cf. *The Wasps,* 725-6.

in his willing submission to the impartial judgment of transubjectivity, even though he hears the other only in order that this other should in his turn hear him.[231]

This same self-ennobling function of other-relatedness in intersubjective intercourse is also present in friendship. Like the virtue of justice, friendship is also a moral habit, has to do with the volitional,[232] is other-oriented,[233] involves equality,[234] and has a unifying, ordering role to play in the polis.[235] In terms of other-relatedness, Aristotle describes friendship as a "friendly feeling toward any one as wishing for him what you believe to be good things, not for your own sake but for his, and being inclined, so far as you can, to bring these things about."[236] Similarly, a friend is "one who will always try, for your sake, to do what he takes to be good for you,"[237] and "who shares your pleasure in what is good and your pain in what is unpleasant, for your sake and for no other reason."[238] These definitions apply most of all to one of the three

[231] For the ideas expressed in this and in the previous paragraph see Vecchio, *ibid.*, pp. 77-81, 83-5, 158.

[232] NE 1157 b 30-3. Aristotle also associates the virtue of justice with the voluntary (NE 1136 a 18: $\tau\grave{o}$ $\gamma\grave{\alpha}\rho$ $\delta\iota\kappa\alpha\iota o\pi\rho\alpha\gamma\epsilon\hat{\iota}\nu$ $\pi\hat{\alpha}\nu$ $\dot{\epsilon}\kappa o\acute{\nu}\sigma\iota o\nu$), with wishing (NE 1129 a 9, 10: $\beta o\acute{\nu}\lambda\eta\sigma\iota\varsigma$), and also with deliberate choice (NE 1134 a 2: $\pi\rho o\alpha\acute{\iota}\rho\epsilon\sigma\iota\varsigma$). In NE 1157 b 30-3, Aristotle uses both the verb $\beta o\acute{\nu}\lambda o\nu\tau\alpha\iota$ and the noun $\pi\rho o\alpha\acute{\iota}\rho\epsilon\sigma\iota\varsigma$ in connection with friendship. Stewart argues (*ibid.*, pp. 376-7) that $\beta o\acute{\nu}\lambda\eta\sigma\iota\varsigma$ is merely a popular word to express the same idea as the technical term $\pi\rho o\alpha\acute{\iota}\rho\epsilon\sigma\iota\varsigma$. Ross notes (*Aristotle*, pp. 199-200) that "it has often been complained that the psychology of Plato and Aristotle has no distinct conception of the will. Aristotle's doctrine of choice is clearly an attempt to formulate such a conception." At any rate, Aristotle nowhere speaks of "the subject of the virtue of justice," meaning the volitional faculty of the soul in which it inheres; he only indicates that it has to do with the irrational part of the soul. St. Thomas, on the contrary, expressly says that the will is the proper subject of justice. Cf. *Expositio*, 889: "Convenienter notificavit iustitiam per voluntatem, in qua non fiunt passiones, et tamen est exteriorum actuum principium, unde est proprium subiectum iustitiae quae non est circa passiones."

[233] *Rhetoric*, 1381 b 35-7: "Things that cause friendship are: doing kindnesses; doing them unasked; and not proclaiming the fact when they are done, which shows that they were done for their own sake and not for some other reason."

[234] NE 1158 b 1; P 1287 b 33.

[235] NE 1155 a 22; P 1262 b 8-9.

[236] *Rhetoric*, 1380 b 35-1381 a 1.

[237] *Ibid.*, 1361 b 37-8.

[238] *Ibid.*, 1381 a 4-6.

kinds of friendship,[239] i.e., to perfect friendship, which is the friendship existing between men who are good and alike in virtue[240] and wish the good of their friends for their friends' sake.[241]

On account of these manifold similarities between friendship and the virtue of justice, it is not surprising that Aristotle expressly associates them with one another. He says that "friendship and justice . . . seem to be concerned with the same objects and exhibited between the same persons,"[242] so that people's friendship is limited by the extent of their association, which also limits justice.[243] Justice is presupposed for friendship, so that there can be no friendship without justice, although there can be justice without friendship.[244] In this sense, there is no need for justice between friends,[245] since their feelings of friendship transcend the demands of strict justice. In other words, for Aristotle friendship is the most perfect form of justice. In it the demands of justice are willingly met in a superabundant way. The friend exhibits the total perfection of all the virtues in a supereminent way. For him, general justice is an authentic way of life and his sole concern is the good of the other, his friend, or, if this other is the polis, the common good. In this way, the loyal citizen is the perfectly just man in his concern for the good of the community. Similarly, patriotism itself is the perfect expression of the common good-oriented political virtue of general justice, the perfection and totality of all the virtues.

Unrestrained individualism and selfish greed in Athens after the

---

239 Aristotle lists three kinds of friendship according to the motives on account of which men befriend one another: 1) friendship of utility (NE 1156 a 11-2); 2) friendship of pleasure (NE 1156 a 13-14, 15-7) and 3) friendship for the sake of good (*bonum honestum*) or of perfect friendship (τελεία φιλία; NE 1156 b 6-23).

240 NE 1156 b 6-7.

241 NE 1156 b 10.

242 NE 1159 b 25-6. Cf. NE 1160 a 8; 1161 a 10-11.

243 NE 1159 b 30-31.

244 Cf. NE 1161 a 30-4, 1161 b 8-10.

245 NE 1155 a 27-9. La Plante says that "friendship in its highest form causes him who has this virtue to consider his friend as a person, as a being to be loved for his own sake, not as something which furthers the self-interest and material gain of the lover." Harry La Plante, "Justice and Friendship in Aristotle's Social Philosophy," *Proceedings of the American Catholic Philosophical Association* 36 (1962), 125. Thus the closest that Aristotle approaches the Christian concept of disinterested love of neighbor is in the highest form of friendship, which also is at the same time the most perfect form of justice.

Peloponnesian War were a rejection of the ancient standards of justice. This unbounded selfishness might have been an occasion for Aristotle to call attention to the venerable tradition of virtuous life in the polis. To counteract the influence of community-destructive, antipolitical immorality, he expounds, under the master notion of general justice, a theory of the truly virtuous, common-good-centered moral life. Just as the advocates of immorality advance claims for the absolute right of the strong, Aristotle upholds the supremacy of a rationally based morality of justice. He indicates that only an other-directed morality is productive of good for the self, and thereby shows the senselessness of a solely self-centered moral or, rather, immoral attitude. Against the praise of expediency by champions of universal injustice, Aristotle praises the transubjective value of general justice and hails it as the complete and perfect political virtue, the very meaning and essence of virtuous life in the polis. He points out that men only want to seem just, without being actually just,[246] and that people give only lip service to justice but in their hearts prefer their own selfish advantage.[247] He states that "what aims at reality is better than what aims at appearance."[248] The whole tenor of his community-conscious theory of general justice seems to be in accord with the judgment of Thucydides who speaks through the mouth of Pericles:

> I am of the opinion that national greatness is more for the advantage of private citizens, than any individual well-being. . . . A man may be personally ever so well off, and yet if his country be ruined he must be ruined with it; whereas a flourishing commonwealth always affords chances of salvation to unfortunate individuals.[249]

In summary, Aristotle's ethics has a psychological basis. Therefore, the first two stages of the development of his psychology mark also the development of his ethics, and, in particular, that of his concept of justice. In his mature ethical thought the notion of justice rests on a bipartite division of the soul.

His ethics is also marked by its rationalism and by the subjection of the moral to the intellectual virtues. Φρόνησις is the virtue of the practical intellect which guides the moral virtue of justice.

---

246 *Rhetoric,* 1365 b 6-7.
247 *Ibid.,* 1399 a 29-31.
248 *Ibid.,* 1365 b 1.
249 Thucydides, II, 60.

In distinction from Plato's heteronomous ethics with its transcendental dimension, Aristotle's ethics is totally autonomous, rational, immanentist, and naturalistic. This ethical outlook is evidenced in Aristotle's theory of justice. In the *Nicomachean Ethics* he first proposes an abstract, formal concept of justice as a moral virtue, to be followed by its concretization in political justice and in law. Justice as a virtue is of two kinds, general and particular.

Other-relatedness and the objective mean of equality are the two characteristics of the formal concept of justice. General justice is the totality and perfection of all virtues. Its other-relatedness directs the moral subject to the common good of the polis, to the political, that is, distinctively human, hierarchy of values in their totality. This political other-relatedness is a more characteristic feature of general justice, the political virtue, than equality. Its mean is the aggregate of all the means of all the particular virtues, including particular justice.

Calasanctius Preparatory School
and Medaille College
Buffalo, N.Y.

5

THE NATURE OF MAN ACCORDING TO PLOTINUS

by

ANGELITA MYERSCOUGH, A.S.C.

I. THE PLACE OF MAN IN THE PHILISOPHY OF PLOTINUS

Man occupies a central position in the philosophy of Plotinus. On this various interpreters seem to agree regardless of their sharp disagreements in their understanding of other aspects of his philosophy or their interpretation of his doctrine on human nature.[1] Vertically, man occupies the metaphysical center of being in Plotinus' conception of reality: at the farthest reach above him is the Absolute, the One; downward from man at the very nadir is the nonbeing of formless matter. Horizontally, too, Plotinus appears to have man at the focal point of his vision of reality, since in every problem he examines he returns again and again to the question of man. For Plotinus, man is the mid-point, both of the metaphysical and the mystical aspects of his philosophy. Whether he considers the order of being or the order of knowing, Plotinus recurrently discourses on man. With Plotinus, there is a firm conviction

---

[1] For example, Thomas Whittaker says: "His psychology . . . is the centre . . . Within the soul, he finds all the metaphysical principles in some way represented." *The Neo-Platonists,* 2d. ed. (Cambridge: University Press, 1928), p. 43. A. H. Armstrong comments that Plotinus' doctrine about man is "not important in itself but a good centre from which to survey his philosophy as a whole," in Plotinus. "Man's Higher Self," *The Downside Review,* 66 (1948), 408. Similar comments are made, e.g., by Sister Rose Emmanuella Brennan, "The Philosophy of Beauty in the Enneads of Plotinus," *New Scholasticism,* 14 (1940), 7; G. Carriére, "L'homme et la réalité chez Plotin," *Revue de Ottawa,* 15 (1945), 103,* 111,* 113;* Paul Henry, in introduction to MacKenna, *Plotinus, The Enneads,* 2d ed. rev. (New York: Pantheon Books, c. 1957), p. xli; K. G. Moore, "Theory of Imagination in Plotinus," *Journal of Psychology,* 22 (1946), 44-45.

that, knowing man, one can come thereby to know the rest of reality, since in man all elements of reality are in some fashion reflected.[2]

When Porphyry set himself the task of "revision and arrangement" of his master's unedited writings, he placed at the very outset of the first Ennead the tractate on "The Animate and the Man," though this was written nearly last. Despite Porphyry's explanation of his arrangement as an intent of "leading off with the themes presenting the least difficulty"[3] it would seem that the centrality of the subject in Plotinus' thought warrants—and may have influenced—this choice. Prophyry himself affirms that his master lived "within himself" in "unbroken concentration upon his own highest nature,"[4] as if from that study he came to discover his whole doctrine.

Bréhier appears justified in presenting his study of the philosopher as an attempt "to make clear a way of life rather than a doctrine in the works of Plotinus,"[5] for it seems that basically Plotinus is concerned with the human problem. The mysticism in his work appears to be a search for the metaphysical basis of a moral philosophy.

Consequently, the image of man that we find in the *Enneads* is dynamic rather than static, since Plotinus is less concerned with an abstract analysis of the nature of man than with a consideration of how man ought to function so as to attain the ultimate realization of his true higher self in ecstatic contemplation of the All. In Plotinus' universe, where the divine hypostases of Nous and Psyche are ordered emanations from the One[6] and the material world in

---

2 *Enneads*, V, 1, 3; VI, 6, 1; III, 2: 3, 8. Unless otherwise noted, all references to and citations from Plotinus in this paper will be from Stephen MacKenna's translation, 2d. ed., revised by B. S. Page (New York: Pantheon Books, c. 1957). The large Roman numeral will refer to the Ennead, the second figure to the tractate, and the third figure to the numbered section. Where more than one section of the same tractate is referred to, a colon will be used instead of the comma following the tractate number.

3 Section #24 of Porphyry's life, in MacKenna, *ibid.*, p. 18.

4 *Ibid.*, #8, p. 7.

5 *The Philosophy of Plotinus*, trans. Joseph Thomas (Chicago: University of Chicago Press, 1958), p. 6; also p. 29.

6 A note is in order regarding certain limitations set for this article: regarding terminology, it has not been possible to weigh carefully the multiple Greek terms Plotinus often uses for the same or slightly different realities. Hence, here the terms will be chosen in their general significance which will normally be obvious. The terms for the three hypostases will be capitalized. Nor has it been possible

turn an emanation downward from Psyche, man's position is at the mid-point; but it is a vibrant mid-point. As one interpreter has aptly expressed it:

> Sarà l'anima del singolo, dentro l'immobile scenario metafisico di Plotino, il vero protagonista della vita cosmica, che conferirà un senso moralmente drammatico a un universo di essenze sovrumane.[7]

Man's original existence—outside the limits of time and space— is in the realm of pure spirit. At a point of time this already existing individual soul in some manner detaches itself from the realm of spirit and plunges downward to join itself to an individual body. It is in this condition that we find ourselves in the present empirical situation. But here we do not remain at a static level of being. Either we become more bestial, descending further toward the non-being of pure matter, or we face upward in the return ascent through the world of intellect to final union with the One. This latter is our destiny. It is the good life for Plotinus, whose view of human nature is decidedly intellectualistic.

Plotinus' own words indicate his placement of man at the central position, and his conception of that as an inherently dynamic place:

> Man has come into existence, a living being but not a member of the noblest order; he occupies by choice an intermediate rank. . . . ever being led upwards. . . . Man is therefore, a noble creation, as perfect as the scheme allows; a part, no doubt, in the fabric of the All, he yet holds a lot higher than that of all the other living things of earth.[8]

---

to examine Plotinus' doctrine chronologically; rather I have attempted to set forth what seems to be his final teaching. Furthermore, I have not essayed an evaluation of Plotinus' sources and influences, since to do more than simply repeat the interpretation of others would have demanded too extensive a knowledge of other philosophers and the whole oriental philosophy which seems to have exerted considerable influence on Plotinus, together with the Platonic heritage.

[7] G. Faggin, "Plotino," in *Enciclopedia filosofica* (Venezia-Roma: Istituto per la collaborazione culturale, 1957), Vol. III, col. 1453; also col. 1457. Armstrong similarly notes the emphasis on life, the dynamic and vital character of spiritual being in Plotinus' philosophy in *Plotinus* (London: George Allen & Unwin Ltd., 1953), p. 34.

[8] III, 2, 9.

Summing up his observations of the empirical human situation, he writes:

> But humanity, in reality, is poised midway between gods and beasts, and inclines now to the one order, now to the other; some men grow like to the divine, others to the brute, the greater number stand neutral.[9]

II. THE STRUCTURE OF HUMAN NATURE IN PLOTINUS' PHILOSOPHY

Each man, for Plotinus, is a sort of microcosm, though he does not use that expression formally. Each of us, he says, "is an Intellectual Cosmos, linked to this world by what is lowest in us, but, by what is the highest, to the Divine Intellect."[1] These words point clearly to the dualism in his doctrine on human nature. Obviously the first problem to be considered in setting forth Plotinus' teaching should be an examination of this double character, to establish with what precision is possible what Plotinus held the "highest" and "lowest" in man to be. Hence we shall look first at the "Couplement" itself, ourselves "the Animate" as we actually exist here and now. This exposition will lead in turn to the question that Plotinus asks as to what it is in us that is our true self. This will evidently be the "highest part," which for him is the spiritual element. After having considered the structure of human nature in Plotinian philosophy, we shall examine his explanation of how the spiritual and material element came to be joined to form empirical man, which will be Plotinus' account of the descent of soul to body.

A. *Duality in human nature*

In the tractate that Porphyry places first in the *Enneads* we find Plotinus speaking of "the Couplement of soul and body,"[2] "this Animate,"[3] "this total We."[4] Further on he writes of every human

9 III, 2, 8.

---

1 III, 4, 3.
2 I, 1, 5.
3 I, 1, 3.
4 I, 1, 10.

being as a "compromise-total,"[5] a "dual thing," and a "living conjoint."[6] There seems to be little doubt about Plotinus' insistence on
this duality in human nature.

It is not this couplement, however, which he holds to be the true
man. "For every human Being is of twofold character; there is that
compromise-total and there is the Authentic Man."[7] Repeatedly
Plotinus insists on this identification of real man with the spiritual
principle. "By 'us, the true human being,' I mean the higher
soul."[8] Again, "man . . . is not the Couplement of Soul and body:
the proof is that man can be disengaged from the body and disdain
its nominal goods."[9] Or again, simply he writes: "the Soul is the
man."[10]

The questions naturally come to mind: if the soul is the man,
then what is this body of ours and how does it stand in relation to
soul? Plotinus' basic answer seems to be found in the concept of
body as instrument of the soul.[11] He writes of the body as "an instrument of ours, a thing put at our service for a certain time."[12]
Beautifully, he compares the soul-body relationship to that of a
musician and the lyre on which he plays:

> the thing bound up with him, the thing which he tends and
> bears with as the musician cares for his lyre, as long as it can
> serve him: when the lyre fails him, he will change it, or will

5 II, 3, 9.

6 VI, 4, 14; IV, 4, 23.

7 II, 3, 9.

8 IV, 4, 18.

9 I, 4, 14.

10 IV, 7, 1; also V, 3, 9; V, 3, 3; I, 1, 10. Here, as throughout this paper,
the references are not intended to be exhaustive but merely indicative, since I
have aimed at substantiating statements by explicit reference to Plotinus' own
words. In referring to his affirmations in various places of the *Enneads,* I have
tried to use his statements as understood in the particular context in which they
appear.

Concerning Plotinus' doctrine on the identification of true man with higher
soul, it is to be noted that the philosopher is not always consistent, as he was
often inconsistent in other matters. For example, in IV, 7, 1, he writes, "We
know that man is not a thing of one only element: he has a Soul and . . . a body."
Cf. also I, 1, 10: I, 8, 8; V, 3, 3; V, 3, 9; VI, 9, 1; VI, 4, 15.

11 I, 1, 3; IV, 3, 23; IV, 3, 26; IV, 8, 7.

12 IV, 7, 1.

give up lyre and lyring, as having another craft now, one that needs no lyre, and then he will let it rest unregarded at his side while he sings on without an instrument. But it was not idly that the instrument was given him in the beginning: he has found it useful until now, many a time.[13]

This passage illustrates the more optimistic side of Plotinus' thought concerning the body, which contrasts rather sharply with other statements of his about the body as the source of evil and corruption to the soul.[14]

The union of the soul with the body is by way of simple juxtaposition,[15] and does not constitute a substantial union. The body is only a temporary associate of the soul. Between the two there is a difference of nature, for they are "two beings united by a revocable bond."[16] Soul simply inhabits the material dwelling of the body,[17] "its noble companion,"[18] with which it is joined in "an artificial unity" since in reality it is of a different nature.[19]

The "Animate," the "Couplement," exists because of the soul.[20] Plotinus prefers to speak of the body as being in the soul rather than the soul as embodied.[21] The soul is present animating every part of the body but is itself without quantity or extension, since it is entirely incorporeal.[22] It is as "Form to this Matter or as agent to this instrument"[23] that soul animates body. Elsewhere Plotinus declares the soul to be "in body as Ideal-Form in Matter,"[24] which however remains separable.

The sense in which Plotinus speaks of soul as "form" animating

[13] I, 4, 16.

[14] Examples of Plotinus' optimism regarding the body-soul couplement in I, 4, 5; II, 3, 9; II, 9, 8; II, 9, 9; III, 2, 9. In IV, 8, 3 and VI, 7, 31, for example, his doctrine is quite pessimistic. Carrière discusses this contrast in *op. cit.*, p. 88.*

[15] III, 2, 4; IV, 8, 7; IV, 4, 18; I, 1, 8: II, 1, 2; V, 9, 3; VI, 4, 3.

[16] Jules Simon, *Histoire de l'école d'Alexandrie* (Paris: Joubert, 1845), I, 504, quoted in Carriére, *op. cit.*, p. 103.*

[17] II, 9, 18.

[18] I, 2, 6.

[19] IV, 4, 18.

[20] I, 1, 7; III, 4, 2; VI, 4, 14.

[21] II, 3, 9; II, 9, 18; IV, 3, 22. G. Carrière stresses this point in Plotinus' doctrine in "Man's Downfall in the Philosophy of Plotinus," *The New Scholasticism,* 24 (1950), 295.

[22] IV, 9, 1.

[23] IV, 7, 1.

[24] I, 1, 4.

the body is quite different from the Aristotelean conception of soul as entelechy. This Plotinus makes clear in the tractate on the "Immortality of the Soul."[25] Here he first refutes the Stoic and Epicurean positions by insisting that soul is not a body, that it is beyond all bodily nature. Then, against the Pythagoreans, he establishes his doctrine that the soul is not a harmony. Finally, in a series of arguments, Plotinus gives his arguments that soul is not entelechy.[26]

Thus while the soul is in the body and animates it, it does not merge with body, but rather shines into it "by giving forth, without any change in itself, images or likenesses of itself like one face caught by many mirrors."[27] Without abdicating its own unity, according to which it is at once divisible and indivisible, the soul is present in every part of the body, and yet dwells "entire in the total and entire in any part."[28]

Plotinus judges that his favorite metaphor of light is most apt to describe the manner of the soul's presence in the "animate." He asks himself the pertinent question and gives his own answer:

> May we think that the mode of the Soul's presence to body is that of the presence of light to the air? This certainly is presence with distinction: the light penetrates through and through, but nowhere coalesces; the light is the stable thing, the air flows in and out; when the air passes beyond the lit area it is dark; under the light it is lit: we have a true parallel to what we have been saying of body and soul, for the air is in the light rather than the light in the air.[29]

For Plotinus, then, body and soul, while mutually related in man's present situation, remain distinct entities. Yet they often seem to function as a single "animate." Hence, for all his insistence on the cleavage between the higher and the lower in "the Couplement," the philosopher recognizes that there is some sort of real union, and that the body somehow ought to be indicated by the

---

25 IV, 7.

26 IV, 7, 8. A careful study of this point was done by Charles J. O'Neil: "Plotinus as Critic of the Aristotelean Soul," *Proceedings of the American Catholic Philosophical Association,* 23 (1949), 156-164.

27 I, 1, 8. A parallel passage occurs in IV, 3, 23, where Plotinus explains how each organ and member participating in soul is thereby adapted to its own function.

28 IV, 2, 1. Cf. Whittaker, *op. cit.,* pp. 44-45.

29 IV, 3, 22.

grammatical first person. A passage that brings this out appears in the second of his tractates on the problems of soul.

> By "us, the true human being" I mean the higher soul, for, in spite of all, the modified body is not alien but attached to our nature and is a concern to us for that reason: "attached," for this is not ourselves, nor yet are we free of it; it is an accessory and dependent of the human being: "we" means the master-principle; the conjoint, similarly, is in its own way an "ours"; and it is because of this that we care for its pain and pleasure.[30]

Such a highly nuanced statement witnesses to Plotinus' efforts to admit a belonging together of body and soul, and yet to insist on the identity of the real human self with the spiritual principle. Empirical observation makes it clear to the philosopher that man actually existent in the body operates on various levels. To explain this fact, he posits an inner structuring of the soul itself.

B. *The phases of the human soul*

Sometimes Plotinus speaks as if there were separate souls[31] and nearly suggests "a distinction of substantial principles"[32] within man. Much more frequently he speaks of the manifold within man's spirit in terms of the "graded powers" of action, or "soul phases"[33] which correspond to distinct levels of being within man. This seems to be Plotinus' genuine doctrine.

In one place he asserts that: "the faculties of the Soul are many, and it has its beginning, its intermediate phase, its final fringe."[34] Again he writes:

> And as to our own Soul we are to hold that it stands, in part, always in the presence of the Divine Beings, while in part it is concerned with the things of this sphere and in part occupies a middle ground. It is one nature in graded powers; and sometimes the Soul in its entirety is borne along by the loftiest in itself and in the Authentic Existent; sometimes the less noble

---

[30] IV, 4, 18.

[31] V, 3, 9; IV, 3, 23.

[32] E. I. Watkin, "Plotinus and Catholic Philosophy," *The Dublin Review,* 190 (1932), 60.

[33] IV, 3, 22; V, 3, 1.

[34] I, 8, 14.

part is dragged down and drags the mid-soul with it, though the law is that the Soul may never succumb entire.[35]

Although these and other passages point to a tripartite structure in the soul, there are other places[36] in which Plotinus speaks of only a twofold division. This leads one interpreter to describe his doctrine on soul thus: "The soul itself is twofold, one part being the agent strictly, and the other, that nature which is the result of the soul's illumining or animating the body, being itself a sort of organ."[37]

However, it would seem that the triple power interpretation corresponds more accurately with Plotinus' teaching. For example, when discussing the problem of self-knowledge in the tractate on the "Knowing Hypostases and the Transcendent," he refers quite explicitly to a "sense-principle," a "reasoning-principle" and the "Intellectual-Principle" in the soul of man.[38]

The sense-principle means soul operating through the agency of the body at the lowest level, including sensation, sense memory and imagination, passions and desires. Here the bodily element seems to predominate "with a trace of Soul running through it."[39] It represents the point of contact of soul with external matter.[40] Our reasoning-principle, Plotinus affirms, "acts upon the representations standing before it as the result of sense-perception; these it judges, combining, distinguishing" It is this reasoning-principle, it seems, which stands "at the fringe of the Intellectual" yet leaves us "fettered to the lower."[41] At the highest level of soul, the "Intellectual-Principle" is our true self.

Despite the "manifold" in our soul there are no parts; it remains

---

[35] II, 9, 2. Cf. also IV, 8, 8, and VI, 9, 8.

[36] I, 1, 7; III, 1, 7; III, 2, 3; IV, 7: 7, 13; IV, 3, 31.

[37] Gordon H. Clark, "Plotinus' Theory of Sensation," *Philosophical Review*, 51 (1942), 375. Crocker, *op. cit.*, p. 24, speaks of (1) the higher part of man's soul as that phase desiring World Soul and through this, Mind, leading to the One; and (2) the lower part, having affinity for matter, mixed with it, and making possible sensation, appetite, and passion. Crocker does not seem to accept Plotinus' distinction of a mid-soul.

[38] V, 3, 1-5. Other indications of the tripartite soul phase doctrine in these passages III, 2, 18; IV, 3: 4, 22, 23; IV, 7, 14; IV, 8, 3; V, 3, 9.

[39] II, 3, 9.

[40] V, 3, 2.

[41] III, 4, 3.

a unity. "Itself a unity, soul confers unity, but also accepts it."[42] Earlier, when describing the condition of ourselves as participants in both the realm of the Intellectual and the sense-realm, Plotinus indicates that it is the one "authentic existent" of our individual soul that is of "divine station but at the lowest extreme of the Intellectual" and yet "skirting the sense-known nature."[43]

In its gradation of powers, our soul resembles the World Soul, with which, as we shall presently consider, it is intimately related. Our souls contain an "Intellectual Cosmos," but

> they also contain a subordination of various forms like that of the Cosmic Soul. The World Soul is distributed so as to produce the fixed sphere and the planetary circuits corresponding to its graded powers: so with our souls; they must have their provinces according to their different powers, parallel to those of the World Soul.[44]

In his exposition of the origin and order of beings, Plotinus explains the dynamism of this correspondence between our soul's manifold and that of the World Soul, as part of the essential hierarchy of reality, whereby each order "takes fullness by looking to its source; but generates its image by adopting another, downward movement," and yet is not "complete severed from its prior."[45] In this cosmic dynamism, the human soul parallels the action of World Psyche since our spirit reaches "away as far down as to the vegetal order" to which it communicates life. At the same time the soul both participates in and images the reverse movement upward toward the Intellectual sphere with which it has ever remained in contact.[46]

The human being who shall have followed the way along which Plotinus seeks to lead him will ultimately, the philosopher insists, arrive at a condition in which he will "inhabit the body in a mode very closely resembling the indwelling of the All-Soul in the universal frame." At this point of arrival "we begin to reproduce within ourselves the Soul of the vast All and of the heavenly bodies."[47]

42 VI, 9, 1.
43 IV, 8, 7.
44 III, 4, 6; also III, 4, 3; II, 3, 10.
45 V, 2, 1; also II, 9: 3, 17.
46 V, 2, 1; also IV, 7, 12; V, 7, 1; V, 3, 9.
47 II, 9, 18.

It is because of this close parallelism between our souls and the World Psyche that Plotinus tells us that we should look at ourselves in order to know the Divine Mind. The passage is worth citing, since in it are indicated all the elements of Plotinus' doctrine on the manifold powers of our human soul which we have been discussing.

> One certain way to this knowledge is to separate first, the man from the body—yourself, that is, from your body; next to put aside that Soul which moulded the body, and, very earnestly, the system of sense with desires and impulses and every such futility, all setting definitely towards the mortal: what is left is the phase of the Soul which we have declared to be an image of the Divine Intellect, retaining some light from that source, like the light of the sun which goes beyond its spherical mass, issues from it and plays about it.[48]

C. *The higher soul, the true self*

That aspect of the soul which Plotinus declares to be "an image of the Divine Intellect" we now examine at closer range. For him, it is our real personality, the true human being, the genuine "We." Though there is uncertainty as to whether this higher self belongs to Nous or Psyche, there is little wavering in Plotinus' conviction about the identification of the true self with the higher realm. What he wrote near the end of his life is consistent in the large with his earlier assertions:

> The beast is the body which has been given life. But the true man is different, clear of these experiences; he has the virtues which belong to the sphere of Nous and have their seat actually in the separate soul, separate and separable even while it is still here below.[49]

Writing of the descent of soul into encumbering body, Plotinus asserts that "in spite of all, it has, for ever, something transcendent."[50] He declares that "the individual soul has an existence in the Supreme as well as in this world,"[51] and again that "this physical

48 V, 3, 9.
49 I, 1, 10. Translation of Armstrong, in *Plotinus* (London: George Allen & Unwin, 1953), p. 129. Cf. also I, 1: 7, 13.
50 IV, 8, 4.
51 V, 7, 1.

life is not the 'We'; the 'We' is the activity of the Intellectual-Principle."[52]

This "authentic man,"[53] as has already been indicated in discussing the nature of existent man as a body-soul "couplement," remains in its own right independent of body, dwelling permanently above the mutabilities of life in the flesh.[54] At the same time it is the authentic soul which animates us in this empirical existence, as Plotinus states, insisting that our souls are not simply copies of ourselves in the intellectual sphere, but "those very originals in a mode peculiar to this sphere."[55]

It is not a contradiction for Plotinus to maintain that we who exist in this sense-world can yet transcend it and have our authentic being in the world of spirit. He was not thinking in terms of a spatial or even quasi-spatial transcendence, since for him the categories that apply to the world of the three great spiritual Hypostases are distinct from those derived from our earth-bound experience.[56] Hence for Plotinus there is no difficulty in affirming that the true "We" exists both on this empirical level and in the transcendent realm of spirit.

It is not easy to determine Plotinus' thought on the exact relationship of this higher self to the three hypostases of the One, Mind, and Soul. Obviously, by the nature of the Plotinian One, we do not form part of it, though our ultimate destiny is some form of union with this "Alone." Sometimes Plotinus speaks of our higher selves remaining in the world of Nous; and again he affirms that we are not the Intellectual-Principle, insisting that "the We is the Soul at its highest."[57]

Though Plotinus' thought seems to have remained undecided on this question, the evidence indicates that he inclined more strongly to consider our souls as belonging to Psyche rather than Nous. This he assumes to be true when he devotes a whole tractate

---

52 I, 4, 9.

53 II, 3, 9; IV, 7, 1.

54 III, 4, 2; III, 6, 1; IV, 3, 5; IV, 7: 11, 13; IV, 8: 3, 4, 5; V, 3, 8; VI, 4, 14; VI, 9: 8, 9.

55 V, 9, 13.

56 IV, 8: 4, 5, 6; V, 1, 4; VI, 1:2, 3; VI, 4:4, 16. Armstrong stresses this interpretation in two of his articles in *Downside Review:* "Plotinus. Man's Higher Self," 66 (1948), pp. 414-415; "The Relevance of Plotinus," 67 (1949), p. 129.

57 V, 3, 3.

to answering the question, "Are all souls one?"[58] Similarly, he assumes this to be the case in his treatise on the "Omnipresence of the Authentic Existent,"[59] where in one place he says unequivocally that "the one Soul so exists as to include all souls," obviously intending to include human souls. Many interpreters of Plotinus find no problem involved here, because to them it seems quite clear that for the philosopher the souls of men are immanent in the World Soul and inseparable from it.[60] For A. H. Armstrong, however, a definite problem seems to exist, which he has studied carefully over the years. Discussing the question in 1948, he admitted that in V, 3, Plotinus makes us to be only Soul, not Nous.[61] Yet he considered that in Plotinus' normal thought our true selves are the Forms of individuals eternally existing in Nous.[62] In a 1953 publication, he seemed to be uncertain—in the introductory section of the volume he states that our individual souls are "Plotinian parts" of Universal Soul.[63] Yet further on in the same book, in the section on "Our Selves," he writes:

> We remain ourselves in the world of *Nous;* our particular personalities at their highest are Intellect-Forms in *Nous,* distinct without separation and united without losing their individuality.[64]

Since then Armstrong has admitted that the problem for him remains undecided, indicating his uncertainty as to whether, in Plotinus' thought, our true self should "be properly described as Intellect or as soul conformed to Intellect."[65] He writes:

> The frontier of the self seems to shift in his thought between Intellect and higher soul. But when he moves our upper limit

58 IV, 9.

59 VI, 4 and 5.

60 For example, in articles already cited, E. I. Watkin, pp. 53-54; Crocker, p. 24; Sister Emmanuella, p. 6; Bréhier, *op. cit.,* ch. V, *passim;* William Inge, *The Philosophy of Plotinus,* 3d ed. (London: Longmans, Green, 1929), I, pp. 213ff. Also G. Capone Braga, "Il problema del rapporto fra le anime individuali e l'anima dell'universo nella filosofia di Plotino," *Revista di Filosofia,* 23 (1932), 106-125.

61 *Art. cit., Downside Review,* 66 (1948), 417-418.

62 *Ibid.,* pp. 416 and 418.

63 *Plotinus,* cited above, p. 38.

64 *Ibid.,* p. 122.

65 "Salvation, Plotinian and Christian," *Downside Review,* 75 (1957), 134.

down to the level of soul he invests higher soul with that kind of invulnerable stability which at the time when he wrote the great treatises on the soul—IV, iii and iv—he was inclined to reserve for Intellect.[66]

Perhaps the nondecisive interpretation is nearest to a true explanation of Plotinus' doctrine, since for him there is not always (if ever) a sharply defined dichotomy between the second and third Hypostases. For example, at the conclusion of the fifth Ennead, he writes:

> And before the particular Soul there is another Soul, a universal, and, before that, an Absolute-Soul, which is the Life existing in the Intellectual-Principle before Soul came to be and therefore rightly called (as the Life in the Divine) the Absolute-Soul.[67]

In the Plotinian construction of the universe there is always an interrelation of each successive hierarchy of being: downward, there is an emanation of the lower from the higher, but upward there is the imaging in the lower of that which is beyond it. Trouillard notes that in the *Enneads* the word *logos* has a relative significance, precisely because it indicates this function: each order is *logos* or expression of its generator.[68] This explains how our individual souls, while conceived by Plotinus as having their being as participants in World Soul, can yet have, and precisely thereby do have, a relationship to Divine Mind. At their highest they are either individual form-intelligences in the realm of Nous, or at least perfectly conformed to the form-intelligences which are their archtypes. On the level of Soul, they are *logoi* of individual form-intelligences, expressions of this form on the level of reality just

66 *Ibid.*

67 V, 9, 14; cf. also II, 9: 3, 8; IV, 3: 12, 13; IV, 7, 13.

68 Jean Trouillard, "La médiation du verbe selon Plotin," *Revue Philosophique de la France et de l'Étranger,* 146 (1956), 65. The author cites V, 1, 3 and I, 2, 3, in support of this statement. Armstrong makes the same point in *Downside Review,* 66 (1948), 412-413, where he affirms: "Mind is timelessly emanated or radiated from the One and timelessly returns upon it in contemplation in just the same manner as Soul is produced from the Divine Mind. With both we can distinguish two stages (not of course successive in time), one of emanation as a potency and one in which the potency returns upon its principles and becomes informed and actualized by contemplation of it." Armstrong reiterates this interpretation in *Downside Review,* 67 (1949), 125-126.

below.[69] Downward, they have their place in the operation of World
Soul in its appropriate task in the universe. Producing some share
in reality in the lower strata, they participate in the "activity of the
Intellectual-Principle, which thus, while itself remaining in its
identity, operates throughout the Soul to flood the universe with
beauty and penetrant order—immortal mind, eternal in its un-
failing energy, acting through immortal soul."[70] Situated at the mid-
point of this cosmic dynamism, the individual human being, the
authentic man, enters this world of matter and sense, and yet remains in its individual self-identity in the realm beyond.

In view of this doctrine of the higher self, it is not surprising to
find Plotinus teaching the immortality of the soul. Our soul, the
authentic "we," pre-existed our present mode of being in association
with body; it continues to exist in some fashion in the intellectual
realm even now; and it will go on existing when it has laid aside its
body-instrument. "To Real Being we go back, all that we have
and are; to that we return as from that we came."[71]

Plotinus devotes an entire tractate to proving the immortality of
the soul.[72] A large part of his argument (already referred to above)
is devoted to showing that soul is not a body, which is for Plotinus
always a composite, "something put together."[73] Body itself, he
argues, could not exist without soul—certainly not a living body—
and the facts of bodily movement and growth prove that some
incorporeal soul exists and causes these phenomena. Furthermore,
Plotinus claims that if the soul were a corporeal entity, "there
could be no sense-perception, no mental act, no knowledge, no
moral excellence, nothing of all that is noble."[74] He argues thus
from the need for a unitary percipient in order that there be perception; this need is filled only by the non-material soul. A similar
argument he adduces from the fact of pain and other bodily sensations, as well as from the intellectual act, all of which would be
impossible if the soul were a kind of body. It is because of his doctrine of the soul's immortality that he rejects the concept of soul as

[69] Armstrong, art. cit., Downside Review, 67 (1949), 410-411; also Crocker, art.
cit., p. 29.
[70] IV, 7, 13; also II, 3, 18; IV, 8, 7.
[71] VI, 5, 7; also IV, 8, 4; V, 3, 6; VI, 4, 4; VI, 9, 9.
[72] IV, 7.
[73] IV, 7, 2.
[74] IV, 7, 6.

entelechy, since he considers that the latter doctrine makes the body in some way author of the soul. Rather, he insists, the soul "is an Essence which does not come into being by finding a seat in body; it exists before it becomes also the soul of some particular."[75]

Plotinus' principal argument for the eternity of the soul considered as participant in the All-Soul is based on the principle of sufficient reason. The only adequate explanation of the existence of life in contingent beings is the eternal existence of Soul.

> Not all things can have a life merely at second hand; this would give an infinite series: there must be some nature which, having life primally, shall be of necessity indestructible, immortal, as the source of life to all else that lives.[76]

Plotinus also appeals to our own experience in proof of the immortality of soul. Once we have entered into true intellection, "the only authentic knowing," having purged the soul of all "commerce with the bodily as far as possible," we will recognize our own immense splendor and grandeur. When this is grasped, Plotinus reasons, there will be perforce recognition of "the immortality of such a value."[77] Finally, he argues that if every soul were dissoluble, the universe itself would long since have ceased to exist, for it is the Soul which alone lives by its own energy and communicates this energy to all things.

It is the self-identical individual existing here who will likewise continue to exist beyond bodily dissolution. The absurdity of the opposite supposition, Plotinus assumes, needs only to be stated to be self-refuted:

> May we suppose the Soul to be appropriated on the lower ranges to some individual, but to belong on the higher to that other sphere? At this, there would be a Socrates as long as Socrates' soul remained in body; but Socrates ceases to exist, precisely on attainment of the highest.[78]

Elsewhere, too, Plotinus teaches the immortality of individual men by the exigency of their receiving a reward for their moral worth in this life.[79]

[75] IV, 7: 8, 5.
[76] IV, 7, 9.
[77] IV, 7, 11.
[78] IV, 3, 5.
[79] I, 9; I, 7, 3; III, 2: 1, 9; III, 4, 6; IV, 3, 24.

At times Plotinus speaks of a *transmigration of souls*, which seems contradictory to his more carefully reasoned conviction on the immortality of individual human souls. In the third Ennead, he writes at some length of the soul's becoming something else after death, in conformity with the faculty most developed during its "normal" human existence.[80] These successive reincarnations, he writes elsewhere, are like one dream after another, or like sleep in different beds.[81] Inge interprets these passages as a Plotinian attempt at myth, rather than serious philosophy. In the final analysis, Inge believes, Plotinus pays minimum attention to this problem that so intrigued the ancients simply because he was uninterested in it, as somewhat beside the point of genuine philosophical grasp of reality.[82]

For Plotinus, the true way to view the structure of human nature is to see empirical man as a dual being, with the authentic part of him spiritual in nature, his true higher self. This is soul in its highest phase. In the present temporal condition, man's characteristic function is discursive reasoning, which is the operation of the mid-phase of soul. At a lower level, spiritual man imparts living form to his body, making vital operations of vegetal and sentient life possible. Plotinus' explanation of how the eternally existent individual human soul, which is the true higher self of each of us, enters "into the body from the aloofness of the Intellectual,"[83] is the problem to which we now address ourselves. We shall also examine briefly the functioning of soul through the instrumentality of its material body, and summarize the main features of Plotinus' concept of man's moral and mystical destiny.

III. THE DESCENT OF MAN'S SOUL TO HIS BODY

In several places in the *Enneads* Plotinus has recorded his searchings for a satisfactory explanation of how and why man's soul comes into association with his body. The problem is most completely discussed in the eighth tractate of the fourth Ennead, entitled in MacKenna's translation "The Soul's Descent Into Body," where the philosopher treats of the problem of the human soul's

80 III, 4, 2.
81 III, 6, 6; also, IV, 3: 13, 15.
82 Inge, *op. cit.*, II, pp. 29-34.
83 IV, 7, 13.

joining itself to its body partner, in the context of the problem of universal Soul. The opening paragraph is worth citing because of its beauty of expression, the convergence in it of nearly all the lines of Plotinus' doctrine, and the feeling of personal contact with the philosopher that it gives us.

> Many times it has happened: lifted out of the body into myself; becoming external to all other things and self-centered; beholding a marvellous beauty; then, more than ever, assured of community with the loftiest order; enacting the noblest life, acquiring identity with the divine; stationing within It by having attained that activity; poised above whatsoever within the Intellectual is less than the Supreme: yet, there comes the moment of descent from intellection to reasoning, and after that sojourn in the divine, I ask myself how it happens that I can now be descending, and how did the Soul ever enter into my body, the Soul which, even within the body, is the high thing it has shown itself to be.[1]

A. *The problem and nature of the descent itself*

The concept of the original nexus of body and soul as a "descent" Plotinus accepted from previous Greek thinkers, especially Plato. What puzzled him was the nature of this descent: was it a good or an evil? was it necessary or free? The contrariety in the answers that others gave to this same problem is discussed by Plotinus.[2] He was especially harassed, it seems, by the two opposing explanations given by Plato himself: the earlier one, especially in the *Phaedrus,* which explained the descent as an evil; and the *Timaeus* account which allowed it as a good thing, necessary to the order of the universe. Plotinus' conviction appears to be that the two accounts can be reconciled, though his interpreters generally agree that his work never offers a well-reasoned solution.

That evil for man arises from the union of soul with body seems to be a definitive conclusion of Plotinus. However, this does not indicate that he necessarily considers the descent of soul to body to be an evil. Rather the evil seems to come from the soul's excessive plunging into the depths of its material body. The descent itself of the soul to body rather appears to be a necessary part of

1 IV, 8, 1.
2 IV, 8, 1 to 5.

universal providence, an ineluctable part of the cosmic emanations of being from higher to lower, from unity to multiplicity.[3]

According to Porphyry's chronological listing of the tractates, the first in which Plotinus speaks of the descent is that on beauty. There he seems to take a pessimistic view of the descent:

> So . . . a Soul becomes ugly—by something foisted upon it, by sinking itself into the alien, by a fall, a descent into body, into Matter. The dishonour of the Soul is in its ceasing to be clean and apart . . . let it be but cleared . . . emancipated . . . purged of all that embodiment has thrust upon it, withdrawn . . . in that moment the ugliness that came only from the alien is stripped away.[4]

Again, in the tractate on evil he speaks of the entry of the soul into matter as a crushing back of the soul and as the source of its weakness.[5] Similarly, he speaks of our existence here as lying in "gloom and mud,"[6] and of the soul's being "evil by being interfused with the body."[7] Perhaps the most dramatic description of the embodiment of man's soul is that found in the fourth Ennead.

> Before we had our becoming Here we existed There, men other than now, some of us gods: we were pure souls, Intelligence inbound with the entire of reality, members of the Intellectual, not fenced off, not cut away, integral to that All. Even now, it is true, we are not put apart; but upon that primal Man there has intruded another, a man seeking to come into being and finding us there, for we were not outside of the universe. This other has wound himself about us, foisting himself upon the Man that each of us was at first . . . now we have lost that first simplicity; we are become the dual thing, sometimes indeed no more than that later foisting, with the primal nature dormant and in a sense no longer present.[8]

---

3 Bréhier, *op. cit.,* p. 55, very perceptively observes that a contrast exists in the thought of Plotinus between "Soul conceived as the organizing force of bodies and the soul conceived as the seat of destiny." From the former viewpoint, the contact of Soul with body follows its normal function and is good and necessary; according to the latter viewpoint, the connection is a result of Soul's impurity and of its vices.

4 I, 6, 5.

5 I, 8, 14.

6 I, 8, 13.

7 I, 2, 3.

8 IV, 4, 14.

This mythical account of the descent undeniably illustrates Plotinus' conviction that some evil accrues to the higher self from its partnership with material body.

Nevertheless, the more dominant thought, evident throughout the *Enneads,* seems to be that man's embodiment is a necessary part of the total dynamism of the universe. Plotinus nearly always associates the individual man's descent with the work of universal Soul bringing lower beings to reality as images of itself. Soul in turn is a likeness to Nous, which again reflects in its own order the utterly transcendent One. Thus the union of our souls to our bodies may be an imperfection from one viewpoint, but it is one which is itself a part of the nature of things and according to the dispositions of universal providence.[9] It may be designated a fall, rightly or wrongly, but this fall itself belongs to the cosmic order and occurs for the good of the whole.[10]

It is necessary for every level of being to exist in order that the whole order of things be complete, with full actualization of the potentialities of production of the lower which exist in the higher stages of being.[11] Thus already existing individual human souls have a predisposition to descend to bodies, for these are "the dwellings prepared for us by our good sister Soul (the All-Soul) in her vast power of labourless creation."[12] Likewise our bodies are apt to be ensouled, as Plotinus indicates when, for example, he says that the dramatically intruding body "had a certain aptitude and it grasped at that to which it was apt."[13] Answering at greater length the question of how the intruder found entrance, Plotinus writes:

> In its nature it was capable of soul . . . this body is not a husk having no part in soul, not a thing that earlier lay away in the soulless; the body had its aptitude and by this draws near: now it is not body merely, but living body. By this neighbouring it is enhanced with some impress of soul—not in the sense of a portion of soul entering into it, but that it is warmed and lit by soul entire.[14]

[9] Armstrong notes this harmonizing of particular evils within the universal order in "Plotinus, Soul and Body," *Downside Review,* 67 (Autumn, 1949), 411. Theodore Roeser discusses this problem in "Emanation and Creation," *New Scholasticism,* 19 (1945), 85-116.

[10] IV, 8, 5; III, 2, 14.

[11] Armstrong, *art. cit.* in #1, p. 407.

[12] II, 9.

[13] IV, 4, 14.

[14] IV, 4, 15.

Elsewhere Plotinus speaks of the descent as an illumination of body by the soul.[15] Struggling with the problem of whether and how the descent to body may be a sin for the higher soul, he again uses the image of light and speaks of the body as the object which takes up the light from above and "lives by its life."[16] It is soul which furnishes "body with the power to existence."[17]

As Armstrong notes, "in Plotinus' thought there is a real two-way relationship between higher and lower."[18] The two are unthinkable apart: the lower is altogether dependent on the higher for its being, and the higher cannot exist without producing the lower.[19] Plotinus writes of the soul's impulse outward toward the sense realm:

> There is that which has acquired appetite, and by this accruement, has already taken a great step outward; it has the desire of elaborating order on the model of what it has seen in the Intellectual-Principle: pregnant by those Beings, and in pain to the birth, it is eager to make, to create. In this new zest it strains towards the realm of sense.[20]

Writing of the individual soul's inclination to its own body, Plotinus produces another dramatic description of the descent, but one distinctly optimistic in tone:

> In that archetypal world every form of soul is near to the image (the thing in the world of copy) to which its individual constitution inclines it; there is therefore no need of a sender or leader acting at the right moment whether into body or into a definitely appropriate body: of its own motion it descends at the precisely true time and enters where it must. To every soul its own hour; when that strikes it descends and enters the body suitable to it as at the cry of a herald; thus all is set stirring and advancing as by a magician's power or by some mighty traction.[21]

Both the tractates on Providence and that against the Gnostics[22] emphasize this "mighty traction" among all phases of reality as

15 I, 8, 14.
16 I, 1, 12.
17 IV, 8, 2.
18 *Art. cit., Downside Review,* 67 (Autumn, 1949), 407.
19 II, 9: 3, 17; III, 2, 14; IV, 8: 5, 7; V, 4, 1.
20 IV, 7, 13.
21 IV, 4, 13.
22 III, 2 and 3; II, 9.

necessary, and therefore, ultimately good for the totality. For example, Plotinus avers: "The Divine Reason is the beginning and the end; all that comes into being must be rational and fall at its coming into an ordered scheme reasonable at every point."[23] Since the going forth of our soul to union with our body is part of this whole harmony of being, there is no question of either compulsion or free will, at least not of freedom of choice, for it is an instinctive "leap of the nature" of our higher self.[24] There is an inherent tendency in our soul to its union with body, and in this sense the descent seems voluntary.[25]

Ultimately, Plotinus affirms, "there is no inconsistency or untruth in saying that the Soul is sent down by God; final results are always to be referred to the starting-point, even across many intervening stages."[26] Human life is like a drama, in which each man is assigned a role appropriate to him, but in his playing the role he exercises power of choice to play it well or ill. The true value of the drama, however, depends in the last analysis on its author, who assigns each one "his own quite appropriate place."[27]

Plotinus does not offer a real solution to the great problem of reconciling human freedom with divine causality and teleology, as it concerns either the original embodiment of our higher self, or on the level of our empirical existence on this earth. Nonetheless, he recognizes that the solution cannot be the denial of either member of the apparent antinomy. For him, man's origin is "a voluntary descent which is also involuntary," for "the necessity includes the choice."[28] Plotinus is not merely juxtaposing words; he is expressing his conviction of the truth.

The choice that the individual soul makes at the point of its descent is a choice to be joined to matter. This involves its separation in some fashion from universal Soul in order to govern a particular body.[29] This declaration of independence from world Soul is

23 III, 2, 15.

24 IV, 4, 13.

25 IV, 8: 4-5.

26 IV, 8, 5.

27 III, 2, 17. This same facet of Plotinian doctrine is brought out in the discussion of the beauty of the universe by Fiammetta Bourbon di Petrella, *Il Problema dell'arte e della bellezza in Plotino* (Firenze: F. Le Monnier, 1956), p. 97.

28 IV, 8, 5.

29 IV, 8, 4.

a fault in so far as it is motivated by audacity and desire for separation, and leads to fragmentation.[30] Yet the whole process is a necessary effect of the inner dynamism of the universe: "better for the Soul to dwell in the Intellectual, but, given its proper nature, it is under compulsion to participate in the sense realm also."[31]

B. *Positive value of the descent for human knowledge*

The dark picture that Plotinus draws of the human soul's imprisonment in the body "in bitter and miserable durance . . . a victim to troubles and desires and fears and all forms of evil"[32] is only partially true. Later in the same tractate that expresses this pessimism, Plotinus points out the positive value of embodiment for the soul, in terms of self-realization and experiential knowledge. He makes it clear that the soul that lives here as it should

> will have taken no hurt by acquiring the knowledge of evil and coming to understand what sin is, by bringing its forces into manifest play, by exhibiting those activities and productions which, remaining merely potential in the unembodied, might as well never have been even there, if destined never to come into actuality. . . . The act reveals the power, a power hidden, and we might almost say obliterated or non-existent, unless at some moment it became effective.[33]

A little later Plotinus adds: "Where the faculty is incapable of knowing without contact, the experience of evil brings the clearer perception of Good."[34] Similarly he affirms that "the loveliness that is in the sense-realm is an index of nobleness of the Intellectual sphere, displaying its power and its goodness alike" for "all things are forever linked."[35]

By reason of the union of soul with body, man the "living conjoint" has opened up to him a mode of knowledge not possible to him prior to this descent.

---

[30] IV, 8, 4-5; V, 1, 1.

[31] IV, 8, 7. Faggin, *op. cit.*, col. 1457, declares that the descent "non é dovuta a una colpa o a un caso irrazionale, ma a quella legge di necessitá che governa la gerarchia degli esseri e il processo della generazione divina."

[32] IV, 8, 3. Admittedly, Plotinus is here describing Plato's concept from the *Phaedrus.*

[33] IV, 8, 5.

[34] IV, 8, 7.

[35] IV, 8, 6.

It is by means of the sense organs of its body that the soul can engage in sense perception,[36] which is a genuine means of contact with reality. According to Plotinus' doctrine of sense perception, the soul itself is the agent in sensation, not the passive object of sense impressions.[37] The bodily organs act as the soul's instruments, since they enter directly into contact with corporeal objects. This is possible because they are essentially homogeneous with material things and hence capable of being modified by them.[38] At the same time, animated by soul, they have with it a spiritual affinity so that the impression received in the bodily organ is transformed in such a way that it can be perceived by the higher reasoning faculty.[39] Thus, for Plotinus, "bodily organs are necessary to sense-perception . . . the Soul entirely freed of body can apprehend nothing in the order of sense."[40]

Sense perception has a triple value for man as long as he exists in embodied soul: for utility, for the enjoyment of beauty, and for knowledge. It can be useful for him as a warning signal to avert dangers, which is highly useful.[41] Similarly through sense faculties there is made possible the intellective perception of the beauty of form communicated to material things by the divine world Soul when it stamped them with Ideal-forms.[42]

Much more important for Plotinus is the fact that through sense knowledge man can begin his noetic ascent upward to pure contemplation. Certainly the philosopher holds that the ideal situation would be for man to establish as little contact as possible with corporeal things and to enter immediately within the realms of unalloyed intellective activity. This, he admits, is not possible for the majority of men.[43] For them, salvation for Plotinus is intellectual rather than volitional and begins with knowledge of sensibles, which serve as a springboard for higher knowledge. In the tractate

36 IV, 4: 23, 24.

37 III, 4, 2; also IV, 4, *passim*, and V, 3: 2-3.

38 IV, 4, 23.

39 IV, 3, 23.

40 IV, 3, 23. Cf. IV, 3, 23, where Plotinus explains in some detail his theory of the process of sense perception by means of the various sense organs.

41 IV, 3, 17; IV, 4: 22, 24, 28; V, 3: 1, 2.

42 I, 6, 3. Sister Rose E. Brennan, *art. cit.*, brings this point out in her discussion of the Plotinian doctrine of beauty: also, perhaps with deeper insight, does F. Bourbon di Petrella, *op. cit.*, pp. 94-103.

43 V, 9, 1.

on the knowing hypostases and the transcendent, he describes
clearly:

> Anyone not of the strength to lay hold of the first Soul, that
> possessing pure intellection, must grasp that which has to do
> with our ordinary thinking and thence ascend: if even this
> prove too hard, let him turn to account the sensitive phase
> which carries the ideal forms of the less fine degree, that phase
> which, too, with its powers, is immaterial and lies just within
> the realm of Ideal-Principles. One may even, if it seem neces-
> sary, begin as low as the reproductive Soul and its very pro-
> duction and thence make the ascent, mounting from those ulti-
> mate ideal principles to the ultimates in the higher sense, that
> is to the primals.[44]

The reason why Plotinus grants that sensation is the beginning of
genuine knowledge is based on his theory of ideas and emanations.
Since sensible objects are ideas extended in space, they are corporeal
images of eternal realities. Consequently by means of sense perception we are truly in touch with reality. Though sensation may not
give us a very firm grasp on it, yet it is a contact, from which we
can mount to "the ultimates in the higher sense."[45]

It is in the lowest phase of soul, the sense-principle, that this most
elemental contact with reality takes place. The next higher phase,
the reasoning principle, coordinates the empirical data furnished in
sensation, elevating the sense perceptions to the level of intelligibility.[46] As a process, reasoning involves a development of the impressions received through coordination with previous knowledge
stored in both sense and intellectual memory.[47] Reason judges, combines, distinguishes,[48] and thus arrives at opinions or judgments.[49]
This process of discursive knowledge involves mental effort, but it
is an effort that only man in this embodied life is capable of.

> Our intelligence is nourished on the propositions of logic, is
> skilled in following discussions, works by reasonings, examines
> links of demonstration, and comes to know the world of Being

44 V, 3, 9.

45 VI, 7, 7; also IV, 8, 8; V, 3: 2, 3. Clark, *art. cit.*, *Philosophical Review*, p. 382,
stresses this importance of sensation in Plotinus' theory. The entire article is a
detailed and convincing study of the Plotinian doctrine of sensation.

46 Faggin, *op. cit.*, col. 1460.

47 IV, 3: 28-32; V, 3, 3.

48 V, 3, 2.

49 III, 6, 4.

also by the steps of logical process, having no prior grasp of Reality but remaining empty, all Intelligence though it be, until it has put itself to school.[50]

In this mid-phase of the soul, man is already reaching upward toward the full dominance of his higher self, which has joined itself to the corporeal element.

Nevertheless it remains subject to the weaknesses and downward attraction of the body, as the following passage indicates:

Reasoning is for this sphere; it is the act of the Soul fallen into perplexity, distracted with cares, diminished in strength: the need of deliberation goes with the less self-sufficing intelligence.[51]

Despite his comprehension of the positive value of the body for man as he exists in the present condition, Plotinus never permits himself to forget that the corporeal part of man is radicated in matter. This problem must be examined to complete the picture of the descent of soul to body in Plotinian philosophy. It is not necessary to delay long in explaining the nature of body to which the soul descends, since Plotinus is chiefly concerned with body in its relationship to soul, whence it derives its reality and whatever positive value it may have.

C. Negative aspect of the fall: evil in the human situation

For Plotinus, body is ontologically evil in so far as matter is its substratum, since in his philosophy matter is the primal evil.[52] In the hierarchy of emanations there is unceasing diminution from the One, which is transcendentally All, down to the final terminus of emanations in matter, "perfect non-being."[53] As the good, which is pure being, exists necessarily, so must its contrary, which is the infinite evil,[54] the "perfect poverty"[55] of matter. As Plotinus affirms:

Given that the Good is not the only existent thing, it is inevitable that, by the outgoing from it, or, if the phrase be pre-

50 I, 8, 2.
51 IV, 3, 18.
52 I, 8, 7.
53 I, 8, 7.
54 I, 8, 8.
55 I, 8, 3.

ferred, the continuous down-going or away-going from it, there should be produced a Last, something after which nothing more can be produced: this will be Evil . . . this last is Matter, the thing which has no residue of good in it: here is the necessity of Evil.[56]

For Plotinus, matter never really unites with form substantially, but "remains an underlying darkness in material things . . . spoiling and corrupting the forms they receive from soul."[57] Matter is a pure receptacle, in which forms are received only as in a mirror,[58] or like dreams of good.[59] Fundamentally, matter remains completely without determination, always in flux,[60] forever non-being, "Authentic Non-Existence."[61]

Since man's body has matter as its substratum it is necessarily tainted with evil in the metaphysical sense. The soul's contact with this unreality can readily become for it a source of moral evil.

Ideally, the soul should simply and quickly fulfill its cosmic function of communicating its image to the body and then turn back at once to the intellectual sphere.[62] In practice, Plotinus admits, this does not happen. Like Narcissus, the soul allows itself to be enticed by its own reflection in the body and plunges lower and lower into matter.[63] Like "the steersman of a storm-tossed ship who is so intent on saving it that he forgets his own interest and never thinks that he is recurrently in peril of being dragged down with the vessel," so our souls "are intent upon contriving for" their bodies and hence are pulled down by them.[64] Thus the body is the occasion for man's weakness and debasement. Because the individual soul must live in contact with its body to govern it—unlike universal Soul directing the corporeal world from above with facility— it happens that in practice a man comes nearly to be mastered by body and to be imprisoned in it.[65] The light of soul streaming into the body becomes dulled as it mingles with matter.[66]

[56] I, 8, 7.
[57] Armstrong, *art. cit., Downside Review,* 67 (Autumn, 1949), p. 416.
[58] III, 6, 13.
[59] VI, 7, 28.
[60] I, 8, 4; III, 4, 5; III, 6, 7.
[61] II, 5, 5.
[62] IV, 8, 5.
[63] IV, 3, 17.
[64] *Ibid.;* also V, 9, 1.
[65] IV, 8: 7, 2.
[66] I, 8, 14.

This occurs because the soul's intimate contact with the non-being of matter renders the accomplishment of its proper functions more difficult—in extreme cases, close to impossible. The modifications and troubles we feel arise from our embodiment. Intermingling with body hinders the soul's intellective act, filling it with desires, pleasures, pain and fear, which have their origin in the body.[67] Embodiment is particularly the cause of fear, since the greatest fear arises from the dread of death; and mortality is owing to the body.[68] All this is found in several places in the *Enneads,* and is well summarized in the tractate on evil when Plotinus writes:

> What soul could contain Evil unless by contact with the lower Kind? There could be no desire, no sorrow, no rage, no fear; fear touches the compounded dreading its dissolution; pain and sorrow are the accompaniments of the dissolution; desires spring from something troubling the grouped being or are a provision against trouble threatened.[69]

Nevertheless, the moral evil is not in body itself.[70] It is the soul which has the power to choose how far it will plunge into matter, and thus yield to the attraction freely. Just as Plotinus holds firmly that the higher self's initial descent to body is voluntary within a framework of cosmic necessity,[71] so he holds that man in his empirical existence likewise acts voluntarily, though his choices fit within the universal schema.[72] In his treatise on fate he writes:

> There must be acts and thoughts that are our own; the good and evil done by each human being must be his own; and it is quite certain that we must not lay any vileness to the charge of the All.[73]

Refuting the idea that our lives are controlled by the stars, he denies that "our acts of will and our states, all the evil in us, our entire personality" are to be ascribed to a control beyond us.[74] Man

---

67 I, 8: 4, 8, 13; III, 1, 9; IV, 8: 2, 3; V, 9, 1.

68 IV, 7, 1.

69 I, 8, 15.

70 In spite of occasional expressions to the contrary, this seems to be Plotinus' real conviction, as witnessed to especially in his treatises on Fate and Providence and against the Gnostics.

71 Cf. *supra,* pp. 24-25.

72 II, 9, 8; III, 1: 1, 8; III, 2: 10, 14, 17; IV, 4, 44-45; VI, 8: 1, 2, 6, 12.

73 I, 3, 4.

74 I, 3, 5.

is not wholly a creature of his inheritance or his environment, though these have an influence on him. In his comparison of life to a play upon the stage, Plotinus affirms that "these actors, souls, hold a peculiar dignity; they act in a vaster place than any stage: the Author has made them masters of all this world; they have a wide choice of place."[75] Plotinus admits that man's freedom resides in his will, which is the power of self-disposal, independence, deliberateness, that distinguishes man from beasts.[76] Admittedly, the power of self-disposal relates to reason, and is in part conditioned by man's rationality in attitude toward himself and things.

Man can exercise his freedom even to the point of so far sinking into the defiling allurement of material life that he becomes in practice a slave to his bodily impulses.[77] It is then that the pessimistic image of man drawn by Plotinus applies:

> We are become dwellers in the Place of Unlikeness, where, fallen from all our resemblance to the Divine, we lie in gloom and mud: for if the Soul abandons itself unreservedly to the extreme of viciousness, it is no longer of good: it has taken to itself another nature, the Evil, and as far as Soul can die it is dead. And the death of the Soul is twofold: while still sunk in body to lie down in Matter and drench itself with it.[78]

In this condition of abandonment to sense life, genuine freedom is not exercised:

> We admit, then, a Necessity in all that is brought about by this compromise between will and accidental circumstances . . .

[75] III, 2, 17.

[76] VI, 8: 1-3, 5-6; III, 2: 4, 7, 9, 17. On the point of Plotinian doctrine concerning freedom and the existence of a faculty of will, interpreters reach contradictory conclusions. Whittaker, op. cit., p. 76, calls Plotinus a "determinist." G. H. Clark, "Plotinus' Theory of Empirical Responsibility," New Scholasticism, 24 (1950), pp. 22ff., agrees. Inge, op. cit., II, 185, opposes Whittaker's interpretation. The careful study of Crocker, "The Freedom of Man in Plotinus," Modern Schoolman, 34 (1956), 23-35, concludes convincingly that Plotinus teaches human freedom, especially in VI, 8.

[77] Bruno Switalski, in Plotinus and the Ethics of St. Augustine (N. Y.: Polish Institute of Arts and Sciences in America, 1946), p. 22, quotes the paradoxical formula of Kristeller, to the effect that in Plotinus the soul has "liberty" to possess liberty or to be deprived of it. According to his interpretation, Plotinus looks upon freedom of choice as applying to the general ethical disposition rather than to individual actions.

[78] I, 8, 13. Cf. also I, 2, 3; I, 8, 14; III, 2: 4, 10; III, 3, 4; III, 4, 5; IV, 8: 2, 4: V, 9, 1.

when the Soul has been modified by outer forces and acts
under that pressure so that what it does is no more than an
unreflecting acceptance of stimulus, neither the act nor the
state can be described as voluntary.[79]

When the individual allows himself to act under the impulse of
ignorance, or as led by chance, imagination or bodily passions, his
action is not a truly independent act.[80] This happens because having
isolated itself from universal Soul, the human soul allows the
initial contact with matter to deepen to a state of complete satura-
tion so that the reasoning-faculty itself, to the extent of the fall
into corporeality, "becomes wholly indeterminate, sees darkness,"
for "it has taken Matter into itself."[81] Once men are enslaved, "the
Evil which holds men down binds them against their will."[82]

At times Plotinus pessimistically admits the fact that many men,
even the majority, may live enslaved to bodily passions, yet he never
concedes that the higher self in human nature as such is irretrieva-
bly self-enslaved. In nearly all the passages in which he writes of
the degradation of man, he goes on to add that such a condition
lasts only until man summons up his spiritual forces to rise above
material desires. For example:

> As the Soul is evil by being interfused with the body and by
> coming to share in the body's states and to think the body's
> thoughts, so it would be good, it would be possessed of virtue,
> if it threw off the body's moods and devoted itself to its own
> Act—the state of Intellection and Wisdom.[83]

Elsewhere he declares that in spite of the depth of the fall there
always remains something transcendent which is able to recover
itself.[84] Rightly disposed, man can resist the allurements of his own
body and material things:

> Alone in immunity from magic is he who, though drawn by
> the alien parts of his total being, withholds his assent to their
> standards of worth, recognizing the good only where his au-

79 III, 1, 9. Also I, 8, 4; III, 1, 8; V, 1, 1.
80 Crocker explains this well, *art. cit.*, pp. 27-29.
81 I, 8, 4.
82 I, 8: 5, 14; also IV, 4, 44; IV, 8: 4, 7, 8.
83 I, 2, 3.
84 IV, 8: 4, 7, 8. Also I, 8, 14; III, 2: 4, 18; III, 3, 4; VI, 8, 12.

thentic self sees and knows it, neither drawn nor pursuing, but tranquilly possessing and so never charmed away.[85]

We can conclude that in Plotinian doctrine, man remains a responsible agent, who can and ought to live according to the rational principle. On this level he can freely exercise his power of self-disposal. Then his actions are truly reasonable, truly conformed to all that is noblest in him. They are then, in Plotinus' understanding, fully voluntary because then our soul is acting at one with the world Psyche in its governance of the universe. In the third *Ennead*, we find this clearly expressed:

> But when our Soul holds to its Reason-Principle, to the guide, pure and undetached and native to itself, only then can we speak of personal operation, of voluntary act. Things so done may truly be described as our doing, for they have no other source; they are the issue of the unmingled Soul.[86]

Contrariwise, human evil exists when men separate themselves from universal Soul by following their individual attractions to material things. Moral evil does not belong to material things as such, but to the human person which acts according to its lowest phase rather than under the command of its higher element. Trouillard expresses this concept well when he writes:

> Le dualisme du pur et de l'impur n'est donc pas celui de deux substances, mais de deux structures mentales: il n'est pas celui de l'esprit et de la matière, mais celui de la pensée affranchie et de la raison confisquée, de l'esprit éveillé et de l'âme en sommeil. Le mal-négation devient une lourde réalité dans le jugement désorbité, et une manière d'ordre inversé.[87]

In the measure then that the descent of soul to body is the occasion of the spiritual man's plunging into the defiling depths of material absorption, it can be called the reason for evil in the human situation. Yet one must not forget that for Plotinus this descent is also a part of the total cosmic dynamism of emanation, within the human microcosm, and as such is a good. For the human soul, apt for body, is only individually personalized in its becoming conjoined with body. Though man's creation may be envisaged by Plotinus as a fall, it still remains true that it is man's coming

85 IV, 4, 44.
86 III, 1, 9. Also I, 8, 11; III, 6, 2; IV, 4, 25.
87 *Art. cit.*, pp. 68-69.

into being. The philosopher recognizes that in the present schema, the human person attains his ultimate goal of contemplative union with the All, only consequently to his union with the instrument-body.

IV. MAN'S CONTEMPLATIVE DESTINY

In order to attain his goal of ecstatic contemplation, empirical man must follow in reverse the path of descent: from the nadir of his immersion in matter he must begin the upward ascent. The further down he has plunged, the longer will be the return journey. This involves a purification and a positive action of virtue. Fundamentally, the goal is to be attained by a noetic rather than a volitional process, although man's exercise of freedom will determine whether or not he will follow the promptings of his higher intellectual nature.

The mystical identification with the One which is the final term of man's destiny is possible only to the man who has become in some way like to the One. To approach Him, man must in a fashion become divine. To behold the pure Light, man must be illumined, and to communicate with the One, he must return from multiplicity to inner unity.[1] This means that man must enter the way of dialectic purification in order to be able to achieve the hoped-for term.

A. *The way toward the goal*

At the lowest level, man must withdraw from the fragmentizing effects of contact with matter. His sense desires, passions, appetites, and fear itself must be brought under full control of his higher soul.[2] It must be purified from the stains resulting from traffic with corporeal things.[3] For man this involves ascetic self-discipline, in which even attention to food and drink will lie outside the soul's attention.[4] The man of such disposition attains a kinship with the

---

[1]Maurice Burque, *Un problème plotinien, l'identification de l'âme avec l'Un dans la contemplation* (Roma: Pontificia Universitas Gregoriana, 1939), p. 8.

[2] I, 2, 3; III, 4, 2; VI, 5, 12; VI, 4, 14; III, 6, 5.

[3] Switalski, *op. cit.*, p. 5; H. Van Lieshout, *La Théorie Plotinienne de la vertu* (Freiburg, Schweiz: Studia Friburgensia, 1926), pp. 63-64.

[4] I, 2, 15.

powers of the heavens, and thus becomes good; it arrives at a condition that Plotinus describes as an inhabitation of the body "in a mode very closely resembling the indwelling of the All-Soul in the universal frame." This, he continues, "means continence, self-restraint, holding staunch against outside pleasure and against outer spectacle, allowing no hardship to disturb the mind."[5]

Our task is "to work for our liberation from this sphere, severing ourselves from all that has gathered about us."[6] We must break away from the alien in us, and rise toward our true destiny.[7] In the tractate on beauty, Plotinus exhorts his reader to enter courageously on the ascetical way:

> Withdraw into yourself and look. And if you do not find yourself beautiful yet, act as does the creator of a statue that is to be made beautiful: he cuts away here, he smoothes there, he makes this line lighter, this other purer, until a lovely face has grown upon his work. So do you also: cut away all that is excessive, straighten all that is crooked, bring light to all that is overcast, labour to make all one glow of beauty and never cease chiselling your statue, until there shall shine out on you from it the godlike splendour of virtue, until you shall see the perfect goodness surely established in the stainless shrine.[8]

Virtue itself is cathartic: the flight hence, we read in the tractate on evil, is a matter of "acquiring virtue, of disengaging the self from the body; this is the escape from Matter, since association with the body implies association with Matter."[9] Virtue itself is not the Good, but the means whereby man can free himself from entanglement with matter in order to come to the good.[10]

It is the so-called civic virtues that Plotinus delineates and places as the necessary first phase of the upward ascent of the soul.[11] These are the four virtues of prudence, fortitude, sophrosyny and rectitude.[12] Their value is primarily personal, not social, in Plotinus' doctrine. As long as we remain in the passing life here, the philosopher teaches, these virtues are a principle of order and

5 II, 9, 18.
6 II, 3, 9; III, 6, 5; V, 3, 17.
7 III, 4, 2.
8 I, 6, 9.
9 I, 8, 7.
10 I, 8, 6. Crocker, art. cit., p. 26.
11 Van Lieshout, op. cit., pp. 68-71.
12 I, 2, 1.

measure, aiding us to overcome the disharmony and unmeasured evil of sheer matter.[13] They ennoble us by setting bound and measure to our desires and to our entire sensibility . . . dispelling false judgment."[14] Because in the first stage these virtues simply bring about moderation and perfect the single parts of our soul, they are not yet pure and perfect virtues, remaining characteristic of the sensible, temporal sphere.[15] Nevertheless, they already begin to etch in us some likeness to the divine, thus preparing us remotely for contemplative union.

In the next higher stage of man's ascent, which still remains in some measure ascetical, Plotinus again names and places these same virtues, but he now calls them "purifying virtues,"[16] and he justifies this appellation by detailing how they indicate that man has become good by having stripped himself of the body's entanglements and devoting itself finally to its own proper intellectual acts. The result is a deepening of the traces of divine image.

In the positive aspect of the ascent, sensible beauty is a point of departure for the soul, which from beautiful sights and harmonious sounds, can rise to consider intellectual beauty, soul-beauty. From the sense domain it is to ascend to the higher region of beauty of acts and habits, virtues and knowledge.[17] Arrived at the stage of enlightenment, the soul's likeness to the divine has become more profound, as it has at the same time disengaged itself more and more from the alien corporeality of its body-instrument. The practice of dialectic established it in a world of ideas; it concentrates all its attention there. It devotes itself to reason; and then, bypassing reason, begins to ascend to the sphere of pure intellect and to grasp true being.[18] The light streaming down from above penetrates the soul, which is now able to perceive this light.[19] Unity replaces multiplicity. In such a condition of "inner unity," where man finds himself wholly true to his essential nature, he himself becomes "very vision."[20] Ugliness, disharmony, fragmentation, dark-

13 III, 6, 2.

14 I, 2, 2.

15 Inge, *op. cit.*, II, pp. 166-167.

16 I, 6, 6; I, 2, 3. Whittaker, *op. cit.*, pp. 92-93.

17 I, 6: 6-9; IV, 7, 10; IV, 8, 4-8; V, 9: 5, 9. Sister Rose Emmanuela, *art. cit.*, pp. 29-30; Faggin, *art. cit.*, col. 1458; Bourbon di Petrella, *op. cit.*, pp. 102-105.

18 I, 3, 3; VI, 7, 35.

19 I, 8, 15; V, 3, 17.

20 I, 6, 9; V, 3, 9. Trouillard, *art. cit.*, p. 72.

ness, the taint of contact with matter, all are laid aside. The new
phase has begun by a new orientation, says Plotinus, and now "the
soul must thrust towards the light."[21]

B. *The goal of man, contemplative union with the One*

The light toward which the soul must tend streams into it from
the source of Light, the primal One. Deep within itself, the soul
finds this light, so that the ecstasy of contemplation is not a spatial
ascent, but an intuitive vision of the One, which is in no particular
place because it utterly transcends all spatial and temporal categories.[22] On arriving at this point the soul has passed through the
intellectual realm, and beyond it, to arrive at the ecstatic vision of
the Deity with which it enters into real contact. The soul has come
full circle from its initial descent to its ultimate point of ascent.

In this dynamism, a double impulse is noted by Plotinus. The
descent came from a drive toward self-affirmation; the return represents the impulse to reascend whence it came forth. The double
rhythm is a harmony which has its source in the One. It is not
simply a self-generated impulse that urges man to rise from alien
matter; rather it is a yielding to an attraction from above. The
power of return in contemplation is the greatest gift of the One:
"the illumination and the passionate desire are *given*."[23] The soul
"loves the Supreme Good" because it is "from its very beginnings
stirred by it to love."[24]

Prepared by both natural disposition and training, the soul is
ready for the contemplative vision with the One.[25] In this "contemplative operation within itself . . . alone is Happiness."[26] When
man has reached the term of this ecstatic union with the All, he has
attained his goal:

> And this is the true end set before the Soul, to take that light,
> to see the Supreme by the Supreme and not by the light of
> any other principle—to see the Supreme which is also the

21 I, 2, 4; VI, 9, 8.

22 V, 9, 13; VI, 5: 12, 13; VI, 7, 34; VI, 8, 11.

23 Armstrong, *art. cit., Downside Review*, 75 (1957), 128. The same concept
is expressed by Faggin, *art. cit.*, col. 1458.

24 VI, 7, 31.

25 II, 9, 18.

26 I, 5, 10.

means to the vision; for that which illumines the Soul is that which it is to see.[27]

In this state, entirely emptied of its attention to things and even to itself and prepared by a perfect intellectual catharsis, the soul is absorbed into the unifying and beautifying ecstasy.[28] The man who contemplates the Supreme is totally turned to it and drawn to it. Such a soul

> has seen that presence suddenly manifesting within her, for there is nothing between: here is no longer a duality but a two in one . . . all distinction fades: it is as lover and beloved here. . . . This she sought and This she has found and on This she looks and not upon herself; and who she is that looks she has not leisure to know . . . she is of perfect judgment and knows that This was her quest, that nothing higher is.[29]

Lost in this ecstatic union, the soul is in some manner identified with the One, for there is "no longer a duality but a two in one." This union is not a metaphysical loss of self-identity of the soul, nor a physical absorption of the being of the soul in the substance of the First Principle. Examined carefully, Plotinus' doctrine is seen to hold that this mystical union is an intentional union,[30] entirely resulting from a noetic dynamism. It is an intuitive vision in which, though there is in one sense no longer a duality, there yet remains ontologically a twoness, "two in one."

At this final terminus where man has attained his destiny, he still remains man. True, he has left behind him—at least in the order of intention, if not actually through the severance of death[31]—his

---

[27] V, 3, 17.

[28] V, 7, 35.

[29] VI, 7, 34.

[30] Such is the conclusion reached by Maurice Burque, *op. cit.*, after careful study of this problem of the identification of the soul with the One. He takes note of the divergence of interpretation on this question, explaining how two fundamental answers are given as reflecting Plotinus' thought. One is that of those who hold for an absolute identification, veering toward pantheism: among this group he cites M. de Corte, J. Simon, E. Vacherot, Rodier, Zeller, Bréhier, Inge. Rejecting identification as the correct interpretation, are Lindsay, Arnou, Marechal. After a careful verbal study, and a detailed study of the contemplative union of the second Hypostasis with the One, he concludes as above indicated.

[31] For Plotinus ecstatic contemplation was possible in this life; IV, 8, 1. Porphyry says that Plotinus four times experienced this intuitive vision.

bodily partner. The unmeasure and darkness of matter no longer affect him, for he has been freed from their trammels. The higher phase of his soul completely dominates the mid-phase of discursive reason and the sense-phase: all activities of sense, imagination, memory both sense and intellectual, discursive reason and judgments, have receded and been cast aside. Man, the "pilgrim of the universe"[32] of Plotinian thought, has gone forth on his descending journey to the nadir of the utmost reaches of being, and has returned upward reversing his journey, to be absorbed in blessed union with the One. The final words of the *Enneads* as Porphyry has arranged them succinctly express this beatitude:

> This is the life of gods and of godlike and blessed men—liberation from the alien that besets us here, a life taking no pleasure in the things of earth—a flight of the alone to the Alone.[33]

V. CONCLUSION: SOME OBSERVATIONS ON PLOTINUS' PHILOSOPHY OF MAN

Within the span of the fifty-four tractates of the *Enneads* only the first two are explicitly dedicated to a study of human nature. Yet it is evident that throughout his writings, Plotinus returns again and again to the question of man. Though he deals with a large range of philosophical problems, his chief intent seems to have been to encourage men to rise to the spiritual level of existence. Even in tractates where he deals with the great realm of being above and beyond man, Plotinus never allows him to forget that within himself he reflects the entire cosmos.[1] Even so, Plotinus' doctrine on human nature is but a limited part of his total philosophy; hence, the readily admitted limitation of these few concluding observations on Plotinus' teaching on man.

On the positive side, perhaps the greatest value attaches to the stress given to the spiritual element in man. Without a doubt this is the basic orientation of Plotinus' entire philosophy, and in par-

---

32 Faggin, *art. cit.*, col. 1458.

33 VI, 9, 11. Translation is that of Grace H. Turnbull, from *The Essence of Plotinus* (New York: Oxford University Press, 1948), p. 222.

---

1 P. Henry in introduction to MacKenna's *Enneads* says that the philosophy of Plotinus "is throughout implicitly present as a totality in each particular theme" (p. xli). Clark, *art. cit., Phil. Review*, makes a similar observation, p. 357.

ticular of his concept of human nature. Plotinus rightly perceives that the power of reason is man's distinctive characteristic. He recognizes that the material universe is at the service of man; and that through a moderated use of things, appreciation of their beauty, perception of the truth through the beginnings of knowledge by way of sensation, man can develop his fullest potentialities. In his very origin man is a dependent and has an existence that is participated being. His life on earth is not a purposeless wandering between two blank nothings. A basic teleology permeates Plotinus' doctrine on human nature. Man is destined to an immortal life hereafter, where his true happiness will be the beatifying ecstatic contemplation of divinity. Even in his present bodily condition, man can anticipate this final mystical union.

Certainly Plotinus has recognized some of the fundamental problems in a philosophy of human nature. Regarding the basic question of what man is, though he has seen that both a material and a spiritual element must be considered, he has failed to recognize the body as substantially joined to soul. This failure to some extent influences pejoratively his doctrine on man's knowing processes and his view of man's final destiny. Though he clearly would agree with a Catholic theologian that "the end of life is life, not death,"[2] he would limit immortal life to man's soul. For Plotinus, there is no room for a doctrine of corporeal resurrection. Nor, for the same consideration, is there in his doctrine anything paralleling the Aristotelean-scholastic concept of the rule of reason to be established within the emotional and physical dynamisms of human nature.

Though he refutes Gnostic-Manichaean errors on matter and evil, Plotinus fails to perceive in matter as such anything at all except evil, though his concept of it as a counter-balance to positive being at the other extremity of the hierarchical structure of the universe, leads him to describe it as infinite evil. This is the source of Plotinus' inability to appreciate rightly the positive value of the corporeal element of human nature, or to grant it a place in the "true self." Similarly, this misapprehension leads him to identify, or nearly so, creation and the fall. He seems to have had an intuition of some original disturbance in human nature. However, he makes man's coming into being in bodily form itself the source

[2] Raimondo Spiazzi, *Maria santissima nel mistero cristiano* (Milano: Massimo, 1955), p. 153.

of evil. Nevertheless, Plotinus recognizes that in the last analysis the evil in the human situation arises from man's free choice of dispositions contrary to his higher destiny, rather than from the matter which occasions the evil.

To Plotinus' concept of matter is also to be attributed his lack of a clear conception of the social dimension of human nature. Whereas others may have erred in the past or at present by over-emphasizing the physical aspects of man's natural appurtenance to society, Plotinus bypasses this completely. He does, however, recognize a certain fundamental intellectual community among men.[3]

Though his solution of the problem of free will within a divine providential governance of the universe is not satisfactory, Plotinus has perceived the fundamental nature of the problem, and has seen that the solution must lie in a reconciliation of both divine causality and human freedom. When Christian theologians have divided so sharply in their explanations, credit must be given to Plotinus for so handling the problem that he cannot be justifiably accused of having rejected either of its basic elements.

Concerning human freedom, Plotinus has seen that it is owing to man's rational nature. However, while recognizing the existence of the faculty of will, he de-emphasizes it in contrast to his strong insistence on the intellectual dynamism of man's achievement of his destiny. Some interpreters have criticized Plotinus for attributing too great a self-sufficiency to man in the attainment of his goal. Good pagan that he was, it would seem proper to forgive his failure to perceive the revealed doctrine of divine grace, particularly in view of the fact that he unmistakably did recognize man's dependence on the attraction of the divine being in his upward journey toward the beatifying vision.[4]

In spite of the shortcomings of Plotinus—his obvious errors, lack of systematization, apparent contradictions, and mixing of philosophy, myth, and mysticism—high tribute must be paid him as the greatest of the Neoplatonists. Furthermore, it was he whose writings were a powerful instrument of Providence in the formation of so great a Christian thinker as St. Augustine. Of all the pagan philosophers of antiquity, the influence of Plotinus is incalculably greatest for the development of Christian mysticism in both East and West.

[3] IV, 9, 1; VI, 5, 10.
[4] Cf. *supra,* p. 40.

While rejecting his errors, Christians have known how to use the true insights of Plotinus. Even when his concepts are false his language has often been useful.[5]

A.S.C. Provincialate, Ruma, Illinois

---

[5] One of his best present-day interpreters expresses well the value of Plotinus for Christians:

> To the Christian, a very great deal that Plotinus says about Intellect and the higher soul seems to be true, but true not about something that we are or have by nature but about something which God has, and is giving us by grace in conforming us to the likeness of his Son, the Uncreated Wisdom. . . . It is Christ in Christian thought who corresponds to the 'true man', the 'true self' of Plotinus.

Armstrong, *art. cit., Downside Review,* 75 (1957), p. 135.

6

DUNS SCOTUS ON THE OMNIPOTENCE OF GOD

by

FELIX ALLUNTIS and ALLAN B. WOLTER

INTRODUCTION

The text that follows is a translation of the whole of question seven of the *Quaestiones quodlibetales* of John Duns Scotus and is taken from the English version of that work being prepared by Alluntis and Wolter with the support of a grant from the Penrose Fund of the American Philosophical Society. Alluntis's recent Spanish translation of this same work[1] is accompanied by what virtually amounts to a new edition of the Latin text found in the Luke Wadding edition[2] and reprinted by L. Vivès.[3] He has introduced a new numbering system for the paragraphs and has divided each question into appropriate articles and subdivisions. Our English version will follow this numbering system, but for the convenience of footnote cross references, we add to each paragraph number the number of the question as well. Thus 6.44, for example, refers to question six, paragraph 44 in the Alluntis edition. In the text that follows all paragraphs are preceded by a 7.

Unlike some of Scotus' other works, the *additiones* to the *Quaestiones quodlibetales* found in the Wadding and Vivès editions do not seem to be in any instance the work of Scotus himself. This is certainly the case for those additions where reference is made to Scotus in the third person, but even where this is not the case there are subtle differences of doctrine in some additions that betray the

[1] *Cuestiones Cuodlibetales (Obras del Doctor Sutil Juan Duns Escoto)*, Latin text and Spanish translation with an introduction, summaries and notes by Felix Alluntis, O.F.M. (Madrid: Biblioteca de Autores Cristianos, 1968)

[2] *Ioannis Duns Scoti opera omnia*, 12 vols. (Lugduni: sumptibus Laurentii Durand, 1639).

[3] *Ioannis Duns Scoti opera omnia*, 26 vols. (Parisiis: apud Ludovicum Vivès, 1891-1895).

hand of an editor or commentator rather than that of Scotus himself. For one or the other of these reasons we have omitted the two additions intended to supply the lacuna at 7.38 in the text.

Footnote references to Scotus' major commentary on the *Sentences* of Peter Lombard (called the *Ordinatio* by the editors of the new critical Vatican edition[4] and *Opus oxoniense* or 'The Oxford Commentary' by earlier writers on Duns Scotus) are made to the Vatican edition for Bk. I, but the Wadding-Vivès edition for Bks. II to IV. Because the Vatican edition numbers the paragraphs within any distinction consecutively, it is unnecessary to mention the question or the parts into which some distinctions are subdivided. This is not the case for the Wadding-Vivès edition. The Roman numeral within brackets refers to the volume in the respective edition, and the arabic numeral that follows gives the page or pages in the respective volume.

The *Quaestiones quodlibetales* represent the last and most mature work of Scotus. Its twenty-one questions, he tells us, are organized according to two great categories, God and creatures. Each question is a complete treatise touching on numerous theological and philosophical problems. Scotus employs the usual scholastic method of his day, beginning each question with initial arguments *pro* and *con;* this is followed by what is commonly called the 'body of the question' and the question ends with answers to the initial arguments. The arguments themselves are generally constructed in the form of a syllogism.

The present question is important for assessing Scotus' final position on a number of philosophical problems. His main concern is to determine whether natural reason can prove or disprove demonstratively that God can produce directly whatever can be caused. This necessitates distinguishing between infinite power (which God admittedly has) and omnipotence as Christian theologians understand it. In turn, this provides an occasion for explaining not only Aristotle's theory of demonstration and 'scientific' or epistemic knowledge, his position on omnipotence, and why in principle he had to admit that God created the angels, but also Scotus' own views on how God's existence and infinite perfection can be demonstrated, on the basic structure and methodology of metaphysics, on the distinction between intuitive and abstractive cognition, the

---

4 *Ioannis Duns Scoti opera omnia* (Civitas Vaticana: typis polyglottis Vaticanis, 1950 ....).

nature of theology as a science, why no science of 'existence' is possible, and what is necessary and eternal about contingent facts.

TEXT

Can it be demonstrated by natural and necessary reason that God is omnipotent?

7.1 So far we have investigated what pertains to God internally and in particular the relationships of person to person.[1] Now it remains to study what pertains to God considered externally, i.e., properties that imply a relationship of God to creatures. Here two sorts of questions could arise, one about the subject of the relation,[2] the other about the term or object to which it relates.[3]

7.2 Two questions were raised about the subject, one general, the other particular. The first question is this: Can it be demonstrated by natural and necessary reason that God in general, and not just one particular person, is omnipotent?[4] The second question pertains to one person in particular, Has the Son or Word of God some causality of his own as regards the creature?[5] Consider the first of these.

INITIAL ARGUMENTS PRO AND CON

7.3 First, the *argument for the affirmative.*

'God is omnipotent' seems demonstrable by natural reason, since natural reason can demonstrate that God has infinite power and, therefore, is omnipotent. Proof of the antecedent: The Philosopher[6] proves that God has infinite power from the fact that he produces motion over an infinite span of time. Proof of the implication: No power could be greater than the infinite. One could not even think of anything greater. If a power could be surpassed, it would not be infinite. But every power which is not omnipotence could be thought of as surpassed by a power which is omnipotence.

1 Cf. *Quodlibet* qq. 1-6.
2 Cf. *Quodl.* qq. 7-8.
3 Cf. *Quodl.* qq. 9-11.
4 Cf. Duns Scotus, *Ordinatio* I, d.42 (VI, 341-349); d.2, n.111ss (II, 189ss).
5 Cf. *Quodl.* q. 8.
6 Aristotle, *Physics* VIII, c.5 (256a12-256b2); *Metaph.* XII, c.6 (1071b-22).

7.4 Arguments to the contrary:

If it can be demonstrated that God is omnipotent, it can also be demonstrated that God can generate the Son. The consequent is false because this is a matter of pure belief and hence cannot be demonstrated by natural reason. The implication is proved from Augustine:[7] "If the Father did not generate a son equal to himself it was because he was either unable or unwilling to do so." And he argues further: "If you say he was unwilling, you accuse him of envy; if you say he was unable, where is the omnipotence of God the Father?" His point is, if the Father could not beget a son equal to himself he would not be omnipotent. Conversely then, if he is omnipotent, he can generate a son equal to himself and thus if the antecedent is demonstrable, so also is the consequent.

7.5 Furthermore, if God's omnipotence could be demonstrated, it could also be demonstrated that he could create anything that could be created. The consequent is false, for an angel can be created and still it seems impossible to demonstrate by natural reason that an angel can be created by him. The Philosopher following natural reason did not assume that the Intelligences were created by God; rather he assumed them to be necessary of themselves, that is, they were not effects produced by anything else. In the *Metaphysics*[8] he shows that a separate substance[9] has no magnitude on the following grounds. It has infinite power and infinite power cannot have magnitude. Then he asks whether there are one or many separate substances, and concludes there are many. According to him, then, not only the first, but any immaterial substance is infinite, and by the same token it is necessary of itself.

BODY OF THE QUESTION

7.6 We must first make two necessary distinctions and then solve the question accordingly.

---

[7] Augustine, *Contra Maximinum*, II, c.7; PL 42-762.

[8] Aristotle, *Metaph.* XII, c.7 (1073a3-12); c.8 (1073a14).

[9] Literally, *substantia separata*, i.e., a substance that exists apart or in separation from sensible or material things, hence an immaterial entity or spiritual substance. Here it refers to the Intelligences or intelligent beings responsible for the orderly movement of the stars and planets. Medieval thinkers considered the Aristotelian Intelligences other than God to be some sort of angel.

ARTICLE I

The Necessary Distinctions

1. Demonstration of Simple Fact and of the Reasoned Fact.

7.7 The first distinction is taken from the *Posterior Analytics,*
namely, there is a difference between (1) a demonstration of the
reasoned fact [*propter quid,* διότι] i.e., by way of the cause and (2)
a demonstration of simple fact [*quia,* ὅτι] i.e., by way of the
effect.[10]

This distinction is proved by argument. Every necessary truth
that is not evident from its terms but is connected necessarily and
evidently with another necessary truth that is evident from its
terms, can be demonstrated by means of this other evident truth.
Sometimes this truth is derived from the cause, sometimes from the

---

[10] In this passage, Scotus explains his interpretation of Aristotle's well known
distinction between a demonstration of fact and a demonstration of the reasoned
fact. Cf. *Analytica posteriora* I, c. 13-14 (78a22-79a33). Both are syllogistic argument forms that fulfill Aristotle's technical requirements for demonstration in
that they yield a conclusion that can be called 'scientific or epistemic knowledge'
(scientia, ἐπιστήμη). Scotus cites four basic conditions for knowledge of this
sort: (1) it must be certain and not just an opinion; (2) it must be a necessary
truth, not just a contingent one; (3) it must not be immediately evident but
it is known by means of other evident and necessary truths; (4) it is derived
from these latter truths by way of some form of syllogistic or discursive reasoning
process. Cf. *Ordinatio,* prol., n.41 (I, 23-24); *ibid.* I, d.2, n.39 (II, 148-149); d.3,
nn. 230ss (III, 138ss); *ibid.* III, d.24, n.13 (XV, 44b); *Reportata parisiensia,*
prol., q.1, n.4 (XXII, 7b-8b); *ibid.* III, d.24, n.16 (XXIII, 454). *Demonstratio
propter quid* or διότι, uses as its middle term something which expresses an
ontological cause or reason why the predicate of the conclusion inheres in the
subject. The essential definition of the subject or any one of its four Aristotelian
causes might serve as the middle term. Following the Oxford translation of
Aristotle, we have called a syllogism of this sort a 'demonstration of the reasoned
fact' and the conclusion it yields 'knowledge of the reasoned fact.' *Demonstratio
quia,* or ὅτι, which we have translated as 'demonstration of the simple fact,'
uses as a middle term something that logically connects the predicate to the
subject, but does not give what Aristotle or the Scholastics would consider to
be the real reason or the ontological cause why the subject in question has such
a predicate. It is not clear whether Scotus equates *propter quid* and *a priori*
on the one hand, and *quia* and *a posteriori* on the other as Ockham expressly
does (Cf. Ockham's *Summa Logicae* III, pars 2, c.17). For Aristotle, demonstration
through a remote cause (an *a priori* principle), however, is only a *demonstratio
quia.*

effect, for not only can truths about causes entail certain truths about effects, but truths about effects can also entail truths about causes. Therefore, some true propositions can be demonstrated either (1) by means of another evident truth derived from the cause and in this case the demonstration is of the reasoned fact or (2) by means of a truth derived from the effect and then the demonstration is one of simple fact.

From this a corollary seems to follow. Principles that are immediate or evident from their terms cannot be demonstrated by a demonstration of the simple fact. If this be true, there are some truths intermediate between the first truths and the last conclusions and they alone are demonstrable by simple fact through such ultimate truths as are themselves evident. How a truth based on an effect can be evident whereas the truth taken from the cause is not evident becomes clear if one considers the way of acquiring scientific or epistemic knowledge by experience which Aristotle describes in the *Metaphysics* and *Posterior Analytics*.[11] Through the experience of many individual instances perceptible to the senses, we know that an effect occurs, and yet we do not know the reason why it does so, because the cause is not given through sense perception but requires further investigation.

2. Two Meanings of Omnipotence.

7.8 The second distinction refers to omnipotence and presupposes the following general meaning of the term. Omnipotence is not passive but active, and not just any type of active power, but a causal one. This implies that omnipotence refers to something causable in essence that is distinct from the cause. For there is no causality except as regards something simply distinct. Hence it is a power or potency related to the possible. 'Possible' is not understood as opposed to 'impossible' nor as equated with 'producible' insofar as this is opposed to 'absolutely necessary of itself.'[12] Rather,

11 Aristotle, *Metaph.* c.1 (980b28); *Anal. post.* II, c.19 (100a3-12).

12 Scotus' point here is to distinguish a divine person like the Son or the Holy Spirit from the divine essence on the one hand, and from something causable like a creature on the other. The deity or divine nature is shared perfectly and hence is possessed perfectly by all three persons. It is said to be 'absolutely necessary of itself.' The process whereby it is shared or communicated is called a 'divine procession' or 'production' and is twofold. The Father, or first person of the Trinity, communicates or shares his divine essence with the second person, called

'possible' as the correlative of 'omnipotence' is equated with 'causable' because it represents the term of a causal power.

As the component *omni,* i.e., 'all' or 'every' in the word indicates, omnipotence also asserts some sort of universality. This does not refer to potency, considered simply in itself (for omnipotence is not formally all or every instance of power, for it is not a power of the creature). The power's universality is not taken simply but with reference to the causable (i.e., the possible or what can be created), so that the meaning is this: 'Omnipotence is that active power or potency whose scope extends to anything whatsover that can be created.' But this can still be understood in two ways. In the first sense it is taken disjunctively to mean the power can produce 'everything that can be created either mediately or immediately.' In the other sense, it means the power can produce 'everything that can be created,' and can do so immediately, at least so far as causes are concerned. In other words, no other active cause need intervene.[13]

ARTICLE II

Solution of the Question

7.9 In the second article we must see whether omnipotence can be demonstrated (1) by a demonstration of the reasoned fact or (2) by a demonstration of the simple fact.

7.10 There are three conclusions about its demonstrability as a reasoned fact.

---

the Son, or the Word, or *Logos.* The Father and Son, as a single principle, communicate their essence to the Holy Spirit. Because it is one and the same numerical essence that is shared or communicated in the Trinity, medieval theologians felt justified in distinguishing such divine productions or eternal processions from a causal production where, not only is the cause really distinct from the effect, but the effect has a nature or essence that is numerically distinct from that of the cause. According to this technical usage, for example, the Father can be called a 'producer' (*producens*) or a 'principle or source' (*principium*), but not a 'cause' (*causa*). The Son and Holy Spirit conversely cannot be called 'effects' or said to be 'caused' but they can be called 'producibles' or 'possibles' (in the sense of not being something 'impossible') or *principiata* (singular *principiatum*) in the sense that they represent something 'which proceeds from a principle.'

[13] Cf. Duns Scotus, *Ordinatio* I, d.8, n.302-306 (IV, 326-328); d.20, n.24-34 (V, 313-318); d.42, n.8-9 (VI, 342-344).

The first is this: 'God is omnipotent' (in either sense of omnipotence) is a truth that, in itself, is demonstrable as a reasoned fact.

Second conclusion: This truth can be demonstrated to a person in the present life under certain conditions.[14]

Third conclusion: This truth cannot be demonstrated to one in the present life in terms of what he knows naturally and according to the present dispensation.[15]

7.11 As for the demonstrability of omnipotence as a simple fact, there are two conclusions:

The first is this: The proposition 'God is omnipotent in the sense that the scope of his power extends immediately to every possible' is true, but we cannot demonstrate it by a demonstration of simple fact.

The second conclusion: 'God is omnipotent in the sense that his power extends mediately or immediately to every possible' is a proposition that can be demonstrated as a simple fact by a person in the present life.

[14] The Latin text reads '*istud verum est demonstrabile viatori stante simpliciter statu viae.*' As Scotus subsequently explains (cf. 7.19), this means that without destroying his status as a pilgrim in this life, a man could have, or be given, such a perfect concept of God that he would be able to use it as the middle term of a syllogism to demonstrate that God is omnipotent. Scotus considers only the beatific vision itself, or some such ecstatic or mystical experience in this life in which God is seen face to face, to be inconsistent with man's status as a pilgrim. This leaves open the question as to how such knowledge could be communicated to him. Presumably it would have to be given somehow directly by God. According to Scotus, if one had at some time intuitive knowledge of God, this would suffice for him to form an abstractive concept of God (so-called because it 'abstracts' from the fact of whether the subject still exists or does not exist). Since God can cause immediately whatever he can cause through secondary or created causes, he could infuse such a concept directly into the human mind. Scotus' point is that given the existence of such a concept in the mind, whether it be acquired, infused, or what have you, man in virtue of his native ability or natural power to reason and to draw conclusions, could use such a concept to demonstrate this truth as a reasoned fact.

[15] We have translated '*de lege communi*' (literally, 'according to the common law') as 'according to the present dispensation.' This refers not only to man's natural endowments, but to such supernatural gifts as are available to the generality of mankind. What is excluded are such special supernatural or mystical experiences as those had by the patriarchs, prophets or apostles to whom God imparted his original revelation. Such chosen individual presumably possessed a direct experiential knowledge not given to the ordinary believer to whom they communicated what God revealed to them.

7.12 We have five conclusions then, which, taken together give a complete answer to the question.

1. Concerning the First Conclusion

7.13 Proof of the first conclusion:[16]

If a truth can be demonstrated as a reasoned fact from another prior truth, it possesses this property in virtue of its terms.[17] 'God is omnipotent' (in either sense of omnipotence) is a truth of this sort. Therefore, [it is demonstrable as a reasoned fact].

7.14 The major is clear: A truth of this sort is the kind of truth it is in virtue of what its terms mean. Consequently, a truth that is self-evident is one that is known to be such from the meaning of its terms and from this it follows that the truth is self-evident to any intellect which conceives the meaning of these terms.

7.15 The minor is proved. A truth that in virtue of its terms is necessary, but not immediately known, also has the property of being demonstrable as a reasoned fact in virtue of its terms. 'God is omnipotent' (in either sense of omnipotence) is a truth of this sort. That we are dealing with a truth that is both true and necessary is clear, but we do not prove it here because it is not in question. Our problem refers only to the way in which this truth can be known or proved.

7.16 There are two arguments to prove that this necessary truth is known mediately.

First, the sequence or order in which things can be known is the same as it would be were they really distinct. It makes no difference how the mental existence of one is to be distinguished from that of the other. But if nature, intellect, will and external power were really distinct from one another, their real order or sequence would be this: (1) the nature, because it has (2) such an intellect and (3) such a will, would be (4) externally potent in the way that it is. Therefore, no matter what kind of distinction exists between these things their order of knowability is always the following: (1) the divine nature, because it has (2) such an intellect and (3) such a will, has (4) the sort of potency that is omnipotence. It is obvious then not only that some medium for this necessary

16 Cf. *supra* 7.10.
17 Cf. Duns Scotus, *Ordinatio I*, d.2, n.14-24 (II, 131-137).

truth exists, but also what that medium is, namely that the divine nature has intellect or will or both.

7.17 A second proof that this is a mediate truth would be this: Every necessary truth is either mediate or immediate, but this truth is not immediate, therefore, [it is mediate]. Proof of the minor: One of the conclusions we arrived at in solving the first question[18] was that the personal or notional properties pertain more immediately to the essence than properties implying relationship to the external. But the notional does not pertain to the divine essence as immediately as does something essential, as the proof in the solution of the same question shows, for the property of perfect memory is the medium in virtue of which 'speaking'[19] pertains to the divine essence. *A fortiori* therefore omnipotence, which asserts a relationship to external things, does not pertain to God or to any divine person with an immediacy that is absolute.

7.18 To the first of these two proofs a further clarification could have been added as to just which power is formally omnipotence or, to be more exact, which is the immediate foundation of omnipotence. Is it the divine intellect or the divine will? For our purpose, however, it is not necessary to determine which of these it is, since what we are trying to prove follows just as well from either alternative.

2. Concerning the Second Conclusion

7.19 [*Exposition and proof*] The second conclusion[20] should be understood in this way. A demonstration of God's omnipotence as a reasoned fact (taking omnipotence in either sense) is possible

---

18 Cf. *Quodl.* q.1, 1.44.

19 Following St. Augustine, the medieval theologians generally explained the eternal procession of the Son from the Father as involving the divine intellect and that of the Holy Spirit involving the divine will. To the extent that intellectual memory in recalling an object or situation that is no longer present gives to that object or situation some kind of 'existence' or status as an object of thought, the intellectual act whereby the Father 'begets' the Son was ascribed specifically to the Father's 'memory.' Since the Son is also called the *Logos*, or Word of the Father, Scotus calls this act of eternal production by the Father an act of 'speaking' the Word (*dicere Verbum*). Since the Holy Spirit proceeds from the Father and Son by an act of love, his eternal production is called an act of 'spiration' or 'breathing.'

20 Cf. *supra* 7.10.

for a person in this life who possesses nothing repugnant to his status as a pilgrim, whether this be something passing like St. Paul's ecstasy or something permanent [like the beatific vision].

Proof of this conclusion: Any intellect that can have a simple concept that includes virtually an immediate truth together with another mediate truth can also know the mediate truth through a demonstration of the reasoned fact. But the human intellect in the present life, apart from any permanent or transient knowledge inconsistent with its pilgrim status, can possess a simple concept which virtually includes both the truth 'God is omnipotent' as well as another truth from which it follows immediately. Therefore, ['God is omnipotent' can be known through a demonstration of the reasoned fact].

7.20 This minor seems obvious at least as regards the assertion that some simple concept virtually includes the truth ['God is omnipotent'] by means of another immediate truth. For this would follow from what was established in proving the first conclusion,[21] namely that God's omnipotence is a mediate truth.

What still remains to be proved is that such a concept can exist in the intellect of a person in this life who has the status of a simple pilgrim, in other words, one who neither is in a state of rapture nor possesses the beatific knowledge. This is proved first by an example, secondly by an argument.

The example is this: Something can be understood only incidentally. For example, man is understood only in terms of something accidental to him when we think of him as 'the white one' or 'the one able to laugh.' Further knowledge of man would be in terms of something essential to him but still general. For example, to think of animal is also to think of man. Thirdly, something can be understood in terms of what is both essential and specific and yet the knowledge in a techenical sense is confused. Such would be the case if I understood what a man is [in the sense of being able to apply the name correctly] but did not know how to define him or even what the more generic elements were that would enter into such a definition. Of course, one could distinguish between the absolute and the relative as the first step in that direction. However, the final step in knowing some object with scientific knowledge, or more precisely, with knowledge immediately preceding scientific knowledge, is the knowledge of its definition. For

21 Cf. *supra* 7.16-7.17.

this knowledge is the most distinctive and the most specific essential knowledge one can have of it. It goes far beyond that vague knowledge of which the Philosopher speaks in the *Physics*[22] in expressing how names are related to definition. In such knowledge by definition at least we have a concept which includes evidently and virtually all the necessary truths about such an object.

7.21 This example provides the following argument. Apart from the immediate vision or intuitive knowledge, it is possible to have a most distinctive conception of an object which precedes scientific knowledge, and such a concept, which would include in the most evident way truths about principles and about conclusions, would suffice for having scientific knowledge of such an object. But for a person in the present life, any knowledge of God, except immediate vision or intuitive knowledge, is simply compatible with his pilgrim status. Therefore, it is possible for him to have such a concept of God that is both consistent with his pilgrim state and sufficient to know propositional truths [including that of God's omnipotence].[23]

7.22 The major of this syllogism[24] is evident from the example cited above as well as from the distinction between abstractive and intuitive knowledge explained in the first article of the sixth question.[25] I repeat it here briefly. Although abstractive knowledge can be either of the non-existent or the existent, intuitive knowledge is only of the existent as existing. Abstractive and definitional knowledge of man, however, can be of the non-existent as well as the existent. This appears clear from what was said there [in question six]. It is also obvious in itself, because the same knowledge is there whether the thing exists or does not exist. Therefore, this definitional knowledge which is non-intuitive, is of the universal defined object.

7.23 The minor[26] also appears clear from what was said [in question six].[27] For only intuitive knowledge of the divine essence puts man beyond the status of the pilgrim, either permanently if

---

[22] Aristotle, *Physics* I, c.1 (184b10).
[23] Cf. Duns Scotus, *Ordinatio,* prol., n.61-65, 141ss (I, 37-40, 95ss); I, d.3, n.25-26, 56, 58, 61 (III, 16-17, 18, 38-39, 40, 42); *ibid.,* n.158-161 (III, 95-100).
[24] Cf. *supra* 7.21.
[25] Cf. *Quodl.* q. 6, 6.18-6.19.
[26] Cf. *supra* 7.21.
[27] Cf. *Quodl.* q. 6, 6.20.

he possesses such knowledge permanently or for the time being if he has it only for a time. The example provides proof of this.[28]

It is also proved by argument in this way: Where any object of science is concerned, apart from intuitive knowledge, it is possible to have abstractive knowledge that is most distinct. Now God as such is an object of some science. Therefore, besides intuitive knowledge of him it is possible to have a most distinct knowledge of this sort, which was what we set out to prove. For such knowledge does not put one outside the pilgrim state and yet it would include virtually and evidently all necessary truths about God.

7.24 Proof of the major:[29] Every science is concerned with the thing but not precisely as existing. I understand this to mean that although the existence itself is seen to be something in the object or associated with the object, it is not necessarily required that existence actually pertains to the object insofar as the object is knowable by way of demonstration.

This is evident from the mind of the Philosopher:[30] "Demonstration concerns necessary truths and definition is a scientific process. Now just as scientific knowledge cannot be sometimes knowledge and sometimes ignorance, so neither can demonstration nor definition be sometimes the sort of things they are and at other times not the sort of things they are." From this he concludes:[31] "Therefore, neither definition nor demonstration are possible in relation to perishable individuals for perishing things are not revealed to those who have scientific knowledge when they have passed from our perception. Though their meaning remains in the soul unchanged, there will no longer be a definition or demonstration." I understand the meaning of the Philosopher to be this: If there were definitions or demonstrations of the contingent or the perishable as such, these would exist at one time and not at another. For even though the concept of the perishable object remained in the soul, it would still follow that one would know it at one time and not know it another time and there would be a demonstration of it at one time and not at another. But this is impossible.

28 Cf. *supra* 7.20.

29 Cf. *supra* 7.23.

30 Aristotle, *Metaph.* VII, c.15 (1039b30-1040a7); *Anal. post.* (71b15-16); (75b24-25).

31 Aristotle, *Metaph.* VII, c.15 (1040a-10).

7.25 From the foregoing,[32] then, I obtain this proposition: Since the notion can remain in the soul even if the actual existence of the object does not remain, it follows that such existence is not essential to the object insofar as it can be known scientifically. For the scientific definition or notion cannot remain the same in the soul if what is essential to such knowledge does not remain. But whether an object that can be known scientifically is able or not able to exist in reality, at least its notion as an object of scientific knowledge can remain the same in the soul even if its existence does not continue. Scientific knowledge, therefore, abstracts from existence in the sense that actual existence is not included in its definition as an object that can be known scientifically [i.e., by way of demonstration].

7.26 In accord with this conclusion one could draw this following corollary. It is clear how theology can exist as a science in the intellect of a person in this life who retains his pilgrim status. For the intellect that can possess a concept which virtually includes all necessary truths about that object, both those that are immediate and those which are known by means of the others, can have a complete science of that object. The intellect of the pilgrim can have such a concept of God. Therefore, [it can have a theology or scientific knowledge of God].

7.27 The minor is manifest. A most distinctive concept of the subject of theology (which is God) is possible apart from intuitive knowledge and such a concept contains virtually and evidently all necessary truths about that subject. However, it cannot contain contingent truths, for these are not apt by nature to be included in the notion of any subject, for only such truths as are necessary are included sufficiently in any simple concept.

However, there are some necessary truths about contingent things, not indeed about their actuality but about their possibility. Such truths can also be known scientifically in the aforesaid way. Truths of this type, for instance, are 'God has the power to create, the power to raise from the dead, the power to beatify' and so on with all the other articles of faith that concern the contingent. Beyond these necessary truths about what God can do, however, nothing can be known about him in a properly scientific way so far as this property [of omnipotence] is concerned.

---

[32] Cf. *supra* 7.24.

Therefore, a pilgrim in this present life would be a theologian in a perfectly scientific way, if, in virtue of the most distinct concept of divinity obtainable apart from intuitive knowledge, he knew all necessary truths in an orderly fashion, both those which refer to intrinsic properties which are there necessarily and those which concern what is possible externally.

7.28 [The view of Henry of Ghent][33] From this it follows that if theology is assumed to be properly science in some light other than the light of glory but more than the light of faith, and that such light would be the knowledge or the concept of the object, then such an opinion would be true. But the one who defended this opinion concerning the light [namely Henry] apparently did not understand it in this way, for according to him the light would be that in which the object would be known and not be, it seems, the formal meaning or the formal knowledge of the object itself, as is claimed here.

3. Concerning the Third Conclusion

7.29 [*Exposition of Proof*] Our third conclusion[34] is this. By his purely natural endowments, man in the present life cannot demonstrate as a reasoned fact that God is omnipotent. Proof of this conclusion: A mediate proposition cannot be known as a reasoned fact except by means of the appropriate immediate proposition. This can be known simply from its terms especially from the meaning of the subject term, namely from the fact that the subject includes the predicate and therefore includes the truth or knowledge of the proposition immediately. Therefore, the coordinate knowledge of the reasoned fact is only possible to an intellect possessing a concept of the subject that virtually and evidantly includes the whole coordination. But such a concept of God is not possible to a person in this life by purely natural means so long as he remains in the pilgrim state.

7.30 Proof of this: The only concepts such a person can have naturally are those caused by the agent intellect working with sense

[33] Henry of Ghent, *Quodl.* XII, q. 1 (Paris, 1518 ed., photoreprint Louvain; Bibliotheque S.J., 1961) fol. 483, Y-Z; q. 22, fol. 498, D; *Summa quaestionum ordinariarum*, art. 13, q. 2 (Paris, 1520 ed., photoreprint St. Bonaventure, N.Y.: Franciscan Institute, 1953) I, fol. 91r.

[34] Cf. *supra* 7.10.

images, for by God's common dispensation no other factor moves the mind of the pilgrim naturally. But agent intellect and sense images cannot give rise in us to a concept so distinctive of God that it contains virtually and evidently the whole orderly sequence of demonstrable truths including that of his omnipotence in either sense.[35] The proof for this last statement depends on [my] solution to the question: 'In what manner is God knowable to one in this life?'[36]

7.31 This brief sketch of the salient points, however, can be given here. The most perfect simple concept a pilgrim can attain of God by natural means does not transcend the most perfect idea of God possible to the metaphysician, for the knowledge of faith does not yield a simple concept of God. It only inclines us to assent to propositions which are not evident from the meaning of the simple terms they contain. Faith produces no simple conception, then, that goes beyond all simple concepts of the metaphysician. Added evidence is this. A believing and an infidel metaphysician have the same concept, for when the believer affirms something of God that is denied by the infidel, they do not contradict each other in words alone but in what they mean.

7.32 Now the most perfect simple concept a metaphysician gets of God, however, does not include evidently an orderly sequence of truths extending all the way to this proposition: 'God is omnipotent, where omnipotent is understood in either sense. For many philosophers have presumably had concepts of God that are the most perfect it is possible for one in this life to reach by natural means. And still they were unable to arrive at a knowledge of this truth. But it would have been possible to do so had they had such a simple concept. Indeed it would have been almost necessary for them to do so, for by means of such a concept they would have perceived the immediate truth of the proposition from which omnipotence follows, and by making the necessary deduction they would have reached this mediate truth.

7.33 There is another way to prove this point. The first principle proper to God reached by the metaphysician is known to him only as a simple fact. But it would have been known to him as a reasoned fact if he could have a concept of God that included virtually

35 Cf. Duns Scotus, *Ordinatio,* prol., n.41 (I, 23-24); I, d.2, n.39 (II, 148-149); d.3, n.230ss (III, 138ss).
36 Cf. Duns Scotus, *Ordinatio* I, d.3, n.1-5, 10-68 (III, 1-3, 4-48).

and evidently the orderly sequence of truths about God. Therefore, [he had no such concept].

7.34 Proof of the first proposition, namely the first principle
proper to God reached by the metaphysician is known to him at
best as a simple fact. The premise which provides the means for
inferring anything proper to God is always some particular proposition in which a predicate pertaining to a created being is asserted
of some being. From such a premise the metaphysician draws a
conclusion in which a predicate proper to God is affirmed of some
being. He argues, for instance, in this way: 'Some being is caused,
therefore something is an uncaused cause,' or 'Some being is finite,
therefore some being is infinite,' or 'Some being is possible, therefore some being is necessary.'[37] Proof that all these conclusions follow is found in the fact that the less perfect condition cannot be
true of anything unless the more perfect condition also is true of
something, for the imperfect depends upon the perfect. All these
inferences, it is clear, are only proofs of the simple fact.

7.35 [*Objections*] To the foregoing these objections are raised:

According to the first proof of the first conclusion,[38] the will
provides a means for inferring omnipotence of God by a demonstration of the reasoned fact. And the intellect of one in this life
can know there is in God a will, in fact the first and most perfect
will. Therefore, the intellect can also know God is omnipotent
through a demonstration of the reasoned fact.

7.36 Also, every true and necessary proposition whose terms are
primitive or irreducibly simple concepts is self-evident. But a proposition asserting any attribute of God is this sort of proposition.
Therefore, [it is self-evident].

7.37 Furthermore, the known properties of a natural being imply
that God has certain perfections. Imperfection in what is mobile
implies perfection in the first mover. From natural effects, therefore,
the philosopher of nature can know God by demonstration of the
simple fact. If the metaphysician could only know of God through
proofs of simple fact, his knowledge would not transcend physics
or natural philosophy.

---

[37] Cf. Duns Scotus, *Ordinatio* I, d.2, n.41-147 (II, 149-215).
[38] Cf. *supra* 7.16.

7.38 [*Answer to the Objections*] Look for the answers else-where.[39]

4. Concerning the Fourth Conclusion

7.39 Next we must consider the conclusions involving a demon-stration of the simple fact, the first of which is about immediate omnipotence with respect to every possible.[40] Here we shall first explain what immediacy means; second, what the philosophers held; third, what our position should be.

1. *The Meaning of Immediacy*

7.40 The mediacy of a cause to an effect can be understood in two ways; (1) a cause that causes by means of some intervening cause, or (2) a cause that causes by means of some effect. For not every effect that is intermediate with respect to a further effect is also a cause of the latter. Consequently the immediacy of an active cause to its effect can be understood either as excluding every intermediary active cause or as excluding every prior intervening effect.

7.41 If 'immediacy' means both types of mediacy are ruled out, then I say that not only philosophers but also theologians would deny God is immediately omnipotent, for they admit that God cannot cause a relation without first (either in time or in the order of nature) causing its foundation. And so he is not able to cause immediately every effect whatsoever, i.e., without causing previously, by a priority of nature, some intermediate effect as it were.

7.42 Hence, the problem is limited to immediacy in the sense of excluding an intervening efficient cause. The effective intervention is understood quite generally to cover the case where the causation of the intermediate cause extends either (a) to the main effect, or (b) only to some effect that is prior or dispositional with respect to the main effect.

---

[39] Cf. Duns Scotus, *Ordinatio* I, d.2, n.29 (II, 140-141); d.3, n.65 (III, 46-47). The two additions found in the Wadding-Vivès edition, in the translators' judg-ment, cannot be ascribed to Scotus himself.

[40] Cf. *supra* 7.9.

2. The View of the Philosophers

7.43 What the philosophers held was our second point.[41] It seems they felt that not only was God's immediate omnipotence undemonstrable, but that it was simply impossible that he could be omnipotent in this way. The basis for their view seems to be this proposition: "A source or principle that is necessary and absolutely perfect is not related immediately to anything in a contingent fashion." The proof is this: No novelty or contingency could be ascribed to what immediately emanates from such a source. To begin with, this principle, since it is simply necessary, can behave in but one way. And given this uniform behavior there is nothing else needed for it to act nor is there anything to impede its action. It is not an imperfect principle and therefore it cannot be impeded or be insufficient or require anything else.[42]

7.44 If the aforesaid proposition were true (viz. that a necessary and sufficient principle could not produce anything immediately and at the same time contingently), it would follow at once that it could not cause every possible thing immediately. This implication is proved first generally. Then it is proved specifically of motion, for it follows that God cannot cause movement immediately, whether this be locomotion in particular or, more specifically, the circular movement of the heavens.

7.45 This implication can be proved, it seems, according to the mind of the Philosopher.

First, generally, if God could cause every effect immediately without any secondary cause, he could deprive secondary causes of their proper action. But from the exegesis of the Commentator[43] on a text of the *Metaphysics*, "When beings have no action of their own, they have no essence of their own," it is clear the Philosopher considers it incongruous that God should be able to destroy the essences of all other things, since he holds that some things other than God are formally necessary.

7.46 Confirmation: If God could cause any effect independently of the ordered sequence of causes in the universe, the causal order that exists between the causes would not be simply necessary.

41 Cf. *supra* 7.39.

42 Aristotle, *Physics* VIII, c.6 (259b32-260a19); *Metaph.* XII, c.7 (1072a-20-25).

43 Averroes, *Metaph.* IX, com. 7 (*Aristotelis opera cum commentariis Averroes* [Venetiis: Apud Juntas, 1512], VIII, fol. 231v, H).

Consequently, it would not be essential either—something the philosophers would consider incongruous.

7.47 Secondly, the implication is shown to hold particularly of movement. According to the Philosopher in the *Physics*[44] an infinite power cannot immediately move a body in time. If it could, some finite power could move the body in equal time. For, as he argues there, if the motive power were increased, the time it takes to move would be shortened. Therefore, according to Aristotle's mind it follows that God could not immediately cause motion properly so-called. For, since motion involves succession, it necessarily will take time.

7.48 Suppose this objection is raised. By an instantaneous change without any succession, God can cause the thing moved to pass to that stage to which it is moved in time by a finite cause. Answer: This does not solve the difficulty for God cannot cause immediately the circular movement of the heavens. He cannot cause it in time as is admitted, nor in an instant, for in that instant the heavens as a whole and each of its parts would be in the same place as they were before. Therefore, in that instant the heavens would not be moved.

7.49 Thirdly, it seems that the same point can be established as regards every material effect, for it seems that such effects are produced by a transmutation of matter. In the *Metaphysics*[45] Aristotle proves, apparently against Plato, that what is separated from matter cannot transmute matter immediately. The Commentator says in the same place:[46] "It is impossible that a form separated from matter transforms matter. Nothing transmutes matter except what is in matter, and this is relevant to those who say the world is generated and that the one who transmutes it is an individual thing or something individual like a particular body."

7.50 Finally, it seems that these proofs can be confirmed from the mind of the Philosopher in the *Physics*.[47] What he wants to say there, apparently, is that everything God can cause immediately and as total cause, he causes necessarily. For it seems that when the effects depends totally and exclusively on the agent, the only grounds for introducing contingency as regards causing or not

44 Aristotle, *Physics* VIII, c.10 (266a24-266b6).
45 Aristotle, *Metaph.* VII, c. 8 (1033b25-1034a8).
46 Averroes, *Metaph.* VII, com. 28 (VIII, fol. 178r, C).
47 Aristotle, *Physics* VIII, c.6 (259b32-260a19).

causing is some mutability in the agent. If God could cause immediately everything causable, every one of these things would depend totally and exclusively on him, and consequently, God would
cause everything causable necessarily. From this many incongruities
would follow, namely that secondary causes would be deprived of
their activity, which the first reason[48] touched on; that God would
cause immediately every movement, which the second proof[49] mentioned; and that God would cause immediately every material effect, which the third reason[50] brought up.

3. Solution

7.51 As regards the third point, it should be maintained: (a) according to the common opinion of the theologians, God is so omnipotent that without any other agent, he can cause everything
causable, and still (b) this fact cannot be demonstrated even by a
demonstration of the simple fact.

(a) According to the theologians God has immediate omnipotence

7.52 The first point is proved by authority: "In the beginning
God created the heavens and the earth." [Genesis 1:1][51]

7.53 A reason is also adduced to prove this. The active power of
any secondary cause exists in the first cause in a more eminent way
than in the second cause. Now what possesses the active power more
eminently can cause the effect, it seems, without the intervention
of what possesses it only in a lesser degree. To produce an effect no
imperfection is required in the active power. For imperfection is
not essential to acting, it is rather an impediment.[52]

Confirmation: We see equivocal causes producing effects as perfect as those of univocal causes. This would not happen unless they
possessed active power sufficient for perfect causation. But they do
not possess univocal power, only eminent power. Therefore, [this
eminent power suffices].

7.54 This reasoning,[53] although it seems probable, would not be
a demonstration for the Philosopher. For he would deny this propo-

48 Cf. *supra* 7.45.
49 Cf. *supra* 7.47.
50 Cf. *supra* 7.49.
51 Genesis 1:1.
52 Cf. Duns Scotus, *Ordinatio* I, d.8, n.223-306 (IV, 279-328).
53 Cf. *supra* 7.53.

sition: 'Everything that possesses in itself eminently or virtually the active power of the proximate cause, can produce the effect of this proximate cause immediately.' For he would say, a cause with such eminent power can indeed produce the effect of such a power, but only in its own orderly way, which means it functions precisely as a higher and more remote cause.

7.55 To the claim that no imperfection is required for causing[54] he would give this reply. When I say 'cause immediately' I assert two things: (1) causation—which requires perfection, and (2) immediacy or the way it takes place—which requires some measure of imperfection. Consequently, imperfection is needed in the agent, not indeed as the basis for causing but as a necessary condition for causing immediately.

For where an essential order exists, nothing can be adjacent to the least perfect unless it is in some measure imperfect. If it were right next to the most imperfect, the perfect would be equally immediate to every other member distinct from itself. And then an essential order would not obtain among these things, even as there would be no such order or sequence among the natural numbers if each proceeded from unity with equal immediacy.

7.56 From this it appears that the Philosopher would deny 'The more perfect a cause, the more immediately it causes,' if by 'more immediately' we mean the exclusion of intervening causal agents. Furthermore, he would say 'The more perfect the superior cause, the more the intermediary causes through which it acts.' These intermediary agents are not required to contribute causal perfection. This exists already in all its fulness and perfection in the first cause alone. They are needed to tone down the perfection gradually until the least perfect effect is achieved. Such a tempering occurs only where there is a diminution of perfection and some measure of imperfection is introduced.

(b) *Immediate omnipotence is not demonstrable as a simple fact*

7.57 Proofs for the second point,[55] namely that this truth is not demonstrable by a demonstration of the simple fact.[56]

---

54 Cf. *ibid.*

55 Cf. *supra* 7.51.

56 Cf. Duns Scotus, *Ordinatio* I, d.2, n.118-120, 178-181 (II, 193-197, 234, 236); d.42 (VI, 341-349).

The first proof is from authority. Philosophers could have arrived at a knowledge of such truths as are demonstrable as simple facts. Now they were unable to reach a knowledge of this truth. Indeed they held the opposite view. This hardly seems probable if the truth in question were demonstrable as a simple fact.

7.58 The second proof is from reason. Nothing about the way causes are ordered or interrelated implies the superior cause can produce the same effects with or without the inferior cause. The sun alone, for instance, cannot generate a man without a father's intervention though it can do so with the father. By the same token then, nothing about the way causes are interrelated implies that a first cause can produce the same effect without the secondary cause that it can produce together with it.

7.59 For other kinds of causes this is even more obvious. Suppose it were true, as some claim, that an essential order exists among materials or material causes. Suppose, for instance, that the matter immediately informed by the intellectual soul is the body with its organs, and that this in turn is composed of other materials, and ultimately of matter that is primary in an unqualified sense and is the matter proper to the first substantial form. It is not necessary that this primary matter be able to be the immediate matter of every form that can inform a secondary or higher form of matter.

7.60 It is clear the same holds good of forms. There is no need that everything that can be immediately informed by a secondary form can also be immediately informed by the first form. This is true whether the forms be first and second in the order of generation or that of perfection.[57]

What was said of the material and formal causes would be more convincing if the theory of a plurality of forms, which is not at issue here, were true. For our purposes, however, it suffices that if there were such an order among material and formal causes, the first cause would not have to be the immediate cause of everything causable. Still less then, among efficient causes where such an order does in fact exist, must the first cause be able to be the immediate cause of everything.

7.61 This also appears clear in the case of the efficient causes of knowledge. As the *Physics*[58] puts it, principles are the causes for

57 Cf. Duns Scotus, *Ordinatio* IV, d.11, q.3, n.22-57 (ed. Vivès, XVII, 388-438).
58 Aristotle, *Physics* II, c.9 (200a15-16).

knowing conclusions. The first principle has truth most evidently. It also contains eminently and virtually the truth of all the propositions that follow from it. Its ability to be the immediate cause of knowing each of these propositions, however, is not required. Indeed to acquire knowledge of a remote conclusion it is necessary to use intermediary steps in an orderly way.

7.62 Lastly, it appears clear in the case of final causes. It is not necessary that the last in a chain of final causes be the immediate end of each of the links. An end close at hand is only linked to the ultimate end by some intervening cause. For example, the exterior organs for eating and drinking are aimed at health only by means of their own ends or purposes, namely eating and drinking.

(c) The opposite view cannot be demonstrated

7.63 Although the theologians' view is not demonstrable, since it is in fact true, its opposite is not demonstrable either. For this reason the arguments adduced for the philosophers' view should be answered.

To the first:[59] The theologian might well concede the first cause can deprive these caused causes not only of their activity but also of their entity, for it can annihilate them. In calling the eviternal perpetual, however, he does not agree with the Philosopher's statement that all perpetual things are formally necessary. For it is simply possible for the eviternal not to exist even though this is not by reason of some intrinsic passive potency like that found in perishable things.

7.64 Another answer is this. God could deprive secondary beings of their activity simply by anticipating their causality and producing the effects they might have caused. He would not need to deprive them of their entity. They could remain in existence and yet not produce their effects because these were caused immediately by another cause. Still they could have caused those effects. This particular fire, for instance, might remain in existence without producing fire in this wood because this was anticipated by a stronger agent which set it afire. Yet it could have caused this effect for it has the form of fire which is the source for setting things on fire.

---

59 Cf. *supra* 7.45.

7.65 As for the Commentator's dictum: 'If beings have no action of their own, they have no essences of their own,'[60] how is the antecedent to be understood? Actually or dispositionally? Not just actually! For in such a case his argument would be: 'If the less fundamental is removed, so too is the more fundamental.' But this would be a fallacy of the consequent, for the absence of action could be due to other factors. A stronger agent might anticipate the action or a counteragent might prevent it. Hence his meaning must be: 'Dispositionally or virtually they have no action of their own.' In such a case, it would indeed follow that they have no essence of their own, for every agent by its own form and power possesses its action virtually even when it is not actually producing it.

That the antecedent should be so interpreted can be gathered from the preceding remarks of the Commentator. "These agree that no being has any natural action of its own." And he adds: "If beings have no action of their own"—i.e., naturally or dispositionally in accord with their proper nature—"they have no essences of their own." The 'moderns,' against whom he argues here, assume one agent produces all beings without benefit of any intermediary. But this is not what Christians claim. As Augustine[61] says: "God administers the things he has created in such a way that he lets them exercise their proper functions." God could have done everything. By so doing he would not have destroyed the entities of things, although he would have left them idle and barren. Still he preferred to endow them with active powers and actions of their own even as he gave to each its entity. For he did not deprive them entirely of the perfection of which they were capable.

7.66 Answer to the *third* reason:[62] The Philosopher does not deny the material form is induced in matter immediately by God. Later on in the question on good fortune[63] we shall discuss what Aristotle thought about the intellectual soul. But what about that text of the *Metaphysics*[64] where the Commentator is cited to the effect that nothing immaterial can transmute matter immediately? The theologian would deny this, particularly if this is understood of

[60] Cf. *ibid.*

[61] Augustine, *De Civit. Dei* VII, c.30; PL 41,220.

[62] Cf. *supra* 7.49. Scotus apparently forgot the original sequence in which these objections occurred. He calls this 'the second reason,' and calls the second objection, which he answers in 7.70, 'the third reason.'

[63] Cf. *Quodl.,* q. 21.

[64] Aristotle, *Metaph.* VII, c.8 (1033a25-1033b11).

God, as seems to be the case from the Commentator's allusion to those 'who say the world is generated.'[65] He repeats the same opinion later on in the third comment:[66] "What moves matter has to be a body with an active quality." And he ascribes this view to Aristotle.

7.67 If the text of Aristotle can be given a sound interpretation whereas that of the Commentator cannot, it seems better to make sense of Aristotle and argue that Averroes misunderstood him. This can be done here, it seems. For the present I will only touch the problem briefly, but it appears Aristotle here is arguing against Plato to prove the Ideas are not necessary for generation, since this individual suffices to beget that individual. What is more, the Ideas cannot beget an individual [since they are universals]. If the one generating is not an individual, what is generated will not be individual either.

7.68 Both inferences suffice to show a Platonic Idea begets nothing, but they must not be applied to the present case, namely where God is concerned.

For if an Idea would generate, it would function as a univocal cause, for [a prototype and its effect must be] of the same species. No univocal cause is necessary, however, unless it be composite and material like the thing generated. This is the proof of the first part of the argument, viz. that the ideas are unnecessary.

7.69 The second part, namely that the ideas cannot generate, makes this point. If the univocal generator is not an individual material composite, what it generates will not be individual.

Now God can be a cause of generation and he is required for generation, not as a univocal cause but as an equivocal cause. And in this role he acts as the supreme equivocal cause in virtue of which every other cause, be it univocal or equivocal, exercises its function.

7.70 Answer to the *second* reason:[67] We have to concede absolutely that both Aristotle and Averroes[68] denied that God could immediately move a body. And on this point the theologian must contradict them both. They did hold, however, that God could move the heavens mediately, that is to say, by means of an Intelli-

65 Averroes, *Metaph.* VII, com. 28 (VIII, fol. 178r, C).

66 *Ibid.*, com. 31 (fol. 181v, G-H).

67 Cf. *supra* 7.47.

68 Averroes, *Metaph.* XII, com. 41 (VIII, fol. 323v-325v).

gence which is the proper mover of the heavens. Of this we will say more in answering the third of the arguments at the beginning of the question.[69]

7.71 Answer to the *fourth* argument[70] used to confirm the first three proofs: One can say it was not the mind of Aristotle that God is an absolutely necessary cause of whatever he causes immediately, i.e., without some intervening agent. This will be discussed later in speaking of the intellectual soul in the question on good fortune.[71] Only if every medium whatsoever be excluded, be this (1) an agent productive of the effect itself or of some prior disposition towards the effect, or (2) some medium caused or prior to the effect, did Aristotle believe that God does necessarily whatever he can do immediately. Whatever can act without benefit of any intervening prior effect or previous agent, acts necessarily. And he gives this reason. Since the effect *in toto* depends immediately on God alone, he would say, any novelty in being or contingency it might have would be traceable in the last analysis to some novelty in God. He makes this point in Bk. VIII of the *Physics*.[72] For if no prior effect, no other agent, no dispositional cause is involved or intervenes, this novelty in the pattern of change or in the absolutely first effect, whatever this may be, would come immediately from God.[73]

7.72 But consider something God can cause immediately in the sense that he effects it directly and not just through some vicarious agent, and yet he makes use of some dispositional cause or at least some prerequisite effect. Now Aristotle would not claim it was with simple necessity that God causes such an effect. It is the necessity of inevitability only, and presupposes the dispositional causes and prerequisite effects are given.

7.73 On neither of these points of course would the theologian agree with Aristotle, since he claims God by his will relates contingently and freely to every external thing that can be caused. Not only is necessity of immutability excluded but that of inevitability as well.

---

69 Cf. *infra* 7.99ss.

70 Cf. *supra* 7.50.

71 Cf. *Quodl.* qq. 21, 21.45.

72 Aristotle, *Physics* VIII, c.6 (259b32-260a19).

73 Cf. Duns Scotus, *Ordinatio* I, d.8, n.223-306 (IV, 279-328).

7.74 Hence I admit Aristotle would in principle claim there are many things God is unable to cause immediately, for example, everything whose production is simply contingent and neither immutably nor inevitably necessary. But the theologian would contradict him here, as was said.

7.75 [*Conclusion*] Consequently, our fourth main conclusion about demonstration is this. It is true that God is omnipotent immediately as regards everything causable but we cannot demonstrate this by a demonstration of simple fact.

5. Concerning the Fifth Conclusion

7.76 [*Exposition and Proof*] The fifth main conclusion[74] is this: It can be demonstrated as a simple fact to a person in this life that God is omnipotent mediately or immediately. That is to say, he can cause everything causable either immediately or by means of something subject to his causality.

7.77 The proof of the conclusion is this. There must be an end to efficient causes, as Bk. II of the *Metaphysics*[75] proves. Put briefly, Aristotle's argument is this. The totality of effects itself has a cause which is not part of the whole, for then the same thing would be cause of itself. Hence it is something outside the totality as a whole. Consequently, if causes cannot ascend indefinitely, not only will each effect be caused, but the whole multitude will be caused, and hence by something outside the whole multitude. And here it will end with a cause that is simply first.[76]

7.78 But another proof of this conclusion can be given. It is this. The higher the efficient cause, the more perfect its causality. Therefore, if above a given cause there is another infinitely superior in causing, this will be infinitely more perfect in causality, and hence will possess an infinitely perfect causality. But no causality that is caused or dependent in causing is infinitely perfect, because it is imperfect with reference to that on which it depends. Therefore, if the causes ascended *ad infinitum,* some cause will be uncaused in an absolute sense and independent in the exercise of its causation. Hence, with this the sequence of causes will end, so that this will be an efficient cause that is not itself caused nor dependent in

74 Cf. *supra* 7.11.
75 Aristotle, *Metaph.* II, c.2 (994a-20).
76 Cf. Duns Scotus, *Ordinatio* I, d.2, n.41ss (II, 149ss).

causing. And from it a lesser cause will get all its causality or at least will cause in virtue of it.

7.79 From this our thesis follows. Everything causable mediately or immediately by a lesser cause can be caused by a higher cause, at least by means of the proximate cause. Consequently, the first cause is omnipotent in the sense we understand it in this conclusion.

7.80 [*Objections to this argument*] This argument,[77] it seems, could be challenged on two counts:

First, one could say the order of efficient causes indeed ends with one efficient principle; yet this is not God but some Intelligence which moves the first heaven. All natural reason deduces is that beyond such a motor, God 'moves' immediately, but only as final cause. The Philosopher, it seems, attributed this manner of moving to God in Bk. XII of the *Metaphysics*[78] where he says God moves as loved and desired.

7.81 Secondly, one could say there is no proof the first efficient cause, whatever it may be, has power to cause everything in some way, namely immediately or mediately. Its only power is over those effects related to it through a chain of causes. What needs proof is that there are no other possible effects outside this concatenation.

7.82 [*Answer to the objections*] The fact that there is but one being that exists of itself and does not come from another rules out both of these assumptions. From this it follows that there is but one unique agent, independent in its acting. For what is dependent in its being, is dependent in its acting, if it acts.

REPLY TO THE INITIAL ARGUMENTS

1. Reply to the Argument about Infinite Power

7.83 As for the first of the initial arguments,[79] two aspects must be investigated, first the antecedent and afterwards the implication itself.

[*To the Antecedent*] As for the antecedent, some say Aristotle thought the First Being did not have infinite power intensively. In

---

[77] Cf. *supra* 7.78.
[78] Aristotle, *Metaph.* XII, c.7 (1072a25-1072b15).
[79] Cf. *supra* 7.3.

other words, his power was not infinite in depth. It was just that what power he has is exercised over an infinite time span.[80]

7.84 For the reason he gives entails only that the First Being moves with a movement that is infinite. But this movement is only infinite in duration and for this a power infinite in duration suffices.

7.85 This is challenged on two counts: first, that it misrepresents the mind of Aristotle; second, that the proof given is no good.[81]

Consider the first.[82] From the antecedent 'God is of infinite power,' Aristotle concluded 'Therefore, this power cannot be in magnitude or have magnitude, be this infinite or finite.' For there is no such thing as infinite magnitude, he argued, and for any power of finite magnitude, there can be some power which is greater. What Aristotle understood by infinite power in the antecedent, then, was something, that to his mind, was not consistent with the opposite of the consequent, viz. to be in magnitude or to have magnitude. To say he thought the opposite of the consequent was compatible with the antecedent, would be to claim he drew an inference which to his mind was invalid. Now a power of infinite duration is compatible with having magnitude, which is the opposite of the consequent. For it is clear the heavens have magnitude, and yet—according to him—they have a power of infinite duration. Indeed according to his statements in Bk. IX of *Metaphysics* and Bk. I of *On the Heavens and Earth*,[83] and many other places he claims: "Everything perpetual is formally necessary and thus if it is active, it has an active power of infinite duration." Hence, in the antecedent, according to his mind, Aristotle did not understand infinite power to be one of duration, but rather some other kind, one that was incompatible with magnitude. But this could only be intensive infinity. I agree therefore with this conclusion that Aristotle—whether or not he proved his point sufficiently—was thinking of intensive infinity of power.

7.86 The second point about the proof remains to be discussed, namely whether it is any good.[84] About this I say: One can infer

---

80 Cf. Duns Scotus, *Ordinatio* I, d.2, n.111ss (II, 189ss).

81 Cf. Duns Scotus, *Ordinatio* I, d.2, n.74ss (II, 174ss).

82 Cf. *supra* 7.83.

83 Aristotle, *Metaph.* IX, c.8 (1050b-8, 20-22); c.7 (1072b10-15): *De caelo* I, c.12 (283b6).

84 Cf. *supra* 7.84.

as much about the perfection of a power from what it is able to do as from what it actually does. Now Aristotle's antecedent, namely 'God moves with a movement that is infinite,' is false according to the theologians. Nevertheless many of them concede that he could have moved with a movement that was infinite. They admit this also as regards the past, even as all concede he can continue future movement *ad infinitum*. Where they part company with the Philosopher, however, is in his assumption that this power is necessarily actualized. For between two related extremes each of which is immutable in itself, the relationship that holds is absolutely necessary. Such are God and the heavens. They are necessarily related with a necessity of immutability. From this it follows further that the movement caused in the heavens by God is also necessary, though not with the necessity of immutability, but with that of inevitability; therefore, it cannot cease. The theologian not only disagrees with Aristotle's first proposition that a necessary and absolute relation holds between God and the heavens. He also rejects the second proposition about [the necessary motion of the heavens], for the theologian does not assume that God moves the heavens necessarily. He only claims that God could produce movement for an infinite period of time. Now one could conclude that his power is infinite from the fact not only that he does move in this way but that he can move in this way.

7.87 But does this imply the power is also intensively infinite? I say it does. For no power can move for an infinite time unless it does so of itself or in virtue of another power. Even if we assume the latter, we must eventually end up with some first power which moves of itself. Therefore, Aristotle argues that the power of the first mover is such that it moves of itself and not in virtue of another. From this it can be inferred that such a power is intensively infinite. Something that has active power of itself also has entity of itself. What possesses something of itself possesses it in all the fulness it is possible to have. For nothing possesses a limited amount of anything unless it gets it from some agent which limits it to that specific degree. Suppose one being possessed of itself the plentitude of entity whereas another of itself had only a limited entity. There would be absolutely no more reason why one rather than the other had the plentitude of being. On the contrary, it would seem to be pure chance that this is so and there can be no chance in things which exist of themselves. From this, then, it follows that the first mover moves by itself and hence exists of itself. Since the fulness of active power and of entity is not possible without intensive infinity, it follows that the first mover possesses infinite power intensively.

7.88 An objection is raised to the statement in the antecedent that it moves with infinite motion.[85] According to you, the intended conclusion would follow just as well if the first mover moved with infinite motion but did so of itself.

I grant that the main strength of the argument comes from the fact, that it moves of itself. However, the argument based on infinite movement has some evidence in its favor for according to Aristotle the first movement is primarily infinite and that is why it is more appropriate to the first mover. Now it is the primacy of movement that provides the means for inferring the intended conclusion, so that in the antecedent the phrase 'it moves with an infinite movement' must be understood of the first infinity, namely that which is not derived from the infinite movement of another but exclusively from the mover's own power.

7.89 [*To the implication*] Let us consider the implication in the first main argument.[86] Although an infinite active power is truly omnipotence, this inference does not follow: 'Natural reason can prove God has infinite power, therefore natural reason can prove God is omnipotent.' For it is not known by natural reason that infinite power is the same thing as omnipotence in the sense that the scope of God's power extends immediately to everything that is possible.

7.90 Consider the proof for the implication[87] that infinite power is omnipotence, namely 'No power can be greater than the infinite; one cannot even think of anything greater. But every power which is not omnipotence could be thought of as surpassed by a power which is omnipotence.' The Philosopher's answer would be this. The power that is supreme is not omnipotence as we understand omnipotence. Nevertheless it is infinite power. Because it is intensively infinite, we cannot even think that it is surpassed in intensity. Even though one could somehow think of it as being exceeded extensively (for it is not omnipotence as we understand it), one could not really think this in the technical sense of 'to

85 Cf. *supra* 7.3.
86 Cf. *supra* 7.3, 7.83.
87 Cf. *supra* 7.3.

think' or 'to understand,' since we cannot do so without contradiction. For the Philosopher would claim that the very idea of one and the same subject being omnipotent immediately as regards every possible is self-contradictory, since it would do away with the essential order of causes.

7.91 While it is true that the supreme or infinite active power is omnipotence, it is not known by natural reason that the highest power possible, even if it be intensively infinite, is omnipotence properly so-called, namely the power of causing immediately everything possible.

2. Reply to the Argument About the Generation of the Son.

7.92 [*Causal vs. Productive Powers*] As for the first negative argument, namely the one referring to the generation of the Son,[88] I have this to say: Active power can mean two things: (1) a causative power whose correlative is the possible, i.e., the causable—and this is the proper sense of the term—or (2) it can be understood in a wider sense as a productive power whose correlative is the possible, i.e., the object producible. Therefore, omnipotence can be understood in two ways. (1) As a causative power of everything causable and (2) as a productive power of everything producible. If it is understood in the second sense, only the Father is omnipotent. He is the fruitful source for producing anything producible. The Fathers of the Church, however, do not speak of omnipotence in this sense. They only speak of it insofar as it implies causative power in regard to everything causable, i.e., possible.[89] In this sense, neither the Son nor the Holy Spirit are 'possibles' although they are producible, for they are not able to be caused or produced with a distinct nature of their own. If we take omnipotence as the Fathers of the Church understand it, i.e., as a causative power of everything causable common to all three persons, it must be admitted absolutely that omnipotence does not refer to an intrinsic notional act [productive of a divine person]. Therefore, even if it could be demonstrated that God is omnipotent, it could not be demonstrated that he is potent as regards such notional acts.

---

88 Cf. *supra* 7.4.
89 Cf. Duns Scotus, *Ordinatio* I, d.20, n.24-34 (V, 313-318).

7.93 [*To the authorities cited*] It does seem, however, that the texts cited from Augustine[90] and Richard[91] conflict with what has just been said. To the citation from Augustine used against us, it can be replied, 'If the Father cannot generate the Son, or cannot generate a son equal to himself, he is not omnipotent,' is not a formal consequence or implication in the same way that an argument from the destruction of a quantitative part to the destruction of the whole would be a formal consequence.[92] But it is [a material consequence] from the destruction of something posterior which follows necessarily, to the destruction of what is prior. If the Father could not generate the Son or an equal son, it would be because this ability is neither a part of his essential perfection nor a personal property of his. The second possibility is excluded because that person [i.e., the Father] exists of himself, and therefore it is not repugnant to what is peculiarly his own to produce something actively. If the first alternative is the case, he would not have the perfect nature which in some person is able to produce everything producible. Therefore, even though the denial of the notional act does not formally entail the denial of omnipotence, by reason of its matter the consequence is valid for this person for whom such a notional act is compatible by reason of what is proper to him as a person.

7.94 Against this it is objected that, according to Richard,[93] the proper object of omnipotence seems to be God or a divine person. He says that if there were two omnipotent beings, one would make the other completely impotent. This would not follow unless the object of one's omnipotence was the other omnipotent.

7.95 This can be answered like the argument from Augustine[94] was. The inference 'He is omnipotent, therefore he is powerful as regards another God or omnipotent' does not hold like the consequence about the whole in quantity. For, if another God were assumed to exist, he would not be the object of omnipotence properly so-called, but would exist of himself necessarily. However,

90 Cf. *supra* 7.4.

91 Cf. *infra* 7.94, note 91.

92 For the distinction between material and formal consequences see E. A. Moody, *Truth and Consequence in Medieval Logic* (Amsterdam: North Holland Publ. Co., 1953), pp. 70-80.

93 Richard of St. Victor, *De Trin.* I, c.25; PL 196, 902.

94 Cf. *supra* 7.93.

the consequence holds for extrinsic objects. With his will one omnipotent agent could produce all possibles and everything that could coexist with them. The other omnipotent agent, however, could by his will impede the production of the same set of possible objects. Therefore the second would render the first totally impotent, not by acting or doing something to him but to the objects of his power.

7.96 If you say the two could always agree with each other about the objects to be willed, I answer: Although this seems to be pure fiction as regards objects to which both wills relate contingently and with an equal degree of independence, it would still follow that one omnipotent could make the other completely impotent, because there cannot be two total causes for one and the same effect. Either the effect would receive existence twice or else each cause as distinct in itself would not be the complete cause. But this omnipotent, who, according to your assumption, would agree with the other about the objects to be willed, could by his own will be their complete and total cause. Therefore, the other could not be a distinct total cause of the same set of objects. And what holds for two objects, holds for all. Just from the standpoint of the objects then, the will of one omnipotent agent could reduce the other to impotence in the sense that the second would be unable to actualize anything since the will of the first as a distinct and total cause of the same would prevent the second from doing anything.

7.95 To these answers[95] to the authorities of Augustine and Richard this objection is raised. The following are all formal consequences: 'If the Son is omniscient, he knows of the generation of the Father,' 'If he wills all things, he wills this generation.' Similarly then, 'He is omnipotent, therefore he can generate the Son' is a true and formal consequence and not just one that holds by reason of its matter.[96]

7.98 In answer one could say that the distribution in all these terms 'omnipotent,' 'omniscient,' and 'willing all' is not over acts but over objects of the same act. That is why one can infer formally that they hold for this object, for that object, and hence for any object whatsoever of such an act. Now the notional act is

---

[95] Cf. *supra* 7.93-94.

[96] Giles of Rome, *Sent.* I, d.20, princ.1, qq.1,2. in corp. (Venetiis, 1521, photoreprint Frankfurt am Main: Minerva, 1968), fol. 114-115.

a simple object of the divine knowledge and will of any divine person; but the notional act is not an object of omnipotence. That is why 'omniscient' and 'willing all' formally entail the knowledge and volition of the notional act whereas 'omnipotent' does not entail the power of producing that act. The reason for this difference is that the notional act is something that can be known and willed, but it is not simply a possible insofar as 'possible' means 'causable.' For although the notional act has the characteristic of being good and true, it does not have that of being causable or caused.

3. Reply to the Argument about the Creation of the Angels

7.99 As for the second argument[97] about the creation of the angels,[98] I concede that just as the proposition 'God can cause everything causable mediately or immediately' is demonstrable, so too one can demonstrate specifically that God can cause a particular causable, but only when the minor by which the conclusion is to be inferred is evident and demonstrated; not otherwise. As the Philosopher says:[99] "It happens that every mule is known to be sterile. But it is not known to hold for this mule, unless the minor 'This is a mule' is known to be true." Now the minor that allows one to conclude 'God can cause an angel' is the proposition 'The angel is causable.'

7.100 [*Two Questions. Is it demonstrable that the angel can be caused? What did Aristotle think about this?*] Some say this minor is merely believed but is not demonstrable.[100] Hence the conclusion is merely believed even though the major be demonstrable.

7.101 Secondly it is claimed that according to the Philosopher, one must deny the minor and hence the conclusion also. For they say it is clear from the *Metaphysics*[101] that the Philosopher held that since every Intelligence is necessary, each exists of itself. What is caused by another, however, is of itself nonbeing and in itself is only possible. On the other hand, the simply necessary is in no sense just a possible. Aristotle consequently did not hold both of these two contradictory propositions, viz. 'An Intelligence is neces-

97 Cf. *supra* 7.5.
98 Thomas, *Summa theol.* I, q.46,a.2 in corp.
99 Aristotle, *Anal. post.* I, c.1 (67a33-36).
100 Cf. *supra*, 7.96.
101 Aristotle, *Metaphysics*, XII, c.7 (1072b10-15).

sary' (a point he clearly held) and 'Nevertheless it is caused by another.'

7.102 Some[102] also say Aristotle held an Intelligence is infinite and from this it follows that it exists of itself, for finite is only what exists by means of another. Proof of the antecedent: In the *Metaphysics,* Bk. XII, chapter [7],[103] Aristotle states again that it was proved that the first mover cannot have magnitude because he has infinite power and no finite being has infinite power. And immediately afterwards, at the beginning of chapter [8],[104] he asks whether it is necessary to postulate one or several substances of this sort and decides that there are several depending on the distinct number of celestial movements. Therefore his intention, to put the two conclusions together, is to show there are many substances without magnitude because many have infinite power. And further on in the same chapter he says:[105] "It is clear then that there must be many substances which are of the same number [as the movements of the stars] and in their nature eternal and in themselves unmovable and without magnitude, for the reason mentioned above" in the previous chapter, namely, that they have infinite power, which cannot exist in finite magnitude; neither can it exist in infinite magnitude since there is no such thing.

7.103 We ought not to attribute to any author a false or absurd opinion, however, unless he states such expressly or unless it follows evidently from what he does say. Now the proposition 'An angel is a being which exists of itself' is not only false (as is obvious) but is absurd as well (since its opposite can be demonstrated, as we shall see). Since no text of Aristotle expressly states such a proposition, it seems unreasonable to attribute it to him.

7.104 [*Answer to the First Question. It is demonstrable that the angel is causable.*] In opposition to what has been said, therefore, I make two observations regarding this minor 'The angel is causable.' First, it is demonstrable; second, Aristotle admitted it.

Proof of the first. Two intellectual natures that are simply infinite cannot coexist. But an intellectual nature that exists of itself or is uncaused is simply infinite. Therefore, there cannot be several

---

[102] Henry of Ghent, *Quodl.* VI, q.14 in corp. (f.253); *Summa* a.25,q.3 in corp. (I, fol. 154r, H).

[103] Aristotle, *Metaphysics,* XII, c.7 (1073a4-12).

[104] *Ibid.,* c.8 (1073a15).

[105] *Ibid.,* c.8 (1073a37-b2).

intellectual natures that are simply uncaused. Now the first intellectual nature is uncaused; otherwise it would not be first. Therefore every other nature is caused.

7.105 The first proposition of this deduction [i.e., that two infinite intellectual natures are impossible] is proved at length in the question on the unicity of God.[106] Here I will touch on only one proof.

Each of these natures would understand the other most perfectly, that is to say, in all its intelligibility and comprehensibility. Similiarly each would love the other insofar as it is capable of being loved. Each would also comprehend and love himself in the same way. Thus each would be beatified in intellect and will not only by himself but by the other as well. And yet it is impossible that one and the same potency should simultaneously comprehend two objects each of which is infinitely adequate, for each would be fully equal to the total strength of that potency. Furthermore, one and the same power or potency cannot have two objects that are first to the same degree. But the essence of one would be the first object of his intellect; the essence of the other consequently could not be its first object, but neither could it be its secondary object. For since it is just as infinitely perfect as the first, it could not be posterior to it in entity. Consequently, it could not be posterior to it in intelligibility either. It is also impossible for one power to comprehend the essence of the other nature as perfectly as its own, particularly if its own nature does not include the other nature eminently, or if the other is not essentially dependent upon it, or if the two natures are not the same sort of thing. Yet all of these situations would be true on the assumption that God and an Intelligence were both infinite.

7.106 The second proposition of this deduction,[107] viz. a nature which exists of itself is infinite, appears clear from what was said above[108] about how the Philosopher proved the prime mover to be infinite because it has its power of itself and hence has the plentitude of power.

7.107 [*Answer to the Second Question. According to Aristotle, the angel is causable. Proof from the Metaphysics*] Proof of the second

---

106 Cf. Duns Scotus, *Ordinatio* I, d.2, n. 157-190 (II, 222-243).

107 Cf. *supra* 7.104.

108 Cf. *supra* 7.87.

point, namely that Aristotle admitted this minor[109] [i.e., that the angel is causable].

First proof from his mind in Bk. XII of the *Metaphysics*.[110]

He admits all things have an essential order to one another and even more so to one First Being. Now the intensively infinite cannot be subordinate to another as its end, for an infinite good does not exist for the sake of some other good. The good of the whole universe, however, is subordinated in two ways, namely (1) in the way one being is ordered to another and (2) in the way they are all ordered to something best which exists apart. Neither can the infinite be subordinated to some higher source for its active power is infinite. And also, according to him at the end of Bk. XII, "Things refuse to be governed badly, therefore one ruler let there be."[111]

7.108 It may be objected that Aristotle admitted an order among beings that have no matter because the second cause, although it is not produced by the first, still depends upon the first cause, as happens in the case of species of numbers and figures.[112]

7.109 Answer: Nothing depends for its being on anything that is not some kind of cause. The same holds true of its continuing to exist. What is said of number does not contradict this, for a lesser number taken potentially or materially is a part of a greater number. But a part functions as a material cause, as one gathers from Bk. V of the *Metaphysics*:[113] "Parts are causes of the whole in the sense that they are that out of which the whole is made." And Aristotle adds in the same place: "The parts are causes in the sense of being the substrate." If the smaller number be taken actually and formally, however, it is not a part of the larger number nor does the latter depend upon it for its being.

7.110 Furthermore, in the same Bk. XII of the *Metaphysics*[114] Aristotle declares that the first mover moves as the object of thought and desire. What can be known and loved, however, moves without being moved. It is in this way that God moves the Intelligence closest to him. Therefore, he is the cause of this Intelligence's intel-

---

109 Cf. *supra* 7.104.
110 Aristotle, *Metaphysics* XII, c.10 (1075a18-19).
111 Aristotle, *Metaphysics* XII, c.10 (1076a-5).
112 Aristotle, *Metaphysics* V, c.2 (1013b18-25).
113 *Ibid.*, V, c.2 (1013b18-25); cf. *Iliad*, 11, 204.
114 Aristotle, *Metaphysics* XII, c.7 (1072a27-28).

lection and they say this intellection, according to Aristotle, is identical with the substance of the Intelligence.

7.111 It may be objected that 'to move' in this case is understood metaphorically and that properly speaking it does not mean 'to cause something.' Answer: Every intellection not identical with its object is caused by that object, and according to the Commentator,[115] it appears this means it is caused efficiently, for he says there: "The bath insofar as it is in the mind moves as an efficient cause, and insofar as it exists outside the mind it moves as a final cause."

7.112 [*Proof from the Physics*] The same point[116] can be proved from Aristotle's mind in Bk. VIII of the *Physics*.[117] Here he shows that an infinitely powerful mover cannot move immediately. Now the heavens are moved; therefore they are moved immediately by someone with finite power. Such a proper mover is an Intelligence. Therefore, Aristotle wants to say the Intelligence is finite and hence does not exist of itself. The validity of this implication was established earlier.[118]

7.113 Another argument from the same Bk. VIII is this. There the Philosopher wants to show that a mover of infinite power moves the heavens with an infinite movement. But, as we said,[119] he does not do so immediately; therefore, he does so mediately, i.e., by means of an Intelligence. And the Commentator[120] affirms it to be the mind of Aristotle that a finite mover moves the heavens immediately and the infinite mover moves it mediately. So far as the heavens go, therefore, there are two ordered movers.

From this I argue that wherever several agents are essentially ordered, what the second receives from the first is either (a) its existence (e.g. the heavens and the sphere of fire) or (b) some influence, if not its existence (e.g. to put a ball in motion a bat must be given movement by the hand), or (c) both produce the same effect immediately, but according to a certain order, namely one is the major, the other the minor agent, but both achieve the same effect (e.g. the father and mother in the generation of off-

---

115 Averroes, *Metaphysics* XII, com. 36 (VIII, fol.318v,I-K).

116 Cf. *supra* 7.104.

117 Aristotle, *Physics* VIII, c.6 (259b32).

118 Cf. *supra* 7.86-7.88.

119 Cf. *supra* 7.47.

120 Averroes, *Metaphysics* XII, com.41 (VIII, fol.323v-325v).

spring according to the opinion that maintains the mother plays an active role).

In which of these three ways, I ask, are these two agents related to each other in moving the heavens? Certainly not in the third way, for it would follow immediately that the finite and the infinite power would move for an equal time, indeed for the same time period, since both cause the movement immediately as their proper effect. If it be the second way, we have what we intend to prove, since nothing receives from an Intelligence anything other than its essence according to Aristotle. If they are related in the first way, this is clearly our proposal. Obviously then Aristotle conceived these agents to be so ordered that the second came from the first. The first, in such a case, would move mediately and would give being and power to the immediate mover. And because it would give these perpetually, the first agent would be the cause of the perpetuity of the motion whereas the finitude of power which is not distinct from the angel's nature would be the cause of the succession in the movement, for the mobile could offer some resistance to a finite power, something it could not do to an infinite power.

7.114 [*Confirmation from Averroes and Avicenna*] A third proof for our claim[121] is to be found in what Averroes thought of the matter. Speaking of Aristotle's mind in *De substantia orbis*,[122] he writes: "The heavenly body not only needs the power of locomotion but also a power which gives it being, substance and eternal permanence," etc. Then he adds: "Some have said that he, viz. Aristotle, did not say that the sky had an efficient cause, but only a moving cause, and this was most absurd." Aristotle then maintained that the heavens, like the Intelligences, were formally necessary. For he held as a universal principle that every perpetual substance is formally necessary. This is obvious from Bk. IX of the *Metaphysics*[123] "Nothing perpetual is potential," etc. What his mind was on this subject appears obvious enough from Bk. XII of the *Metaphysics*.[124] That God be the cause of the being and substance of the Intelligence, then, is just as consistent with the mind of Aristotle, as is the view that he caused the being and substance of the heavens, which Averroes interpreted him to mean.

121 Cf. *supra* 7.104.
122 Averroes, *De substantia orbis*, c.2 (IX, fol. 6v,I; 7r,A).
123 Aristotle, *Metaphysics* IX, c.8 (1050b7-10,15-30).
124 Aristotle, *Metaphysics* XII, c.7 (1072b10-15.)

7.115 Furthermore, it is the express view of Avicenna[125] that every Intelligence is caused by the First Being. And perhaps he not only did not contradict Aristotle here but explained the manner and order of their production which Aristotle did not go into. If it be maintained that Aristotle thought that every Intelligence was produced immediately by the First Being, then Avicenna would indeed contradict him as to the order of their production, but not as regard the conclusion we set out to establish, namely that the Intelligence is produced. On this they would agree. As for the way it was caused, we know well enough that Avicenna did not think of it as involving change or novelty. According to him the complete being of the Intelligence would be always emanating from the First but its essence would be distinct and separate. It would be similar to the way we believe the Son to be always proceeding from the Father except that Father and Son have same essence. Or according to Aristotle, it would be like the perpetual light in transparent bodies that never fall into the shade of any body that could cause shadows in the universe. And still the sun would effectively cause this continual light in the luminous bodies, for such light is not said to exist of itself. If it did, it would not be the same kind of light as that in a part of a transparent body which is not always illuminated. For when it is illuminated anew, this is certainly caused by the sun. What is caused, however, is not the same in kind as what exists of itself.[126]

7.116 As for the proof that Aristotle thought the angel was not caused, because he held it to be formally necessary, I say that Aristotle did not consider 'caused' and 'formally necessary' to be mutually repugnant, since he says in the *Metaphysics*:[127] "The principles of perpetual things must be always most true, for they are the cause of truth in other things." Hence he admitted that perpetual things, which are formally necessary, have principles. Again he says in the chapter 'On the necessary' in the *Metaphysics*:[128] "There is nothing to prevent some necessary things having other causes." This also appears clear from the case of principles and conclusion, namely where the principle is the cause of the conclusion being true.

125 Avicenna, *Metaphysics* IX, c.4 (104v-105r).
126 Cf. Duns Scotus, *Ordinatio* I, d.8, n.232-262 (IV, 282-302).
127 Aristotle, *Metaphysics* II, c.1 (993b26-30).
128 Aristotle, *Metaphysics* V, c. 5 (1015b9-15).

7.117 As for the argument that the caused is of itself nonbeing and properly speaking is only possible being,[129] we must reply that this means it is not being of itself or better, it is not being which exists in and through itself. Thus what is required is that it does not have the mode of being characteristic of the self-existent, not that some kind of nonentity pertain to it. A negation of this first sort, however, is compatible with the necessary whereas negation of entity is not.

7.118 As for the dictum 'The caused is of itself only possible,'[130] if 'possible' means that subdivision of being that is opposed to 'actual,' then this is not necessarily found in everything caused, but only in such cases where the caused is something new. Causation and novelty were not necessarily connected for Aristotle, nor are they for those theologians who claim God could have produced something from eternity. Yet everything caused is a possible in the sense of being an object of a causative power, but this 'possibility,' although it is incompatible with 'necessity of itself,' was not repugnant to 'formal necessity' according to Aristotle.

7.119 The opinion attributed to Aristotle [131] about an Intelligence being infinite, however, must be rejected. The opposite is not only true but, in itself it is demonstrable and, as we have shown above, it represents the mind of Aristotle.[132]

7.120 [*Reply to citations to the contrary*] Therefore I answer those texts adduced by those who would ascribe this opinion to him.

Reply to the first:[133] The final conclusion of chapter [7] is not that the first mover is without magnitude because it is of infinite power, but rather another conclusion which he says has been proved earlier, viz. "It is impassive and unalterable, for all other changes are posterior to change of place."[134] Now this substance is not capable of local motion, as can be proved from what he had said before. Then he concludes, therefore, it cannot be moved by any movement that presupposes local motion, and thus it is un-

129 Cf. *supra* 7.101.
130 Cf. *ibid.*
131 Cf. *supra* 7.102.
132 Cf. *supra* 7.104-7.116.
133 Cf. Aristotle, *Metaphysics* XII, c.7 (1073a2-12), where he says that the first mover cannot have magnitude because he has infinite power. Cf. *supra* 7.102.
134 *Ibid.*, XII, c.7 (1073a10).

alterable. Next follows his question at the beginning of the subsequent chapter: "Is there one substance of this sort or more than one, etc.?"[135] Hence this refers to the unalterable being of which he was just speaking and not to a being of infinite power mentioned earlier. For what continuity would his words have if they did not refer to what he had just been talking about but to something he has said previous to that?

Or if he was referring to the earlier remark, one could say it must be the conclusion he meant, namely that it has no magnitude. And I concede that there are many things without magnitude just as there are many that are unalterable and impassive.

7.121 To the other text,[136] I have this to say. By demonstration of the reasoned fact, a negation can be inferred of some subject using as many media as there are causes why the opposite affirmation is repugnant to that subject. Now if some single thing were the adequate cause of such repugnance, it would be an adequate means of establishing such a negation. Intensive infinity is one cause why it is impossible to have magnitude but it is not an adequate cause. To have intellectuality without matter, however, is adequate. For the middle term to be sufficient, however, it is necessary to have both intellectuality and immateriality conjoined, since intellectuality alone does not suffice according to Aristotle (as is clear from the case of man); neither is immateriality alone sufficient (as is clear from the case of the heavens).

7.122 Consequently, my answer to the text in question would be this. Absence of magnitude can be inferred from infinite power. It is in fact so inferred in the penultimate conclusion of chapter [7][137] and also in Bk. VIII of the *Physics*.[138] But it can also be inferred from immateriality together with intellectuality. Something purely intellectual [i.e., without matter] cannot have magnitude. The intellectual form itself cannot be extended, but if something intellectual is also something quantitative, it is because it has matter perfected by an intellectual form. It receives quantity, not because of its intellectuality, but because of its materiality which

135 Cf. *ibid.*, c.8 (1073a15).

136 Cf. *ibid.*, c.8 (1073a37), where Aristotle says such substances are "in their nature eternal and in themselves unmovable and without magnitude, for the reason mentioned above." Cf. *supra* 7.102.

137 Aristotle, *Metaphysics* XII, c.7 (1073a2-12).

138 Aristotle, *Physics* VIII, c.10 (266b7-8).

is perfected by an intellectual form as is the case with man. 'A nature with infinite power has no magnitude' is a true proposition, but this proposition is also true: 'An intellectual nature that has no matter has no magnitude.' In the passage cited toward the end of the [seventh] chapter,[139] it is proved that the first mover has no magnitude because he has infinite power. But this means is not adequate so far as this predicate goes. In the previous chapter,[140] near the beginning, it is stated that immovable substances must be without matter because they must be perpetual and if something is perpetual in actuality, it is without matter in actuality. Later on, at the beginning of the [seventh] chapter[141] it is explained how these moving substances are intellectual natures.

7.123 From these two we have a second means for eliminating magnitude, namely intellectuality without matter. And so far as this predicate is concerned, this middle term is adequate. Therefore, when it is said in chapter [8][142] that there must be many substances without magnitude "for the reason mentioned above," this must be taken to refer to the adequate cause (i.e., intellectuality without matter, which was mentioned at the beginning of both chapters six[143] and seven)[144] and not to the proposition about infinity of power at the end of the [seventh] chapter.[145] This interpretation does not do violence, it seems, to the words of the text, for intellectuality without matter is the proper cause, indeed the adequate cause, as regards this predicate [i.e., 'to be without magnitude']. 'To have infinite power,' however, is not its proper or adequate cause, because this predicate pertains to every intelligence whereas the middle term [viz. 'to have infinite power'] pertains to God alone, to whom be honor and glory into ages of ages.

The Catholic University of America

139 Aristotle, *Metaphysics* XII, c.7 (1073a2-12).
140 *Ibid.,* c.6 (1071b21).
141 *Ibid.,* c.7 (1072b16-25).
142 *Ibid.,* c.8 (1073a30).
143 *Ibid.,* c.6 (1071b21).
144 *Ibid.,* c.7 (1072a20-25).
145 *Ibid.,* c.7 (1073a2-12).

7

THE MODE OF EXISTENCE OF BEAUTY:
A Thomistic or a Kantian Interpretation?

by

CAROLINE CANFIELD PUTNAM

Those of us who have been brought up on Thomistic critiques of this and that can readily fall into the trap of producing them. Caution tells us to be wary in comparing one philosopher with another, especially when one lives in the thirteenth century and the other in the eighteenth. However, there is always the hope that some new clarification may occur through the juxtaposition of forceful ideas. In the present case, the disinterested pleasure in the beautiful appears to be a common principle for Thomas Aquinas and Immanuel Kant, while the question of how beauty exists appears to divide them.

I.

What, then, is beauty, and what is its mode of existence? The Kantian doctrine is eminently subjective. It passes through a slow evolution. In the precritical writings, beauty is treated superficially. The *Observations on the Feeling of the Beautiful and Sublime,* published in 1764, compares the phenomenal aspects of beautiful things, always small, refined, and delicate, with the majestic, digni- fied, "oceanic" aspects of the sublime.[1] Kant's early thought on the matter stems from Baumgarten and Meier.[2] Although he does not seem to be versed in Platonic or Aristotelian doctrine, he is quite familiar with the writings of English philosophers on the subject. He knows the hedonistic theories of Lord Shaftesbury and Francis

[1] On the empirical-psychological character of this work, see the translation and comments of John T. Goldthwait, Berkeley, University of California Press, 1960.

[2] Cf. P. Menzer, *Kants Aesthetik in ihrer Entwicklung,* Berlin, Akademie Verlag, 1952, pp. 35ff.

Hutcheson,[3] the moral view of Henry Home,[4] and David Hume's discussion of an empirical "standard of taste." Edmund Burke's *Enquiry into the Origin of Our Ideas of the Sublime and the Beautiful,* written before 1764, was not translated into German until 1773. Kant makes no mention of it in the *Observations,* but refers to it later in *The Critique of Judgment.* From this earliest phase, two factors in Kant's final theory emerge: the distinction between aesthetic and sensuous enjoyment, and the notion of a special faculty of taste.

With the publication of the first *Critique* in 1781, his views become more original and profound. The aesthetic of *The Critique of Pure Reason* is "the science of all *a priori* principles of sensibility"[5] and its two pure forms of space and time. Here the term receives its broad Greek meaning of αἴσθησις, perception. In the *Metaphysics Lectures,* he calls the rules of taste "*a priori,* but not immediately so." They are based on "universal rules of experience."[6] At this time, too, he determines the relation of beauty, not as one of knowledge and the object, but of knowledge and the subject. In a famous letter to Carl Reinhold, December 28, 1787, Kant speaks of three *Critiques* each dealing with a faculty and its sphere of operations: *The Critique of Pure Reason,* for the faculty of knowledge and theoretical philosophy; *The Critique of Taste* (later changed to *The Critique of Judgment*) for the feeling of pleasure and pain and the area of teleology; *The Critique of Practical Reason,* for desire and the realm of practical philosophy.[7]

The Critique of Judgment, encompassing Kant's definitive aesthetic, was finally published in 1790. In structure, it follows the plan of *The Critique of Pure Reason* and, as a result, some of its conclusions appear forced. The work was not assembled at one sitting. There are repetitions and changes which indicate a chronological development. Section 38, for example, gives an early treatment of the problem of the universality of beauty. The second and

3 *An Enquiry into the Original of our Ideas of Beauty and Virtue,* 1725; translated into German 1762.

4 *Elements of Criticism,* published 1762; translated into German 1763.

5 Tr. J. Watson, *Modern Clasiscal Philosophers,* ed. B. Rand, Boston, Houghton Mifflin, 1936, p. 382. What is *a priori* is independent of experience.

6 O. Schlapp, *Die Anfange von Kants Kritik des Geschmacks und des Genies, 1764-1775,* Göttingen, 1899, p. 162.

7 *Briefe,* Vol. 9, p. 345.

fourth moments handle the problem with increasing clarity, while the Introduction, section vii, contains the most conclusive discussion.[8]

II.

The four moments of the beautiful indicate its character and position. Consistent with Kant's critical plan, each moment or determination must correspond with one of the fundamental categories of quality, quantity, relation, and modality. According to the first moment of quality, beauty gives enjoyment without interest. Positively, it is contemplated for its own sake; negatively, it is without interest.[9] According to quantity, the second moment, beauty gives universal pleasure without any concept. Positively, it is universal; negatively, it is without a concept. The second moment follows from the first, since beauty becomes universal by being abstracted from personal interest. According to relation, the third moment, beauty is the form of purposefulness without purpose. This follows from the second moment. If there is to be universality, there must be cognition; a cognition consequent upon the intuition of the imagination. This requires the free play of the understanding and the imagination in a so-called "finality without final end."[10] According to modality, the fourth moment, beauty yields a necessary satisfaction without a concept. This moment is obviously like the second and should be classed with it.[11]

Here then are many indications of the nature of beauty. It is disinterested, conceptless, universal, necessary, and purposive. Elsewhere, Kant distinguishes between "free" and "adherent" beauty, between beauty and perfection, between beauty and moral good. These qualifications will be considered successively; then perhaps some decision as to whether beauty is subjective or objective may be reached.

---

[8] B. Dunham, *A Study in Kant's Aesthetics, the Universal Validity of Aesthetic Judgments*, Lancaster, Pa., 1934, Ch. I.

[9] H. Cohen, *Kants Begründung der Aesthetik*, Berlin, Dümmlers, 1889, p. 209.

[10] J. C. Meredith, *Kant's Critique of Aesthetic Judgement*, Oxford, Clarendon Press, 1911, "Introductory Essays," p. lxiv.

[11] *Kritik of Judgment*, tr. J. H. Bernard, London, Macmillan, 1892; quality, p. 55; quantity, p. 67; relation, p. 69; modality, p. 96.

Beauty is disinterested[12]

Beauty has no moral, social, utilitarian, or hedonic interest. Interest is limited to "the existence of a certain object or a given action."[13] "It must please in virtue of itself," Kant had said earlier.[14] He was to say later:

> The pleasure which is not necessarily connected with the desire of the object, and which, therefore, is at bottom not a pleasure in the existence of the object of the idea, but clings to the idea only, may be called contemplative pleasure or *passive satisfaction.*[15]

Beauty is grasped without a concept

Kant distinguishes between general and conceptual knowledge. Although there is no concept, there is an idea in the form of knowledge he calls "general." Ideas are "representations referred to an object . . . in so far as they can never become a cognition of it."[16] An aesthetic idea is an intuition of the imagination. With the beauty of nature, for instance,

> . . . the bare reflection upon a given intuition apart from any concept of what the object is intended to be, is sufficient for awakening and communicating the idea.[17]

The aesthetic judgment is not cognitive; it "contributes nothing towards the knowledge of its objects,"[18] yet, as T. M. Greene points out,

12 Israel Knox lists a number of philosophers who characterize beauty as disinterested: M. Mendelssohn, Schopenhauer, S. Alexander, Shaftesbury, Hutcheson, Alison, Lipps, Kames. *The Aesthetic Theories of Kant, Hegel, and Schopenhauer,* New York, Columbia University Press, 1936, p. 22. Meredith, *op. cit.,* p. liii, includes Thomas Aquinas.

13 A. Aliotta, *L'Estetica di Kant e degli'idealisti romantici,* Rome, Perella, 1942, p. 61.

14 *Reflections,* #827.

15 *Metaphysics of Morals, Werke,* Vol. VI, p. 212.

16 Meredith, *op. cit.,* pp. 202-210. An idea is defined in *The Critique of Pure Reason,* p. 228, as a "necessary conception of reason, to which no corresponding object can be discovered in the world of sense." Since then, "an *idea* signifies a concept of reason, and an *ideal* the representation of an individual existence as adequate to an idea," he concludes that beauty is properly an ideal. Meredith, p. 76.

17 Meredith, *op. cit.,* p. 184.

18 Bernard, *op. cit.,* pp. 37 and 166.

[Kant's] identification of beauty with aesthetically satisfying form . . . commits him to the view that taste does involve a type of cognition in which conceptual interpretation must assume an essential role.[19]

Beauty is universal and necessary

Kant speaks of an "imputed" or "normative" universality, and an "exemplary" necessity.[20]

Because the foundation of the aesthetic evaluation is not a concept, it is clear that no rule can be given, according to which one is bound to recognize the beauty of a thing . . . yet it has for us a universal appeal, it exacts the consensus of all, supposing, not an object principle, but a common subjective rule.[21]

This universality is within the knowing subject. It is located with the disinterestedness of pleasure, with pleasure resting on an *a priori* judgment, or with a pleasure that is not of sense.[22] The harmonious interplay of the imagination and the understanding results in a satisfaction which is universally communicable, because "such an accord is an exigency for all knowing subjects in the universality of their formal structure."[23] Man seeks in the beautiful object to reach "timeless universality in value of a more beautiful conceptual form."[24]

Beauty is purposive

Kant has called *The Critique of Judgment* teleological. However, the finality he means here is a finality apart from a final end. "Aesthetic purposiveness is independent of any concept of a purpose." It has purpose "only in so far as the object makes us feel

19 "A Reassessment of Kant's Aesthetic Theory," *The Heritage of Kant,* ed. G. T. Whitney, Princeton, Princeton University Press, 1936, p. 342.

20 Bernard, *op. cit.,* p. 94.

21 Aliotta, *op. cit.,* p. 64.

22 R. von Schubert-Soldern, "Die Grundfragen der ästhetik unter kritischer Zugrundelegung von Kants Kritik der Urteilskraft," *Kant-Studien,* Vol. 13, 1908, p. 252.

23 Aliotta, *op. cit.,* p. 71.

24 G. Denckmann, *Kants Philosophie des aesthetischen,* Heidelberg, 1910, p. 74.

the harmony of our faculties of representation."[25] Meredith explains:

> Purposiveness without purpose, or, rather, finality apart from an end is only a pleasure projected into a given object, and depending upon a peculiar mode of interpreting the sensation of its effect upon the mind.[26]

The finality, then, is rather a resultant unification than a predetermined goal.

> . . . [What] specifies aesthetic knowledge is that to the objective representation is added an awareness of self, a presence of the soul, especially quickened through the harmonious interplay of faculties, the senses and the intelligence; harmonious interplay which realizes their unity.[27]

Resulting from the harmony of imagination and reason, the pleasure is pure, disinterested, and not empirical.[28]

"Free" beauty differs from "adherent" beauty

In distinguishing between "free" or "pure" beauty and "adherent" beauty, Kant reveals the narrowness of his own culture. He calls beauty free and natural if the form in and of itself "awakens an immediate interest";[29] if it involves no more than "an aesthetically agreeable play of sensations induced by the formal arrangement of sensuous qualities."[30] In this class he places what does not imply utility or unfulfilled perfection. Few man-made beauties and not even all natural beauties can be thus classified. So Kant is left with flowers, some birds, seashells, drawings, and free delineations. These, he claims, are superior in their "unconstrained" simplicity[31] to "adherent" or dependent beauties which

25 H. W. Cassirer, *A Commentary on Kant's Critique of Judgment,* London, Methuen, 1938, p. 204.

26 "Introductory Essays," pp. lxix-lxx.

27 A Marc, S.J., "Métaphysique du beau, I," *Revue Thomiste,* Vol. 57, 1951, p. 116.

28 Cf. Kant, *Analytic of the Beautiful from The Critique of Judgment, with Excerpts from Anthropology from a Pragmatic Viewpoint, Second Book,* tr. W. Cerf. New York, Bobbs-Merrill, The Library of Liberal Arts, 1968, introduction, p. xx.

29 Meredith, *C. Aesth. J.,* p. 158.

30 Greene, *op. cit.,* p. 335.

31 *Reflections,* #1855.

involve an additional reference to moral, cultural, or utilitarian considerations requiring the use of concepts.[32] The beauty of nature, whether free or not, is a *"Beautiful thing"*; the beauty of art, dependent or not, is always a *"beautiful representation"* of a thing."[33]

Beauty is not synonymous with perfection

Perfection consists in the "agreement of the manifold in a thing with an inner character belonging to it as its end."[34] It is irrelevant to the beauty of nature, but must be taken into account when considering a work of art. The beautiful, since it regards the form, implies limitations.[35] What perfection it has refers to the subject.[36] Actually, Kant prefers to posit perfection of the sublime.

> Intellectual and intrinsically final (moral) good, estimated aesthetically, instead of being represented as beautiful must rather be represented as sublime.[37]

He works out the following analogy between beauty and morality:[38]

Beauty	*Morality*
I. The direct pleasure *in the intuition*	—*in the concept*
II. Pleasure without any interest	—with interest, but for the judgment rather than for enjoyment
III. Freedom of imagination (law of the understanding)	—of the will (universal law of reason)
IV. Subjective universality	—objective universality

32 Greene, *op. cit.*, p. 333.
33 Meredith, *C. Aesth. J.*, p. 172.
34 *Ibid.*, p. 173.
35 *Ibid.*, p. 90.
36 *Reflections*, #1780: "logical perfections refer to the object."
37 Meredith, *C. Aesth. J.*, p. 123.
38 Menzer, *op. cit.*, p. 185.

Is beauty subjective or objective?

This is the paramount question. It is the one which puzzles all students of Kant's aesthetics. It certainly puzzled Kant himself. Theoretically, there is little doubt that he held beauty to be subjective. "The beautiful lies in the ideas."[39] Beauty is not a property of the object;—the beauty is "in the mode of taking it is."[40]

> [As] beauty is not a property of the object considered on its own account, the rationalism of the principle of taste can never be placed in the fact that the finality in this judgment is regarded in thought as objective.[41]

Taste "merely judges its object *as if* beauty were an objective quality."[42] In practice, the famous *als-ob* is to take the place of objectivity, so that one may talk of the "objective conditions" of the beautiful. Menzer lists the following objective indications of beauty found in Kant's *Reflections:* suitable relations, order, unity, symmetry, harmony, contrast of color, consonance of colors next to each other.[43] While the objects of nature are phenomenal, "their apparent design, harmony, purposiveness are noumenal."[44] The full notion of the interplay of faculties requires that the aesthetic relation meet existence from the phenomenal world.

> The aesthetic idea works functionally in the viewer and brings him face to face with the object of his intuition. The beautiful is in the object, thus it is objective. The emanation of the beautiful . . . is an objective fact.[45]

This does not mean of course that the beautiful object is presented as a thing-in-itself. It is rather a "becoming phenomenon."[46] Dunham accepts this "objectivity" when he gives an inclusive Kantian definition of the beautiful:

> An object is beautiful to the extent and degree in which, by its form and sensuous qualities, it excites all the activities

39 *Reflections*, #1855.
40 Meredith, *C. Aesth. J.*, p. 137.
41 *Ibid.*, p. 216.
42 Greene, *op. cit.*, p. 345.
43 Menzer, *op. cit.*, p. 73.
44 Knox, *op. cit.*, p. 18.
45 Denckmann, *op. cit.*, p. 71.
46 *Ibid.*, p. 72.

of the human self to the most refined and harmonious inter-play of which they are capable.[47]

However, when one considers that "objectivity" for Kant means only an appearance of a thing, only "its validity for a subject in-dependent of the empirical subjective condition,"[48] one is faced with some confusion. It is the fundamental problem of *The Critique of Pure Reason,* indeed of all Kantian thought: How can there be external reality if it cannot be known? Perceptive critics of the Kantian aesthetics, such as Victor Basch, point out that Kant never comes to a uniform solution of this problem.[49] He cannot without abandoning his beautifully worked out theory.

Beauty and the supra-sensible

The beauty which Kant speaks about cannot be described as metaphysical or transcendental. It would then partake of the "trans-cendental illusion."[50] Beauty is in no way transcendent, since it is "entirely confined within the limits of possible experience."[51] Yet, in beauty, "nature gives clear indication of the presence in the uni-verse of a *super-sensible substrate,* both teleological and moral."[52] Beauty gives super-sensible unity to man's powers in the unitive action of the aesthetic intuition.[53] Having insisted earlier that "beauty is the substratum of itself," Kant now affirms, in the in-troduction to *The Critique of Judgment* (probably the last part of the work to be written), that this substrate lying at the base of nature is irrational and unknowable.[54] Here again is the same fundamental Kantian contradiction. Beauty is termed subjective, but for reasons of convenience it may be treated as if it were ob-jective. If, basically, it belongs to the noumenal order, or if it is

47 *A Study in Kant's Aesthetics,* p. 131. Cf. also, p. 69.

48 Denckmann, *op. cit.,* p. 72.

49 V. Basch, *Essai Critique sur l'esthétique de Kant,* Paris, Alcan, 1896, pp. 502ff. Cf. also D. P. Dryer, *Kant's Solution for Verification in Metaphysics,* Toronto, University of Toronto Press, 1966, pp. 193ff., T. M. Greene, *Moral, Aesthetic, and Religious Insight,* New Brunswick, N. J., Rutgers University Press, 1957, pp. 75-78, W. Cerf, *Analytic,* introduction, pp. xxii-xxx.

50 *C. of Pure R.,* tr. M. Müller, *Modern Classical Philosophers,* p. 424.

51 *Ibid.*

52 Bernard, *C. of J.,* pp. 104, 176f., 250.

53 Denckmann, *op. cit.,* p. 40.

54 Meredith, *C. Aesth. J.,* p. 6.

identified with the "super-sensible substrate" it is unknowable;
if not, it is purely ephemeral. One is reminded of Hopkins' Leaden
Echo which struggles to "keep back beauty" from "vanishing away."

III.

The answer of Thomas Aquinas to the problem of beauty is based
on a different metaphysics. In sum, he would answer with Hopkins:

> Give beauty back, beauty, beauty, beauty, back to God,
> beauty's self and beauty's giver.

The most extensive discussion of the subject is found in his *Commentary on The Divine Names*. That, and the opusculum *De pulcro
et de bono*,[55] so long attributed to him, will form the basis of an
analysis of the nature of beauty in general, of beauty and participation, of beauty and analogy, and of the divine beauty itself.

The nature of beauty

The Divine Names of Denis the pseudo-Areopagite contains a
full chapter on goodness and beauty as names of God. Declaring
his Platonic allegiance, Denis makes the beautiful-and-good central
in scheme of reality:

> The beautiful is the same as the good, inasmuch as all things
> in all things . . . desire the beautiful and the good; nor is
> there anything in the world but has a share in the beautiful
> and good.[56]

Aquinas in his *Commentary on The Divine Names* follows Denis:

> Since in various ways the beautiful is the cause of all things,
> it follows that the good and the beautiful are the same, since
> all things desire the beautiful and the good . . . And there
> is nothing that does not participate in the beautiful and the
> good, since each thing is beautiful and good according to its
> proper form.[57]

[55] This opusculum forms part of the long *Commentary on The Divine Names
of Albertus Magnus*. Cf. G. Meersseman, *Introductio in Opera Omnia Beati
Alberti Magni, O.P.*, Bruges, 1931, and P. Mandonnet, *S. Th. Aq. Opuscula
Omnia*, Paris, 1927, p. 426.

[56] *In Librum Beati Dionysii De divinis nominibus expositio*, ed. C. Pera, O.P.,
Turin, Marietti, 1950, Ch. IV, #7.

[57] *Ibid.*, Ch. IV, 1. v, 355.

The opusculum *De pulcro et de bono,* however, makes distinctions between *pulchrum, bonum,* and *honestum.* Although this work is currently attributed to Albertus Magnus, it bears a close relationship to the subsequent thought of Aquinas and the distinctions made are important. The beautiful considered as the "splendor of form" is distinct from the good and the *honestum* (the good sought for its own sake). In so far as it draws desire to it, the beautiful is not distinct from the good. In a fundamental way, they are the same in things, although distinguished in the intentional order.[58] Later, he clarifies the relationship. The good by its nature is the end of desire. The *honestum* adds, over and above the good, a certain force and dignity whereby it attracts the desire. The beautiful contributes a sort of "resplendence and clarity on proportioned things."[59] (This description has been taken by Maritain and others as the classic scholastic definition of beauty.[60]) Denis has already spoken of beauty as the cause of harmony and splendor; Thomas Aquinas will later posit three indications of beauty: integrity, proportion, and clarity.[61]

In the mature thought of the *Summa Theologiae,* Aquinas applies an intentional distinction to beauty and goodness. The two are identical as regards the thing; their foundation is its form . . .

> but they differ in concept. For the good, strictly speaking, regards the appetite, that being good which all men desire; and, therefore, it partakes of the nature of an end, for the appetite is as it were a sort of movement to the thing. The beautiful, however, concerns the force of knowledge, for things are said to be beautiful when they give pleasure at sight. Therefore, beauty consists in proper proportion, because the sense derives pleasure from things properly proportioned.[62]

What is added to the good, he notes in the *Commentary* and later in the *Summa Theologiae,* is the "formal ordination to the cognitive power."[63] The good must gratify the appetite. The beautiful

---

58 *De pulcro et de bono,* ed. P. Letheilleux, Paris, 1881, Ch. IV, l.v., Sol 2.

59 *Ibid.,* Sol. 6.

60 J. Maritain, *Art and Scholasticism,* tr. J. F. Scanlan, London, Sheed and Ward, 1932, p. 25.

61 *Summa Theologiae,* I, Q. 39, 8.

62 *S. Th.,* I-II, Q, 27, 1 ad 3. Cf. on this point, A. Feder, S.J., "Des Aquinaten Kommentar zu Pseudo-Dionysius 'De Divinis Nominibus'—Ein Beritag zur Arbeitsmethode des hl. Thomas," *Scholastik,* Vol. 1, 1926, pp. 247ff.

63 *In Lib. De div. nom.,* Ch. IV, 1. v, 356.

"gives pleasure by mere apprehension."[64] "Beauty is the power of reality to please in being contemplated."[65]

Beauty and participation

How is the "splendor of form on what is well-proportioned" to come about? Denis answers that it is by participation. "All things participate in Him, nor does He depart from anything that exists."[66] The theory of participation stems from Plato. Socrates' speech at the banquet traces the beautiful through its manifestations in lesser beings to its consummate expression in Absolute Beauty. This beauty, "separate, simple, and everlasting, . . . is imparted to the evergrowing and perishing beauties of all other things."[67] According to Durantel, Denis seems to teach participation in a form of Platonic Idea, a Universal, inspired also by the χωρισιόν of Plotinus.[68] Whether the Very-Good and the Very Beautiful which he speaks of are to be equated with the Divinity, or to be considered as separate types or principles, it is certain that Denis considers God to be the source of all. "Everything which is has its being in Him."[69] He keeps beings united in Him and projects them by a sort of inexpressible embrace. As Durantel explains:

> . . . In calling beings to participation in it, the Divinity becomes a separable, multiple thing, numerous in its works, without at the same time dividing itself, losing its simplicity, leaving its unity; through the multipilicity, the production, the distinction of all things, it remains identical, unalterable, indivisible.[70]

This mode by which the multiple proceeds from the one is not by way of division, nor of production of varieties of the same type; rather, according to St. Thomas, it is a mode of effusion, "the mode

64 *S. Th.*, I-II, Q. 27, 1 ad 3.

65 G. Phelan, "The Concept of Beauty in St. Thomas," *Aspects of the New Scholastic Philosophy*, ed. C. Hart, New York, Benziger, 1932, p. 129.

66 *De div. nom.*, Ch. V, #5.

67 *Symposium*, 211 C.

68 J. Durantel, *Saint Thomas et le Pseudo-Denis*, Paris, Alcan, 1919, pp. 17, 179. Although there is much detailed information in this classic presentation, it is not always accurate.

69 *De div. nom.*, Ch. I, #7; Ch. V, #4.

70 Durantel, *op. cit.*, p. 20. Cf. also *De div. nom.*, Ch. I, #5; Ch. II, #11.

of a stream which comes forth from the fullness of a spring without dividing or lessening it."[71]

This doctrine of participation becomes the basis of the henological argument. "More and less are predicated of different things, according as they resemble in different ways something which is maximum."[72] Since inferior beings cannot explain the imperfect degrees of perfection found within them, they require a higher being who is perfection itself. That is why Garrigou-Lagrange holds that the fourth way of presenting the existence of God "contains in condensed form all the dialectics of Plato."[73]

In relation to beauty, the Thomistic teaching is derived from that of Denis. The beauty of a creature is "nothing else than a participated similitude of the divine beauty in things."[74] God grants to all creatures something of his own light.

> These gifts of the brightness of the divine ray must be understood as a participation of similitude; and they are also 'beautifying,' that is, causing beauty in things.[75]

Because of consonance, creatures are ordered to God as to an end. There is also a consonance in the order of one creature to another,— God brings together all things for the same end.

> This can be understood in the Platonic sense, that the higher things are in the lower by participation, and the lower in the higher by a certain excellence; and thus all things are in all things. And from the fact that all things are found in all things in this kind of order, it follows that all things are ordained to the same ultimate end.[76]

Later on, in the Sixth Lesson of the *Commentary*, where he again treats of the harmony of parts, Aquinas stresses the point that it is not by one mode that all things are in all. By diverse modes "all things have some communion with all things."[77]

---

71 *In Lib. De div. nom.*, Ch. II, 1. vi, 214.

72 *S. Th.*, I, Q. 2, 3.

73 *God: His Existence and His Nature*, tr. Dom Bede Rose, O.S.B., St. Louis, Herder, 1941, Vol. I, p. 308. Cf. pp. 302-345.

74 *In Lib. De div. nom.*, Ch. IV, 1. v, 338.

75 *Ibid.*, 340.

76 *Ibid.*, Ch. IV, 1. v, 340, 350.

77 *Ibid.*, Ch. IV, 1. vi, 364.

The analogy of beauty

Since it is of diverse modes, this sharing or participation cannot be one of equality. It cannot be univocal. Yet neither can the relation be purely equivocal; for the infinite, as the source of being, must be Being Itself. Thus there is a separation and a union which can only be regarded analogically.

The beauty shared by creatures is related to them as the beauty of God is related to him. The likeness is not in the beauty, but in the relationship. Such an analogy, in the sense of a relation of one thing to another, is that of proper proportionality.[78] It does not necessarily imply "similarity of perfection," but rather "similarity of proportion."

This relationship involving identity on the one hand and distinction on the other can give no knowledge of what God is since it merely points out his dissimilarity to creatures. The analogy of attribution, taken as a causal relation in which the analogon is only in the primary analogate, can do no better. However, since the causal relation in question is in the transcendental order, the analogon is not extrinsic to the lesser analogates but rather existing in them in a finite manner. An analogy such as this makes possible affirmations about God.

Knowing this, we can see that Denis (and with him Thomas) has used both analogies. His favored way of negation is bound up with the analogy of proper proportionality. God is known by what he is not. "God is known in all things and apart from all things . . . and he is not in anything in the world nor is he known in anything."[79] In relation to creatures, the divine beauty, as the primary analogate in an analogy of attribution is either efficient, exemplar, or final cause.[80]

As efficient cause, it produces "harmony and splendor in all things"; it flashes forth "beautifying communications."

> From this beautiful [reality] all things possess their existence, each kind being beautiful in its own manner, and the beautiful causes the harmonies and sympathies and coming together of all things. By the beautiful, all things are brought into one,

[78] *S. Th.*, I, Q. 12, 1 ad 4.

[79] *De div. nom.*, Ch. IV, #7, #10.

[80] *Ibid.; De ver.*, Q. 2, 11; *De prin. nat., IV Met.*, L. 1. In these texts, the analogy is spoken of as a relation of the many, or the one, to the one as efficient, exemplar, and final cause.

and the beautiful is the source of all things in so far as it is the creative cause which moves the world and holds all things in existence.[81]

In the opusculum *De pulcro et de bono,* a distinction is made between the created beauty which is the form of beautiful things and which makes things beautiful "formally, not effectively," and the beauty which is the form of the first mover and which makes beauty come to be effectively as well, "not by physical action, but by acting through his essence."[82] "From God emanates the beauty of all beautiful things."[83]

Thomas explains that God, who is the supersubstantial being, is called "beauty" because he gives beauty "to all created beings according to the property of each."[84] He is the cause of clarity by granting to creatures some of his brightness, which must be "understood as a participation of similitude," which "beautifies" or causes beauty in things.[85] Every form through which a thing has existence is a certain participation of the divine clarity,[86] a sort of radiation from it. God is also the cause of harmony. "What pertains in any way to consonance proceeds from the divine beauty."[87] Agreement in intellectual matters, friendship in matters of affection, communion in action, and unity attained in any way by creatures,— all these are reached only "in virtue of the divine beauty."[88] Where Denis says that the beautiful "gives existence, moves, . . . and conserves all things," Thomas shows that these three functions belong to the nature of an efficient cause and further, that as an imperfect agent acts out of desire for an end not yet possessed,

> . . . it belongs to a perfect agent to act through the love that it has, and this is why he [Denis] adds that the beauty which is God is an effective, moving, and containing cause 'through the love of his own beauty.' For, since he possesses his own beauty, he wishes it to multiply in so far as this is possible, namely through the communication of his likeness.[89]

81 *De div. nom.,* Ch. IV, #7.
82 *De pulcro et de bono,* Ch. IV, 1, v, Sol. 4 and 6.
83 *Ibid.,* Sol. 3.
84 *In Lib. De div. nom.,* Ch. IV, 1. v, 339.
85 *Ibid.,* 340.
86 *Ibid.,* Ch. IV, 1. v, 348; 1. vi, 360, 367.
87 *Ibid.,* 1. v, 348.
88 *Ibid.,* 1. vi, 367.
89 *Ibid.,* 1. v, 352-353. Cf. also 1. vi, 365; 1. viii, 389-390.

The divine beauty is also the exemplar cause of all. "It is their model (παραδειγματικόν, the ultimate law of their being, their idea, or type) from which they derive their definite limits."[90] As his own beauty, God acts through his essence *exemplariter* in all things. All things are determined according to divine beauty. "However much a thing has of beauty, so much does it have of being."[91] As God is the "fountain of all derivative beauty," such beauty pre-exists in him "not in a divided way, but uniformly."[92] It is the "rule of actions." Its validity lies in the fact that "no one cares to act as an image of or to represent anything except the beautiful."[93]

Lastly, beauty is a final cause as the "goal of all things and the object of their yearning (since the desire of the beautiful brings all into being)."[94] The beautiful, for the author of *De pulcro et de bono*, "draws things to itself," and is "that in which action terminates."[95] For Aquinas, created beauty and "clarity of form and measurement" require an end.[96] Creatures share in a graduated harmony and "from the fact that all things are found . . . in this kind of order, it follows that all are ordained to the same ultimate end."[97]

> The beauty which is God 'is the end of all as the final cause' . . . for all things are made that they should imitate in their own separate ways the divine beauty.[98]

> All 'turns toward the beautiful and the good' desiring him as an end. And he is not only the end as desired, but also in so far as all substances and actions are ordered in him as in an end. . . . Things move not only because of some extraneous end, but reach their goal through him and because of him.[99]

Thus, through the beauty dwelling in creatures, we are able to affirm something of the divine beauty in its causal relation to them.

90 *De div. nom.*, Ch. IV, #7.
91 Ch. IV, 1. v, Sol. 3 and 6.
92 *In Lib. De div. nom.*, Ch. IV, 1. v, 349.
93 *Ibid.*, 354. Cf. also 1. viii, 383; 390-391.
94 *De div. nom.*, Ch. IV, #7.
95 Ch. IV, 1, Sol. 7 and 11.
96 *In Lib. De div. nom.*, Ch. IV, 1. xxi, 554.
97 *Ibid.*, 1. v, 340.
98 *Ibid.*, 353.
99 *Ibid.*, Ch. IV, 1. viii, 382, 390.

The divine beauty itself

God himself, absolute beauty, is the term of the analogical and attributive process just described. Affirmation, based on relation, leads to negation of the relation and the defects of the lesser beings thus linked to the greater. The ultimate result, however, is neither affirmation nor negation but sublimation. Denis affirms the beauty of God through a causal relation,—what has been technically called an analogy of intrinsic attribution, since beauty is present in the finite effect and the infinite cause, although differing not in degree but in being itself.

The negation which follows the affirmation, withdraws all imperfections from the divine beauty. "God is . . . not beautiful in one part, nor at one place."[100] He is without what Thomas terms the dual defects of created beauty: changeableness and particularity.[101] There is no alteration, generation, or corruption of beauty in him. In every way, with no distinction, he is beautiful—"according to himself." We exclude from him whatever is beautiful under only one aspect, place, time, or relation. "What belongs to God first and according to himself, belongs totally and always and everywhere."[102] The "beautiful" and "beauty" which are distinguished in creatures (the former being that which "participates in beauty," and the latter "a participation of that cause making all things beautiful") are not divided in God.[103] In *De pulcro et de bono*, both terms are applied to him, to show either his perfection or his simplicity. Beauty in the abstract does signify a perfect being, and thus "to show the perfection of the first cause, that it really is in him, he must be called beautiful." To show his simplicity, he must be called beauty, for his simplicity requires that these two titles are the same in him.[104] Thomas explains:

> In the first cause, the beautiful and beauty are not to be divided as though they were two different things in him; this is because the first cause, on account of his own simplicity and perfection, alone 'comprehends the whole,' that is, all things in one—so that even though in creatures the beautiful

100 *De div. nom.*, Ch. IV, #7.

101 *In Lib. De div. nom.*, Ch. IV, l. v, 345. Cf. M. T.-L. Penido, *Le Rôle de l'analogie en théologie dogmatique*, Paris, Vrin, 1931, pp. 115-116.

102 *In De div. nom.*, Ch. IV, l. v, 346.

103 *De div. nom.*, Ch. IV, #7.

104 Ch. IV, l. v, Sol. 3.

and beauty differ, God comprehends them both in himself and as one and the same.[105]

In this manner, excluding the imperfections of the finite, one reaches the sublime way of eminence. God is then spoken of as the "super-essential beautiful," as "all-beautiful," "more-than-beautiful," as "eternally, unvaryingly, unchangeably beautiful," from beforehand containing "in a transcendent manner the originating beauty of everything that is beautiful."[106] The beautiful is, therefore, predicated of him according to an excess.[107] The excess may be twofold: that of the comparative or superlative in a genus ("more-than-beautiful"), or that which transcends any genus ("above-the-beautiful"). In both ways we may speak of God, "not that he is in a genus, but that all things in any genus whatever may be attributed to him."[108] "God is in a most excellent way, in himself, and before all others, the fountain of all beauty."[109]

Is beauty transcendent?

To speak of a transcendental, in the scholastic sense, is to speak of a characteristic which runs through all being.[110] It is above all specific and generic modes of being. Objective beauty,—ontological beauty, must be such. By their very existence and in so far as they exist, all beings are beautiful. Subjective beauty, the relational beauty which gives pleasure to the knowing subject, is held by some to be of a lower order, because the subject is not always able to perceive the beauty resident in things.[111]

> [Not] all things are apprehended as beautiful. Yet if it were possible for the mind to abstract from all else, and contemplate the perfection of a thing, it would be in a way to experience its beauty. The fundamental reason for the absence of the experience is not so much in reality itself as in the apprehending mind.[112]

[105] *In Lib. de div. nom.*, Ch. IV, 1. v, 338.
[106] *De div. nom.*, Ch. IV, #7.
[107] *In Lib. De div. nom.*, Ch. IV, 1. v, 343.
[108] *Ibid.*, 342-343.
[109] *Ibid.*, 348.
[110] *In X. Met.*, 3; *Quodlib.* VI, 1.
[111] L. Callahan, O.P., *A Theory of Esthetic According to the Principles of St. Thomas Aquinas*, Washington, D. C., Catholic University Press, 1927, p. 75.
[112] Phelan, *op. cit.*, p. 129.

Beauty is not listed with the transcendentals in *De veritate,* but it is equated with the good in the objective order. They differ only intentionally. Why should it not be a transcendental as well? "It is in fact," says Maritain, "the splendor of all the transcendentals together."[113] Even in its relational character, "it is rooted in existence and in being."[114]

IV.

Kant and Aquinas both indicate that disinterestedness and pleasure are factors in the experience of the beautiful.[115] They hold that beauty is delighted in for its own sake. They find in the experience a "harmonious interplay" of faculties and, if one agrees with Maritain and Gilby, they find the resultant knowledge "conceptless."[116] However, there is a fundamental difference to be considered. For Kant, the starting point is in the subject while the relationship of beauty and objective reality is not clear. For Aquinas, the starting point is being and the scope is as broad as existence itself, while the relationship to the knowing subject is not fully presented. In God, for whom essence and existence are one, beauty has been brought back to its self and giver.

Newton College of the Sacred Heart

---

113 Maritain, *op. cit.,* p. 134.

114 Phelan, *op. cit.,* p. 129.

115 Maritain, *op. cit.,* p. 161, n. 55; a very interesting comparison of the aesthetic theories of Kant and Aquinas.

116 *Ibid.,* p. 162. Cf. *The Range of Reason,* New York, Scribner's 1952, pp. 16, 22-23; *Creative Intuition in Art and Poetry,* New York, Pantheon, 1953, Ch. VI; T. Gilby, O.P., *Poetic Experience,* London, Sheed and Ward, 1934, pp. 9, 79, 107.

8

MAURICE BLONDEL: ACTION AND THE CONCEPT OF CHRISTIAN PHILOSOPHY

by

LEO J. ZONNEVELD

INTRODUCTION

The relationship between philosophy and Christianity is not a particular and isolated area of Maurice Blondel's philosophy; but its very heart.[1] The primary and persistent intention of his work has been to elaborate a philosophy which, in the course of its free and autonomous development, would spontaneously open towards Christianity. It was his desire to build a philosophy that would progress naturally towards the supernatural and would necessarily posit the problem of Christianity without actually making its acceptance a philosophical imperative. To accomplish this he had to construct a philosophy that would develop in an autonomous and natural manner, and at the same time would introduce what one could provisionally call "the Christian hypothesis."

The relation of human nature to the supernatural is the all-pervading problem of the history of Christian thought. Confronted with the objection that the Christian way of life is somehow disloyal to the human dimension of our existence, the Christian philosopher throughout history has had to attempt a reconciliation between the immanent meaning of philosophy and the transcendent meaning of Christianity.[2] Blondel's philosophy examines the actual form of this perennial problem.

---

[1] "Il problema della filosofia cristiana non è semplicemente un capitolo nel sistema blondeliano: ne è l'anima, il centro, il motivo inspiratore." Paolo Valori. *M. Blondel e il problema d'una filosofia cristiana* (Roma: "La civiltà Cattolica," 1950), p. 101.

[2] The term "immanent" refers to the effort of philosophy to find a meaning of reality while remaining within the subject considered. Theology accepts a

Blondel suggests a solution that no modern philosopher can ignore. He gives the finite dimension of human life its full weight, never leaves the human level prematurely, and accepts courageously the insufficiency of the natural order. All the usual categories of contemporary existentialism are there: freedom as risk and commitment, the psychological and irrational elements of existence, the hypothesis of the absurd, the ultimate human choice between the presence and the absence of God.

Blondel has an unlimited confidence in the creativity of the human mind, "the adulthood of man," and the "coming-of-age of humanity," but for him the exaltation of man's creative power does not result in an over-immanentization of God, a secularization of religion, or the "death of God." With acute awareness of the discrepancies between the world of Christian discourse and the world of modern philosophy, he presents us with the tragic greatness of modern man, with his frightful loneliness, and with the absurdity of life which man experiences once the alienation of God from human experience becomes a reality. When the secularization of human existence reveals the existential anxiety of man, Blondel invites man to come fully alive and to follow his reason and heart to the very end where man can meet the Absolute in a living, free and personal encounter.

It is this modernity of Blondel that fascinates the present day reader. His philosophy has a prophetic sound. Beyond the specific polemics of the modernist crisis, which today are mostly of historical interest, Blondel's philosophy has a far more universal significance than is usually given to it. The problems he faced in the stormy days of modernism are quite similar to the problems of de-Christianization we are witnessing in our days. In a prophetic way, his philosophy accepts Bonhoeffer's challenge of "plunging itself into the life of a godless world, without attempting to gloss over its ungodliness."[3]

The philosophy of Blondel is a philosophy of action. Action is for him the most universal, most unitive, and most dynamic phenomenon encompassing the totality of human existence. He sees

---

meaning that transcends or goes beyond what is given in experience. For a definition of these terms as used by Blondel, see Chapter II, footnote 45.

[3] Dietrich Bonhoeffer, *Letters and Papers from Prison* (New York: MacMillan, 1962), p. 222.

action as the mediating force between life and thought; it establishes truth and produces the *adaequatio mentis et vitae*.[4] Without denying that thoughts may help clarify action, he wants to show that action clarifies thought which is even more important.[5] In action the mutual fertilization of life and thought takes place; "Thought has the perpetual tendency to surpass action. . . .; action has the perpetual power and obligation to surpass thought. . ."[6] "Action is the Word Incarnate, thought embodied. . ."[7] "Every thought," Blondel insists, "is incomplete, diffuse, indetermined; not worthy of us and God. It is only in action that we find the decisive, the accomplished, the absolute."[8] "God is Act. Truth is an act. Being similar to God, knowing him and loving him; that is action."[9] "Action is not only real, it is productive of reality."[10]

Blondel proposes to lead us to an interior vision of things and to interpret the relationship between authentic action according to our interior exigencies and the understanding which results from it. To carry into action what we will, think and are, to manifest our existence with all the dynamism of the spirit faithful to the élan of the spirit, is the path to truth. *Qui facit veritatem venit ad lucem*.[11] The truth obtained through action is given to us in recognition of it and becomes at once the light and the goal of our intelligence.

Action is not easily defined. "It should be clearly distinguished from activity."[12] The word "action" expresses what is at the same time principle, means and end of an operation which remains immanent to itself.[13] It is not simply an externalization of an idea, an

---

[4] "Sans doute, la vieille logique est bien étroite, elle a éclaté. La vérité n'est plus *adaequatio rei et intellectus;* et on ne vit plus sur des idées claires. Mais il reste la vérité, et cette vérité qui reste, elle est vivante et agissante; c'est: *adaequatio mentis et vitae." Carnets intimes*, p. 86.

[5] *Ibid.*, p. 97.

[6] *Ibid.*, p. 517.

[7] *Ibid.*, p. 329.

[8] *Ibid.*, p. 224.

[9] *Ibid.*, p. 211.

[10] *Ibid.*, p. 179.

[11] Je me propose d'etudier l'action, parce qu'il me semble que dans l'Evangile il est attribué à l'action seule de pouvoir manifester l'amour et de pouvoir acquérir Dieu." *Carnets intimes*, p. 270.

[12] *Ibid.*, p. 36.

[13] Taymans D'Eypernon, *Le Blondélisme* (Louvain: Museum Lessianum, 1933), p. 19.

artistic production independent of the agent. It is more than a fashioning of the habits and social behaviour of the agent according to an outside intention. Action actualizes thought and intention, expressing the perfect unity of being and knowledge, the synthesis of spontaneity and reflection. Action is the manifestation or epiphany of the silence of being.[14] Blondel's philosophy is a supreme effort to surpass and to reconcile opposite positions; immanentism and transcendentalism, existentialism and essentialism, rationalism and irrationalism.[15] Historically and philosophically, he stands between positivism and immanentistic idealism on the one hand and anti-intellectualism on the other hand.[16] He is opposed to rationalism that negates true religion, the transcendent and above all the supernatural.[17] At the same time he rejects the anti-intellectualism of the believer who feels that no rational justification can be given of the contents of Christianity.[18] Prior to the distinction of anti-intellectualism and intellectualism, is the unity-principle, action, which extends into the realms of intellectualism and anti-intellectualism.[19] Action is a primary indubitable datum of human experience: "To consult the immediate evidence, action in my life is a fact, the most general and the most constant of all . . .

---

[14] James Sommerville, "Maurice Blondel and the Philosophy of Action," *Spiritual Life,* 7 (1961), p. 114.

[15] Aloisio Sartori, *Filiosofia e cristianesimo* (Patavii: Typis Seminarii Patavini, 1953), p. 24.

[16] *Ibid.*, pp. 18-19.

[17] "It is both legitimate and beneficial to enrich intellectualism by searching consciousness itself for more than notional knowledge, for something other than a 'cognition' since, in our immanence, there is a presence, an influence, a motion to which we have to give an 'agnition' which is even more than an assent." M. Blondel, *La Philosophie et l'esprit chrétien*, II (Paris: P.U.F., 1946), p. 122.

[18] "M. Blondel s'est attaché à . . . l'étude des rapports de la pensée avec l'action dans le dessein d'arbitrer le différence entre l'intellectualisme et le pragmatisme par une 'philosophie de l'action' qui enveloppe une 'philosophie de l'idée' au lieu de l'exclure ou de s'y borner." Lalande, *Vocabulaire technique et critique de la philosophie*, 1926, v. 1, p. 19b.

[19] In his foreword to Duméry's book, *La Philosophie de l'action, essai sur l'intellectualisme blondélien* (Paris: Aubier 1948), p. 7, Blondel writes: "Il s'agir de la *compénétration* salutaire et nécessaire de *deux fonctions* que ne se développent que l'une par l'autre et l'une pour l'autre en vue d'une destinée unique et inéluctable."

which no man avoids since even suicide is an act; action manifests itself even in spite of myself."[20]

This irreducible reality is more than the spirit of vitality of the
acting person; it is also the content of the work done. It has all
the richness of concrete life: desires, habits, sentiments combined
with the rigorous strictness of the mind with its ideas and ideals.
It is the deepest awareness of being alive, of simply being. Duméry
says that action must be understood as a spiritual activity in its
source and in the integrity of its development, as a "Cogito-
Existentiel,"[21] the dynamism of a spiritual being, the source from
which will and intellect draw their power to act. This experience of
existence which human knowledge can never completely elucidate
nor effectively escape in this life is the concrete starting point for
Blondel. It is not an easy starting point. As Brightman points out:

> "To be explicit, each metaphysician must begin with his own
> present personal experience, his NOW. It is the 'source of
> evidence' . . . It contains much theorizing, doubting, be-
> lieving, criticizing and the like; much memory, perception,
> purpose, reasoning, references to the beyond, duration spatial
> relations, temporal passage or 'perpetual perishing.' It con-
> tains all presently observable loves, hates, fears, and hopes of
> NOW; all conation, striving and efforts, desires, aversions."[22]

To keep this whole arsenal of human experience present in an
effort to translate this spontaneous energy into a reflective thought
is not an easy undertaking. This is Blondel's precise problem: "to
equate reflective and spontaneous movement."[23] No wonder that
Blondel remarks: "If someone would just have said what I have
in mind to say, I would be very grateful."[24]

[20] M. Blondel, *L'Action, essai d'une critique de la vie et d'une science de la
pratique* (Paris: P.U.F., 1950), p. VIII. This edition is a reprint of the text of his
thesis originally published by Félix Alcan in 1893. This new edition follows
the same pagination as the first edition. Henceforth we will refer to this work
as *L'Action, 1893*.

[21] Henri Duméry, *op. cit.*, p. 31.

[22] Edgar Brightman, *Person and Reality: An Introduction to Metaphysics* (New
York: Ronald Press, 1958), pp. 36-38. Cf. Blondel, *Carnets intimes*, p. 43: "Action
is eminently synthetic, nourished by ideas and sentiments. Action is a concrete
definition, not an abstract analysis of the idea."

[23] *L'Action*, 1893, p. XXIV. Blondel formulates this in Latin as follows: ". . .
mentis et vitae, intelligentis et agentis, volentis et voliti adaequatio." *Ibid.*, p. 303.

[24] *Carnets intimes*, p. 84.

To let action develop all its interior richness and to give a free hand and open mind to its élan requires a sympathetic attitude and a willingness to listen to the immanent voices of our existence. Such an attitude destroys all rationalistic mental security and introduces the continuously surprising newness of life inviting man to unknown and obscure horizons. "What is always new here on earth is action, that is, a movement toward the infinite, a displacement into the immensity, a change into the absolute and the immutable."[25] Blondel's intentions are clear: "I want to show that the highest form of being is to act, that the most complete form of action is to suffer and to love, that the true form of love is to adhere to Christ."[26]

Gabriel Marcel points out: "The reality of the act is by no means exhausted in the apparent accomplishment. It is of the essence of the act to *commit* the agent."[27] Blondel requires this commitment from his reader: "One should insist with all his power on the necessary truths, but not think that one can penetrate into the conscience of others; one only awakens these truths in others and only to the extent that God acts in them."[28] To solicit this commitment from the unbeliever and to awaken the intense desire to act out his life, Blondel wants at the same time something very personal, passionate or compelling, and something impersonal, reserved or unemotional.

> "One should not say anything that cannot accept a cold investigation, but one should say it with a permanent élan, a constant force, hiding behind the appearance of sweetness and patience the controlled but untamable energy which supports, advances and penetrates irresistibly."[29]

In this way Blondel believes that he can legitimately hope to penetrate those places where the philosophical currents are formed and receive proper consideration from them as regards the notion of revelation and even the idea of a Christian supernatural order.[30]

---

25 *Ibid.*, p. 267.

26 *Ibid.*, p. 85.

27 Gabriel Marcel, *Creative Fidelity* (New York: The Noonday Press, 1964), p. 107.

28 *Carnets intimes*, p. 484.

29 *Ibid.*, p. 240.

30 *Ibid.*, pp. 551-552.

I

BLONDELIAN METHOD

The Dialectic of Action

To his personal problem, how to be at the same time an autonomous philosopher and a faithful believer, Blondel intends to give
a scientific answer.[1] Philosophy which is primarily concerned with
man and his destiny cannot pretend to construct itself completely
without seriously taking into account the fact of religion which is
par excellence centered on the spiritual ends of man. On the other
hand, one has to keep in mind that the destiny of man, as revealed
by religion, is supernatural.[2] How then could philosophy instruct
us about man's supernatural destiny if its means are by definition
purely rational and natural? Would not one have to conclude that
philosophy cannot be self-sufficient, that it never will be able to
answer the fundamental demands of man? This has often been
asserted by Christian thinkers, some of whom have expressed a
resolute hostility towards philosophy. Blondel will maintain that
it is the task of philosophy itself to manifest, not accidentally but
essentially, the insufficiency of philosophy, and to indicate how this
insufficiency itself can help us to define the nature of philosophy.

The necessity to admit that the rational order "scandalizes reason" is philosophically humiliating and can only be accepted when
it can be proved that philosophy is obliged simultaneously to state
the problem of human destiny and to admit its incapacity to provide an adequate solution. If this can be done, then it is clear that
man, in following a light which does not come from nature, still
obeys his own reasons and its most profound demands.

The personal intuition original to Blondelian thought and repre-
senting "a line of demarcation between two eras of philosophical

---

[1] Blondel uses the term "scientific", and even "method of verification" or
"laboratory proof" (Cf. *L'Action*, p. XV) to meet the objection of a generation
that put all its faith in science. What he intends is a metaphysical foundation.

[2] "Blondel est à la fois philosophe et chrétien. Comme philosophe, il pense que
la philosophie ne saurait se désintéresser du problème de la destinée ultime de
l'homme, sans quoi elle ne vaudrait pas une heure de peine. Comme chrétien, il
croit que la fin dernière dépasse toute nature, est proprement 'surnaturelle.' "
Jean Lacroix, *Maurice Blondel* (Paris: P.U.F., 1963), p. 14.

speculation"[3] could be formulated in the following way: the aspirations of the human soul point necessarily and of themselves to a fulfillment beyond that which is within the rational sphere. Needless to say, the necessity of the supernatural does not follow from a simple analysis of human nature since the supernatural is by definition that which transcends reason. Hence, no apriori method can prove the necessity of such a supernatural consummation of the natural order. The only possible approach will consist in an analysis that does not apply itself to nature as pure essence but to man in his concrete historical existence. If by existentialism one understands a philosophy that emphasizes the fullness of the concrete order, one may say that existentialism in France began with Blondel.[4] If there is in man a need and aspiration of which his nature cannot give an adequate explication, concrete reflections should be able to tell this. A concrete reflection,[5] according to Blondel, consists essentially in an analysis of human action, including all the different types of human behaviour: metaphysics, ethics, science, and technology. Action, "this privileged datum,"[6] contains the whole field of human knowledge; action unifies sense experi-

---

[3] Maurice Blondel, *Léon Ollé-Laprune* (Paris: Bloud & Gay, 1923), p. 173. In his modesty Blondel contributes the philosophical innovation to his master. His inspiration came first of all from himself. In a footnote on page 85 of the same work he writes: "C'est sans y attacher (à la pensée d'Ollé-Laprune) mon inspiration essentielle que j'ai composé le livre de l'*Action;* et seulement beaucoup plus tard que, du point de vue ou j'étais parvenu et par des techniques bien différentes, j'ai aperçu les convergences que j'essaie de manifester ici . . ."

[4] "On peut dire, en un sens, qu'il est le premier existentialiste français. Mais on peut parler aussi, avec M. Paliard, de son 'anti-existentialisme,' si l'on comprend par là que sa philosophie de l'action, en brisant le cercle de l'immanence, brisait aussi en même temps celui de la subjectivité et d'une liberté solitaire." Albert Cartier, *Existence et Verité* (Paris: P.UF., 1955), p. 41. "On pourrait même dire san paradoxe que l'existentialisme n'a rien à voir avec une philosophie existentielle authentique, c'est ce que M. Blondel et G. Marcel, entre autres, n'ont pas cessé d'affirmer hautement, en répudiant formellement toute qualification de leurs doctrines comme existentialistes, sans laisser par ailleurs d'en revendiquer fermement le caractère existentiel." R. Jolivet, "Maurice Blondel et la pensée existentielle," *Etudes Philosophiques,* 7 (1952), p. 332.

[5] "La réflexion ici, n'est pas une abstraction mutilante, séparatrice. Elle est un détecteur d'essences au sein de l'existence." Duméry, *Raison et religion,* o.c. p. 312.

[6] Jean Lacroix, *op. cit.,* p. 15.

ence with scientific knowledge and philosophical speculation.[7] Action is the whole of man, the substantial bond that constitutes the concrete unity of each being while assuring its communication with all others, bringing together in it thought and life, individual originality and the totality of the social order, science and faith . . . Action is the geometric figure where the natural, the human, and the divine converge.[8]

Blondel thus proclaims that philosophy must study the spontaneous life of the human subject, its relations with the universe and with God: "It is into action that we will have to transport the center of philosophy, because the center of life is also there."[9] How does one study action? Does not action escape the ideal world of philosophy? Must not philosophy be satisfied with the universe of ideas? Blondel's answer is in the negative. For him philosophy is a universal critique of the whole of human life. The philosophical question, "Yes or no, has human life a meaning and man a destiny?"[10] with which he starts his philosophical investigation does not exclude any human experience.

Blondel's criticism[11] of the current philosophical starting point is that the Cartesian *Cogito* abstracts from the concrete order, from everything that precedes, accompanies, and completes reflective thought and the constructions of the mind. The illusion of idealism is to take the concept for the exact substitute of true reality.[12] By

---

7 *L'Action*, p. 42.

8 Cf. Paul Archambault, *L'Oeuvre philosophique de M. Blondel* (Paris: Bloud & Gay, 1928), p. 57, footnote 1.

9 Blondel, *L'Action*, p. XXIII.

10 *Ibid.*, p. L.

11 "Le dualisme cartésien, le criticisme kantien, l'idéalisme et l'immanentisme qui en ont été les consequences diversifiées résultent d'un faux problème initial, en opposant même le sujet et l'objet, l'intelligible et le réel, la connaissance et l'être, la pensée et l'action, la recherche philosophique se condamnait à d'artificielles, insolubles et stérilisantes difficultés." Blondel, *L'Action I* (1936), (Paris: P.U.F., 1949), p. 339.

12 "En constatant que, de l'autre côté, on s'attachait ou à la sensation ou à l'équivoque *Cogito* lui-même, comme si c'étaient là des réalités coupées au couteau et stabilisées, je ne pouvais m'empêcher d' y voir du pseudo-concret, des abstractions artificiellement solidifiées; . . . Et quand je lisais dans Ravaisson que 'Descartes a vu la réalité comme à nu' je sentais douloureusement combien cette vision est insuffisante, combien cette réalité est mutilée. C'était du factice, et je voulais du vivant." Lefèvre, Fr. *Itinéraire philosophique de M. Blondel* (Paris: Spes, 1928), p. 41-42.

identifying the contents of consciousness with its conceptual representation there is no longer a respectful communication with
reality; and philosophy is reduced to a mere bouncing around of
ideas as if they were the things themselves. By objectifying the
concept as a well localized, individual closed atom, the content of
consciousness is cut off from its life-giving source.[13] The narrow
rationalistic starting point of the *Cogito* no longer discerns the
natural ingredients or effective conditions, necessary for the
spiritual functions of man, and ceases to be a perception of the
living unity of all these functions. It no longer is an existential
Cogito.[14]

A philosophy of the concrete universal order does not neglect
anything. There is no isolation from experience, feeling, psychological states, nor is there any negation of the most diverse theses
which de facto exist in the history of human thought.[15] The fruitfulness of a philosophy depends upon the relationship that in daily
life already exists on a prereflective level between man and his
world, between man and his neighbor, and between man and the
Absolute.[16] A study of action requires, therefore, that we approach
life without prejudice and place no obstacle to the immanent pre-
philosophical dialectic which is a normal part of human life. Thus
the object of philosophical reflection is not a static and passive
datum, but the acting agent in all his restlessness and existential
relations.[17]

[13] The philosophy of the *Cogito* presents thought according to a Blondelian
expression as "un enfant trouvé."

[14] "The Cartesian *Cogito* is like that cornerstone which a president or minister
solemnly lays at a dedication—but upon which no one ever builds anything!"
(Gaston Bachelard), as quoted by Tresmontant, *Introduction à la métaphysique
de Maurice Blondel* (Paris: Editions du Seuil, 1963), p. 47.

[15] Maurice Blondel, "Sens, Possibilité et Necessité de Notre Méthode" (extract
from a letter of 1931), *Teoresi*, V (1950), p. 6.

[16] Koenraad Boey, "De Dubbele Oorspronkelijkheid van Blondel's 'Action',"
Bijdragen, 24 (1963), p. 134.

[17] "In the Philosophy of Action, philosophy is given its complete role, that
of being a way of life and not a mere system of ideas. It will have nothing
to do with those who conceive of philosophy as some sort of inviolate realm
of pure thought not bestained by the concrete loves, hatreds, fears and failures,
and aspirations of the living human being as he works out in history and
in himself the destiny of the human race. For while human nature is essentially
the same, it is existentially ever-changing, and so essence must always be discussed in the real world on all levels, theological, historical, biophysical, and

Before the thinker turns to this datum and determines the necessary conditions and inner law of life, it is necessary for him to observe action in its movement and expansion. The methodic doubt that clears the ground for philosophical reflection is not one that ignores some of the data of human life; it is rather a determined refusal to accept the necessity of a particular solution. Initially we suspend judgment and avoid the prejudice of a formal mental category, a predetermined existential apriori, or the affirmation of a divine plan. These are the things which "in approaching the science of action I have been trying to withdraw myself from."[18] While no solution is postulated or taken for granted at the start, the philosopher excludes or ignores no thesis or historical solution apriori. He wants to start his philosophical investigation by considering the totality of the phenomena while withdrawing himself from all premature or unscientific solutions.

Blondel invites us to take a complete inventory of human experience with the greatest purity of mind, intellectual humility, and childlike docility that avoids making ourselves the center and rule of reality. A man should actually let himself be instructed by life, following the light that is given to him who does not claim to generate it himself.

> "To take the viewpoint of all other minds, to find out what light, partial truth, temporary limitations each one contributes, is to practice what one has called 'the method of immanence': this means that one enters as it were into the interior of all consciousness, of all realities, instead of drafting them in the narrow thought we form of them."[19]

Blondel is a careful observer who has the patience, docility and, receptivity to learn from the admirable richness of reality. His cultivated mind and highly sensitive Pascalian heart enable him to taste and to describe the most diverse experiences with exceptional

---

not merely on the metaphysical. The philosopher, then, must join hands with the mystic and the saint, with the artist, the scientist, the economist, the sociologist, the laborer in field and factory, in a living expression and unfolding of truth." E. Sponga, "The Philosophy and Spirituality of Action," in *Proceedings of the 18th Annual Convention of the American Jesuit Philosophical Association* (Woodstock, Md., 1956) pp. 72-73.

18 Blondel, *L'Action*, p. XXI.

19 Blondel, *art. cit.*, p. 7.

insight and accuracy.[20] *L'Action* shows a sense of wonder which is even more fully manifested in his diaries, correspondence, and marginal remarks distributed throughout his writings. His works contain impressive descriptions of the phenomena of human existence, incisive analyses of the world around him, and profound aphorisms and quotable statements. No hypothetical solution, actual, historical, or imaginary, no matter how absurd it may seem, is left undiscussed. He gives all such solutions a chance to shed their light, however dim it may be, on the problem of the meaning of life and destiny of man.[21]

The Blondelian approach touches on the general philosophical problem of the concrete singular and the abstract universal. Blondel admits that philosophy must necessarily work with ideas, generalities, and approximate expressions of reality, but he emphasizes that it is no less imperative to attain to the real being of a thing, the singular concrete. There is, he says, the constant scientific temptation to capture things under general headings and categorize them according to hypothetical solutions. This is the purpose of science. Yet science cannot exhaust the singularity of things in all their depth and produce at the same time communicable and reflective knowledge. To understand reality scientifically we must number it and put a general label on the things we investigate. However, the singularity lost in scientific generalization should not be sacrificed to a childish desire for simplicity, since the universal category, the label that fits every bottle, is the least informative of all. The complexity of the universal truth finds its richest expression in the understanding of the singularity of things. In the name of science itself we are not allowed to sacrifice more of the singularity of the real than is necessary for communicable understanding. This may be difficult but "so much the better, because we must distrust a "philosophy at ease!"[22]

---

20 "On y trouvera, comme on l'a dit, des pages d'une telle richesse et finesse d'observation qu'elles pouraient devenir le bréviaire sans cesse relu des mêmes âmes qui se nourissent déjà de Pascal." Jean Lacroix, *op. cit.*, p. 14.

21 Poncelet, A. "The Christian Philosophy of Maurice Blondel," *International Philosophical Quarterly*, V (1965), p. 568.

22 Blondel, *art. cit.*, p. 9.

Blondel's approach respects the singularity of things because in their singularity things embody the universality that the philosopher is looking for.[23] It also respects universality because from it the singularity of things receives its consistency and ultimate meaning. As Blondel puts it:

"No facts, no experience which would serve to illustrate and support those affirmations which we will be led to make will prevent us from allowing for a further solution, which derives its exact sense and finds its entire justification only in becoming a part of the whole, for, actually, there is no partial solution as such. . . . The particular is the echo, in an original being, of the entire order, just as the universal is present at every real instance which contributes to the harmony of the whole."[24]

The universality that is echoed and manifested in the singularity of things and experiences demands that the philosopher never divorce himself from life. Philosophy is not only the "reflected thematization of the unreflected,"[25] as Duméry puts it, "it is life itself becoming conscious of itself and giving direction to itself."[26] The

---

[23] "Jouons notre rôle et sachons particulariser, relativer l'absolu, afin d'universaliser le relatif et le particulier. Double movement, double caractère indispensable à l'achèvement providentiel de la destinée humaine." *Carnets Intimes*, p. 346.

[24] "Nul des faits, nulle des expériences qui nous serviront à illustrer et à réaliser les affirmations que nous serons amenés à porter ne cessera de réserver la solution ultérieure,—solution qui ne prendra son sens exact et ne trouvera sa justification entière qu'en s'insérant dans l'ensemble, car il n'y a point à vrai dire de solution partielle." *Ibid.*, p. 11. Blondel is, therefore, sympathetic towards the Hegelian effort to overcome the opposition of subject and object and he freely subscribes to Hegel's criticism of a philosophy "which presents the absolute as the night in which, as we say, all cows are black." *Hegel Selections*, edited by Jacob Loewenber (New York: Scribner's Sons, 1957), p. 14. The absolute cannot be imposed upon the singularity without destroying them in their singularity. The absolute must appear from within contingent realities as their unifying and clarifying bond of subsistency. "Le singulier est le retentissement, en un être originel, de l'ordre total, comme l'universalité se présente à chaque point réel qui contribue à l'harmonie de l'ensemble." *Itinéraire Philosophique*, p. 78.

[25] Duméry, *La tentation du faire du bien* (Paris: Edition du Seuil, 1956), pp. 168-169.

[26] Blondel, "Le point de départ de la recherche philosophique," *Annales de philosophique chrétienne*, 152 (1906), p. 239.

philosophy of action is a reflective presence to life.[27] It is interested in the whole human order which cannot be discovered in thought alone, but demands human action "as a living spring and source of intellectual speculation."[28] Philosophy of action demands that the script of life be reproduced systematically and reflectively. Therefore the philosophy of action surrenders itself unconditionally to life and to the innermost dialectical movement of human reality. In this way it assists at its own birth and evolution.

The circuminsession of life and thought, of reflective and unreflective knowledge, of the singular concrete and the abstract universal, should be firmly established before we introduce the necessary distinction between the prospective knowledge of action and the retrospective knowledge of philosophy. Only retrospective knowledge is reflection "sensu stricto." It is this reflection that turns to spontaneous knowledge, or first reflection, in order to analyze it.

Blondel insists continuously on the role of prospective knowledge. This, he holds, is inherent in the unreflected action of man, guides our practical decisions, accompanies our projects, directs us to a goal, and unifies our isolated experiences. The "direct method of verification"[29] is the "practical way,"[30] a method of "direct experience."[31] This method is a prerequisite for anyone who wants to discuss the exigencies of life, for "even to discuss them we must submit ourselves to them."[32] Curiosity of the mind does not cancel practical necessities; thinking does not dispense us from living; the obligation to act is from a different order than the need to know. Philosophers and uneducated people alike should maintain a childlike and naive docility to the "empirisme du devoir."[33] Such practical knowledge gives to all those who listen to the dictates of conscience and practice this living analysis of moral experimentation a complete and valid solution of the problem of life. Deep devotion to life gives evidence of its basic design. A mortifying faithfulness to life itself, along with a method of analytic scrutiny

27 "L'idée représente le réel, est un 'mobile' de l'action." *Taymans d'Eypernon, op. cit.,* p. 71.

28 Blondel, *L'Action, II* (Paris: P.U.F., 1963), p. 11.

29 *L'Action,* p. XI.

30 *Ibid.*

31 *Ibid.,* p. XV.

32 *Ibid.,* p. XI.

33 *Ibid.,* p. XIV.

and synthetic implication, is required to make the meaning of life stand out against the colorful scene of daily existence. The taste of life is not an indiscriminate passion to satisfy the superficial appetites, a "savoir vivre" of the "bon vivant"; it is rather the moral experimentation of giving oneself over to all that conscience and life demand from us. Such prospective experimental knowledge, perfect in its kind, reveals the practical harmony between the necessity which forces me to act and the movement of my own life. "The practice of life itself contains a complete method and makes possible a valid solution of the problem with which each man is faced."[34]

Bouillard's insistence on the inseparability of prospective knowledge and proper philosophical retrospective knowledge should be understood in the light of his criticism of Duméry's idealistic interpretation of Blondel's thought. Blondel writes: "The method of dialectical invention cannot legitimately be separated from the method of effective progress."[35] Every vital process promotes and permits a process of reflection which, in turn, supports and even commands a new movement of life and additional action. As Bouillard points out to Duméry, it is not enough to simply admit this typical feature of Blondel's thought but it should be emphasized that this is the heart of the Blondelian method. Duméry takes great pains to prove that Blondel's philosophy is an "integral intellectualism." In doing so, this great interpreter of Blondelian thought establishes beyond doubt that such philosophy is far removed from the anti-intellectualism of which it has often been accused. Blondel needed, at least historically, a strong defender of the true philosophical character of his work. Duméry is such a defender and he proves his case convincingly. Prospective knowledge itself is not philosophy. Philosophy is retrospective knowledge. "It is the purpose of philosophy to put into practice a thought of this kind. It is the reflective analysis of all that is lived; that is to say of all that is thought, wanted and realized by each one in praxis."[36]

The philosopher wants to determine "what is necessary and in-

34 *Ibid.*, p. XV.

35 Blondel in *Etudes blondéliennes*, II (Paris: P.U.F., 1952), p. 22.

36 Duméry, H., *La tentation de faire du bien, op. cit.*, p. 169.

evitable in the total unfolding of human action."[37] To meet all the requirements of universal, objective, communicable knowledge and to solve the problem of human destiny in a scientific way *"my reasons should not have more value for me than for another."* "What one knows because one does it, one cannot reveal to others who do not practice it; to the eyes of others it is only opinion, belief or faith; for himself *his* science does not have the universal, impersonal and commanding character of *the* science."[38]

Thus in spite of the importance of prospective knowledge, Blondel's philosophical approach to the problem of human action, his "science de la pratique," comes definitely first in the order of intention. It is the design and vocation of his life to be a *philosopher* of action. As such, "it becomes necessary to pose the speculative problem of the practical order."[39] And, as Duméry keeps on repeating, the position of Blondel is clear: philosophy, the philosophical science of action, is possible only by means of the indirect method.

The indirect method lives within and from the totality of human action; it is the rational translation of the direct method of verification, the reflective partner of life lived to the fullest degree. Reflective knowledge may not exhaust life, but it is the only kind of scientific knowledge available to man. The vivid and vital communication between life and thought as manifested in action, is essential; the practical and speculative solution have the same contents although not the same scientific value. The philosopher discovers the same truth as the ordinary man but if "the method of the ordinary man"[40] is sound, it is the task of philosophy to show *why* it is sound. To make the practical solution a rational one is the work of philosophy. "It is the role of the logic of action to determine the chain of necessities which compose the drama of life and lead it forcefully to its dénouement."[41] The dialectical method requires that philosophy and spontaneous life, reflective and prospective knowledge are clearly distinguished. It is this duality in the synthetic unity of action that gives the dialectical method its meaning. Within the unity of action philosophy is the rationally

37 Blondel, *L'Action,* p. 475.
38 *Ibid.,* p. XVII.
39 *Ibid.,* p. XVIII.
40 "méthode des simples et génereux," *ibid.,* p. XVI.
41 *Ibid.,* p. 473.

understood rule or logic of action expressing the determinism of spontaneous life of the agent.

> ". . . everything consists in equating the reflective motion with the spontaneous motion of my will. This relation of equality or distance is determined in action. Therefore, it is very important to study action; it comprises in itself a world which is its original work and which must contain the complete explanation of its history, its whole destiny."[42]

The exigencies immanent to action and spontaneous thought which philosophy has to reproduce reflectively, commands the dialectical movement between the *volonté voulante* and *volonté voulue,* between *pensée pensante* and *pensée pensée,* between existence and essence. Typical of the Blondelian method is not the simple and common observation that there is a distinction between concrete life and the formal conditions of its intelligibility, and it explicitly affirms this also. But when Blondel writes that "action and the idea of action are heterogeneous and irreducible" and "that life and knowledge of life are distinct things,"[43] he touches on the singular fruitfulness of his thought: the logic of action reveals philosophy's most fundamental insufficiency. Philosophy's essential insufficiency shows itself through the method of immanence, and this consists "in trying to equate, in our own consciousness, what we appear to think and to will and to do with what we do and will and think in actual fact—so that behind factitious negations and ends which are not genuinely willed may be discovered our innermost affirmations and the implacable needs which they imply."[44] Philosophy "has as its task to show us both what we inevitably have and what we necessarily lack, so that we may integrate into our willed activity all that is postulated by our spontaneous activity."[45]

[42] *Ibid.,* p. XXIV.

[43] Blondel, "L'Illusion idéaliste," *Premiers écrits II* (Paris: P.U.F., 1956), p. 122.

[44] Blondel, *Letter on Apologetics,* trans. Alexander Dru and Illtyd Trethowan (London: Harvill Press, 1964), p. 157. "En quoi donc consistera la méthode d'immanence, sinon à mettre en équation dans la conscience même, ce que nous paraissons penser et vouloir et faire, avec ce que nous faisons, nous voulons et nous pensons en réalité-de telle sorte que dans les négations factices ou les fins artificiellement voulues se retrouveront encore les affirmations profondes et les besoins incoercibles qu'elles impliquent." Blondel, *Lettre. Premiers écrits I* (Paris: P.U.F., 1956), p. 39.

[45] *Ibid.,* p. 198. The term "immanence" has different meanings, "La notion d'immanence commence par avoir un sens très général, si général qu'elle est

The fruitfulness of the method of immanence becomes evident when the philosopher realizes that he has the impossible task to equate reflective thought and spontaneous movement. When the duality in the unity of life cannot be brought to harmonious and peaceful unity in reflective thought, then the question arises: why this impossibility, what causes the gap, what conditions have to be fulfilled to come to a successful equation of life and thought? As long as philosophy has not answered these questions or shown that they are unanswerable, its task is unfinished.

---

inexploitable, redoutable, à moins d'apporter des précisions. *Immanent,* pour les scolastiques, s'oppose à *transitif.* Pour Spinoza, il s'oppose à *transitif, accidentel, extrinsèque.* Pour Kant, il s'oppose à *hors expérience possible.*" (Duméry, *Raison et religion dans la Philosophie de l'action,* p. 297, footnote 109). From what has been said it is clear that Blondel uses the term in a more general sense. Immanence for him does not exclude all exteriority or heteronomy, only absolute exteriority. Immanence is not opposed to *transcendence* and *supernatural* because these two terms indicate a reality and gratuity to which reason can give a legitimate foundation. "L'immanence est le caractère de l'activité qui trouve dans le sujet ou elle réside non pas sans doute toute principe ou tout l'aliment, ou tout le terme de son déploiement, mais du moins un point de départ effectif et un aboutissement réel, quel que soit d'ailleurs l'entre-deux compris entre les extrémités de cette expansion et de cette réintégration finale . . . L'immanence ne signifie donc pas, comme on paraît souvent le croire, identification; et d'autre part transcendant ne veut pas dire nécessairement séparé et spatialement extérieur. Si en vivant nous dépassons nous-mêmes, si en voulant nous voulons plus que nous-mêmes, si l'action est créatrice, n'est-ce pas qu'il y a un transcendant qui nous est immanent." Cf. Lalande, *Vocabulaire de la philosophie* (Paris: P.U.F., 1956), pp. 468-469. Faithfulness to the method of immanence requires that we define the natural autonomous conditions of human action. If the supernatural order and the divine heteronomy have to be postulated in the definition of the conditions of human action then the method of immanence will include the necessary recognition of the insufficiency of philosophy and lead to the condemnation of a doctrine of immanentism. At one and the same time we have to postulate necessarily the transcendent character of the supernatural order and grasp it under its natural and immanent appearances. "Puisque c'est dans notre action même que se découvre le besoin du surnaturel, ce surnaturel même garde, au regard du philosophe, le caractère d'immanence qui seul mous permet de la saisir en nous sous son aspect naturel." *Etudes blondéliennes* II, p. 103. The presence of the supernatural under natural appearances manifests itself in the form of insufficiency and the impossibility of a purely immanent self-equation.

The Ontological Question

The role of human thought is to project in an ideal order a series of notions and norms which form the intelligible structure of life or action. This ideal order is characterized by a determinism, a chain of necessary and universal ideas which give meaning to living action. The actualization of these ideas in the order of real being does not belong to the level of thought. In themselves the ideas and norms are conditions of living action, therefore they remain merely possible as long as they have not been actualized. As far as they form a logical whole, the ideas are necessary because they constitute an indispensable link in the chain of thought that makes it possible for philosophy to establish itself as a science. Once philosophy has shown that this system of rational requirements rests upon the most concrete living experience and determines the conditions which seem to us necessary if what we think and will is to exist, it is not up to philosophy to produce, "as in a seedbed prepared for it, being itself, the living truth, the gift which brings salvation."[46]

Philosophy cannot fill in the blank spaces it indicates, nor can it establish them in their reality by any resource of its own.

> "To say that the method of immanence, like all methods of a scientific character, shows us nothing more or less than the 'necessary' is not to use the word in an ontological sense as if it were a question of absolute existence or of truths whose contraries would imply contradiction; it is merely to observe that our thoughts are inevitably organized in a close-knit system, and it is this determinism, underlying as it does even the use of our freedom, which makes it possible to constitute philosophy as a science."[47]

Philosophy's work, then, is to criticize all the phenomena of our life by confronting them, by studying their relations, by developing an integral determinism of the conditions of action which is thought. In thinking, we suspend the extramental existence of the objects. "We study, for example, the idea of God not just as God, but in so far as it is our necessary and effective thought of God without attempting to add to this conception what it cannot give us."[48] Thus philosophy has absolute autonomy on the level of the

46 *Ibid.,* p. 160.
47 *Ibid.,* p. 161.
48 *Ibid.,* p. 153.

intelligible conditions of action. It must, however, recognize its fundamental incompleteness. Philosophy never can substitute its rational universe for the universe of reality. In the very exaltation of autonomous reason lies its principle of limitation and insufficiency. It can establish a totally autonomous universe of intelligibility (subjective knowledge, i.e., knowledge of the phenomena), yet it needs the intervention of an option to reach reality (objective knowledge, i.e. knowledge of being).

By defining itself as the constitution of a "complete phenomenalism of thought and action," philosophy extends its field to the whole of human expressions, yet in another sense it is reduced to methodical and systematic reflections.

Philosophy, for Blondel, stands at the service of man's freedom; its true role is to define the conditions of being and acting and to present them to freedom of man, who realizes them in the optional act. Reality is not founded on the necessary appearance of the phenomena, but it is fulfilled in being by mediating action which bestows upon them the being that they manifest.[49]

"Thus, it seems, the chief and indeed the unique aim of philosophy is to assure the full liberty of the mind, to guarantee the autonomous life of thought, and to determine in complete independence the conditions that establish its sway."[50]

The method demands that we at first suspend the ontological affirmation in order to let all phenomena find their place in the chain of necessary ideas. The necessity of thought which philosophy determines on the phenomenal level is the necessity to pronounce and commit oneself; the necessity to act and to make a lived option. Philosophy describes in order to prescribe; it verifies in order to judge.

Blondel avoids all phenomenalism because the very principle of immanence reveals the necessity of transcendent freedom in order to arrive at "objective" knowledge. The "subjective" knowledge of the phenomenal order does not suffice. Theoretical insight is not

---

49 "La réalité des objets connus est donc fondée, non pas en une sorte de double sousjacent, non pas dans la forme nécessaire de leur phénomène; elle est fondée dans ce qui nous impose une option inévitable; elle est realisée dans l'action médiatrice qui leur donne d'être ce qu'ils paraissent. Leur existence est donc en eux, puisqu'ils sont tels qu'ils sont connus, et hors d'eux, puisqu'ils sont connus tels qu'ils sont." L'Action, p. 486.

50 Blondel, Letter on Apologetics, p. 157.

enough to "attain" reality. Through the option of freedom one has to move on to "objective" knowledge. The strength of philosophy lies in its inherent weakness. As an autonomous system of logical and necessary ideas it is not directly concerned with the reality of the phenomena and does not demand a concomitant commitment to the "being" of them. This enables philosophy to pursue its course independently of the option. However, to arrive at being the explicit will has to embrace freely the necessities of the determinism of action. As long as there is only necessity there is no real being.[51] One's grasp of being is more authentic to the extent that there is an increasing adequation between what the explicit will freely accepts and what the logic of action necessarily imposes. Since truth is the equation of thought and reality, "subjective" knowledge proposes and imposes the option so as to arrive at knowledge of being (objective knowledge).

The almost enigmatic statements surrounding the "ontological affirmation" have created a good deal of misunderstanding in the interpretation of Blondel's view:

> "To pose with precision and scientific competence the problem of knowledge and of being, it is necessary first to determine exactly the system of the relations which are interposed between the two extremes. From the (implicit) voluntary to the (explicitly) willed, from the ideal conceived to reality in act, from the efficient cause to the final cause, all the intermediary stages must be covered before one has the right to turn back and see in the fleeting succession of phenomena, the solidarity of being. Moreover, once our thought has embraced the whole of transitive operations, which, little by little, render the final cause immanent in the efficient cause, there is need for it to make the whole series of the objects share in the reality of the term which was already present from the point of departure."[52]

There is no doubt in Blondel's mind that we have a certain knowledge of being of which we cannot rid ourselves. There is absolute correspondence and perfect reciprocity between being and knowing. The affirmation of being is anterior and interior to any attempt to negate it. It is within this "vital and irrecusable certi-

---

[51] "Pour être en nous, il faut que nous voulions que les objects soient pour nous ce qu'ils sont en soi." *L'Action,* p. 437; also: "C'est dans ce qu'il est possible d'agréer ou de refuser en nous qu'il faut voir la véritable réalité des choses." *Ibid.,* p. 436.

[52] Blondel, *L'Action,* p. 427.

tude of being"[53] that the series of necessary conditions unfolds itself. Every necessary truth is considered to be really existing as the objective expression of our being. The dichotomy of thought and external reality, the question as to the independent existence of the objects of our thought, is totally irrelevant to the Blondelian problem of "subjective" and "objective" truth. "I place myself before this dichotomy," he writes.[54] In action the synthesis of subject and object is first. Blondel has no need to establish the reality of things; being is never in the waiting room, neither before nor after the freedom of choice. Every necessary condition reflectively affirmed is a rational expression of an equally necessary truth of reality. His method of immanence guarantees him that there is in every thought a necessary presence of reality; it only can be thought this way because it is this way in reality. The necessity to affirm the reality of all the objects of the intellect and will in their irreducible originality and their infrangible solidarity, is the *leitmotiv* of the last chapter of *L'Action*. There is no trace of voluntarism or idealism. The reality of things does not depend upon the will or the intellect, or anything else for that mater. Reality simply *is*, the affirmation of it is no great problem.

The affirmation of being, however, is the affirmation of the objective existence of all the phenomena in their mutual solidarity. Among the phenomena which the dialectic of action irresistibly manifests to thought, is the great alternative which imposes itself upon every man; to choose for or against God. The objective reality of every particular being finds its ultimate meaning and foundation in the very source of all subsistency. Blondel does not deny that a child has objective existence, but he claims that before we can affirm or recognize it as such philosophically, the necessary conditions, his father and mother, have to be co-affirmed, at least

---

53 Blondel, *L'Etre et les êtres* (Paris: P.U.F., 1963), p. 359.

54 In a letter of December 7, 1910 to Auguste Valensin, Blondel writes: "Vous me remarquez sans doute que M. Wehrlé semble considérer que mon effort est conditionné par le caractère de 'subjectivité' de la philosophie moderne. J'aurais à protester contre cette interprétation qui ne reprend pas d'assez loin la question. Car je ne me place pas, pour commencer, dans le *sujet*, (ce qui suppose une distinction conceptuelle et un travail de l'entendement morcelant), je me place avant cette dichotomie, dans l'action qui est immédiation, synthèse du sujet et de l'objet, opération réele et prospiciente, mais non encore connaissance analytique et refléchissante." Blondel, *Correspondence Blondel-Valenisin*, II (Paris: Aubier, 1957), p. 191.

implicitly. Whatever the smallest phenomenon necessarily requires for its subsistency must be simultaneously affirmed. The whole chain of necessary conditions requires the nail from which it hangs. In unfolding the necessary conditions we recognize the truth and reality proper to each phenomenon; but the dynamism of action, which is at no time absent in the development of thought, cannot be arrested at any one stage, but forces the mind to solidify the consistency of the smallest phenomenon within the unifying firmness of the whole system.[55] Not until the end of the growing expansion when we make "the series of objects share in the reality of the term which was already present from the beginning" can we affirm the reality of the phenomena.

An adherence to one's own reality requires, therefore, an adherence to the totality of being. If the dialectic of action shows that an existential commitment to one's true nature demands that we open ourselves for God's initiative, then a rejection of "the being who illumines all reason and for or against whom everyone pronounces himself"[56] would mean a rejection of one's own reality.

The crucial text in which Blondel combines "objective" knowledge with "subjective" knowledge by means of the option, reads as follows:

"We have the idea of an objective reality, we affirm the reality of things, but in order to do so, it is necessary that we pose implicitly the problem of our destiny, and that we subject all we are and all that is for us to an option. We only arrive at being and beings by passing through this alternative; the way we solve it will inevitably change the meaning of being. The knowledge of being implies the necessity of the option; being in knowledge is not before, but after the freedom of choice. . . The knowledge which before the choice was simply subjective and propulsive becomes afterwards privative or constitutive of being."[57]

[55] "Tout se tient dans le réel, et l'on ne connaît parfaitement quelque chose, que dans la mesure où l'on connaît tout. Car, puisque l'être est un, pour connaître exhaustivement un phénomène quelconque, il faut connaître tout le réel dont il fait partie." *Taymans d' Eypernon, op. cit.,* p. 17.

[56] Blondel, *L'Action,* p. 435.

[57] "Nous avons l'idée d'une réalité objective, nous affirmons la réalité des objets; mais, pour le faire, il est nécessaire que nous posions implicitement le problème de notre destinée, et que nous subordonnions tout ce nous sommes et tout ce qui est pour nous à une option. Nous n'arrivons à l'être et aux êtres

Before the option we have what Blondel calls "a subjective knowledge of the truth," a necessary knowledge which proposes an inevitable alternative. After the option, there is the additional "objective knowledge of reality." If the option is negative the objective knowledge is privative of being; if it is positive then it puts us in possession of being. What Blondel is saying is that subjective knowledge becomes objective by means of an existential choice.

The subjectivity we are dealing with here is the subjectivity of the phenomenological method. It is "that source of spiritual activity which, either in the order of knowledge or in the order of the will, is determined only by the object but in such a way that without it the object could neither be conceived nor willed."[58] The subjective knowledge that precedes and proposes the option imposes itself universally and necessarily upon every individual, whatever his disposition, his willingness or unwillingness to accept it. "What is necessarily present in thought" is called "purely subjective." In traditional terminology it is not subjective at all, it is sound rational or speculative knowledge.[59] Whatever this subjective knowledge conceives is necessarily conceived as really existing. The option does not make this knowledge more objective, in the sense that there is a better *adequatio rei et intellectus*. The subjective knowledge is the best possible *adequatio rei et intellectus*. Nothing can improve on it. The option produces an *adequatio mentis et vitae*. "La vue de la vérité" becomes "la vie de la vérité." It brings thought alive, it makes the knowledge of the truth a possession or privation of the truth. It is a different way of knowing without change of object: speculative knowledge of the truth becomes effective knowl-

---

qu'en passant par cette alternative: selon la façon même dont on la tranche, il est inévitable que le sens de l'être soit changé. *La connaissance de l'être* implique la nécessité l'option; *l'être dans la connaissance* n'est pas avant, mais après la liberté du choix . . . La connaissance qui, avant l'option, était simplement subjective et propulsive devient, après, privative et constitutive de l'être." *Ibid.*, pp. 435-436, 437.

58 Y. de Montcheuil, *Pages religieuses de M. Blondel* (Paris: Aubier, 1942), p. 53.

59 "What Blondel calls 'subjective knowledge of truth,' is precisely what ordinarily is termed objective knowledge and to which Aristotelian and Scholastic tradition attributes an ontological value." Bouillard, *Blondel et le Christianisme* (Paris: Editions du Seuil, 1961), p. 148.

edge of the truth, cognition becomes agnition. Although subjective knowledge always implies and underlies objective knowledge, the option decides whether subjective knowledge becomes effective or privative.

Thus philosophy of action shows the necessity of the option. Without it there will be no solution to the problem of human destiny. It goes even so far as to establish the necessary subjective truth of a positive option, but it is at that point that philosophy reaches its limit. There the "science of action" terminates and action takes over to provide the "objective" possession of the truth, in freedom and choice. Thus the strength of philosophy lies in its weakness. It can construct the autonomous system of necessary ideas; it can do so independently of the optional choice that leads to a possession of the truth, because where there is necessity there is no freedom of choice, and no "objective" being which results only from an option. At that point its strength turns necessarily into weakness because "the fundamental principle on which phi- losophy depends as a specifically defined science is that even the complete knowledge of thought and of life does not supply or suffice for the activity of thinking or living."[60] This necessary re- serve must become the principle of doctrine. Philosophy has as its function to determine thought and the postulates of action, without either providing the being of the notions it studies, or the fulfill- ment of the exigencies it discovers. Actual thought and life are transcendent to the immanence of this integral determinism of philosophy, and it is on condition that reason recognizes the integrity of its immanent system of thought that it will discover its own insufficiency. The more complete and rigid the system of logically linked ideas will be, the more will reason recognize that its power does not lie in the recuperation of freedom and reality, but in its mediating role vis à vis of freedom.

It is clear, from what has been stated, that the immanent affirma- tion of the transcendent, whether freedom or the supernatural, does not touch the transcendent reality of these immanent affirmations. The distinction between subjective and objective knowledge allows the philosopher to study religion from a strictly theoretical stand- point. "Formerly identical with objective faith, subjective faith is essentially at the mercy of rational criticism, while objective faith

[60] Blondel, *Letter on Apologetics*, p. 180.

remains untouched."[61] If, therefore, the study of the conditions of action forces us to include as a final condition the complete gratuitousness of the supernatural, then philosophy will have to include this notion as the final link in the conditional chain of thought.

> "If in the study of sensible reality and even of the lowest form of existence, we find, in so far as we try to disengage some objective element, that our thought loses itself without ever being able to pin down this sensible or scientific or metaphysical phenomenology, it is perhaps because we can never touch being at any point without encountering at least implicitly the source and bond of all being, the universal Realizer. Neither sensation, nor science, nor philosophy terminates absolutely in itself."[62]

Because action cannot complete itself on the natural level, Blondel adds a final link: the supernatural. It is at this point that philosophy and theology meet. "For both faith and reason teach that the supernatural must be humanly inaccessible."[63] Blondel finds in the very principle of immanence the reason for philosophy's autonomy and strength and concomitantly the source of its most fundamental weakness and essential insufficiency. "It is when it is fully developed that [philosophy] becomes most clearly incomplete."[64] The method of immanence thus provides philosophy not only with the possibility of discussing the supernatural without destroying its transcendence, but it turns the possibility into an obligation. The principle of immanence reveals man's most fundamental, philosophically unexplainable, contingency.

The required transition from subjective knowledge to objective knowledge is possible only by adding the hypothetical necessity of the supernatural to the chain of action's necessary conditions. This is what Blondel means, we believe, when he writes that: "we must now face the fact that the question of method which we have had to raise here as a particular problem is at bottom a quite general and essential problem of philosophical doctrine."[65]

The role of philosophy thus consists in building a logical and necessary system, antecedent to the option, that enables freedom

61 *Ibid.*, p. 158.
62 *Ibid.*, pp. 201-212.
63 *Ibid.*, p. 160.
64 *Ibid.*, p. 159.
65 *Ibid.*, p. 163.

to realize itself. Philosophy is nothing but the methodical and systematic organization of spontaneous thought at the service of life and freedom. The essential link between the necessity of philosophy and freedom of the life of action enables philosophy to be an autonomous science.

> ". . . It is the determinism, underlying as it does even the use of freedom, which makes it possible to constitute philosophy as a science."[66]

The very necessity of the supernatural, of a gratuitous gift fulfilling man's deepest aspirations, results from the logic of determinism which by its nature tends necessarily to completeness and serves freedom. The necessity is part of human freedom itself. The necessity of an order of conditions whose realization is to be obtained by freedom is a scientific necessity, a hypothetical necessity. The reality and realization of that which is seen as necessary depends upon another element which remains outside of philosophy. Only the effective praxis of life can produce the possession of this "subjective necessary truth."

The familiar observation that thought and life are not identical does not mean that thought is divorced from life. It simply means that the determinism of thought is not all of life; there is more to life than logical determinism. Life obeys its own rational power which forces it to affirm in freedom (option) the logic of action which is unveiled in philosophy.

> "It is not the question that, by willing, we make reality subsist in itself because an arbitrary decree would have created it in us; the question is that, by willing, we make it exist in us because it is and as it is in itself. This act of the will does not make reality depend on us; it makes us depend on reality."[67]

II

THE INSUFFICIENCY OF PHILOSOPHY

> ". . . by this word (action) we must understand the concrete activity of living thought which expresses to ourselves both ourselves and everything else, although we shall never become

66 *Ibid.*, p. 168.
67 Blondel, *L'Action*, p. 440.

'adequate' to the least of our ideas; and also the initiative by which our instincts, our desires and our intentions are expressed in everything else, although our constantly renewed efforts to attain ourselves never make us 'adequate' to ourselves."[1]

Human freedom is militant. We are neither all powerful dreamers, nor wheels in a mechanism.[2] This is the repeated revelation of action: freedom and necessity are present in the same act and at the same time. We are committed to action but the commitment is not the result of man's own free initiative.

"Judging from the immediate evidence, action appears as the most general and constant fact of life, as the expression in me of a universal determinism. It takes place without me. More than a fact, it is a necessity."[3]

We act without knowing what action is; we are brought into existence without having asked to live. We are involved, we must act. Our actions carry with them the weight of an eternal responsibility and even at the price of blood, action cannot be undone. Even suicide is an act. "Thus, I am condemned to life, condemned to death, condemned to eternity. Why, and by what right, since I have neither known nor willed it?"[4] Man is a prisoner of his actions. As soon as they are accomplished they weigh on his entire life. The past is forever, and what man has done is a burden which he must bear to the end. What we call our freedom is burdened with a weight of necessity. Thus a first glance at man's condition reveals the "impossibility of abstaining and refraining, the inability to be satisfied, to suffice, to break free (from all action)."[5]

1 Blondel, *Letter on Apologetics*, p. 181. ". . . par ce mot (l'Action) il faut entendre l'acte concret de la pensée vivante qui nous exprime à nous-même avec tout le reste, sans que nous égalions jamais la moindre de nos idées, aussi bien que l'iniative par laquelle nos instincts, nos désirs et nos intentions s'expriment dans tout le reste, sans que notre effort perpétuellement renouvelé pour nous atteindre nous égale à nous-même." Blondel, *Lettre, Premiers écrits I* (P.U.F., 1956), p. 65.

2 Cf. A. de Waelens, *Une philosophie de l'ambiguité* (Louvain: Publications Universitaires de Louvain, 1951), p. 321.

3 "A consulter l'évidence immédiate, l'action, dans ma vie, est un fait, le plus général et le plus constant de tous, l'expression en moi du déterminisme universel; elle se produit même sans moi. Plus qu'un fait, c'est une nécessité." Blondel, *L'Action*, p. VIII.

4 *Ibid.*, p. VII.

5 *Ibid.*, p. X.

The awareness of this necessity is at the same time an indication of man's deeper desire to act freely. Man wants to be what he has to be, but freely, because "if I am not what I want to be, that is, what I want to be not merely with my lips, or in desire or imagination, but with all my heart and strength and in my acts, then I am not. In the depths of my being there is a will and love for being, or else there is nothing. . . Were being to be involuntary and forced, it would not be being, so true it is that the last word of all is goodness, and that to be is to will and to love."[6]

Action is not merely a mechanical necessity, it is also an obligation. Man has an obligation to will freely what he has to face and what presents itself as interior impulse or psychological drive. Man has nothing that he has not received, but at the same time it is necessary that everything arise from him, even the being he has received and which seems to be imposed upon him.[7] The problem is inevitable; each man inevitably resolves it; and this solution, right or wrong, but voluntary as well as necessary, each one lives out in his actions.[8]

The Problem of Freedom

The easiest way to solve the problem is to deny its existence. We should, therefore, first investigate whether man can escape the problem of his freedom and his destiny. In the first part of L'Action Blondel shows that man cannot avoid facing the problem of his destiny and the meaning of his life. The escapist who does not deny the necessity of action but simply refuses to take life seriously neutralizes the necessity of action by surrendering himself to its constraint without resistance. The dilettante lends himself to everything without committing himself to anything in particular. He follows necessity everywhere but never questions its demands. He wants to play and enjoy himself and is not really interested in action. When he does act, he affirms everything, both the yes and the no, but in giving himself over to everything, he gives himself to nothing. This refusal to choose is a form of universal detachment which actually is the most acute expression of self-attachment

6 *Ibid.*, p. XXIII.
7 *Ibid.*, p. XXIV.
8 *Ibid.*, p. VIII.

and absolute independence. Everything becomes light and charming, because everything is empty.

> "An enormous burst of laughter, a lugubrious pleasantry, a practical joke . . . nothing, that is what has been made of man and his destiny."[9]

Blondel shows how this escape from the demands of action is practically impossible. At the heart of the most outrageous negations and extravagances of the will, there is an initial movement which always persists and is secretly loved and willed even when it is denied and abused.[10]

To the pessimist who, in addition to not wanting anything, positively wills nothingness, Blondel points out the internal contradiction of such an attitude. The effort to destroy within himself all willing is the fruit of a deeper desire:

> "To conceive nothingness, one must begin by affirming and denying something else, so that thought posits its nothingness only by escaping from it invincibly and by surrounding it as with an eternal presence."[11]

We cannot deny the necessity to will because *nolo velle* is reflectively translated into *volo nolle*,[12] the act of willing underlies the will-not-to-be.[13] Man cannot stop willing, since he always wants something, whatever that may be. He cannot will nothingness because this very act implies the affirmation that there is something. Thus man not only wants that there be something, but he also affirms it necessarily because he cannot destroy the will-to-be without giving a positive solution to the problem: "there is something in our sensations and pleasures, in our knowledge and our actions."[14]

9 *Ibid.*, p. 10.

10 *Ibid.*, p. XX.

11 *Ibid.*, p. 32.

12 "Et 'je ne veux pas vouloir,' *nolo velle*, se traduit immédiatement dans la langage de la réflexion en ces deux mots: 'je veux ne pas vouloir', *volo nolle*." *Ibid.*, p. 12.

13 "On a beau aiguillonner la pensée et le désir: du *vouloir-être*, du *vouloir n'être pas*, du *vouloir ne pas vouloir*, il subsiste toujours ce terme commun, *vouloir*, qui domine de son inévitable présence toutes les formes de l'existence ou de l'anéantissement, et dispose souverainement des contraires." *Ibid.*, p. 37.

14 *Ibid.*, p. 41. "Dans mes actes, dans le monde, en moi, hors de moi, je ne sais où ni quoi, *il y a quelque chose* . . . Ces mots sans doute n'ont aucune précision philosophique: ils précèdent toute profession de phénoménisme, de criticisme ou d'idéalisme; ils traduisent le mouvement naïf de la vie qui s'éprend d'elle-même et de tout ce qui la soutient sans savoir ce qu'elle est."

The Antecedent Determinations of Freedom

After this first affirmation[15] which eliminates the possibility of denying the problem and giving it a negative solution, the way is open to the discussion of the different levels of human activity. Since men's will has an object, the first question to be asked is what is that object is. Blondel shows that the object willed is never equivalent to the primitive élan of the will. There always appears an inadequation between the so-called *volonté voulante* and the *volonté voulue*. It is precisely the task of the philosopher to determine the series of necessary conditions to be integrated in order that the object willed may become equal to the primitive impetus of the will of man. All that appears anterior, strange or consequent upon the will must re-enter the will on a voluntary and conscious level. If he follows the exigencies of the élan of the will to their last implications, the philosopher will know if men's action can be defined and limited to the domain of human activity or whether it surpasses the limits of the natural order.[16]

[15] This affirmation is the positive result of a negation. In the conscious effort to give a negative solution to the problem, man *wants* that there be something. "Cet aveu de la naïve expérience ne m'est point imposé malgré moi: j'ai voulu qu'il y ait quelque chose . . . On a opté pour ce *quelque chose* qui est immédiatement senti, connu, désiré de tous, qui offre a l'activité humaine un champ immense . . ." *Ibid.*, p. 43. Man is committed to further investigation and has to determine the content of this first affirmation.

[16] "On verra ainsi rentrer dans le plan volontaire de notre vie cela même qui paraît antérieur, étranger ou conséquent à la volonté. Et en suivant jusqu'au bout de ses exigences l'élan du vouloir, on saura si l'action de l'homme peut être définie et bornée dans ce domaine naturel . . . : à partir du premier éveil de la vie sensible jusqu'aux plus hautes formes de l'activité sociale, se déploie en nous un mouvement continu dont il est possible de manifester à la fois l'enchaînement rigoureux et le caractère foncièrement volontaire. Ainsi chemin faisant à travers la longue enquête qu'il nous faut instituer, devra-t-on remarquer que l'apparente nécessité de chaque étape résulte d'un vouloir implicite. D'une part, les termes successifs de l'action seront reliés entre eux de telle facon que la rigueur scientifique se communiquera de proche en proche à des études qui ne l'ont pas encore reçue. D'autre part, en découvrant comment nos actes s'épanouissent irrésistiblement et par quelle intime impulsion ils se dépassent sans cesse ainsi que les remous d'une pierre tombée dans l'eau profonde, on sera préparé peu à peu à la question suprême: Oui ou non, pour qui se borne à l'ordre naturel, y a-t-il concordance entre la volonté voulante et la volonté voulue; et l'action qui est la synthèse de ce double vouloir trouve-t-elle enfin en elle-même de quoi se suffire et se définir? Oui ou non, la vie de l'homme se restreindra-t-elle à ce qui est de l'homme et de la nature, sans recours à rien de transcendant?" *Ibid.*, pp. 41-42.

The most elementary objects of man's will are the data of sense experience. However, he cannot hold the dynamism of the will at the level of appearances and be satisfied with a meaning of life that would be realized on the level of its phenomenological origin. The inconsistency and insufficiency of sensation spur man to surpass the purely phenomenological order and to organize these phenomena into an objective system: this is man's response to the purely phenomenological. Science searches for the reason, the why, behind appearances. The objectivity of the sciences, and the solidification and consistency of appearances, require the activity of a subject who possesses the power of coordination to construct a scientific system. Yet positive science does not find in itself the unity and coherence that it employs but does not explain. In raw sense experiences there occurs indeed an awakening of curiosity which is a condition for the possibility of sensation, but the actual acquisition of all positive truth requires the mediation of action, and therefore the presence of a subject without whom no positive truth is possible.[17] Blondel writes:

> "In reflecting upon the development of the exact sciences and the stages of their abstract constructions, one notices that they bring into their successful synthesis an ever increasing element of subjective ideality."[18]

Thus a coherent organization of the phenomena implies the work of a subject and the presence of thought which in its synthetic activity coordinates and fashions the obscure energies from which it emerges. The activity of mind and will expresses itself in an intentional act, which is the purposeful and free possession of the data of experience. As soon as thought and purpose appear on the scene of human activity and reflection begins to control the spontaneity of man, the actions of man become human acts. The act that proceeds from this typically human activity may be called an

---

17 "Qu'on regarde le chemin parcouru dans cette première étape depuis le point où l'on a voulu qu'il y ait *quelque chose*. De la première intuition sensible qui ne paraît simple que parce qu'elle est confuse et qui reste nécessairement inconsistante est né le besoin scientifique. Mais la science positive ne trouve pas en elle-même l'unité et la cohésion dont elle se prévaut sans l'expliquer; de même que, dans la sensation brute, il y a déjà l'éveil d'une curiosité sans laquelle il n'y aurait point même de sensation, ainsi toute vérité positive exige la médiation d'une acte, la présence d'un sujet sans lequel il n'y aurait point de vérité positive." *Ibid.*, p. 101.

18 *Ibid.*, p. 89.

actus humanus, a rational, a voluntary and free act, or just simply action.

It is clear, then, that for Blondel the decisive condition for the possibility of action cannot find its explanation in the sum total of spontaneous forces or in antecedent determinations of the phenomena of sensation.

"There is an irreducible surplus which makes the synthesis surpass the elements of which it is composed."[19]

Man is not aware of conscious action and personal reflective activity unless he sees in such an activity a characteristic of infinity and transcendence. He finds in his actions a kind of a creative sovereignty which is the efficient and final cause of his free activity. The role of action is crucial in the constitution of reason and the birth of the idea of freedom because it is in it and through it that an infinite and transcendent power proper to the agent becomes apparent.[20]

However, man's creative freedom is not absolute, for reflective consciousness is not the fruit of a totally original initiative. The spontaneity and the deterministic progress of life produce necessarily and inevitably the consciousness of freedom; there is a *necessitas libertatis*. This does not mean that freedom gives way to determinism, but it shows that the antecedent determinations result necessarily in an awareness of freedom which in turn ratifies everything that precedes and wills all that enables it to will.[21]

Man has no right to ignore the origin or efficient cause of his freedom. Without it the necessity-character of freedom cannot be explained. Yet, once this is understood, man should focus his attention on the final cause and look towards the future and the unlimited horizons which solicit the will towards final fulfillment. It

[19] Louis Dupré, "Reflections on Blondel's Religious Philosophy," *New Scholasticism*, XI (1966), p. 7.

[20] "Bref, pour agir il faut participer à une puissance infinie; pour avoir conscience d'agir il faut qu'on ait l'idée cet infini pouvoir. Or c'est dans l'acte raisonnable qu'il y a synthèse de la puissance et de l'idée d'infini; et cette synthèse c'est ce que l'on nomme la liberté." *Ibid.*, p. 121.

[21] "Aussi faut-il maintenir à la fois ces deux assertions: d'une part le déterminisme a abouti nécessairement à la conscience de la liberté; d'autre part la liberté, en prenant conscience d'elle-même ratifie tout ce qui précède et veut tout ce qui lui permet de vouloir." *Ibid.*, p. 121.

is there that freedom will find sufficient reason for its free determinations.[22]

Consequent Determinations of Freedom

The freedom of man qualified by antecedent determinations must be further specified by the determinations consequent upon the recognition of freedom. Freedom has to be liberated from the necessity with which it appears into the life of man. Since neither the denial of necessity nor the denial of freedom is possible, there remains only one solution.

> "It is this necessity that must be justified, and how to justify it except by showing that it is in harmony with man's deepest aspirations? Since I am only conscious of my servitude because I envision and long for complete liberation, the two terms of the problem are sharply opposed: on the one side is all that dominates and oppresses the will, on the other side is the will to dominate everything or at least to be able to ratify everything freely."[23]

Blondel will try to integrate necessity into freedom in order to show that the necessity that appeared as tyrannical constraint and the obligation that at first seemed despotic must be seen finally as a manifestation and exercise of the profound action of the will.[24] The integration that Blondel proposes is the equation of the *volonté voulante* with the *volonté voulue,* that is, of that which proceeds from the will (*quod procedit ex voluntate*) with that which becomes the object of the will (*quod voluntatis objectum fit*).[25] The *volonté voulante* is an implicit will, a kind of objective aspiration, a necessary tendency underlying the free activity of man. He describes this aspect of the will as a *"voeu secret,"*[26] *"volonté profonde,"*[27] *"volonté initiale."*[28] The drama of human action consists

---

22 "Quiconque est né pour l'action regarde devant soi; ou s'il cherche d'où il vient, c'est seulement pour mieux savoir où il va, sans jamais s'enfermer dans le tombeau d'un passé mort. En avant, et en haut. L'action n'est action que par là. Il est de science que la cause finale est plus que la cause efficiente; et c'est pour le montrer qu'il était nécessaire de définir le rapport qui les unit." *Ibid.,* p. 123.

23 *Ibid.,* p. X.

24 *Ibid.,* p. XXIII.

25 *Ibid.,* p. 132.

26 *Ibid.,* p. 100.

27 *Ibid.,* p. 277.

28 *Ibid.,* p. 133.

in the failure of the explicit will (*la volonté voulue, la volonté réfléchie, volonté positive*)[29] to be adequate to the implicit will of man. The discrepancy between what man basically wills and what he is consciously willing manifests itself with uninterrupted consistency. Whatever he may be willing explicitly is always insufficient to satisfy man's inner aspiration. The object of a particular act of the will, *id quod volo*, never exhausts the fullness of the act of willing as such, *quod volo*.[30]

Having explained the genesis of freedom and how all powers of nature drive man onward from mere sensation to tendencies which in turn are received in a mental synthesis and represented under the form of an end to be realized, Blondel, as we have seen, went on to show that action must have motives. The conscious presence of these motives engenders the awareness of freedom. The freedom initially experienced by man is so dynamic that it takes up all the necessary conditions for its existence and ratifies all the antecedent determinations.[31] From here on Blondel will follow the established freedom as it is pushed onward by the implicit will towards further development and expansion. Freedom demands in fact, free exercise of the explicit will as well as conscious deployment of its primitive élan.

> "It is a delicate task to show that freedom by exercising itself necessarily does not give up its free appropriation of everything forced upon it by the future. Determinism seems to precede it, to accompany it and to follow it, because it originates, grows and fructifies inevitably."[32]

---

29 *Ibid.*

30 The *volonté voulante* and the *volonté voulue* have no reality outside each other. They are not "entia quae" but "entia quibus." The *volonté voulue* is what we ordinarily understand by will, a conscious decision making power. The *volonté voulante* is more original and could be referred to as a natural drive which is anterior to conscious decisions. It drives our explicit will onward to the point where the latter will openly take possession and freely will the spontaneous choice of the primitive will.

31 "Determinism is an essential part of freedom. It is the self-imposed condition of freedom which never destroys what it conditions. True freedom *makes* its conditions into determinations; it consents to natural impulses only after having provided them with an entirely new efficacy." Louis Dupré, *art. cit.*, pp. 7-8.

32 *Ibid.*, p. 126.

From the established fact of freedom follows a series of necessary actions and relations which step by step will form the framework of man's life and the natural ground of his morality.[33] The centripetal movement of antecedent conditions becomes a centrifugal movement when it goes out to meet the consequent determinations of the outside world and fellow men. Arisen from action, supported and perfected by action, freedom must plunge into further action to make known the moral duty which it implies.[34] Granting that man's real intention has been actualized, although "we almost never do all of what we want to do,"[35] we experience like a real servitude the necessity to lock our intentions up in the narrow frame of an act and in doing so exclude all the other possibilities open to the beautiful agility of thought.[36]

Man's freedom must express itself in an action in which it embodies and realizes itself. "It is by action that the soul (man's free activity) takes a body and the body receives a soul; action is the substantial bond that makes a natural whole out of them."[37] The transcendent power to give a soul to things implies the necessity for man to immanentize this power in a body. Here, as in all other stages of the development of action, "that which is necessary in the obligation to act corresponds to the sincerity of the primitive desire. This very necessity contributes to the realization of the fullness of freedom."[38] The all-embracing yearning of our primitive will accounts for our insatiable exigency and drives us continuously further.[39] At each step the dynamic circle closes itself only to open up even wider and to serve as a point of departure for a new expansion. Action always surpasses its own accomplishments. In this

---

[33] *Ibid.,* p. 137.

[34] "En posant le déterminisme, on en tire la liberté. En voulant la liberté, on exige le devoir. En concevant la loi morale, c'est une nécessité de la produire dans l'action pour la connaître et la déterminer en la pratiquant." *Ibid.,* p. 143.

[35] "nous ne faisons presque jamais tout ce que nous voulons; nous faisons souvent ce que nous ne voulons pas; nous finissons pas vouloir ce que nous ne voulions pas." *Ibid.,* p. 178.

[36] *Ibid.,* p. 193.

[37] *Ibid.,* p. 186. "Le corps est un conséquence et comme un prolongement de notre nature subjective: on veut qu'il soit." *Ibid.,* p. 153.

[38] *Ibid.,* p. 140.

[39] "C'est donc la plénitude de notre volonté originelle qui rend compte de notre insatiable exigence et nous projette toujours plus loin." *Ibid.,* p. 198.

way the center of gravity of the will which gives body to action must be relocated, it must be placed beyond the individuality of man.[40]

Action continues its relentless course. It pours itself out and enters into the world outside itself in search of an equal partner. New determinations from the outside world must be accepted. "In order to act man must accommodate himself to his surroundings, and these surroundings in turn contribute to his way of being and acting."[41] The initiative of the will ("exergy") is modified by the actions of others ("allergy"), which seems to make freedom subject to "coaction" and a prisoner of the activity of others. The world, however, becomes the body of our body and the free activity of man will penetrate the world as it has penetrated his own body. It wants to become the center of all that surrounds it and serves it. In going out into the external world, man discovers his own identity. Projecting himself into action, he mirrors himself and shows himself to others.[42] Action and self-fulfillment are therefore simultaneously communication and dialogue.

Man not only encounters the material world but finds new determinations in himself when he encounters other persons endowed with freedom. The others are not only objects in relationship to which he has to define himself, but also subjects animating and enriching his individuality. In its dynamic endeavor to make the explicit individual will coincide with the implicit will of man,[43] the expansion of freedom leads man towards others; a type of intersubjective union is thus desired which goes beyond simple social cooperation and mutual respect. The will experiences the need for a real, intimate and total union, a union of love, for, in Blondel's characteristic expression: "the will does not want to re-

[40] "L'action ne se restreint pas dans l'enceinte de la vie individuelle. Point de cause efficiente en nous qui n'aille à une cause finale et ne soit un aveu implicite d'insuffisance et une demande de secours . . . Nous sommes forcés de donner, parce que forcément nous avons à recevoir." *Ibid.*, p. 201.

[41] *Ibid.*, p. 214.

[42] "Qui donne reçoit. Mais le reçu, le *donné* sert de guide au donnant." *Ibid.*, p. 224. "L'action est une fonction sociale par excellence. Mais précisément parce qu'elle est faite pour autrui, elle reçoit d'autrui un coefficient nouveau et pour ainsi dire une réformation. Agir c'est évoquer d'autres forces, c'est appeler d'autres *moi*." *Ibid.*, p. 239.

[43] Yves de Montcheuil, *Maurice Blondel: Pages religieuses* (Paris: Aubier, 1942), p. 36.

main alone (*seule*) in order to be more one (*une*)."[44] Man is attracted by others, and especially by the opposite sex. He wants to be loved and he wants to love. He is like a child speaking to himself with candid tenderness and is surprised to find out that he cannot embrace himself.[45] Man, therefore, looks for the arms of a partner to form a union of two persons which objectifies itself in a child. Once again the circle provisionally closed is opened up and expanded. Man seems to lose himself more and more and abandon his freedom to others. He is bound to his partner, to his family, and to society. He is obliged to will his own country and humanity itself.[46] None of these objects are at his service but represent values to be served by him, and are continuously creating new and more extensive duties.

What appears as servitude and limitation of freedom is in reality a further realization of freedom. In man's implicit will family, society and country are immanent. If he gives himself openly and courageously to others, the individual will find himself enriched and realized as a man. Thus individual life tends to identify itself with universal life: "Man seeks, as it were, to unite himself with humanity and to form one will with it."[47]

Blondel is convinced that the individual man's attempt to engage in an all-encompassing way with all that is or was or will be human is the keystone that supports and gives meaning to the aspirations of the will of each individual human being. Moreover it is the foundation in man for his natural morality. Of necessity, man professes a certain "Weltanschauung," a practical utilitarian frame of reference in order to deal with the normal experiences and events of daily life. Everything that presents itself to him will be assimilated according to the norms of this natural morality.

Man establishes for himself a number of universal notions and ideals to which he will conform his feelings and conduct and adopt

44 Blondel, *L'Action*, p. 252.

45 *Ibid.*, p. 255.

46 "Ainsi l'action, issue d'abord de l'intention toute personelle de l'agent, s'est peu à peu incorporé la famille et la cité pour prendre son vol dans l'humanité entière. En exigeant la solidarité totale de tous les hommes, elle vient ce qu'elle veut être; elle veut être, par libre choix, ce qu'elle est deja par l'impulsion de son premier élan." *Ibid.*, p. 277.

47 "l'homme aspire, pour ainsi dire, à épouser l'humanité même et à ne former avec elle qu'une seule volonté." *Ibid.*, p. 275.

the facts of experience. These universal notions and ideals generated in the dynamic expansion of action constitute a metaphysics. In the process of integrating all the data of the real order, man reaches out to the notion of an ideal order that surpasses this universal reality and seems to give it a foundation grounded on absolutes. The ideal order of metaphysics is not simply something of our own construction; it has a necessitating character. As soon as we attempt an explanation of the facts, whatever its simplicity or depth may be, we have committed ourselves to metaphysics. It becomes a norm for further action that in turn commands the absolute of moral duty. Thus we find within man the obligation to be free, an obligation with an absolute character, which in turn is experienced as a further determination. Once again man has to recognize an heteronomy transcending his freedom and obliging him to accept the responsibility to be free.[48]

After having shown that the individual aspires to become all that man can be, it becomes necessary to show that man aspires to become god.[49] In the effort to satisfy the implicit act of willing and to take possession of his freedom, man will try to absorb the absolute which appears in the progressive development of action. The absolute required to fill the insatiable need of the will, will persecute man until he has given it volume, name and significance. *Aliquid superest*,[50] there is a surplus of energy and exigencies of the primitive élan of the will for which the explicit will cannot find meaning, use or adequate fulfillment. Of this surplus of energy and this lack of complete adequation the science of action has to give account. Man is constantly tempted to assign to the excess of human action a finite and manageable object and to fashion for himself a god who satisfies the twofold need of man to create and to master the very god he created. He wants this god to resemble him and at the same time be infinitely different. Man is inclined to choose his god from among the series of objects within his reach

---

[48] "Le terme auquel l'action réfléchie semble éprouver l'impérieux besoin de se suspendre, c'est un absolu, quelque chose d'indépendant et de définitif qui soit hors de l'enchaînement des phénomènes, un réel hors du réel, un divin." *Ibid.*, p. 303.

[49] Yves de Montcheuil, *op. cit.*, p. 35.

[50] Blondel, *L'Action*, p. 305.

and to place it outside this series. This is the phenomenon of superstition.[51]

Blondel gives a remarkable account of this superstitious attitude
as revealed in the practices of civilized man and in the different
forms of pseudomysticism. He places in the category of superstition
the idolatry of science or art, the moralism of Kant, and even the
rationalistic deism that claims to take hold of transcendent being
and in defining and affirming it makes it totally subordinate to the
finite reality based upon it.

The superstitious attitude implies a contradiction, as Blondel
points out. Men make relative realities absolute and finite objects
infinite, and turn to certain phenomena to make them infinitely
more than they really are. In spite of the realization that no finite
reality can exhaustively cover the plenitude of the will's primitive
aspirations, superstition continues in vain to look for and attach
itself to a finite object.

> "From all these probing efforts only this doubly imperative
> conclusion can be drawn: it is impossible not to recognize the
> insufficiency of the whole natural order and not to discover a
> further requirement; it is impossible to find within oneself
> the means of satisfying this religious requirement. *It is neces-
> sary,* and *it is impracticable.*[52] . . . These are roughly the
> conclusions of the determinism of human action."[53]

Sensation, positive science, the affirmation of freedom, the development of individuality, the establishment of family and society,
the acceptance of a metaphysics and morality: all these different
aspects of human life are justified in the philosophy of action by
the impossibility of dispensing with them. All of them are necessary but man cannot limit himself to any one of them. He must go
beyond them because the primitive élan of the will is insatiable

---

[51] "En se répandant, en se réalisant au dehors la volonté ne peut retrouver
dans son oeuvre tout ce qu'elle recèle au sanctuaire de la vie intérieure. Cette
infinitude qu'il sent obscurément en soi et dont il a besoin pour être ce qu'il
veut être, ce qu'il est déjà de désir et d'intention, le sujet la tire de soi; il
s'offre, sous la forme d'un symbole ou d'une idole, son propre besoin d'achèvement et de perfection; il adore l'incommunicable et inépuisable vie dont il porte
la source latente. C'est donc au coeur même de l'action volontaire qui réside un
mystère dont on n'échappe pas au desir de se rendre maître. Comme le spectre
solaire, plus ample que les rayons colorés, l'action est à la fois lumière et chaleur
obscure. Elle va plus loin que notre vue se porte." *Ibid.,* p. 306.

[52] *Ibid.,* p. 319.

[53] *Ibid.,* p. 321.

and does not find full satisfaction within the domain of human activity.

The Insufficiency of Notional Knowledge

The insufficiency of the natural order is the central theme of Blondel's philosophy. Not only action but the whole of reality gives witness to the impossibility of finding meaningful satisfaction in the purely natural domain. The limitation of man's being manifests itself with equal urgency in thought and existence. The material as well as the spiritual dimension of life shows a need for transcendent fulfillment. Everywhere the philosopher is confronted with a need and desire for something more.

In his trilogy, which offers a speculative philosophy and a metaphysics in the classical sense of the word, Blondel illuminates this theme of insufficiency more systematically and more extensively, although perhaps less dramatically, than he does in *L'Action* of 1893. In the two volumes of *La Pensée,* he analyzes the genesis of thought and describes the stages of consciousness antecedent to the appearance of the human *cogito.* Human thought, like human action, does not come to rest on a merely immanent understanding but deploys itself according to an inborn plan that leads man beyond himself towards a destiny of which philosophy, by its own power, cannot determine the contents. However, philosophy can study the functions of thought and the conditions for its fulfillment.

In the first volume of *La Pensée,* Blondel describes the dynamism of thought, its origin, its nature, and its final destination. Thought does not suddenly arise from nothingness, like "un enfant trouvé," but has an obscure birth in the cosmos, in the world as a *solidum quid.*[54] Prior to the subject—object distinction, thought is a *cosmic* thought.[55] The world *is* and it is *thought,*[56] because the global unity

---

[54] Maurice Blondel, *La Pensée I, op. cit.,* p. 35.

[55] The doctrine of cosmic thought is a very much neglected aspect of Blondelian metaphysics. Claude Tresmontant in *Introduction à la métaphysique de Maurice Blondel* (Paris: Editions du Seuil, 1963) rightly emphasizes this aspect of Blondel's thought. For Blondel, cosmic thought, which is immanent thought present in the cosmos from the beginning, is not a divine substance mixed with matter but it is created thought present from the most elementary levels of matter. "La pensée ne surgit pas tout d'un coup par un choc mystérieux ou comme tombant du ciel. Elle suppose des dessous, toute une longue gestation, et, selon la formule scolastique qu'il s'agit seulement de bien entendre, la pensée est inviscérée dans la nature; elle a son fondement dans les choses; c'est dans la matière qu'elle a pour nous son principe d'individuation et son point d'appui

and total interdependency of everything in the universe is more a

---

fondamental." (*La Pensée* inédit, dictée Isambert, 1927). Blondel considers cosmic thought as thought *ut natura,* a thought which is not yet thought by man, a so-called *pensée pensante.* ". . . nous prenous ici la pensée, plus pensante que pensée, à l'etat de spontanéité naturelle et primitive, *cogitatio ut natura, etsi non-dum cogitata.*" (*La Pensée I,* p. 104). The dynamic unity which Blondel defends against a doctrine of static multiplicity reflects itself in action, thought and being to the point where all these spheres of life open up towards a supernatural order and destiny. The dialectics of action, thought and being not only manifest the dynamic unity of life but also assist in bringing it about. The genesis of freedom and thought reflect the progressive evolution of being itself. The *itinerarium ad Deum* begins already at a cosmic and biological level which prepares and supports continuously even the highest intellectual operation. As Tresmontant points out, there is a striking parallelism between Blondel's onto-genesis and Teilhard de Chardin's cosmogenesis. They both think along the same line, the former from a philosophical standpoint, the latter from a scientific standpoint. Teilhard and Blondel knew one another and exchanged memoirs with A. Valensin as a mediator. (Cf. Henri de Lubac, *Blondel et Teilhard de Chardin,* [Paris: Beauchesne, 1965]). Blondel was happy to find that he and Teilhard had certain common views and intuitions. Tresmontant writes: "Si la métaphysique de Blondel est construite selon un dynamisme qui ne s'achève que par en haut, dans un problème suprême. Blondel a appelé le point capital de la métaphysique chrétienne, c'est que cette métaphysique est une métaphysique de la création, soucieuse de suivre la création dans son devenir, dans sa genèse, dans sa consti-tution progressive, dans son dynamisme interne, qui ne s'achèvra que par en-haut, dans un clef de voûte qui n'est pas fournie d'en-bas, par des mains d'homme, mais qui est donnée d'en-haut, par Dieu même. Notons déjà une analogie, une parenté profonde entre la vision du monde de Blondel et celle de Teilhard, qui écrivait: 'Contrairement aux apparences encore admises par la Physique, le Grand Stable n'est pas au-dessous—dans l'infra-élémentaire,—mais au-dessus—dans l'ultrasyn-thétique.' (*Le Phénomène humain,* p. 301). 'Si les choses tiennent et se tienn-ent, ce n'est qu'à force de complexité, *par en-haut*' (*Ibid.,* p. 37). Teilhard est conduit à cette conclusion par les analyses de ce qui apparait dans la réalité cosmique, physique, biologique et humaine, par une description fidèle de la cosmogénèse, de la biogénèse et de l'anthropogénèse, par une phénoménologie de l'évolution dans son sens plénier, c'est-à-dire, du dehors, en savant, en physicien, en naturaliste. Tandis que Blondel parvient à un résultat convergent par une analyse ontologique." (Tresmontant, *op. cit.,* pp. 31-32). There is a re-markable similarity in interest between Blondel and Teilhard but on several delicate points the differences seem to be substantially more than just divergences. Teilhard was happy to find in the explications of Blondel "une résonance exact à sa pensée la plus vivante." (De Lubac, *op. cit.,* p. 14). A great deal of similarity is due to the mediation of Valensin, the mutual respect and intellectual humility of both men, who did not want to hurt each other. They were united in their effort to understand the fullness of Christian revelation from a philo-sophical or scientific standpoint. "Leurs problèmes, quoique semblables, ne coincidaient pas, et ne pouvaient pas coïncider." (*Ibid.,* p. 15).

56 Maurice Blondel, *La Pensée I, op. cit.,* p. 36.

truth than a reality.[57] It is a truth in the sense that such a unity in such multiplicity reveals an immaterial aspect in the center of the most material world. The world is a subsistent thought and a spectacle of intelligibility independent of an intelligent spectator.[58] This cosmic thought is not a compact, immovable, frozen being, identical with itself; on the contrary it reveals itself in multiplicity and diversity which it tends to unify. Thus thought is from its beginning characterized by a duality that corresponds to the relation between the one and the many, between being and becoming, in the structure of the unvirse.

An analysis of organic life reveals an active power that unifies and organizes the diversity in the physical world. Thought appears on that level as *organic* thought. Thought, as we find it in the animal world, manifests more forcefully the tendencies to unify diverse functions, to coordinate opposite forces, and to protect and perpetuate the species. All of this requires a "knowledge without consciousness."[59] Blondel calls this *psychic* thought.

Finally we have a "thinking thought" coinciding with the rise of consciousness. The birth of the latter is at first more thinking thought (*pensée pensante*) than thought already thought (*pensée pensée*). To achieve understanding, thinking thought has to be explicated in a thought already thought. For this, thought has to go through a process of abstraction that will never be able to adequately translate the full contents of the thinking thought. Thought already thought is therefore marked by an inherent insufficiency and incompleteness. There are "two thoughts in each one of our thoughts," Blondel writes.[60] They coexist in each thought

[57] Independently of any explanation the brute fact of the unity and coherency of the universe underlies all our habits of thought and life as a framework of which we are seldom aware but that we implicitly affirm as the condition of all intelligibility. The inner harmony of this unity and coherency is the extramental adequation between the elements of the universe before it is apprehended or affirmed by a subject.

[58] *Ibid.*, p. 34.

[59] "Il arrive un moment où sans ces moyens de défense et d'initiative, la survie deviendrait impossible et c'est ainsi qu'apparaît, comme une réalité physique, l'efficience d'un vie psychique, d'une sorte d'imagerie au de connaissance sans conscience." *Ibid.*, p. 73.

[60] Blondel, *La Pensée II*, p. 13.

man has. Organically and inseparably related, they vitalize the spirit with a ceaseless pulsation.

The first aspect of thought deals with the universal, the rational, and the abstract. The second aspect is concrete thought or real knowledge; it has to do with the singular, the unique, the ineffable.

> "The drama of thought begins and develops in movement and reciprocal stimulation of these two perspectives and these needs which cannot be brought together into a perfect union."[61]

Blondel gives abstract and unifying thought the name "noetic," while the element of diversification and multiplicity is called "pneumatic."[62] These two aspects of thought cannot be identified as

---

61 Blondel, *La Pensée II*, p. 141.

62 "Nous appelons *noétique* l'aspect cosmique de la pensée en tant qu'elle fait de l'univers, en fait et en droit, un *solidum quid, sub specie unius et totius*. Nous appelons *pneumatique* l'aspect cosmique de la pensée en tant qu'elle introduit partout de la diversité, de la singularité, des *vincula* partiels, des centres de réaction, des perspectives différenciées et concourantes. Pulsation incessante, diastole et systole de la natura entière, rythme rationnel et vital de l'homogène et de l' hétorogène qui se poursuivent et s'échangent sans jamais se séparer ni se conjoindre. Or, il importe de noter:

1. que ces deux aspects, en apparences inverses, sont dependant coordonnés, symétriques, s'appelant ou se provoquant l'un l'autre, chacun n'étant possible et intelligible que par l'autre et pour l'autre.

2. que ces deux faits, dynamiquement à la recherche l'un de l'autre, *fonctions* l'un de l'autre, sont cependant incommensurables et irréductibles—quoique indispensables et conspirants.

3. que leur recontre, impossible dans la fini, comme la convergence de deux parrálléles, stimule comme un *optandum* indéclinable le mouvement de la nature et de l'esprit.

4. que le *trou réel* et incomblable est la place préparée, la place attirante où est attendue l'intervention, de l'esprit avec tous les concours éventuels sans lesquels la vie de la pensée ne pourait se parfaire.

5. qu'au cours de tout le développmment de la pensée, les réussites et les ascensions partielles sont comme des amorces, des relais, où se confirment, se relancent, précisent, se font plus urgentes les requêtes de l'Unité et les exigences de la Pensée de plus en plus consciente de sa fonction suprême. (*La Pensée I*, p. 240). Cf. De Jaer and Chapelle, "Le noétique et le pneumatique chez Maurice Blondel. Un essai de définition," *Revue Philosophique de Louvain*, 59 (1961), pp. 609-630. This critical study compares the seventh excursus of *La Pensée I* with the precisions of terminology which were gathered in *Exigences philosophiques du Christianisme*. It strongly emphasizes that the ontic correlate of the noematic condition is the tension which exists between the constitutive principles of unity and diversity of being.

separate thoughts. They are united in their mutual irreducibility. Any attempt to bring about a conscious unification of these two aspects of thought in the full light of explicit knowledge is doomed to failure. This crisis constitutes the very dynamism of thought, which is very similar to the dynamism Blondel finds at the center of the will. This "living duality of our intelligence"[63] is in reality the *conditio sine qua non* for thought as such.

The dialectic of the intellect consists in a continuous exchange between the noetic and pneumatic aspects of thought. Its purpose is "to show the emptiness and void, so to speak, which separates in the most secret part of ourselves the elements of thought."[64] The need, or rather, the duty that thought has to criticize itself, to understand and justify itself, drives noetic thought forward to an integration of the entire contents of pneumatic thought. The hidden truth of life and action must be explicated by noetic thought which by its very nature is unable to handle the total contents of pneumatic thought. The impossibility of arriving at an adequation of life and thought gives us the certitude of a need, an indeterminable principle of disquietude and insatiability.[65] This dramatic need commands the study of the conditions of possibility for the dénouement and completion of thought.

Thus the second volume of *La Pensée* studies "the conditions of possibility for the completion of thought" and the adequation of noetic and pneumatic thought. In the gap which separates these two aspects of thought, an invisible agent must be at work who gives foundation to pneumatic and fulfillment to noetic thought. The impossibility of thought adequation is the rational expression of the inadequation which Blondel observes in the will. Both thought and will are equipped with a surplus of energy, an abundance of light, an insatiable need for transcendent fulfillment. An absolute thought that would unify the noetic and pneumatic aspects of human thought, exhaust the energy, and control the light is not only a desirable answer but an absolute condition for the very possibility and positive fulfillment of thought. Thought transcending the duality of human thought is the only fully ex-

---

[63] Cf. Jeanne Mercier, "La philosophie de Maurice Blondel," *Revue de Métaphysique et de Morale*, XLIX (1937), p. 627: "La dualité vécue de l'intelligence."

[64] Blondel, *La Pensée II*, p. 234.

[65] *Ibid.*, p. 247.

planatory answer which would make human thought possible, give it dynamism, and bring it to completion. Human thought must look for the ultimate meaning of things from the viewpoint of this thought of thoughts: "to think is to think God,"[66] and to understand is to have God's understanding of reality.[67]

Contingency of Being

The inadequation perceived in the drama of human action and thought is enlarged in *Etre et les êtres* to become a drama of the entire universe and total realm of being. While we have an awareness of the inevitable presence of being, none of the realities we experience exhausts our basic idea of being. Matter is being, living organisms, persons, societies, the whole universe are beings. Nevertheless none of these creatures nor the world as a whole suffices to fulfill our primitive exigency for being. While none of these objects is the totality of being either individually or collectively, they do have a certain reality and consistency. It may be possible to call into doubt the existence of a particular object, but it is not possible to maintain a universal doubt concerning the existence of all objects:

> "None of these objects which in common language are called beings respond fully to the essential core of being discovered by reflection on this spontaneous notion of being. At the same time, we cannot annihilate all these realities which, without possessing absolute consistency, support themselves mutually, to the point that we never think of destroying them all together in our thought."[68]

The perception of this inadequation is the recognition of the problem of the coexistence of contingent and absolute being. There is at the heart of every being a presence of the Absolute. The question then is whether this presence of the Absolute destroys the consistency of created being or solidifies it. The thirst for being which characterizes all created being is a need for becoming more than it at first sight is. The consistency, the nature, the well-

66 This expression, which Blondel borrows from Lachelier, is quoted in one of his letters to Blaise Romeyer. Cf. Romeyer, *La Philosophie religieuse de Maurice Blondel* (Paris: Aubier, 1943), p. 334.

67 *"per oculos Dei, per cor Christi."* Blondel, *Exigences philosophiques du Christianisme,* p. 295.

68 Blondel, *L'Etre et les êtres,* p. 145.

rounded definable essence of a being, is not static but dynamically developing toward what it is in fullness within the totality of being. Each degree of being finds its justification and solidity in a spiritual destiny to which it is ordained and to which it contributes. "Matter is that which can be vitalized, life is that which can be spiritualized, the spirit is that which is capable of aspiring to God and can be deified by grace."[69]

In bringing the notion of being and becoming together Blondel does not propose an assimilation of *fieri* and *esse,* but hopes to revitalize the oversolidification of being. Created being is essentially open towards becoming more, and its insufficiency is precisely an expression of the *fieri*-aspect of everything that is. The actuality and existential relations of contingent beings are not simple juxtapositions that are occasionally or artificially brought together. Within the very actuality of their nature contingent beings are unfinished, incomplete, open to unlimited growth, and ready to play a more intensive role in the drama of life which will unveil their ultimate role and destiny.

The universe is ruled by an interior norm, a so-called "ontological norm." If one emphasizes the idea of "becoming" the concept of being is qualified and controlled by this ontological norm which is the built-in logic of things according to which they acquire and express their actuality. This norm is the immanent directrix of every creature to be developed and to be brought to fulfillment according to the plan and design of the creator. There is nothing arbitrary or absurd, nothing left to chance or fatalism in Blondelian ontology. Man is called to cooperate in the achievement of creation according to a well-determined direction of final perfection. This direction is written into the depth of each being, *intimior intimo meo.* Man judges himself by this hidden law in the experience of its appeal and the recognition of its truth. In spite of its transcendence, this logic of being is always infused, as a morphological law, a substantial form directing from within the growth and regulating the interior and exterior relations of beings.[70] This ontological norm is the fundamental framework, the sum total of effective

69 *Ibid.,* p. 263.
70 *Ibid.,* p. 227.

principles that constitute and govern the plan of the creator in the progressive realization of beings.[71]

Blondel's ontology is thus essentially an ontology *in via*. The insufficiency of the created order stares, as it were, the philosopher in the face at each level of being. All the beings, whether taken individually or together, stand in need of fulfillment. They seem to be "indigent and in debt even where they mainfest a specific reality of their own and an apparent efficiency."[72] The experience of this universal insufficiency rebels against any intelligible idea of being.[73] As Jeanne Mercier[74] remarks, Blondel's insistence upon the deficiency of beings is basically nothing else than a more dramatic version of the very fundamental and traditional theme of the finiteness and contingency of beings. It is precisely their contingency that prevents beings from enjoying a true unity, autonomy, and perpetuity and accounts for the fact that they do not realize the fullness of being.

The relative consistency of created beings and the real distinction in contingent beings between essence and existence lead to the affirmation of absolute being,[75] the identity of essence and existence.[76] The duality in beings demands unity, the insufficiency of immanentism imposes the affirmation of absolute transcendence, the natural limitation of beings proves the ontological necessity of Being. The whole of reality is, as it were, a constant prayer for being.[77]

> "The beings, although they really have being, *are not their own being*. Their contingency is tied up with the permanence and internal action of a presence without which they would be, so to speak, less than if they were not at all. . . . All the

---

[71] "Elle est dynamique et dramatique, requérante et édificatrice. Elle est l'explicitation, en connaissance et en action, de la *norme* qui traduit en nous la présence d'un dessein divin et d'une exigence transcendante, exigence à laquelle conspirent notre intelligence et notre volonté selon leur rectitude essentielle, puisque cette règle loin de les refouler est, pour elles, réalisatrice et libératrice." *Ibid.*, p. 526.

[72] *Ibid.*, p. 133. *L'Action, II*, p. 395.

[73] *L'Etre et les êtres*, p. 137.

[74] Jeanne Mercier, *art. cit.*, p. 635.

[75] *L'Etre et les êtres*, p. 370.

[76] "Le cosmos tout entier qui porte son attestation, qui crie son besoin d'autre chose que lui, qui sans se renier . . . ressemble à une parition au seuil . . . de l'existence véritable." *Ibid.*, p. 137.

[77] *Ibid.*, p. 386.

contingent beings imply the necessary, one and unique Being which is all Being."[78]

The One Thing Necessary

Let us now return to the dialectic of action and with Blondel as our guide, see where it leads us. The determinism of action, thought, and being leads man on a three-lane highway to the recognition of the insufficiency of the natural order. The excess of energy in man's deepest aspirations necessarily generates the idea of a possible solution. As Bouillard[79] points out, the notion of necessity and impossibility that appears at this stage of the dialectic is the notion of the supernatural. Blondel does not mention it by name and he cannot do so at this point, but it is here that the solution through the supernatural announces itself in disguise.

The acceptance of such a solution seems at first to be the final blow to human freedom, as well as a total defeat for human action, thought, and existence. Human action finds itself "contradicted and vanquished."[80] The wider it deploys its will, thought, and being, the more do frustrations and limitations appear. At the very same time that man establishes the necessity to be free and autonomous and discovers a more demanding heteronomy at each step he takes, he continues to pursue his basic aspirations to be truly free. He wants to solve this primitive contradiction: he wills, but he did not choose to will.

> "Without doubt most men have neither enough penetration nor perhaps enough pride to feel all the strangeness of this problem. Nevertheless, all have the lively feeling of not belonging to themselves: they know that they find in themselves neither the origin, nor the substance, nor the end of their action."[81]

The result of Blondel's investigations in his first *L'Action* and his more extensive metaphysical trilogy is totally negative in appearance and content. The final product of the dialectic of action, thought, and being is a bottomless pit, a suicidal emptiness, a universal frustration, a necessary and unacceptable insufficiency. The

[78] *Ibid.*, p. 135
[79] Bouillard, *op. cit.*, p. 321.
[80] *L'Action*, p. 328.
[81] *Ibid.*, p. 326.

whole effort and aim of action consists in transplanting the contents of the subject's spontaneous life into what he explicitly chooses as its end.[82] If this were done freedom would at last be fully itself. This effort is hopeless.

The impossibility that the will experiences in choosing itself directly will lead the will to choose itself indirectly by choosing objects *for* itself.[83] The phenomena of the natural order, as has been seen, do not provide man with an object by which the subject can satisfy its infinite yearning. This continuous frustration of willed action manifests the indestructibility of voluntary action, for man would not be aware of this frustration, if there were not in him a will that is superior to the contradiction of life.[84]

> "It is impossible to escape the problem of action, it is impossible to give it a negative solution, it is impossible to find one's own identity, the way we want to be; in short, it is impossible to stop, to retreat or to advance alone. . . It is this conflict which explains the necessary appearance of a new affirmation in man. It is the reality of this necessary presence which makes possible the awareness of this very conflict."[85]

Man cannot be totally and forever separated from himself. He would not exist; he would be a non-being, because he would be absurd, as Sartre holds. Yet action shows us man's existence convincingly and undeniably, so that on the ontological level there must be a presence of man to himself.

> "The religious problem, then, far from being superimposed on the problem of subjectivity constitutes the very center of it."[86]

The "one thing necessary" to furnish this self-possession must be more than a mere idea. The living necessity to will oneself freely is incomprehensible unless we accept the existence of "something beyond" from which man's freedom derives and which he has not yet attained. Man must surrender his freedom to the source from which it originates if he is to exercise it as it demands to be exercised. The actual exercise of freedom is impossible without the actual existence of this source.

82 *Ibid.*, p. 133.
83 Cf. Trethowan-Dru, *op. cit.*, p. 89.
84 Cf. Bouillard, *op. cit.*, p. 86.
85 *L'Action*, p. 339.
86 Cf. Louis Dupré, *art. cit.*, p. 3.

"The proof of the existence of the 'one thing necessary' derives its strength and value from the order of phenomena in its
entirety. All that we will supposes its existence; all that we
are demands its existence. One can, therefore, formulate in
a thousand ways the argument from universal contingency."[87]

The argument *a contingentia* does not look for the necessary outside the contingent but shows that the necessary is already present
within the contingent as a reality. Intead of making the "one thing
necessary" a transcendent but exterior support, the argument reveals that the necessary is immanent at the very center of all that
is. Instead of proving the relative necessity of the contingent, it
reveals to us the absolute necessity of the "one thing necessary."
Per ea quae non sunt et apparent ad ea quae non apparent et sunt.[88]

The traditional theistic arguments are not rejected by Blondel
but they are somewhat interiorized. Blondel accepts the demonstrative force of the traditional proofs, but claims that "as soon as we
regard the 'one thing necessary' from without as a mere object of
knowledge or a mere occasion for speculative study without fresh-
ness of heart and the unrest of love,[89] we are left with little more
than a purely logical, abstract, and partial argument for God's
existence.[90] The traditional proofs need to be supplied with the
dynamism that flows from the total movement of the life of action
in order to have the constraining force which does not leave any
"loophole for the mind."[91]

In spite of some evidence to the contrary, the existence of God
is not simply a postulate requiring an option in the process of which
the *affirmation* of God's existence would take place. The anti-
intellectualist flavor and the role of voluntary commitment which

[87] *L'Action*, p. 343: "Cet unique nécessaire se tient à l'entrée ou au terme
de toutes les avenues ou l'homme peut entrer: au bout de la science et de la
curiosité de l'esprit, au bout de la passion sincère et meurtrie, au bout de la
souffrance et du dégout, au bout de la joie et de la reconnaissance, partout,
qu'on descende en soi ou qu'on monte aux limites de la spéculation métaphysique, le même besoin renaît. Rien de ce qui est connu, possède, fait,
ne se suffit ni ne s'annihile. Impossible de s'y tenir; impossible d'y renoncer."
[88] *Ibid.* This is the text of Blondel's *ex-libris.*
[89] *Ibid.*, p. 352.
[90] "Le Dieu des savants et des philosophes n'est pas le Dieu à croire et
à aimer. C'est un objet don't l'homme s'estime le maître. Loin que l'affirmation théiste soit un achèvement vers la foi au Père céleste, elle est, en fait
souvent un obstacle." Blondel, *Attente du Concile*, p. 44.
[91] *L'Action*, p. 341.

Blondel adds to the purely logical formulation of the theistic arguments are less disturbing to us today than they were to most of the early interpreters and critics of his thought. The cogency of the traditional proofs has frequently been questioned by modern philosophers and the contemporary mind is better conditioned to accept the validity and necessity of the categories of personalistic philosophy in establishing the existence of God.[92] There is considerably less resistance to admit to the domain of metaphysics a lived ontology which keeps the mind from running wild or drying out.

From the mere fact of arriving at God the problem of man's destiny is not thereby solved. The recognition of God is not a one-time declaration of dependence upon the "one thing necessary" after which man can go back to the order of the day and enclose himself in the world of natural phenomena. Man must act out this recognition. The problem of insufficiency is a fruit of action and only action can resolve it.[93] As soon as man thinks he knows God adequately, he no longer knows him; it is simply impossible to immanentize and immobilize the absolute. Since man must admit that God is the ultimate of his thought and life, it is necessary for

---

[92] Blondel would agree with Jolivet: "L'erreur ici se fait de penser que ce qui fait la valeur des preuves de Dieu, c'est leur appareil conceptuel et logique, alors que c'est plutôt l'exigence d'absolu et l'élan spirituel qui les soustient . . . En réalité, la vérité de Dieu est vécue avant d'être connue: les preuves qui ne sont pour elle que des moyens de s'exprimer et de se justifier réflexivement. Ici, plus qu'ailleurs, la spontanéité rationnelle est le principe moteur de toute réflexion." Jolivet, *Le Dieu des philosophes et des savants* (Paris: Fayard, 1956), p. 111. Once the *relative* value of the metaphysical proof of God is understood, there is no longer any reason to minimize or deny its *value*, as is done by some modern philosophers. The more dramatic and more personal dependence upon God experienced by man does not make a cold logical insight into this dependence superfluous. On the contrary it supports it and confirms it, and can help man to acknowledge his radical dependence.

[93] "La pensée de Dieu en nous depend doublement de notre action. D'une part, c'est parce qu'en agissant nous trouvons une infinie disproportion en nous-mêmes, que nous sommes contraints à chercher l'équation de notre propre action à l'infini. D'autre part, c'est parce qu'en affirmant l'absolue perfection nous ne réussissons jamais à égaler notre propre affirmation, que nous sommes contraints à en chercher le complément et le commentaire dans l'action. Le problème que pose l'action, l'action seule peut le résoudre." *L'Action* 1893, p. 351.

him to make his thought and life adequate to this transcendent principle and end of human action.[94]

Thus man wishes to possess the "one thing necessary" which is present to him and to become God in some fashion. But this he cannot attain to or possess by himself and he is thus brought face to face with an inescapable alternative.

> "Man alone cannot be what he is already in spite of himself, what he tends to become voluntarily. Yes or no, is he going to will to live, even to die of it, as it were, by consenting to be supplanted by God? Or will he pretend to get along without Him, profiting by His necessary presence without making it voluntary, borrowing from Him the power to get along without Him, and infinitely willing without willing the infinite?"[95]

In one form or another this dilemma appears to all men, although not with the same clarity and acuteness. Each one of us is aware that something ought to be done with his life and that what he perceives as the most important, the unique necessary problem ought to be solved. The determinism of action produces inevitably this dilemma and man must necessarily make a decision. This the science of action demonstrates convincingly. The option is imposed, one cannot escape it, he cannot not choose, the alternative is there: either "to be god without God and against God, or to be god through God and with God."[96]

The development of action has brought man face to face with this dilemma. The dialectic of action has provoked the option. Philosophy leads man to this precise point with all the compelling force of the science of action. At this point there is a fork in the road. Man cannot stop at the point of bifurcation but has to make a choice as to which direction to take. Philosophy shows him the necessity of the choice but does not force him into either direction. The dialogue between Blondel and his reader at this dividing point is no longer characterized by the necessity of science but turns into

---

94 "Nous ne pouvons donc connaître Dieu sans vouloir le devenir en quelque façon . . . C'est parce que j'ai l'ambition d'être infiniment que je sens mon impuissance, je ne me suis pas fait, je ne peux ce que je veux, je suis contraint de me dépasser; et, en même temps, je ne puis reconnaître cette foncière infirmité qu'en devinant déjà le moyen d'y échapper, par l'aveu d'un autre être en moi, par la substitution d'une autre volonté à la mienne." *Ibid.*, p. 354.

95 *Ibid.*, pp. 354-355.

96 "L'homme aspire à faire le dieu: être dieu sans Dieu et contre Dieu, être par Dieu et avec Dieu, c'est le dilemme." *Ibid.*, p. 356.

an urgent appeal to make a good choice in freedom. Blondel will show to his reader that man can attempt to be self-sufficient without God, and to limit his aspirations to the domain of his own activity. But at the same time he will demonstrate that by doing so, man works against the conditions required for the fulfillment of the primitive élan. To believe that one can find within himself the energy of his action and the means of fulfilling his own destiny is more than simply to ignore an optional and gratuitous gift which does not interfere with the happiness of an average life. It is much more than this, Blondel insists, since it really is to belie one's own aspirations and, under the pretext of loving himself, to hate and to lose himself.

> "The horrifying grandeur of man: he wills that God no longer exist for him and God no longer does exist for him. . . . When God ratifies this solitary will, it is damnation. *Fiat voluntas tua, homo, in aeternum.*"[97]

Such is the message Blondel gives to his reader who at the point of bifurcation chooses to walk alone, to be god without God and not to surrender his freedom to the transcendent source. The hands of the philosopher are tied, for he cannot keep man from choosing this direction. The science of action limits itself to bring forth and show the idea and existence of the "one thing necessary," but it is up to man to freely accept the last meaning of his own being.

When the correct option is made, man opens himself to an action other than his own. He lets the "First Cause take the first place" in his action and recognizes his dependence upon this mysterious guest. This is the only proper way to solve the dilemma. Man must somehow be reborn by an abnegation of himself and by accepting a God present and hidden in the heart of all voluntary action.[98] How can man freely install God in his own life in order that this immanence of the transcendent may finally complete the conscious operation of the will and bring the explicit will and action into equation with the primitive élan of one's freedom? Blondel suggests as a first step that man ought to adhere to what he believes to be good and in

97 *Ibid.,* p. 371.

98 "Car rien de ce qu'il a voulu et fait ne lui est acquis, ni ne peut subsister s'il n'en trouve la possession et la consistance en ce Dieu présent et caché de toute action volontaire. Et ce qu'il faut ici nommer Dieu, c'est un sentiment tout concret et pratique: pour le trouver, ce n'est point la tête qu'il faut se rompre, c'est le coeur." *Ibid.,* pp. 374-375.

accord with his conscience. Man does not have to do all the good he wants to do, *bona omnino facere,* but it is important for him to do well all he does, *bene omnia facere.*[99] A second step is to accept in humility and love suffering, death and mortification. The acceptance of the will of God purifies man's will from all the shadows of self-sufficiency and lights up God's presence in the emptiness caused by mortification and self-denial.

To maintain a good conscience and embrace suffering heroically, sacrifice and self-abnegation are good but insufficient. A third and last step is necessary: "After one has done everything as if expecting nothing from God, he has to expect everything from God as if he himself had done nothing."[100] Ascetic heroism and a life lived according to conscience may still persuade man that he achieve the work of personal salvation by himself and on purely human strength. However, the work of salvation is not achieved by him alone, because he does not even start it.[101]

Thus faced with the problem of his final destiny, man ought to act according to the measure of his light and strength while keeping in mind that he will find nowhere in himself the principle, the means, or the end of his actions. He should never believe that he has reached the end but he should continuously resume his course with the élan of a young soldier and with the timidity of a novice.[102]

The absolute initiative of man has to be replaced freely by the absolute initiative of God. The true will of man is the divine will. To confess his fundamental passivity is for man the highest form of activity. Whoever recognizes that God does everything, to him God gives the grace of having done everything. To appropriate nothing for himself is the only way of attaining the infinite.[103]

The science of action leads man to the recognition of a need that he cannot satisfy himself and that he must fulfill if his life is to have meaning and his primitive aspirations are to achieve their end.

---

99 *Ibid.,* p. 376.

100 *Ibid.,* p. 385.

101 *Ibid.,* p. 385.

102 *Ibid.,* p. 386.

103 "La vraie volonté de l'homme, c'est le vouloir divin. Avouer sa foncière passivité, c'est pour l'homme, la perfection de l'activité. A qui reconnaît que Dieu fait tout, Dieu donne d'avoir tout fait; et c'est vrai. Ne se rien approprier c'est la seule méthode d'acquérir l'infini. Il est partout où l'on n'est plus a soi." *Ibid.,* p. 387.

"The idea of the supernatural is, properly speaking, what is absolutely impossible yet absolutely necessary to man."[104]

The necessary idea of the supernatural is the expectation of the gift of a higher life. The internal logic of human action, therefore, continues in its dynamic search for the understanding of the content of this gift, if this expected gift is given to man. The philosophy of action, in other words, remains essentially unfinished, it is by definition a philosophy of insufficiency. It knows that the supernatural gift which is to satisfy man's need cannot come from within the natural order without losing its supernatural character. Religion would have to fulfill human action and comply with the exigencies of philosophical dialectics. Hence it would have to present itself to a certain degree as coming from without, from within history; more specifically, it would have to possess a supernatural character.[105]

As a Christian, Blondel was anxious to show that the Christian supernatural corresponds to the inner aspirations of man. However, as a philosopher, he could do no more than determine the necessary conditions of such a supernatural that would satisfy man's aspirations. Whether or not Christianity and the Christian supernatural measure up to the inner demands of the will of man is still a philosophical question and philosophy ought to be able to find an answer to it. What philosophy is incapable of doing is to show the necessity or factual realization of the Christian supernatural, not because of dogmatic definitions but because of its own radical insufficiency.

III

THE NECESSARY IDEA OF THE SUPERNATURAL

"Absolutely impossible and absolutely necessary to man, this properly speaking is the notion of the supernatural. Human action passes beyond man, and all the effort of his reason is to see that he cannot and must not stop at this point. This is a

---

104 "Absolument impossible et absolument nécessaire à l'homme, c'est là proprement la notion du surnaturel: l'action de l'homme passe l'homme; et tout l'effort de sa raison, c'est de voir qu'il ne peut, qu'il ne doit pas s'y tenir." *Ibid.*, p. 388.

105 Cf. Jean Lacroix, *op. cit.*, pp. 30-31.

cordial expectation of the unknown Messiah, a baptism of desire that human science is incapable of provoking, because this very need is a gift. Human science can demonstrate this necessity of it, but cannot cause it. Indeed, if it is necessary to establish a real relationship and cooperate with God, how could we presume to succeed in it without acknowledging that God remains the sovereign master of his gift and of his operation? This acknowledgment is necessary but remains inefficacious if we do not call upon the unknown mediator, or if we close our door to the revealed savior."[1]

Faced with the insufficiency of the immanent order of natural phenomena, the logic of action must determine the chain of necessities that could lead the drama of human action to its dénouement.[2] The inner dynamism of action cannot be halted within the realm of immanence. All proposed solutions to do so have shown to be philosophically ungrounded. The appearance of the idea of the Unique Necessary as the explanatory ground of all that exists is therefore not a luxury that man can dispense with, but a hard philosophical necessity. The order of nature is without foundation unless the Unique Necessary provides the solidity which is absolutely indispensable to the existence of this order. There appears in the immanent order of philosophy a necessary transcendence, a supranatural that is absolutely necessary. The will, the intellect, man's total being are forced to acknowledge that there is something else over and above natural phenomena. Their essential insufficiency is repeatedly and consistently revealed in the provisional solutions tried out by man.[3] In these solutions the effect is always greater than the cause. Man must therefore affirm something more than the existence of the phenomenological order; he must affirm the absolute. He must go beyond the immanent and affirm the necessity of the transcendent.

This avowal of insufficiency does not come from outside but from within man. At the very heart of his immanence man finds a need that is not fulfilled by the order of natural phenomena.[4] There is something in him that can never be explained by anything that ap-

---

1 Blondel, *L'Action*, p. 388.

2 *Ibid.*, p. 473.

3 Valensin, A., under "Immanence," *Dictionnaire d'apologétique* (1912), V. II, col. 592.

4 Sommerville, "Maurice Blondel and the Philosophy of Action," *Spiritual Life*, 7 (1961), p. 121.

peared earlier in the movement of the will. It is not a question of inventing something, whatever that may be, nor of adding to voluntary action something that was not already there; it is a question of grasping precisely what is already there, what consequently shows itself necessarily to man's consciousness, and is there always represented in some form. It is an unknown that must be discovered, but more by way of completing an inventory than by a progressive invention.[5]

The very avowal of immanence and its inability to satisfy his implicit aspirations leads man to affirm that beyond nature there is an order that is necessary as well as inaccessible to human action. The Unique Necessary demanded by the immanence of the natural order is thus revealed as an absolute necessity, and at the same time it is clear that it is absolutely inaccessible to our natural powers. Blondel claims that this combination of necessity and inaccessibility provides us with the proper notion of the supernatural. It is at this point, according to Alexander Dru, that Bouillard has made his most important contribution to an understanding of Blondel's thought.[6] The "supernatural," the absolute necessity and absolute inaccessibility of the Unique Necessary, which are revealed by the method of immanence, are, according to Bouillard, not the supernatural in the positively determined form given to it by Christian revelation, but the still undetermined supernatural, that philosophers, even among the pagans, have described.[7] By "supernatural order" we must understand, according to him, the relation of man and the world to the Unique Necessary which transcends the world and human activity. "It simply means that the world cannot do without God. . . It does not say more than the traditional proofs of God's existence."[8]

Between the insufficiency of the natural order and the specifically Christian supernatural order there is, according to Bouillard, a divine order which Blondel considers to be absolutely necessary and absolutely inaccessible to man. This is the order of the so-called "undetermined supernatural." The apparent insufficiency of the natural order makes the affirmation of the absolute necessity of such an undetermined supernatural absolutely necessary.

5 Blondel, *L'Action,* p. 340.
6 Alexander Dru, *op. cit.,* p. 90.
7 Bouillard, *op. cit.,* p. 70.
8 *Ibid.,* p. 98.

One may well question the meaning of the term "supernatural" in such a context. It is obviously not the specifically Christian supernatural. On the other hand, if supernatural simply means the natural relation between man and the Unique Necessary, then one may wonder what is "supernatural" about it. As Bouillard points out, Blondel often uses the term "supernatural" to distinguish man's relation to the transcendent from the phenomenological order of purely human activity.[9] The immanent order of the unbelieving positivist, which Blondel wanted to open up from within, was closed to the intervention of a first cause. The positivist considered the relation of man and the world to the Unique Necessary as alien and supernatural. For the scientist the natural order excluded a transcendent relation to the creator. In *L'Action* Blondel addresses himself to this kind of audience. He intends to break open the closed natural order and to show them the absolute necessity of affirming a super-phenomenological order, a transcendent relation, a "supernatural" foundation of the natural phenomena.

If Bouillard's interpretation is correct, then it must be admitted that Blondel sometimes fails to realize that he is slipping from one sense of "supernatural" into another,[10] even if one likes to believe that the distinction itself is always present to his mind and influences all his work. Duméry denies emphatically that the "supernatural" ever has this relative meaning.[11] He points out to

---

[9] *Ibid.*, p. 84.

[10] Duméry does not accept this. He writes: "Il est déjà fâcheux que Blondel attribue deux sens différents au même mot, dans le même livre, et même à deux pages d'intervalle." Duméry, *Raison et Religion dans la Philosophie de l'Action*, o.c., p. 35. He is referring to the last page of the fourth part of *L'Action*, p. 388, and the first page of the fifth part, p. 389.

[11] "Au plus fort de l'orage, quand on lui reprochait de tirer le surnaturel de la nature, Blondel-aurait eu cent fois l'occasion de dire: 'vous me méprenez: il m'arrive d'employer le mot *surnaturel* dans un sens large, selon une acception banale, non technique.' Il n'a jamais fait cette réponse. Il ne pouvait pas le faire. Le vrai est que, sur ce point, il n'a jamais varié. Il ne rencontre qu'un seul surnaturel, celui dont il déclare en 1893 que la philosophie peut en toucher la 'simple *notion*', mais non pas en atteindre '*l'essence*', celui encore dont il répète dans un lettre de 1894 qu'il 'élève l'homme au-dessus de tout être créé ou concevable', celui enfin qu'il définit en 1896: '. . . il n'y a de chrétien, de catholique, que ce qui est *surnaturel*,—non pas seulement transcendant au simple sense métaphysique du mot, . . . mais proprement surnaturel.' Bref, pour Blondel, . . . *surnaturel* signifie surnaturel, au sens propre, au sens catholique." Duméry, *op. cit.*, pp. 34-35.

Bouillard that Blondel often includes in the natural order the fundamental relation of creature to his creator and the knowledge of this order by the natural light of reason.[12] If "supernatural" in the fourth part of *L'Action* means what is absolutely impossible and absolutely necessary to man, then the idea of God which arises necessarily in man's conscience cannot be the total contents of this undetermined supernatural. The idea of God is not absolutely impossible to man. As has been remarked earlier, Blondel accepts the demonstrative force of the traditional proofs of God's existence. If the idea of God's existence were impossible to man, then the existence of God could never be demonstrated unless one resorted to intuitive knowledge and divine illumination.

However, the proof of the Unique Necessary derives all its force and validity from the order of phenomena.[13] The idea of God, which appears logically in the chain of necessary conditions of the determinism of human action, impresses upon human action a mark of transcendence. Man aspires to possess freely that which reveals itself as necessary for the achievement of the dynamism of the will. As soon as this idea arises, man wants to possess and become in some fashion the God who appears to be present to the very core of his existence. To be freely what he is of necessity man must integrate this further determination into his freedom. At this point of the development of action, the idea of God necessitates man to capture, as it were, God, the source of his vitality and action. The necessity of this enterprise appears to be absolute, but the possibility or impossibility to bring it to successful completion has not yet been clearly established at this stage of the dialectics of action. To the absolute necessity of the idea of God and man's necessary reaction to it, one must add the absolute impossibility of achieving what is necessary to man before he can properly speak of the idea of the supernatural.

To equate voluntary action with the positive aspirations of the will, an infinite power is required and requested, for man does not find in himself the strength to fulfill this requirement and to answer this request. The effort made by superstition has been proved to be a failure. The lesson learned from superstition is that the absolute cannot be controlled and localized in the material and immanent

---

[12] Duméry, *op. cit.*, pp. 35-37.
[13] Blondel, *L'Action*, p. 339.

order, it simply does not fit into the finite and natural domain of human activity without losing its infinity. But the dynamism of life, action, and thought will not come to rest until man freely wills this infinite power, incorporates it voluntarily into his life and places it at the very heart of his freedom as the source of all voluntary actions. The very impetus of the interior will is a living and existential testimony of the presence of this infinite power. Since man does his utmost but cannot exhaust or satisfy this dynamism of the will, the need and aspirations he experiences cannot be of his own making. The "need itself is already a gift";[14] the insatiable dynamism is not the result of man's own initiative but must have a transcendent origin. Therefore, "the absolute initiative of man has to be replaced by the absolute initiative of God."[15] It may be that man does not know how to define the form and shape of God's initiative, but whether he recognizes it distinctly, suspects it to be there, or flatly denies its existence, each of these attitudes requires and presupposes its necessary presence.[16]

It is in regard to this necessary presence and initiative of God that the explicit will has to take position. If man is unwilling to attribute the initiative to God and attempts to will infinitely without willing the infinite, and "uses God against God,"[17] then the affirmation of God is no longer an admission of his transcendence and initiative. In that case man has seemingly done the impossible and immanentized, as it were, the transcendence. This is the voluntary death of the impetus of the implicit will. The explicit will re-

---

14 *Ibid.*, p. 388.

15 *Ibid.*, pp. 386-387.

16 "Et qu'on ne s'imagine pas que, pour insérer dans notre vie ce caractère de transcendance, il faille toujours discerner la présence ou reconnaître distinctement l'action de Dieu en nous. Pour l' avouer, pour en user, il n'est pas indispensable de le nommer ou de le définir: nous pouvons même le nier, sans ôter à nos actes leur portée nécessaire. Car, en le niant, on ne fait que déplacer l'objet de l'affirmation; mais la réalité des actes humains n'est point atteinte, dans son fond, par le jeu superficiel des idées et des paroles. C'est assez que, même masqué et travesti, le bien universel ait secrètement sollicité la volonté, pour que la vie entière reste marquée de cette impression indélébile. Pour entendre son appel ou éprouver son contact, nul besoin de le dévisager. Ce qui surgit forcément en toute conscience d'homme, ce qui a, dans la practique, une efficacité inevitable, ce n'est pas la conception d'une vérité spéculative à définir, c'est la conviction vague peut-être, mais certaine et impérieuse, d'une destinée et d'un fin ultérieure à atteindre." *L'Action*, pp. 352-353.

17 *Ibid.*, p. 371.

fuses to accept the absolute impossibility of the absolute necessity.

Of course, on the level of voluntary action the affirmation of God still stands, but the negative option makes a destructive use of this affirmation. The gift of God's presence and God's initiative is used to strip man's voluntary action of the presence of God's infinite power. The dependence is affirmed but not recognized, the initiative is used but not attributed to God, the gift of God's action is changed into a personal possession.

The idea of the supernatural is, therefore, not simply identical to the idea of the Unique Necessary or to the logical affirmation of God's existence. Both are necessary to man but not impossible. Impossibility appears on the scene and has to be added to necessity when man translates the affirmation of the existence of the Unique Necessary into action and attempts to capture the Infinite and to control it within his own freedom. He discovers that he cannot master it, that it is not his, that it is a gift, a necessary gift.

The insufficiency of the natural order, the idea of the Unique Necessary, the affirmation of God's existence, the recognition of man's inevitable dependence upon God's initiative, are all stages in the genesis of the idea of the supernatural, but the actual birth of this idea takes place when man gives it independent existence and recognizes that he gave life to it because it first had given life to him.[18]

Bouillard states that "sovereign action of God is what is absolutely impossible and absolutely necessary to man, and that is what the word 'supernatural' here indicates."[19] What makes it

---

[18] "Car cette inquiétude persévérante n'est bonne que dans la mesure où elle stimule l'activité présente, alors même qu'elle ne nous permet jamais de nous y borner. C'est l'action même qui doit nous donner, avec l'aliment rassasiant, cette vigueur renaissante de la santé et cette faim insatiable qui est la marque d'une volonté saine et intègre. Jusqu'à notre désir de bons désirs, il faut que nous replacions hors de nous l'origine de ce mouvement volontaire. Même quand nous ne faisons que demander d'avoir de quoi donner, cette prière n'est pas toute de nous; et ce n'est prière qu'autant que l'aveu en est au moins implicite. A l'initiative absolue de l'homme, il est nécessaire de substituer, librement, comme elle y est nécessairement, l'initiative absolue de Dieu. Ce n'est pas à nous de nous le donner, ni de nous donner à nous-mêmes; notre rôle c'est de faire Dieu soit en nous comme il est de soi, et de retrouver au principe même de notre consentement à son action souveraine sa présence efficace. La vraie volonté de l'homme, c'est le vouloir divin." *Ibid.*, pp. 386-387.

[19] Bouillard, *op. cit.*, p. 98.

properly supernatural, undetermined supernatural, if one prefers that expression, is not solely the essential relation of creatures to their creator, but the recognition of the unilaterality and gift-character of this relation. The recognition of the gratuitousness is an essential ingredient of the idea of the supernatural. This idea is not purely logical but comes to life within action, is defined by the necessity of action and the impossibility of its achievement.

The philosophical idea of the supernatural has to include the existential recognition that action cannot come to completion unless God gives himself to us. Even when man desires "to be God without and against God," he uses and abuses the essential relation between God and creatures. If man wishes that God no longer exist for him, God does no longer exist for him.[20] In that case the gift of divine action is for man not supernatural at all; it appears to him as belonging entirely to himself. While borrowing from God the infinite power to act, man refuses to give credit to God. The proper idea of the supernatural does not exist for him. If the idea of a gratuitous supernatural gift is not accepted, then, at the moment of their birth, the ideas of the Unique Necessary, the Absolute, the Infinite, and the Transcendent deliver a still-born child.

The Philosophical Supernatural

Although the first confrontation with the Unique Necessary is already an implicit confrontation with the idea of the supernatural, the idea of the Unique Necessary that has to be affirmed with logical necessity needs to be accepted by a positive option before it becomes an explicit idea of the supernatural. Faced with the inevitable alternative the two possible options take a stand in regard to the Unique Necessary and the supernatural fulfillment of man's destiny. The positive option, however, will generate the idea of a gratuitous supernatural fulfillment, while the negative option will undermine the gratuitous character of the supernatural fulfillment and immanentize what is essentially transcendent. The negative option does not go far enough in its recognition of the Unique Necessary and stops short of the idea of gratuity; it arrests human action before it can generate the ideas of inaccessibility and gratuitousness that characterize the idea of the Unique Necessary.

[20] Blondel, *L'Action,* p. 370.

The idea of the supernatural which Blondel introduces at the end of the fourth part of *L'Action,* is the idea of the Unique Necessary accepted and existentially recognized as the Absolute to whom man has to surrender his will and to whose action he has to open himself. The idea of the Unique Necessary develops under the influence of an existential choice into an idea of the supernatural. It is human action and reaction which make it apparent that the absolutely necessary is absolutely inaccessible to man and, therefore, must be a gratuitous gift. An increasing awareness of man's inability to achieve by himself the transcendent fulfillment, which everyone must necessarily recognize, gradually begins to show "more supernatural" characteristics. The deeper man penetrates into this impossibility the sharper the character of the fulfillment of human destiny as a gift begins to stand out. In exploring the impossibility to which the logic of action has led man, the human will plays an important role. Man can resist the evidence and systematically refuse to accept the gratuity which at each step shows itself more and more convincingly. In his unwillingness to accept such a solution he can and sometimes does turn his eyes away from the gratuitous gift. On the other hand, if he admits the gratuitous character and inaccessibility of this gift, the idea of the supernatural characterizing human life will become gradually more authentically supernatural.

One can hardly speak of an idea of the supernatural before its gratuitous character and inaccessibility are conceived along with it. Although the philosophical idea of the supernatural is implicitly conceived in some way by all men without exception and with philosophical necessity, it develops into an explicit idea of the supernatural only under the influence of a positive choice. Since "under its rational aspect the word supernatural indicates what is essentially inaccessible to us in the Transcendent,"[21] the inacessibility must first appear in the idea of the Unique Necessary before it becomes an idea of the supernatural.

The idea of the supernatural thus appears as the result of the affirmation of the Transcendent. The rational demonstration of God is then distinguished from the possession of God, which becomes imperative once reason has shown his existence. The impossibility to take possession of God generates the idea of the necessity

21 Blondel, *L'Action II,* 1937, p. 521.

of a gift from above. As soon as this idea appears—and it appears necessarily—man either accepts the apparent heteronomy or refuses to recognize it. When he makes a negative choice regarding this alternative he attempts to destroy, not the Transcendent, but its gratuitous character. In other words, the negative choice is not primarily directed against the existence of the Unique Necessary but rather against the "grace" given by the Unique Necessary. When a positive choice is made, the apparent heteronomy is welcomed as a "grace" since through it "man becomes what he wants to be."[22] He will receive the "grace," if given, of possessing the living reality of God.

The necessity of the idea of the supernatural is thus absolute; the negative option rejects the necessary consequences of this absolute necessity, namely, the necessity to make the ultimate fulfillment of human action gratuitous and supernatural. This idea of the supernatural is therefore properly supernatural, philosophically supernatural. One must agree with Bouillard that the idea in question does not have the determinations of the Christian revelation, but it has all the determinations to make it formally supernatural. It is the idea of a gift of God, or of God who gives himself to man, and this makes it formally supernatural.

Blondel's originality and the specific character of his thought lie precisely in the thesis that after the philosopher has demonstrated the existence of the Unique Necessary, he must pose to himself the problem of the philosophical supernatural. It is here that Blondel surpasses all natural theism and develops under the impetus of the logic of action the necessary consequences of the existence of the Unique Necessary.

Bouillard's interpretation of Blondel's idea of the supernatural has the advantage of creating an area of "natural supernaturality" between the insufficiency of the natural order and the specifically Christian supernatural. Yet Bouillard's idea of the "undetermined supernatural" suffers from such a lack of determination that it is hardly possible to call it an idea, let alone an idea of the supernatural. It is successively described as "an idea of the Transcendent," "more precise than the idea of the Transcendent," "an idea close to the idea of transcendence," "an idea on its way to the Christian idea," "a presentiment of the Christian idea."[23]

22 Blondel, *L'Action*, p. 355.
23 Bouillard, *op. cit.*, pp. 90-91.

We have no quarrel with Bouillard about the lack of material determination or the confused and vague material contents which he assigns to Blondel's idea of the supernatural. The philosophical idea of the supernatural does not show that kind of determinations. However, the idea of the supernatural which appears at the end of the fourth part of L'Action, is formally and fully determined; it is the idea of a gift, a gift necessary to man for the completion of human action. It is in regard to this formally determined idea of the supernatural that man has to take a position.[24] To be the object of a far reaching choice, the idea has to be determined. One can hardly make a choice in regard to a formally undetermined supernatural. The necessity to make such a choice could never be established unless the idea of the supernatural carries enough determinations to force an act of the will. The great alternative is concerned with the heteronomy which appears in man's life and the specifically supernatural attitude which makes it possible for man to accept this heteronomy so "graciously" that no violation of man's autonomy is possible. Bouillard is the first interpreter of Blondel's thought to qualify the term "supernatural." Others have concerned themselves with qualifying the word "necessity" or "absolute" of the famous Blondelian formula: "The notion of the supernatural is properly speaking what is absolutely impossible and absolutely necessary to man."

The desire to prove his point has created in Bouillard a certain amount of obscurity and led him to make the supernatural a little too natural. Anything that is not specifically the Christian supernatural, he calls an undetermined supernatural and thus, in final analysis, is reduced to a natural theism or little more than a religious unrest resulting from the affirmation of the Unique Neces-

---

24 Since the option is "l'acte de la volonté par lequel le transcendant, qui ne peut être vivifiant en elle que s'il est librement agrée par elle, est accepté ou repoussé par la volonté", the choice is "non pas entre l'affirmation ou la nègation de l'existence de cet unique nécessaire, mais entre l'acceptation ou le refus de la libre adhésion aux exigences de cet unique nécessaire qui s'offre à l'homme comme le complément infini de sa vie." Taymans, Le blondélisme (Louvain: Museum Lessianum, 1933), p. 175. Taymans defines the supernatural as follows: "ce qui dépasse les exigences et les possibilités de l'homme et de l'univers tout entier. Ce qui néanmoins est, dans l'ordre actuel et concret, le seul terme définitif de l'action, le seule destinée gratuitement offerte à l'homme et que l'homme a une obligation de réaliser avec le secours divin qui n'est refusé à personne." Ibid., p. 183.

sary. In Blondel's thought the idea of the Unique Necessary is not properly speaking supernatural, but it is included in the idea of the supernatural. The necessary recognition that the Unique Necessary has to give himself to man and the idea of God as actually giving himself to man, are less natural and consequently more supernatural. The positive choice which pursues the gratuitous character of this necessary presence of the Unique Necessary makes the idea of the supernatural more properly supernatural. As Blondel points out, inaccessibility is the supernaturalizing characteristic of the Transcendent. The positive choice, precisely because it is a choice, increases the supernaturality of the affirmation of the Unique Necessary but reduces the absoluteness of its necessity. This is because it is subject to the placing of a positive existential choice which commits itself to the contents of the idea of the supernatural.

We believe that according to Blondel the idea of the supernatural is absolutely necessary to man in its most primitive form as the idea of the Unique Necessary. It is not hypothetical in any sense for the Unique Necessary exists and its demonstration is logically and ontologically valid. If the gratuitous character of the existing relation between God and man is increased in the idea of the supernatural, the logical necessity of the idea of the supernatural becomes less absolute and depends on the state (natural, transnatural, or supernatural) of the person to whom this logical necessity appears. If we give the idea the highest philosophically possible degree of supernaturality, the absoluteness of the necessity of the idea of the supernatural will gradually become only hypothetically necessary for it is subject to the choice man makes when he first encounters such an idea.

The idea of the supernatural is dynamogenic. At one stage of its development it may have a less determined content than at its next stage, but at no time is it really undetermined. In his answer to Duméry's criticism of the term "undetermined supernatural," Bouillard states that the idea of an undetermined supernatural means "an idea that does not yet have those specific, positive and historical determinations, which are only contributed by the Christian message."[25] He admits further that "this idea is progressively engend-

---

25 Bouillard, "Philosophie de l'action et logique de la foi," à propos d'un ouvrage de M. Henry Duméry, *Archives de Philosophie*, XXVII (1964), p. 115.

ered and defined by the constant disproportion between the exigency of the human will and its power. . . In this sense, it is formally determined by the way of negative determinations."[26]

If Bouillard avows that the idea of the supernatural is formally determined and therefore philosophically determined as a *donum Dei*, then the undetermined supernatural simply means that the precise form under which God gives himself to man is philosophically undeterminable. The free initiative of God cannot be caught by the determinism of action. Of necessity, the actual contents of this gift are excluded from the necessity of philosophical determinism. Were it not, it would no longer be a "grace" and would thus cease to be formally supernatural. With equal necessity the reality, the actual gift of supernaturalization, cannot be proven by philosophy. In as far as the Unique Necessary is absolutely necessary, its existence can be affirmed with logical necessity, as Blondel does in regard to the affirmation of the existence of God. Philosophy's competence concerning the *reality* of the *donum Dei* is not, however, so easy to admit as the *Esse Dei;* the more the gift-character of the Unique Necessary appears to the logic of action, the less absolute becomes the affirmation of its existence. As soon as the idea of God's totally free initiative colors the idea of the Unique Necessary, the philosopher has no longer the power and the right to pronounce himself on its existence. Were he able to establish the existence of such a supernatural, this would no longer be supernatural, or else we would have to abandon the purely philosophical viewpoint. Duméry writes in this connection:

"I hold with Blondel that one should distinguish the notion and the reality of the supernatural. I hold that the notion has to be rationally, and philosophically, determined. I hold that the reality is indeterminable for a philosopher, that it remains totally, definitely, undetermined."[27]

26 *Ibid.,* p. 116.

27 Duméry, "Blondel ou l'occasion d'apprendre à lire," *Archives de Philosophie,* XXVIII (1965), p. 65. See also Duméry in *Raison et Religion dans la Philosophie de l'action:* "Il n'y a qu'une seule idée de surnaturel, une seule notion immanente, rationnelle, du surnaturel, celle qui est amenée par le 'jeu même du déterminisme mental.' Blondel la détermine progressivement, à partir d'abord du dépassement des fins naturelles (quatriéme partie de *l'Action*), à partir ensuite d'une réflexion sur la donnée révélé (cinquième de *l'Action*). Il y a là deux temps dans la recherche, ainsi que dans l'exposition. *Mais il y a homogénétié et continuité formelles,"* p. 57.

310 STUDIES IN PHILOSOPHY

We have not an undetermined but a determined idea of the supernatural which remains undetermined as to its reality. This idea of the supernatural, formally determined and undetermined or further determinable as to its contents but not as to its reality, is absolutely necessary to man. Man cannot deny or ignore it. To do so would be contrary to the spirit of philosophy. The philosopher must recognize that he has no access to this supernatural domain; to show its necessity as well as its impossibility of attainment by man's natural powers is the task of philosophy. "It belongs to the rational science to study the absolute independence and the necessity of this higher order."[28]

Philosophy and Christian Revelation

In the fifth part of *L'Action* Blondel confronts the Christian supernatural order with the philosophical idea of the supernatural. This absolute necessity of the latter is the fruit of human action; the supernatural is existential and historical in the sense that it does not live in isolation from the many forms of religion present in the world. Far from terminating in an abstract idea, the dynamism of human action overflows the boundaries set by philosophical logic and enters the outside world in search of a reality that could satisfy it. It knocks on the doors of all existing religious institutions to see if they can satisfy the supernatural necessity that it experiences but is unable to satisfy without external help.

If it is the claim of Christianity that it can bring human action to completion and thus satisfy the exigencies of the dynamism of the will, then it is not "scientific to study the letter and spirit of all the different religions except one (the Christian religion)."[29] Nor is there any philosophical reason to investigate all religions except Christianity; on the contrary, philosophy must include Christianity in its field of research if it wants to be truly scientific. Incompetent to pass judgment on the necessary existence of the

---

[28] "Montrer qu'il est impossible à la philosophie de repousser ou de constituer par ses seules forces une vérité, une action, une vie supérieure à la nature, c'est encore oeuvre de philosophie. . . Loin d'empiéter sur un domaine réservé, il faut montrer que tout empiétement réel est impossible: de cette impossibilité même ressort une relation nécessaire; et c'est encore à la science rationnelle d'étudier l'indépendance absolue et la nécessité de cet ordre supérieur," p. 389.

[29] Blondel, *L'Action*, p. 391.

Christian revelation, the philosopher can consider the contents of the idea of the supernatural as proposed in the teachings of the Christian religion. Philosophically speaking, however, the confrontation of philosophy and revelation is hypothetical on two counts. First, the idea of the Christian supernatural is presupposed, accepted as a hypothesis, proposed to the philosopher from the outside. As an idea it does not come from within. Secondly, the Christian supernatural is hypothetical in so far as philosophy cannot prove its necessary existence, even in the case that it had demonstrated the philosophical necessity of the Christian revelation as an idea.

The incurable disproportion between the élan of the will and the term of human action makes it necessary to explore the philosophical idea of the supernatural under these hypothetical conditions with the Christian revelation as an outside guide. It would be unreasonable not to do so after man has experienced the impossibility of completely fulfilling the requirement of his action "without admitting an action other than his own."[30] Being in such need, man has to look into the Christian supernatural, give it a hearing, and see what it has to offer.

Recognizing that the Christian supernatural is a gift coming from above, and realizing that such a gift is necessary for the fulfillment of human action, man should ask himself if this gift is perhaps the one that would meet all the necessary requirements, if it were actually given. It is therefore legitimate to pursue the philosophical search "to the point where we feel that we have to desire something analogous to what, from the outside, the dogmas propose to us."[31] It is legitimate to confront these dogmas with the fundamental exigencies of the will, and to discover in them, if possible, the image of our real needs and the expected answer. We can accept the dogmas by way of hypothesis, as the mathematicians do when they work on a suggested solution and verify it by way of the analytic method.[32]

---

30 *Ibid.*, p. 356.

31 *Ibid.*, p. 391.

32 "Non qu'il faille, pour l'examen même, admettre la vérité formelle du dogme; il va suffire, à la façon des géomètres, d'étudier les relations intrinsèques et les convenances certaines d'une hypothèse dont, au nom même du déterminisme de l'action humaine, l'analyse découvre simplement la nécessité et la cohérence." *Ibid.*, pp. 400-401.

Clearly Blondel suspends judgment as to the reality of Christian revelation and works exclusively with the idea of it as a kind of possible blueprint that could reveal the determinations of the exigencies of the will. If it becomes evident that the acceptance of the Christian idea of the supernatural is an indispensable condition for the completion of human action, then man will have to accept the Christian supernatural as a philosophical necessity. This necessity will be hypothetical as to its existence, but absolute as to its logical exigency.[33]

The idea of the Christian revelation is "necessarily engendered."[34] In the first two chapters of the fifth part of L'Action Blondel shows that what Christian revelation proposes corresponds to the conditions of fulfillment of human action. He specifies, first of all, the formal characteristics of divine revelation: "If it exists, divine revelation has to present itself as independent from human initiative."[35] It necessarily demands from man an act of submission and obedience, an inevitable sacrifice. The movement toward the supernatural which proceeds from man, the élan of the search that brings man to God, has in principle to be a gift. It cannot come totally from the outside, nor can it be totally immanent.[36] If it becomes too immanent, it ceases to be supernatural; if it is too independent from our initiative and our will, the idea of the supernatural loses its character of necessity. It is impossible not to conceive the necessity of divine assistance, since there is a "gaping hole"[37] that separates us from what we want to be. We want this hole filled. The question is how to let the indispensable and inaccessible help descend to us and fill the emptiness which remains wide open at the center of our life. The synthesis between necessity and gift, between divine and human initiative, requires, to be become an actuality, that human and divine action form an alliance. In other words, man must perform acts of faith which he cannot impose upon himself

33 "Même après qu'on a posé, à titre d'hypothèse nécessaire, l'ordre surnaturel comme un postulat scientifique, il faut se garder de croire qu'on en pourrait prouver la vérité réelle par le développement de ses conséquences ou par ses convenances internes. Affirmer qu'il est, cet aveu ne vient jamais de nous seuls." Ibid., pp. 491-492.

34 Ibid., p. 406.

35 Ibid., p. 398.

36 "Elle devrait, ce semble, venir toute d'une source extérieure à nous; et elle devrait nous être tout entière immanente." Ibid., p. 401.

37 Ibid.

for purely natural reasons, for purely natural actions have proven to be insufficient. Confronted with the hypothesis of the Christian supernatural solution, man performs actions that are required by it. He has good reasons to perform these supernatural actions as if they were natural, he must give these actions a chance to bring him the solution he is looking for. He must experiment and, while acting in fully conscious detachment from his natural initiative, seek to discover whether everything that is revealed, is presented to him as coming from God. "One only knows this through effective experimentation."[38]

Man therefore should act as if he already has faith although he does not actually possess it. In such actions the depths of man's élan will be revealed. God is active in this type of action and the thought that follows upon such actions is richer in contents than the one that preceded it. It enters into a new world where philosophical speculation can neither lead nor follow.[39]

One need not admit the truth of revelation and the reality of the divine gift to perform such actions. All that is necessary is to study revelation as a hypothesis in order to determine not only its abstract possibility but, which is even more important, to define the particular fruitfulness of the theandric action in which the will of God and the will of man become coextensive.[40] The Christian supernatural is a gift, but as a gift it has to be at the same time integrally acquired and naturalized in human action.[41]

At the end of our search we do not claim to have arrived at the reality of the Christian supernatural, nor at the demonstration of the possibility of a revelation; all that the study of the determinism of action leads us to is the necessity of such a supernatural if human action is to come to completion. Science owes us nothing more and nothing less than the necessary; it has nothing to say about the actualization of the required conditions, but in case these conditions are actually fulfilled, their realization becomes an absolute and practical obligation. Philosophy must go as far as it can. Too often, Blondel says, it has neglected the most crucial area of its domain. The question of the supernatural must be included in a philosophy of action. Man's inability to equate voluntary action

38 *Ibid.*, p. 402.
39 *Ibid.*, pp. 402-403.
40 *Ibid.*, p. 403.
41 *Ibid.*, p. 405.

with his primitive aspirations is a "cry of nature" which makes it-self heard. The rationality of the supernatural answering this fundamental need of man is properly the object of philosophical investigation. It is the role of philosophy to express the inevitable exigencies of thought as the natural prayer of the human will.[42]

This prayer of the human will must find its answer in action. The only access to the domain of the supernatural is generous experimentation and a faithful submission to the demands of the hypothetical supernatural. Not thought but action is the receptacle large enough to receive the desired gift.[43] The idea of the supernatural is the fruit of action and at the same time the point of departure for further action. The obscurity of the ideas obtained through a reflective presence to life works as a stimulus for further action. Thought asks action for further clarification as long as it does not understand itself. It commissions action to translate its doubts into experiments so that it may find the desired clarity and understanding. This dialogue between the idea of the supernatural and the experimentation carried out in practice reveals that this hypothetical supernatural implies the idea of a mediator and savior,[44] the necessity of positive prescriptions[45] and dogmas.[46] These are all hypothetical necessities implied by the idea of a supernatural that would bring human action to completion. Philosophy is incapable of deciding about the actual existence of

---

[42] *Ibid.*, p. 407.

[43] "On voudrait que tout fût clair à la pensée et qu'il y eût un centre unique de perspective; il n'y en a pas, ce centre est partout; mais ce qu'on ne peut voir clairement, on peut le faire pleinement: le vrai commentaire est la pratique." *Ibid.*, p. 411.

[44] "Il faut donc que même l'élan de la recherche qui nous porte à Dieu soit, en son principe, un don. Sans cette indispensable médiation, nous ne sommes et nous ne pouvons rien. Il n'y a donc de révélation, donnée ou recue, que par un médiateur: première et essentielle exigence." *Ibid.*, p. 398.

[45] ". . . c'est donc une nécessité que cette action soit elle-meme l'objet d'un précepte positif, et qu'elle parte, non plus du mouvement de notre nature, mais de l'ordre divin." *Ibid.*, p. 416.

[46] "Pour que ces actes rituels ne se réduisent pas à une fiction idolâtrique et pour qu'ils égalent la foi dont ils doivent être la vivifiante expression, il est requis qu'ils soient, non pas une invention de l'homme et l'effet toujours imparfait d'un mouvement naturel, mais l'expression de préceptes positifs et l'imitation originale du dogme divinement transcrit dans des commandements distincts." *Ibid.*, p. 416.

this supernatural, but it can determine the implied logical necessity.[47]

A religion that permits the human will to will itself freely and allows human action to achieve its completion is hypothetically necessary. This philosophy can demonstrate. That Christianity is the religion that satisfies the requirements of the determinism of action, or, in other words, that the Christian supernatural is the full answer to the unfulfilled contents of the philosophical supernatural cannot be affirmed by the philosopher. Such an affirmation requires that the hypothetical necessity of the supernatural order as determined by Blondel be freely accepted as a real order existing in the Christian revelation. This is an act of faith, not a philosophical demonstration. This is a reasonable act but not a necessary one. Yet, at the very end of *L'Action,* Blondel adds:

"It is the task of philosophy to show the necessity of posing the alternative: 'Is it or is it not?' It is its task to show that the unique and universal question which encompasses the whole destiny of man, imposes itself upon everyone with the same urgency. 'Is it or is it not?' It is its task to prove that one cannot avoid in practice to declare himself for or against this supernatural: 'Is it or is it not?' It is still the work of philosophy to examine the consequences of either one of the solutions and to measure the immense gap: it cannot go any further nor say in its own name, that it is or that it is not. But if we are allowed to add a word, one which exceeds the domain of human science and the competence of philosophy, the only word in regard to Christianity capable of expressing that part— the best part—of certitude which cannot be communicated because it arises only from the intimacy of an action wholly personal, a word which itself is an action, this is the word that must be said: 'It is.' "[48]

Philosophy and the Supernatural Order

If the supernatural appears within the determination of action and formally surpasses the idea of the Unique Necessary, there is the danger that the necessity of the supernatural would destroy its gratuity. "To speak of *necessity* may seem to make a dangerous con-

[47] "Encore une fois, la réalité de ce don reste, il est vrai, hors des prises de l'homme et de la philosophie; mais c'est l'oeuvre essentielle de la raison d'en voir la nécessité, et de déterminer les convenances naturelles qui règlent l'enchaînement des vérités surnaturelles elles-mêmes." *Ibid.,* p. 418.

[48] *Ibid.,* p. 492.

nection between the two orders and to bring the freedom of the
divine gift within the system of human action in a way which is
illegitimate."[49] To say that the supernatural appears to the philosopher as "necessary" and as inaccessible at the same time, the word
"necessary" must not be understood in an ontological sense as if it
were referring to an absolutely necessary reality. What is necessary
about the supernatural is the appearance of the idea in the development of the determinism of the logic of action. "What is necessary
is that, in some form which cannot be defined to cover particular
cases, the thoughts and actions of each one of us together make up
a drama that cannot reach its conclusions unless the decisive
question arises, sooner or later, in consciousness."[50] The decisive question about which man has to decide is his supernatural
fulfillment. It is not the "supernatural as a historic reality, nor as a
simple possibility like an arbitrary hypothesis, but as something indispensable and at the same time inaccessible to man."[51]

The development of the will forces us to avow our insufficiency,
it leads us to recognize the need of a further gift, and it gives us the
aptitude to receive it. Moreover, it offers us that "baptism of
desire" which presupposing God's secret touch, is always accessible
and necessary apart from any explicit revelation, and which, even
when revelation is known, becomes, as it were, the human sacrament immanent in the divine operation. The philosophical supernatural is not necessary to man because of an explicit revelation,
but because the idea of a supernatural fulfillment appears within
the determinism of action. It is accessible to man even though he
may remain ignorant of an actual divine initiative. The idea of the
philosophical supernatural which lacks all the specific determinations of the Christian revelation, is formally determined as an idea.
This seems to presuppose that man shares in a hidden way the
efficacy of that which he does not know. Blondel refers to "God's
secret touch," "a sort of prevenient grace which is of necessity," a
built-in gift which begins to make itself felt towards the end of the
expansion of human action. This is what he calls the "human
sacrament immanent in the divine operation." The fact that man
does not always need to recognize this divine operation clearly does
not mean that he does not always need the efficacy of a real media-

49 Blondel, *Letter on Apologetics*, o.c., p. 161.
50 *Ibid.*, p. 162.
51 *Ibid.*, p. 161.

tion.[52] If human action without any further aid (*sine addito*) [53] breaks down, the breaking point becomes the precise point of insertion where the supernatural, the *donum Dei,* attaches itself necessarily to the natural order in order to bring the natural requirement of the will to fulfillment. What is "naturally required" is the supernatural which at this stage does not have, as yet, all the determinations of the Christian revelation but is formally determined as a gift necessary to man. There is no reason to make this "supernatural" formally undetermined, as Bouillard seems to maintain.[54] Philosophically speaking, it is supernatural in the proper sense of the term. While necessary to man, it is at the same time a gift that man expects necessarily whether he knows it or not, and that because of its free character on the part of God, man cannot claim as a right. Thus while necessarily expecting this gift, man does not necessarily receive it. This is the necessity which connects the supernatural and the natural orders without infringing upon their independence.[55]

The supernatural in philosophy is controlled by reason. All philosophy can do with the supernatural is, as it were, to naturalize it and point out its natural necessity. However, the light of faith is required to show a *real* continuity between the natural and the supernatural. The more supernatural the idea of the Unique Necessary appears to be, the less absolute becomes the necessity of its actual existence for the philosopher. The reality or the realization of what is proposed as necessary is subordinate to another factor which is outside the domain of philosophy as a science.[56] Philosophy works from the point where human action breaks down and the idea of the supernatural appears with a hypothetical necessity. The legitimate scope of philosophical conclusions stops short at the threshold of the real operation in which the human act and the divine act, nature and grace, can unite. Philosophy therefore remains and cannot but remain on the outside of that mysterious union. It will be up to us to gain a full understanding of this limitation of philosophy with all its necessary complications.

52 *Ibid.,* p. 163.
53 *Ibid.,* p. 162.
54 Bouillard, *op. cit.,* pp. 104-105.
55 Blondel, *op. cit.,* p. 163.
56 *Ibid.*

IV

THE THREEFOLD MEANING OF "CHRISTIAN PHILOSOPHY"

"One wants for philosophy its own and independent domain; theology wants the same for itself. They both demand a separation of competences; they remain distinct from each other in view of an effective cooperation: *non adjutrix nisi libera; non libera nisi adjutrix philosophia.*"[1]

The competence of philosophy in regard to the supernatural is limited. Philosophy of action provides man with a formally determined idea of the supernatural without supplying its material determinations. While the existence of the Unique Necessary is a demonstrable fact, philosophy remains unable to determine whether or not the Unique Necessary has *de facto* fulfilled all the exigencies of the dynamism of the will. Philosophy can determine the logical and hypothetical necessity of what we have called the "philosophical supernatural," if man's life is to have a meaning and find fulfillment. The Christian supernatural, the specific, historical, and divinely revealed gift of God, can be investigated according to the methods of philosophy. The result of such a logical investigation of revealed truth may show in this doctrine an unexpected answer to our longings and a striking similarity with the requirements of the philosophical supernatural.

Autonomy and Separatism

It is obvious that Blondel's philosophy is fully orientated towards Christianity, circles around it, and frequently seems to penetrate into it. It touches the Christian supernatural, it works its way into the most specifically Christian ideas, and borrows its terminology from theology. Is this close relationship to Christianity sufficient to make it Christian philosophy?

Blondel himself disapproves of the expression "Christian philosophy" if by that is suggested that the method of philosophy employed by Christians is different from the method employed by others.[2] He clearly distinguishes between philosophy and theology.

---

1 Blondel, *L'Action, op. cit.,* p. 393.
2 Blondel, *Letter on Apologetics, op. cit.,* p. 128.

"Philosophical knowledge and theological knowledge differ radically *principio et objecto*."[3] He emphasizes the importance of distinguishing what belongs to human science from what is of divine inspiration.[4] Theology presupposes "a rational organization of elements which are not themselves the product of reason."[5] In doing so theology may give a philosophical form to elements that are foreign to philosophy, but the results will always remain different from rational truths reached by rational processes.

Philosophy consists in "the autonomous application of reason to itself," and not in a "heteronomous application of reason to some material or to some object."[6] Blondel's primary intention is not to investigate revealed truth with a philosophical method but to open up the dynamism of thought, being, and action to its last and most intense expression. In this way philosophy not only becomes capable of treating all questions about the Christian consciousness without betraying its own nature, but must examine them in the same spirit as all other questions which ultimately form one same determinism.[7]

The delimitation of philosophy's scope enlarges its competence so that it can include the religious problem.[8] In its autonomy philosophy demands the complete development of the dynamism of action and thought and protests against the restrictions of a "separated philosophy."

Blondel's insistence upon the autonomy of philosophy and the "absolutely precise distinction between theological and philosophical functions of human thought"[9] may give, at times, the impression that he accepts the idea of a "separated philosophy" instead of rejecting it. The separation that Blondel defends is not a "false separatism" that isolates the religious problem from philosophy, but one which is commanded by the constituent principles of philosophy and theology. The formal object of philosophy clearly distinguishes it from theology, and this formal object is the natural light of reason. It is under this natural light of reason that Blondel intends to work, and as far as specification of methods is concerned,

3 *Ibid.*, p. 188.
4 *Ibid.*, p. 189.
5 *Ibid.*, p. 186.
6 *Ibid.*
7 *Ibid.*, p. 187.
8 *Ibid.*, p. 186.
9 *Ibid.*, p. 193.

there is no difference between Blondel's philosophy and the philosophy of those who admit a formal difference between philosophy and theology.[10] Blondel may have had certain nonphilosophical intentions, perhaps apologetic ones, but this does not change his philosophy into apologetics. What a man intends to do with philosophical conclusions does not affect the philosophical character of these conclusions.[11] If Blondel wishes to confront these conclusions with the teachings of Christianity his philosophy does not therefore become theology. Blondel is a philosopher; he is one because he worked out a philosophy even if he only intended his philosophy because he had the heart of an apostle.[12] It can be easily admitted that he would never have produced his philosophy of insufficiency, that the idea of the supernatural would never have appeared to him as a rational problem, that he would never have looked for suggestions and solutions to the enigmas of reason in Christianity, if he had not believed in the truth of the Christian revelation. Perhaps one may say, with Duméry, that without the gospel, without the Church, without theology, Blondel's philosophy is inconceivable. He philosophizes for the sake of Christianity. His initial intention is "to take the catechism and to translate it philosophically."[13] He expresses the conviction that the Christian philosopher can no longer keep his beliefs discreetly at a distance from his own

10 "Reprenons et résumons: du point de vue de la spécification des méthodes, il n'y a pas de différence entre la philosophie selon Blondel et la philosophie selon les auteurs qui admettent l'hétérogénéité formelle de la philosophie et de la théologie. Je dirai même que, sur le point précis du caractère logique et rationnel de la philosophie, il n'existe pas de différence entre Blondel et M. Jacques Maritain." Duméry, *Raison et Religion dans la philosophie de l'action*, *op. cit.*, p. 509.

11 "Le raisonnement qui consiste à dire que la blondélisme est une apologétique (sous-entendu: non une philosophie) parce que Blondel a voulu défendre sa foi et y rallier ses pairs, ce raisonnement est un sophisme. Autant dire que Paul Claudel est un exégète, non un poète, parce qu'il a chanté la Bible, ou que François Mauriac est un théologien, non un romancier, parce qu'il a décrit le duel de la chair et de l'esprit, l'affrontement de la grâce d'en haut et de la grâce d'en bas. Sous peine de ne plus savoir de quoi on parle, une oeuvre se définit par son genre littéraire, par son type culturel, non par des intentions subjectives, cachées ou avouées. Est philosophique ce qui respecte l'essence de la philosophie, ce qui respecte sa méthode. Si Blondel conçoit la philosophie selon un patron strictement rationnel, s'il s'efforce de la pratiquer conformément à cet idéal, nul n'est admis à lui contester sa qualité de philosophie." *Ibid.*, p. 508.

12 *Ibid.*, p. 509.

13 *Notes semailles*, no. 1132.

thinking.[14] "We have to rethink the totality of philosophical problems in function of the idea that Christianity and its *rationale
obsequium* provide us with the unique and supreme destiny which
is *de facto* ours by obligation."[15] It is not improper to have the
doctrine of the gospel penetrate and "ferment the philosophical
dough."[16]

Blondel's defense of the autonomy of philosophy does not result
in a "separated philosophy." His call for autonomous philosophy is
voiced from within his firm belief in the truth of Christianity. The
"truly catholic idea" promotes "a philosophy which is the more
appropriate as it is the more autonomous."[17] It is the Christian
orientation of Blondel's thought which claims an absolute autonomy, purity, and integrity for philosophy. Philosophy becomes
properly universal, all inclusive, Catholic philosophy, if its autonomy is safeguarded and promoted.

The distinction between the essence and the state of philosophy,
as proposed by Maritain,[18] could clarify perhaps how the autonomy
of philosophy is maintained while being conceived from within and
oriented towards Christianity. Blondel's philosophy taken in a
certain state is perhaps impossible "without the gentle and secret
influence of the Christian spirit."[19] But as to its essence, it is authentically philosophical and does not require the truth of Christianity. His philosophy studies the dynamism of human existence
from within the privileged state of Christianity, but under the
essential philosophical light of reason. Whatever is part of the

---

[14] Blondel, *Letter on Apologetics, op. cit.,* p. 170.

[15] Blondel, *Le Problème de la philosophie catholique* (Paris: Bloud & Gay,
1932), p. 39, footnote 1.

[16] *Ibid.*

[17] Blondel, *Letter on Apologetics, op. cit.,* p. 206.

[18] According to Maritain: "La spécification de la philosophie dépendant toute
de son objet formel, et cet objet étant d'ordre naturel, la philosophie prise en
elle-même, que ce soit dans une tête païenne ou dans une tête chrétienne, relève
des mêmes critères intrinsèques strictement naturels ou rationnels." According
to its formal objective philosophy is not Christian. It is Christian "en tant
qu'elle est placée dans les conditions d'existence et d'exercice absolument
caractéristiques où le Christianisme a introduit le sujet pensant: à raison de
quoi certains objets sont *vus,* certains *assertions établies valablement* par elle qui,
dans d'autres conditions, lui échappent plus ou moins." Maritain, "La Notion de
philosophie chrétienne," *Bulletin de la Société française de philosophie,* 1931,
p. 62, 69.

[19] Blondel, *Letter on Apologetics, op. cit.,* p. 204.

existential situation of the philosopher should be included in the material object of philosophy. Philosophy will have to include everything that makes up human existence. Truly autonomous philosophy recognizes that "it cannot ignore the problem of the supernatural."[20] What faith imposes as real upon the believing mind, reason has to conceive as necessary under its natural and rational aspect. When faith and reason speak about the same thing, they speak about it differently; for faith sees as real what philosophy investigates under the aspect of its necessity and rationality.

> "What faith imposes upon us as a reality, reason conceives as necessary but impracticable for us. The one declares to be gratuitously given what the other can only postulate as inevitable, so that they coincide not by overlapping but because one is empty and the other full. Even when their affirmations seem to cover something of the same ground *sub specie materiae seu objecti,* they remain radically heterogeneous *vi formae.*"[21]

THE MEANING OF "CHRISTIAN PHILOSOPHY"[22]

If the autonomy of philosophy as well as of theology has to be safeguarded, the term "Christian philosophy" is an "awkward expression." In the third chapter of the *Le Problème de la philosophie*

---

20 *Ibid.,* p. 206.

21 *Ibid.,* p. 206.

22 The terms "Christian philosophy" and "Catholic philosophy" are used in this context without any distinction. It is not necessary to distinguish between the Protestant idea of the supernatural and Catholic idea of the same reality. The supernatural is philosophically inaccessible as such and any specific determinations supplied by the Catholic or Protestant idea are consequent upon what one can formally say as a philosopher about the openness of philosophy towards a supernatural solution. According to Blondel the expression "philosophie chrétienne" is less precise and less justifiable than the expression "philosophie catholique"; "car, outre que le Christ est tout autre chose que le maître éponyme d'une doctrine proprement philosophique, le terme *catholique* est à la fois plus comprehensif et plus restrictif, puisque d'une part, il s'applique à l'universalité des hommes de bonne foi qui participent à la grâce même innommée et à l'âme de l'invisible Eglise, et puisque d'autre part le catholicisme, ainsi que nous le montrions en discutant les critiques de M. Bréhier, réussit seul à specifier ce qui est surnaturellement chrétien. D'ou le soin avec lequel nous parlons de 'philosophie catholique' plutôt que de philosophie chrétienne quand nous parlons en notre nom." (*Problème de la philosophie catholique, op. cit.,* p. 172, footnote 1).

catholique Blondel investigates the possible meanings of such an expression. He considers three successive possibilities.

1. Whatever the hypothesis may be concerning the existence or nonexistence of a supernatural order, is there anything at all that would make philosophy Christian?

To this question Blondel assumes that a being endowed with reason can know with certitude that God exists, can desire to know more about God, and can strive towards beatitude. At the same time he is capable of recognizing that, while he naturally desires it, beatitude is inaccessible to him. This desire is at the same time natural and inefficacious.[23] It is an essential disposition and permanent mark of every finite intelligence, every contingent will, and all created beings. This universal, necessary, fundamental truth expresses the real distinction of essence and existence within every conceivable reality other than God. This is not a particular thesis among many others, *una e multis,* but a central thesis which supports and guides all philosophical speculation on the world, humanity, and man's destiny. On this point there is unity, *in necessariis unitas,* in the shadow of which different legitimate schools of thought can be developed.[24] In so far as any particular system attaches itself to this central and permanent core, it has no need of any epithet. One may speak of such a philosophical system as universal and essential philosophy, *philosophia perennis.* It does not make much sense to add the term "catholic" to philosophy because in principle philosophy is one and universal. Only for a variety of accidental reasons could one accept the epithet "catholic": to underline the unity and universality of philosophy, to distinguish it from and protect it against partialities, errors, intolerances, transitory contingencies or variable applications, or to indicate that outside a catholic atmosphere the essential and indispensable attitude for an accurate development of rational and moral doctrine cannot be defined with the necessary precision, or be preserved from a mixture of illusions and errors, or kept alive and healthy. "As Fénelon wisely observed, a philosophy which without deviating, erring, or stopping short runs the full course of its development to its legitimate goal is really a 'romanticizing philosophy.' "[25] The presence of another source of light as found in revelation is a blessing for the catholicity of philosophy, not be-

[23] *Ibid.,* p. 160.   [24] *Ibid.,* p. 161.   [25] *Ibid.,* p. 163.

cause it provides solutions and adds information but because it invites reason to examine its conscience and its potentialities.[26] Certain contradictions can stimulate useful reflections. In an indirect way, philosophy can profit from an atmosphere and viewpoint which are kept alive and healthy through the intellectual influence of Christianity as far as the basic directions of the human mind are concerned.

Such a "catholic philosophy" includes a number of fundamental truths, one of which is the central theme of all philosophical thought: by all the avenues a bold philosophy ought to follow we come to unveil certain real profundities of being whose existence we cannot plumb. In so doing we understand the philosophical sense of the following assertion by which some wish to summarize the Thomistic doctrine of finite being: "If the mind recapitulates in itself the whole of nature, this is because it is essentially capable of God and because our reason is made for being, in all its variety and plenitude."[27] Catholic philosophy is, therefore, a philosophy that is open to the supernatural and Christianity, fructified by it in its own domain, but independent of it in its method and constitution. Universal or "pure" philosophy determines which hypothetical possibilities and necessities it must recognize as conceivable from a fully rational viewpoint. It does not exclude the possibility of a supernatural order in spite of the fact that revelation will be required to define it and propose it explicitly.

2. What would be the function of philosophy if the rational hypothesis of the supernatural is supposed to have been realized? How should philosophy behave itself in such a concrete order which imposes upon man's destiny an exact and unique solution?

In addition to a so-called "pure" philosophy there is, says Blondel, a sort of "mixed philosophy"[28] which studies the possible

[26] "Il est traditionnel d'admettre que si la médiation des vérités révélées est *fructuosissima*, ce n'est pas seulement pour donner quelque lumière, quelque connaissabilité aux mystères eux-mêmes, c'est aussi pour purifier, confirmer, approfondir les acquisitions rationnelles qui, par là même et en une sorte de catalyse, prennent en leur domaine propre une activité accrue et féconde, quoique tenues d'autant plus à respecter l'hétérogénéité des deux modes d'information, qu'aucune déduction ne doit identifier." *Ibid.*, p. 162, footnote 3.

[27] Blondel, *Exigences philosophiques du christianisme* (Paris: P.U.F., 1950), p. 109.

[28] Blondel, *Le Problème de la philosophie catholique, op. cit.*, p. 167.

relations between the essential necessities of universal philosophy and their contingent realizations. The task of such a philosophy is to build a possible bridge between the hypothetical necessities of pure philosophy and the concrete data which make up the world we live in. This calls for unique precautions since between the order of ideal necessity and the actual contingent order there exists a basic incommensurability. The necessity of a hypothetical supernatural can never be turned into a concrete necessity without risking confusion between the domain of reason and the domain of positive religion or the "not-to-be-naturalized" supernatural.

It is perhaps this philosophical alliance, subject to many qualifications, which would earn for philosophy the epithet "Christian." In the supposition that the hypothetical necessary has been realized, and has therefore penetrated the concrete order of contingent reality, we may speak of a symbiosis of philosophy and revelation within an irreducible heterogeneity. But we have no right to abuse, either *sub ratione cognoscendi* or *sub ratione essendi,* the de facto union which exists between these two orders.[29] This does not entitle us to rationalize Christianity and to give to the expression "Christian philosophy" a meaning that would secularize it. Despite the fact that within this concrete situation reason and revelation coexist peacefully and are helpful to each other, the epithet "Christian" glued to the word "philosophy" remains in many respects ambiguous and demands to be used with discretion and reserve, *secundum quid* and not *simpliciter.*[30]

A comparison may help us to understand this situation. We listen to an opera. Although we hear voices singing, we do not catch the singer's words. Put under our eyes a libretto and we immediately discern without difficulty the text that is being sung. Do we, therefore, say that the libretto alone causes us to hear the words? No, because we already perceived the opera's melody, and without this perception the written text would not have instilled in us the musical and literary joy derived from it. In somewhat the same way revelation confirms, makes precise, purifies, and universalizes many truths that in themselves are not beyond our rational capacity.[31]

29 *Ibid.,* p. 168.
30 *Ibid.,* p. 169.
31 *Ibid.,* p. 169. Blondel warns us against these analogies "sans doute adjuvantes et partiellement fondées comme cette allégorie dont nous avons usé pour

If we suppose that the supernatural has been realized, we must turn on more brightly the dim light already available to us in philosophy and distinguish between what can and ought to be accessible to well-ordered reason and what is accessible only by revelation. In such a situation revelation becomes an actual light that not only invites but encourages and guides reason in its autonomous search for an understanding of the truth. This does not mean that revelation answers philosophy's questions; it rather helps it to question further. Revelation gives philosophy an impetus to think, and this impetus gives the Christian philosopher an advantage over the non-Christian. The more one wonders, the more one asks; the more deeply one will be able to penetrate into reality, the more will he be able to unveil the inexhaustible transcendentality of being. The influence of revelation, therefore, lies on the side of the questions, not of the answers. According to this second meaning, the expression "Christian philosophy" indicates philosophy as undergoing Christian influence inasmuch as in its actual exercise it confronts the philosophical truths with the truths proposed by revelation.

3. If the thesis that man has a positive vocation to a supernatural destiny is accepted, prudence requires that we first consider certain questions of philosophy of religion in their mutual relationships before we apply their answers to a certain supernatural solution. Such an analytic study will safeguard us against all superstitious presumptions, as well as against all naturalistic magic and false mysticism.[32] Ideas such as those of sacrifice, asceticism, rite, prayer,

---

faire comprendre comment l'enseignement révélé peut accroître la précision et la portée de la raison: dans un concert, j'entends un chant musicalement accompagné; mais je ne discerne pas les paroles et malgré l'harmonie expressive je n'en devine pas le sens; mais qu'on me mette sous les yeux le libretto, aussitôt les sons que je percevais confusément et intelligiblement prennent une netteté et une signification, quoique l'image visuelle et le renseignement intellectuel n'aient rien ajouté au témoignage propre de l'ouïe . . . Toutefois cette comparison péche doublement et gravement. Elle rapproche des données sensibles qui, quoique diverses, sont d'un même ordre, ce qui n'est nullement le cas du naturel même métaphysique et du surnaturel même incarné. Elle suggère l'idée inexacte que le discernement des vérités révélées et des états de grâce pourrait, après leur révélation et leur possession, être opéré naturellement et réellement selon leur caractère original, ce qui n'est pas. *Ibid.*, p. 168, footnote 2.

[32] *Ibid.*, p. 170.

and sacrament need to be purified and organized according to a state of mind that will be strictly in conformity with reason and faith.

This confrontation and alliance between pure philosophy of religion and Christian revelation enables us to study the repercussions that the different states—transnatural, supernatural, or rebellious—will have on man as a natural being. These different states cause in man's consciousness and will certain reactions that differ from those of the "pure state of nature." If the purely human order becomes untenable, if the alternative arises either to fall below the human order or to accept and utilize a higher vocation, if "not to be changed"[33] becomes a loss, then we may say that there is an obligation to a higher fulfillment which is not totally unconscious or unintelligible. Thus, Christianity offers to philosophy as a normal area for investigation what may be called a philosophical study of Christianity or, more properly, "Christian philosophy."

To sum up, the first meaning of "Christian philosophy" is simply identified with pure and universal philosophy, which attempts to discover in its own autonomous way and in an atmosphere of catholicity and universality the truth concerning the fundamental relations between God and his creatures. The second meaning of the expression "Christian philosophy" indicates a philosophy that is guided in its search for the truth in so far as revelation gives an impetus to further questioning and challenges reason to develop itself to its ultimate possibilities. In the third meaning philosophy applies openly itself to Christianity proper in order to determine its logical contribution to the solution of the problem of the destiny of man.

This third meaning of the expression follows logically from the second, while both the second and the third are consequent upon the first meaning of "Christian philosophy." If philosophy is essentially directed towards a supernatural vocation of man (first meaning) then it is not surprising that revelation invites philosophy to investigate in an autonomous way the nature of this vocation (second meaning), and that philosophy approaches Christianity for a philosophical contribution to the understanding of the supernatural vocation of man (third meaning).

Blondel is primarily interested in a philosophy that deserves the

[33] *Ibid.*, p. 171.

epithet "Christian" according to the first meaning.[34] All other possible meanings presuppose that essentially philosophy is by its very nature open to and directed towards a supernatural vocation of man. It would be premature and dangerous to look for any agreement between philosophy and Christianity if this fundamental question has not been deepened and philosophy has not been made immune to the temptation either of ignoring or of remedying the deficiency of nature and the infinite aspirations of man. Without such a radical sanation the whole development of Christian philosophy is compromised and the whole organism of autonomous philosophy runs the risk of being dangerously intoxicated and sterile.[35]

The complexity of the term "Christian philosophy" as proposed by Blondel is not without its difficulties. The controversy that broke out in France in 1931 on the question of Christian philosophy, made it necessary for Blondel to define more clearly what he meant by it. It is hard to be entirely satisfied with the rather fine distinctions and complex sentences with which Blondel attempts to express his firm belief in the autonomy of philosophy and the truth of Christianity. He has to find between the two a connection that will help him to work out a philosophy that keeps its independence and at the same time leads to Christianity. At the end of *Le Problème de la philosophie catholique* he writes that the task he had set out to accomplish is infinitely more complex, more revolutionary, more intractable than he had first suspected.[36]

Before looking for a correspondence between the problems of philosophy and the doctrine of revelation, it is necessary to establish as long and as consistently as possible the autonomy of philosophical research. A philosophy that develops within the hypothesis of the truth of Christianity, although it does not depart from this truth as a presupposition, must be completely sincere with itself. This is even more necessary if it intends to prepare for the acceptance of faith. The only way to safeguard such philosophical honesty is to disassociate, as it were, philosophy from Christianity, to eliminate until the very end the hypothesis of a divine revelation, and to control the desire to show the correspondence between philosophy and the Christian message. It is necessary to

34 *Ibid.,* p. 171.
35 *Ibid.,* p. 172.
36 *Ibid.,* p. 174.

become exclusively a philosopher and ignore, as far as possible, the solutions offered by Christianity until philosophy itself begins to ask for such solutions. Before establishing that "real philosophy" which takes into account factual data and organizes them in a science, it is necessary to show the competence, limits, and desiderata of the metaphysical order. One must show in a special way the incurable deficiency of all thought and of the entire realm of created realities, which, inasmuch as they are created, cannot be self-sufficing. It is only by fulfilling these necessary requirements that one will be able to relate the order of possibles to the order of singular existences, historical data and religious solutions. Only under these conditions will essential philosophy "correspond" with Christianity and accept the epithet "Christian" without losing its own name and independence.[37]

The notion of Christian philosophy does not give philosophy an additional function or competency in regard to Christianity. The adjective "Christian" simply indicates the essential direction that philosophy must have towards Christianity. Blondel emphasizes that the only sort of philosophy compatible with Christianity is philosophy itself.[38] It is a philosophy that avoids the pitfalls of a false Christian connotation and a rationalism of an exclusive and inconsequential type. The identity of "Christian philosophy" and "philosophy itself" would make the adjective "Christian" superfluous except for the fact that philosophy has been gradually transformed and determined precisely by the rejection of the activity of the Christian idea.

An autonomous philosophy that does not go outside the field of strictly rational study or break the necessary continuity of the dialectical process is Christian in its essential constitution. It is essentially Christian because through history it has undergone a permanent and profound transformation that affects its intrinsic nature. In a historical section of the *Letter* Blondel describes "how autonomous philosophy has been transposed and defined under the immanent influence of the religious problem."[39] The provisional equilibrium established in the Middle Ages between philosophy and Christianity resulted in a down-grading of autonomous phi-

---

37 *Ibid.*, p. 175.
38 Blondel, *Letter on Apologetics, op. cit.*, p. 170.
39 *Ibid.*, p. 171.

losophy. To divorce faith from reason and restore the equilibrium between the two disparate elements was not an easy task, because scholasticism had opened to human reason the immense horizons of faith. Left to itself, reason could not forget the world it had once glimpsed or give up hope of finding its equivalent. "No, things are not and cannot be what they were."[40] Thus, even while claiming full independence and transforming itself according to its own autonomy, it has been influenced by the Christian idea from which it tries to be set apart. "In triumphing, it returns upon its tracks, but it is very different from what it was when it set out upon its course. It is vanquished in its apparent victory, victorious in its apparent overthrow."[41]

In its effort to acquire full independence from Christianity, philosophy has shown its own incompleteness and has forcefully been led to recognize the necessity of transcendent truths which are immanent in human life and activity. Christian philosophy is thus a normal result of the history and evolution of philosophy itself.

> "What is it, then, that triumphs? It is philosophy itself, thanks to the gentle and secret influence of the Christian spirit which it seemed to combat and which seems to resist it; the philosophy which springs from the evolution of human thought not as a passing phase but as an acquisition justified in itself."[42]

The Option as the Decisive Moment

The intermediary between philosophy and faith is man's concrete existence. Human action is the meeting ground of reason and faith, of the rational and revealed truth that answers man's quest for meaning. Within human action reason and faith are in constant dialogue and it is not an easy task to determine precisely what reason contributes to the understanding of life and what is contributed by faith. The logic of action does not provide man with an exhaustive understanding of life. Understanding requires a commitment to what is understood, and this commitment generates a light that permeates man's total existence. This practical knowledge, supported by reason and joined in living conversation with reason, is the breeding ground of natural faith and the point of in-

40 *Ibid.*, p. 175.
41 *Ibid.*, p. 176.
42 *Ibid.*, p. 204.

sertion for supernatural faith. The commitment to what is rationally understood is a "complement of intelligibility."[43] Bouillard points out that the philosophy of action does not order us to make an option, it simply shows that each man necessarily makes an option.[44] The inevitability of making an option reveals the necessity to solve the problem of human destiny. At the point where the supreme option is made our understanding ceases to be exclusively rational or philosophical. The knowledge before the option was "subjective knowledge"; it did not have the consistency and value of the "objective knowledge" which results from a free commitment.[45] The option is "the most reasonable but at the same time the most freely chosen act."[46] In so far as it is a reasonable act philosophy can show us the necessity to make an option, but in so far as it is a free act the object of choice escapes the rational necessity of philosophical science. The knowledge that one obtains after the supreme option is, properly speaking, no longer exclusively philosophical. The option changes the perspective. Before the option, knowledge consists in determining the cause by the effects; after the option there is also knowledge that determines the effect by the cause.

The change of perspective takes place between the fourth and fifth part of *L'Action*. Commitment to the hypothetical supernatural destiny of man marks a clear line of demarcation between philosophy and fundamental theology. In the first four parts of his work Blondel speaks clearly to the unbeliever whom he introduces *per gradus debitos* to philosophy and helps to penetrate into the uncommitted knowledge of being. At the beginning of the fifth part the dialogue with his reader continues in the supposition that he has made a positive option in regard to the hypothetical necessity of the supernatural that enables him to explore Christianity as an indicated field of research. From this point on it becomes a dialogue between believers who have committed themselves to the hypothetical necessity of the Christian revelation.

The threefold notion of "Christian philosophy" is reflected in *L'Action*. Through the first four parts Blondel stays within the normal definition of philosophy. The chain of logical necessity is uninterrupted and rigorous. By purely philosophical methodology

---

43 Taymans D'Eypernon, *Le Blondélisme, op. cit.*, p. 78.
44 Bouillard, H., *Blondel et le christianisme, op. cit.*, p. 236.
45 Cf. Chapter 2.
46 Cartier, *Existence et Vérité, op. cit.*, p. 173.

he shows the essential insufficiency of the natural order and man's natural and inefficacious desire for fulfillment of his being. Philosophy remains open at the top and asks questions it cannot answer. It is a philosophy that is "not yet Christian," but orientated, perhaps unknowingly at this point, towards a Christian solution of man's essential natural insufficiency. It shows the necessary character of philosophical solutions with unconditional strictness. It is pure, universal, catholic philosophy. The epithet "Christian" added to philosophy could be deceiving at this stage of the Blondelian notion of "Christian philosophy." There is really nothing that would deserve or require such an epithet, except that possibility and necessity for further development which remains at the end of a philosophy of insufficiency. The recognition that a supernatural fulfillment is not excluded, but rather desirable although inaccessible to philosophy, gives a special significance to the incompleteness of the natural order of philosophy. It constitutes the decisive point of insertion of a hypothetical Christian solution. It is a philosophy that is open to Christianity, although the seat prepared for the supernatural remains at this point unoccupied.

As Bouillard notes,[47] the most important stage in the development of the notion of the supernatural is not the fifth part of L'Action but the end of the fourth part. The hypothetical necessity of the philosophical supernatural appears at that decisive moment in the determinism of action. We are here on authentically philosophical ground and whatever appears within the determinism of action as necessary is the result of essentially rational reflection. At this point the adjective "Christian" applied to philosophy translates the inherent insufficiency of the natural order and the necessity of a gift, a grace, that can fulfill this insufficiency. Philosophy is "Christian" not because it is itself lacking in anything, but because it marks out the territory in which the supernatural, if given, will operate. The insufficiency speaks loudly. It tells us about the need to be fulfilled and shows us the conditions of the object that will achieve philosophy's innermost desire. Not just any object or subject can occupy the empty seat.

Philosophy can determine the size, shape, quality, and conditions of this object or subject by looking carefully at the insufficiency, need, and emptiness at the very heart of man's life. Christian philosophy does not require that this supernatural object exist; it re-

47 Bouillard, op. cit., p. 97.

quires that it should be possible. "It is the hypothesis of the supernatural, not its reality in actual fact, that conditions the validity of natural ontology."[48] Christian philosophy at its first stage is a philosophy that is true to its vocation, and, therefore, cannot dispense itself from raising the religious problem. Once it has raised the problem, it cannot exclude the supernatural perspective or regard it simply as optional. It may be suggested that at this point the notion "Christian philosophy" indicates philosophy first, as insufficient in itself to satisfy the innermost desires revealed in human action, secondly, as demanding a hypothetical supernatural, thirdly, as marking out this hypothetical supernatural, fourthly and finally, as not yet Christian but unconsciously oriented toward Christianity.

For Blondel philosophy taken formally as such can recognize the supernatural precisely as supernatural. It therefore can properly be called both Christian and philosophy.

> "His original thought was . . . to dominate the order of external and conventional relations in which philosophy and religion had hitherto been placed so as to establish a philosophy which should be religious, not by accident, but by nature, without being so as a result of prejudice."[49]

At the beginning of the fifth part of *L'Action* the notion of Christian philosophy receives a further determination. Once the supernatural as defined by Christianity has been accepted as an hypothesis, philosophy becomes more closely associated with it. In its actual exercise it confronts its rational truths with the truths proposed by revelation. Thus philosophy comes under the influence of a hypothetical Christian supernatural. The actual truths of the Christian revelation are accepted as a working hypothesis to stimulate reason in its effort to develop its last and highest possibilities. From the beginning of the fifth part of *L'Action* Blondel's

---

48 Duméry, *Blondel et la Religion* (Paris: P.U.F., 1954), p. 118.

49 Victor Delbos in the introduction to the work of Th. Cremer, *Le problème religieux dans la philosophie de l'action* (Paris: Félix Alcan, 1912), p. VII. Cf. also Albert Cartier, *op. cit.*, p. 213: "Il veut faire une philosophie qui, pour être fidèle jusqu'au bout à ses propres principes, se trouvera *par surcroît* constituer une apologétique." André Hayen suggests that one could even say that a philosophy faithful to its own principles to the end will consequently (*par conséquence*) see itself develop into apologetics. (André Hayen, "La philosophie catholique de Maurice Blondel au temps de la première 'Action,'" *Revue Philosophique de Louvain*, 59 [1961], p. 266).

original intention becomes evident: to develop an autonomous philosophy within the hypothesis of the truth of Christianity, which is not affirmed and never will be affirmed by philosophy. Here the Christian phenomenon and its rational structure are subjected to a philosophical investigation in order to determine the rationality of faith. While working as a believer convinced of the truth of the Christian supernatural, Blondel addresses himself to the unbeliever with the request to accept by way of hypothesis the truth of Christianity for the sole purpose of developing a rational argumentation.

Following the option in favor of a supernatural fulfillment of human destiny, the unbeliever is confronted with the rational elements contained in what the believer accepts by faith. The rational investigation of reality within the defined boundaries of Christian revelation demands from the unbeliever a willingness that is not generated by philosophical necessity. The unbeliever is not asked to accept anything on the authority of revelation, but he is requested to apply the natural light of his own reason to what is known by a hypothetical revelation. The reasonableness of such a request from a person who has made a positive option in regard to the philosophical supernatural is unquestionable but it is not philosophically necessary. It is a logical consequence of the philosophy of insufficiency which indicates Christian revelation as an obvious candidate to fill the vacancy that man realizes within himself. As a philosopher he feels the need of entering into the domain of Christianity and investigate "what is of reason and antecedent to or merely consonant with faith on the plane of reason."[50]

By entering into Christianity as a logical field of research philosophy does not become theology. However, one must agree with Bouillard that in doing so philosophy fulfills at the same time and by this very fact a function normally carried out by fundamental theology. This alliance between philosophy and the hypothetical Christian supernatural could result in what we may call a "Christian philosophy." To the extent that it is *fides quaerens intellectum,* philosophy gives a rational foundation to the truths revealed in Christianity. To the extent that it follows upon an option in favor of a supernatural solution, it becomes *intellectus quaerens fidem.*[51]

[50] Blondel, *Letter on Apologetics, op. cit.,* p. 189.

[51] *Ibid.,* p. 193: "There are two aspects which must always be envisaged simultaneously, if one is not to leave faith without reason or to close reason against faith: *fides quaerens intellectum: intellectus quaerens fidem*—it is this

It is through this second function that philosophy transcends the option to which it led the unbeliever and effects an essentially Christian determination of the formally determined supernatural. As previously mentioned, this process of Christian specification calls for unique precautions inasmuch as a basic incommensurability exists between the order of philosophical necessity and actual contingency.[52]

It is here that the term "Christian philosophy" becomes most meaningful and the delicate equlibrium between the necessity of philosophy and the transcendence of the hypothetical supernatural finds its most successful expression. As soon as one overburdens the term "philosophy" in this expression, the Christian supernatural loses its character of transcendence and gratuity. On the other hand, if one overemphasizes the word "Christian," philosophy withers. In either case Christian philosophy is compromised; the noun absorbs the adjective or vice versa.[53]

Blondel here offers us a theory based on the critical awareness of our insufficiency and on the duty of leaving nothing undone to discover on what conditions this insufficiency can be remedied. Before philosophy can enter Christianity and determine whether the rational structure of Christian revelation corresponds to the demands of the hypothetical supernatural, it is required that Christianity be subjected to a rational purification. Philosophy applied to historical data and contingent conditions of the Christian supernatural must recognize its essential incompetence in regard to whatever is not rationally necessary. An analysis of Christianity, a philosophy of religion, as proposed explicitly in the two volumes of *La Philosophie et l'esprit chrétien,* investigates such notions as sacrifice, redemption, prayer, sacraments, incarnation, and Trinity in order to distinguish in them what is essential and necessary from what is contingent and historical. This is a study of Christianity as historically actualized, practiced, and preached. By eliminating the contingent and historical conditions of the Christian revelation, the rational structure is brought into focus. It is only in this essential rational structure that philosophy can possibly hope to find a corre-

double truth which results from an absolutely precise distinction between the theological and the philosophical functions of human thought."

[52] Blondel, *Problème de la philosophie catholique, op. cit.,* p. 145.

[53] Cf. Nédoncelle, *Is There a Christian Philosophy?* (New York: Hawthorn, 1960), pp. 112-113.

spondence with the essential requirements of the supernatural as revealed in philosophy.

Applied in this way to Christian revelation, philosophy is no longer philosophy in the strict sense of the term but has become speculative theology. Reason is used in organizing and determining the rational and essential relationships of the data of revelation known to us by the light of faith. The term "Christian philosophy" means here little more than a philosophy of Christianity in its actual historical realization.[54]

To sum up: the threefold notion of Christian philosophy is progressively more specifically Christian. At its first stage it indicates the insufficiency of the natural order and proclaims the possibility of a formally supernatural solution to human destiny; it is thus implicitly open to Christianity. After the option in favor of a supernatural solution, the philosopher develops and defines the philosophical supernatural in order to reveal philosophy's most urgent problem and to formulate what it expects of the word from heaven if heaven would speak. "The absolute thus grafted upon human thought is present to it in only a tragic and prospective sense; it works upon it through a sort of fruitful absence."[55] At the third stage philosophy enters openly into the historical Christian supernatural to lay bare the rationality of revelation and to compare it with the hypothetical philosophical supernatural whose demand had become, at the previous stage, more specifically determined under the influence of the hypothetical truth of Christianity.

It is at the first stage that the notion of Christian philosophy is most easily acceptable, inasmuch as it emphasizes the absolutely necessary and universal character of philosophical conclusions. At the second stage the epithet "Christian" becomes most meaningful but the adjective and noun do not make an altogether peaceful pair; they clash in spite of their attraction for one another and

---

[54] As Blondel points out, it is a question of analyzing Christianity in terms of what it has "de pensable, de cohérent avec notre réalité humaine, de relativement intelligible, de naturellement indécouvrable et cependant de parfaitement désirable et bon, malgré ce qu'il réclame de nous et ce qui surpasse, sinon nos vagues aspirations, du moins nos possibilitiés naturelles et nos réclamations humaines." *La Philosophie et l'esprit chrétien*, I (Paris: P.U.F., 1950), pp. 211-212.

[55] Nédoncelle, *op. cit.,* p. 113.

they involve a paradox, for they are both heterogeneous and in-
dissoluble at the same time.[56] The intervention of the option in
favor of the hypothetical solution and the Christian direction of
the search following upon the option seems to be less a result of the
logic of action than of the dynamism of the life of action which
testifies to man's restlessness and the insufficiency of the natural
order. The uneasiness and tension at this stage are witnesses to the
marriage of necessity and gratuity, the natural and the supernatural
which find here their point of mutual insertion.

At the third stage the term "Christian philosophy" stands for the
study of different Christian mysteries and man's supernatural vocation. Here the truth of Christianity and its dogmatic expression are
confronted with the philosophical enigmas. The problems experienced by human action are given all the importance they deserve
in the presence both of the data of revelation and of the contents
of the Christian message. Probing deep into the Christian revelation, Blondel attempts to provide it with "the greatest intelligibility
and lovable acceptability."[57] Although this is not the exclusive nor
the primary task of philosophy, the application of philosophy to
the data of faith will bring forth the religious significance of the
Christian mystery for man. However, the correspondence discovered
between the Christian solution and the philosophical enigmas does
not lead man to necessary philosophical conclusions concerning the
truth of Christianity, since it is not the task of philosophy to think
or rationalize the transcendent gift and living meaning of Christian
revelation. It must therefore be said that at this stage Christian
philosophy consists in a confrontation—nothing more but also
nothing less than a confrontation—of the insufficiency of philosophy
with the fullness of the Christian spirit. Although no philosophical
conclusions can be drawn from this confrontation, it may be said
that:

> "Philosophy will find out that the atmosphere in which Chris-
> tianity flourishes . . . is also the atmosphere in which there can
> be developed, in the most complete and free manner possible,
> without any restrictive epithet, that discipline which deserves

---

56 *Ibid.*, p. 114.

57 Poncelet, "The Christian Philosophy of Maurice Blondel," *International
Philosophical Quarterly*, V (1965), p. 592.

to be called, in the strong, unique and total meaning of the word, 'philosophy.' "[58]

CONCLUSION

The problem of the relationship between philosophy and Christianity occupies a central place in Blondel's thought. Blondel attempts to show that philosophy not only can be open to the Christian idea, but that it is necessarily oriented towards Christianity. Philosophy by its very nature asks questions that it cannot hope to answer. It remains always open towards the transcendent.

Blondel therefore refuses to subscribe to an abortive neutrality that attempts to enclose philosophy within the narrow confines of immanence. Although philosophy may never cross the threshold of faith, he assigns to the philosopher the role of a prophet who has to admit the inherent insufficiency of reason in its effort to realize the ultimate condition for man's achievement. Like the Precursor who baptized with water, prepared the way and removed the obstacles, philosophy announces the necessity of the supernatural while insisting that it has no access to it in and by itself.[1] In other words, Blondel claims for philosophy a qualified competency in regard to Christianity. He asks the philosopher to recognize the essential insufficiency of reason in solving the problem of human destiny, and he expects the theologian to take the prophetic role of philosophy seriously by allowing reason to point out the mysterious desire for what transcends its natural power. This essential relationship between philosophy and Christianity gives a meaningful content to the notion of Christian philosophy, without compromising either philosophy or Christian revelation. We venture to

---

[58] Blondel, *Exigences philosophiques du christianisme* (Paris: P.U.F., 1950), p. 403.

[1] "Remarquons, en effet, le contenu de la prédication du Baptiste. Il n'est qu'un précurseur, non seulement annonçant la venue du Messie, mais indiquant le dispositions nécessaires pour le reconnaître, pour le suivre, pour profiter de sa grâce . . . Il s'agit bien de vérités d'ordre humain et d'obligations s'imposant à une volonté droite dans l'ordre naturel, préludant à une éventuelle vocation plus haute. Cette rectitude de la raison et de la volonté apparaît comme antécédente et préparatoire à la compréhension et à l'acceptation de ce que doit être l'oeuvre messianique et le caractère supra-terrestre du royaume de Dieu." Blondel, *La Philosophie et l'esprit chrétien* (Paris: P.U.F., 1950), pp. X-XI.

suggest that the emphasis upon the insufficiency of philosophy and consequently upon its essential openness towards Christianity, as expressed in the Blondelian notion of Christian philosophy, can be of great value in the philosophical discussions of our times.

Blondel's return to lived experience as the synthetic a priori of thought and reality, has impregnated the thought of many contemporary philosophers. The central intuition from which their philosophies proceed is the synthetic reality of living or "existence." Blondel would have welcomed the penetrating analyses of man's restlessness on the existential plane of experience as presented by contemporary philosophers. With great force they bring out the insufficiency of an exclusively this-worldly meaningfulness and the impossibility of self-satisfied immanence. They condemn the Satrian "grave man" with a Blondelian contempt for idolatry and invite us to accept courageously the existential anxiety, boredom and despair. Inevitably they arrive at the great alternative facing modern man, the tragic choice, so dear to our contemporaries, between love of God and the absurdity of his absence: "the choice by which man prefers to remain his own master, uncommitted to anything outside himself, or surrenders himself to the divine command, of which he has become, more or less, vaguely conscious."[2]

The choice of atheistic existentialism by which man prefers to remain his own master or of the "death of God" theology which seeks to build a secular city, form a contemporary challenge to Blondel's philosophy. Faced with the unbelief of the present time and a humanism excluding personal communion with God, the philosophy of action will continue to illuminate the choice which each person has to make for himself.

Blondel's notion of Christian philosophy confirms the great insights into the human situation that an intense reflection upon the existential and personalistic dimension of man have produced. This notion, as dynamic as the experience from which it proceeds, is gaining in importance for contemporary philosophy which attempts "to describe the gropings of man in search for his destiny."[3] The philosophy of action embraces all human experiences and the dynamisms of personal and historical conditions. It does not ex-

---

2 Blondel, *L'Action*, p. 487.

3 "Je veux décrire le tâtonnement de l'homme en quête de sa destinée." Blondel, *Etudes blondéliennes* (Paris: P.U.F., 1952), p. 21.

clude the questions and problems of contemporary Christianity. On the contrary, it frequently anticipates them.

Blondel's philosophy, therefore, has an "undeniable up-to-dateness."[4] It is prepared to assimilate whatever may appear in the human situation and to lay bare the exigency that arises out of any existential experience. In the always up-to-date experience of action, philosophy will show the exigency of nature to constantly go beyond its own level and the necessity to open itself to the dynamism of transcendence. Such a notion of philosophy demands that the philosopher of action relates to the question of man's destiny everything human and never halts the dynamism of human action at the level of nature alone. It issues continuously an invitation to go on and to go beyond. Blondel's notion of Christian philosophy is a rediscovery of the authentic openness of the *philosophia perennis.*

Blondel expressed years ago a "maddening desire to be heard and to have disciples."[5] This wish is slowly being fulfilled. The philosopher of Aix has affected the thought and behavior of many people who never read his works or perhaps even heard his name but became his unconscious disciples. His vision of the dynamic role of philosophy, in regard to the Christian orientation of man's destiny will give him a permanent place among the masters who continue to influence contemporary Christian thought.

Missionhurst, Arlington, Virginia

---

4 Jolivet, *art. cit.,* p. 592.
5 Blondel, *Carnets intimes,* p. 527.

9

REDUCTION AND CONSTITUTION

by

Thomas Prufer

Transcendental reduction is disengaged and disinterested contemplation of the horizon "world" and "man." This abstention, neither corroborating nor shattering the thesis "world" and "man," is beyond both dogmatism and scepticism. (Manifesting obscurity as obscurity does not do away with obscurity by transforming it into clarity.[1]) The obscure thesis (*Geltungsvollzug*) of the prevenient horizon "world" and "man" becomes theme and phenomenon (constituted in evidence) of a new attitude (anticipation of experience), experience, and science: the transcendental. (The shift from unthematized thesis to thematized thesis: *actus exercitus et actus signatus*.) The transcendental ego is worldless insofar as, through a distancing from and loss of sympathy with the concerns of the mundane ego (*Weltstück*), it thematizes the *cogito mundum et me in mundo* as a phenomenon but does not itself repeat (*setzt nicht mit*) the thesis "world" and "man." The being of experience of the world (*Welt-Haben*) is not worldly being (*gehabte Welt*).[2] Within the transcendental reduction the thesis "world" and "man" has a being-as-phenomenon, a being-manifest, purified of all worldly and human sense, but it is not for that reason *hinterweltlich*, still natural, although no longer worldly and human.[3] By quoting the

---

[1] Cf. III 184, 33-38; IX 478, 4-19. Unless otherwise noted, references are to volume, page, and line of the *Husserliana*.

[2] Cf. IX 532, 20-21.

[3] Cf. Aristotle, *Metaphysics* 997b3ff; Wittgenstein, *The Blue and Brown Books*, New York: Harper and Row, 1958, 47: ". . . the queer role which the gaseous and the aethereal play in philosophy, — when we perceive that a substantive is not used as what in general we should call the name of an object, and when therefore we can't help saying to ourselves that it is the name of an aethereal object."

natural *Ich-Rede*,[4] the transcendental ego objectifies as its own the previously anonymous and silent constitution of the horizon "world" and "man." The will to *Umwertung* recapitulates the world of the world-child, manifesting it as *Erscheinung* and *Setzung* of a life at first hidden ("forgotten"),[5] beyond the thematization and clarification of which no anticipation is meaningful. World-constitution (*Urstiftung des Weltseins*;[6] *Weltbildung*) is itself constituted in evidence within the *epochē* by the transcendental ego as its own, for itself, in distance. This science of the *doxa* presupposed by worldly sciences[7] is a contemplation different from the Aristotelian *noēseōs noēsis*, anticipated by the science of nature, and like the Hegelian, anticipated by the science of experience, insofar as it contemplates othering and the other as its own. Why the fall (*metabasis; die mich selbst verweltlichende Apperzeption*[8]) of transcendental subjectivity into the natural attitude?

What motivates the abstention, distancing, loss of sympathy? The possibility of a whirl of appearances (*ein Gewühl von Erscheinungen*); questioning (*Rückfrage:* bringing all horizons to speech)[9] as dissatisfaction with what is incomplete and therefore abstract; freedom (*Willentlich-sich-loslösen*);[10] uncovering and reappropriating the origin (*Urstiftung*) of philosophy?[11] How do such possibility,

---

4 VIII 75, 24.
5 VIII 90, 1/91, 19.
6 IX 463, 26; Husserl puts *Urstiftung* in quotation marks.
7 VI 158, 18-24.
8 Cf. IX 294, 13-26; 343, 1-10.
9 VIII 223, note.
10 VIII 98, 22-23.
11 The sense of philosophy can be achieved only through a mediation of worldly being by thematization of the experience of worldly being (cf. *Ideen* I, #33-#46; XI 3-24); thematization of the experience of worldly being is in turn mediated by the primordial *fungor*, a dimension, ignored in transcendental naiveté, of *Strömen-Stehen* (*Quellen*) even more fundamental than both the synthesis, through "the standing form" of the temporality of experience, of *Urdatum* (*bewußt ohne gegenständlich zu sein*) and distention (retention and protention), and the reflection, open to indefinite iteration, and self-objectification made possible by this synthesis; cf. X, Beilagen VI & IX; VIII 468, 38-47 (583 ad loc.); XI 392, 13-15; see Klaus Held, *Lebendige Gegenwart* (Phaenomenologica 23), den Haag: Nijhoff, 1966. The formulation *verzeitigte vorzeitliche Zeitigung* is comparable (not equivalent) to the Heideggerian *die Entbergung der Zwiefalt von Anwesen und Anwesendem und die Erörterung dieser Entbergung in die Lichtung* (*Lichtung:* not clarification or bringing forth out of obscurity into

questioning, freedom, recovery differ from their worldly and human forms, which do not lead to the transcendental reduction? Do they presuppose the very irreducible radicality (presuppositionlessness) and totality (concretion not part of a more fundamental whole) which they motivate?

An act of the worldly and human *cogito* cannot achieve the reduction, and the transcendental *fungor* is anonymous until the act of reduction is achieved (more precisely: it is anonymous until the reduction of the reduction, the phenomenology of phenomenology, overcomes transcendental naiveté); for the worldly and human *cogito*, reduction breaks in as an anonymous and unmotivated act, a violence or a grace. This break with the natural attitude (*Einstellungsänderung, Interessenwendung*) is a differentiation: *cogito* [*mundum et me in mundo* (*mundum et me*) *cogitantem*] *qua cogitatum*.

Transcendental reduction regains in clarity and certainty the obscure and dubitable "world" and "man" which it seemed to lose: "*Konstitution ist nichts anderes als die Wiederaufbaubewegung, die der vollzogenen Reduktion folgt.*"[12] The impossibility of a worldly unity of subjectivity as world-constituting and as within the constituted world justifies the distinction between mundane ego and transcendental ego,[13] but this justification presupposes that world-constitution is a justifiable theme. In what way do world and man as such come to be questionable?[14]

The Catholic University of America

---

clarity, i.e., an iteration of *Entbergung*, but rather the clearing within which bringing forth out of obscurity into clarity takes place and then comes into view).

[12] H.-G. Gadamer, "Die phänomenologische Bewegung," *Philosophische Rundschau* XI (1963), 32.

[13] I 212-214 (R. Ingarden on 75, 27-29); VI 515, 6-10; 516, 3-10 (E. Fink).

[14] Jacques Derrida, *L'écriture et la différence*, Paris: Éditions du Seuil, 1967, 251.

10

THE EMPIRICAL HEDONISM OF MORITZ SCHLICK

by

Martin A. Bertman

Moritz Schlick, the foremost spokesman of the Vienna Circle, in his work, *Problems of Ethics* (*Fragen der Ethik*), sets himself the task of using the logical positivist methodology[1] to explore normative problems. This article contends that the methodological assumptions of logical positivism are unfruitful in dealing with normative matters and, further, that Schlick's attempts to use the pleasure principle as a basis for ethics within his empirical orientation is unjustifiable.

In the *Problems of Ethics,* as elsewhere, Schlick asserts that philosophy is an intellectual enterprise which by its very nature cannot discover truth. Science alone is capable of doing this. "Philosophy's task" Schlick says, "consists in making clear the content of scientific propositions, that is, in determining their meaning."[2] In another work, Schlick addresses himself to the role of the philosopher in this situation—"The philosopher as such is not interested in the facts of experience as such, for each fact is only one of in-

---

[1] Cf. Gustav Bergmann, *The Metaphysics of Logical Positivism* (Longmans, New York, 1954), p. 2.

> "Logical Positivists could still agree that they (a) hold Human views on causality and induction; (b) insist on the tautological nature of logical and mathematical truths; (c) conceive of philosophy as logical analysis, i.e., as a clarification of the language we speak in everyday life; and (d) that such analysis leads to the 'rejection of metaphysics' in the sense that, e.g., the points of dispute among the *traditional* forms of idealism, realism, and phenomenalism could not even be started in their original intent, in a properly clarified language."

[2] Moritz Schlick, *Problems of Ethics (Fragen der Ethik)* (Dover, New York, 1962), p. 19.

definitely many possible facts. Rather he is interested in the possibility of facts."[3]

Consequently, in this view, the traditional questions of philosophy are reconstructed so that the substantive materials are presented by the sciences and then philosophy provides possible—or, more usefully, probable—arrangement, through criticisms, for the purpose of clarity, coherence, non-contradiction and systematic coordination of the methods, boundaries, and conceptual techniques of science.

From this vantage normative material can be handled by philosophy in two ways: 1. Philosophy may dirempt itself totally from the empirical. It may construct a normative system based on some few assumptions. These assumptions may come from any quarter and the pragmatic importance of the system so constructed is beside the point. Such arbitrary constructionism would have the same interest and fascination as pure mathematics seems to have for its practitioners. 2. Again, philosophy may use the research of the social scientists and sort through their findings, criticizing and clarifying their methodologies, for the purpose of asserting certain generalities, or even laws, about human behavior. These investigations may, of course, also include man's own interpretations of his behavior. Schlick finds it preferable to choose the second option. Therefore, for him, a meaningful discussion of ethics must be involved with the social sciences, especially psychology.

Consequently, when Schlick uses normative terminology, such as "good," his task is to find how the connotation is ordered within general connections imposed by the social sciences. That is, the usage is meaningful—useful and factual—through its operative function within the context of a scientific discipline. Schlick, speaking for the expectation of logical positivists about sentences capable of inclusion within a scientific framework, says, "We expect instruction as to the circumstances in which the sentence will form a true proposition, and of those which will make it false."[4] It is because Schlick is committed to operating on a "given" that the normative usage must find its place through the techniques of the

[3] Schlick, "On the Relation Between Psychological and Physical Concepts," in Feigl and Sellars, *Readings in Philosophical Analysis* (Appleton-Century-Crofts, New York, 1949), p. 399.

[4] Schlick, "Meaning and Verification," in *ibid.*, p. 147.

empirical social sciences and, further, the confirmation of appropriate usage takes place by a reductive integration of generalizations in the light of specific problems.

It is in this manner that Schlick seeks to avoid a basic error of traditional metaphysical ethics: the reification of certain of the value trails presented by personal, theological, and social milieus. The strength of his approach is that it allows for the reformulation of normative usages when new conditions and relations arise or are discovered. This linguistic flexibility attempts to escape the divagation between connotation and denotation occurring whenever older formulations of normative language have confronted changing conditions.

However, this linguistic flexibility raises a crucial problem. It attaches us to a methodology which necessitates both a provisional and a perspectival interpretation of normative behavior. First, our insight into norms must be partial since they depend on necessarily incomplete surveys and, second, they involve the presentation of evidence whose selection presents an assumption of some prior awareness of value. The last is a very important point which I understand as going further than the difficulties of inclusion and integration within a scientific framework. It is in the nature of normative material that their assignation presupposes prior normative assumptions. This situation is overlooked if we start from a statistical survey of normative behavior or some similar technique. Schlick realizes this constant trend of such an approach toward relativism and would avoid it by finding some essential and universal psychological disposition of mankind. Schlick finds this in hedonism. It is only from such a universal principle that behavior of persons can be related as appropriate or inappropriate. The dilemma of this method is then that without a universal principle it is superficial, and with such a principle it must establish its right to have chosen the opted principle.

Since Schlick's hedonistic principle, based on an assumption of a general behavioral disposition of mankind, cannot be validated by empirical data it becomes a transscientific theory which breaks away from scientific verification. Unacceptably, its introduction results in a destruction of the public, descriptive credentials of empiricism which Schlick understands to be a necessary condition of scientific method. Thereby, it is in opposition to the "tough minded" approach which Schlick sometimes demands, as when he says,

"Ethics has to do entirely with the actual."[5] Nevertheless, Schlick does not wish to follow a logical positivist view which either ignores normative issues or asserts value relativism or agnosticism.[6]

Schlick's ethical position disregards the difficulty. His strategy, despite the incompatibility, is to affirm hedonism as the central ethical principle on an inductive basis. Therefore, he says, as he must in order to be faithful to the inductive character of his scientific allegiance, that "Ethics has to do only with resolutions,"[7] where "resolutions" means more than decisions, including habitual as well as conscious action: the "given" or the "actual." However, there seems some contradiction between this statement which allows for the inclusion of habitual as well as intentional behavior, with the following statement: "The decisions of life, they alone deserve the name 'conduct'; all else is mere activity."[8] Can there be any reconciliation of these two statements? The first statement seems in concert with Schlick's methodological commitment to the observable, whereas the second statement seems to be demanded by an *a priori* acceptance of a rational hedonism.

Actually, there is no reconciliation between the two. The very commitment of logical positivism to empirical methods in the construction of ethical theory refuses reconciliation since values cannot be established by descriptions of the empirical sort, nor can general value principles, as in this instance, hedonism, be so established. Let us but consider Schlick's use of hedonism for explanation and we will see the weakness of adopting a general normative principle for a behavioristic approach.

Even if we allow it to be epistemologically justifiable, which we do not, Schlick's adoption of hedonism has at least the difficulty of offering no adequate interpretation of human experience. His choice of pleasure as the essential disposition of mankind lacks the ability to provide adequate guidance for making ethical discriminations. Of course, Schlick wishes to maintain such a principle so that a standard of what is appropriate and inappropriate—of what

---

5 Schlick, *Problems of Ethics,* p. 21.

6 Carnap and Ayer represent this direction. For them ethical concepts "are unanalyzable . . . they are mere pseudo-concepts. The presence of an ethical symbol in a proposition adds nothing to its factual content." This quote is from A. J. Ayer, *Language, Truth, and Logic,* 2d edition (Dover, New York).

7 Schlick, *Problems of Ethics,* p. 32.

8 *Ibid.,* p. 32.

is "healthy"—exists for instrumental recommendations, i.e., for the transfer from the empirical evidence of the sciences to normative judgments; however, if nothing else, the complexity of human experience precludes this rather naturalistic turn. Again, Schlick's own epistemological "relativism" concerning "facts" puts such a transfer under suspicion: as he remarks, "It is, however, possible to indicate indentically the *same* set of facts by means of *various* systems of judgments; and consequently there can be various theories in which the criterion of truth (unique correspondence) is equally well satisfied. . . . They are merely different systems of symbols, which are allocated to the same objective reality."[9]

Let us consider two instances where Schlick shows the weakness of his approach in dealing with normative behavior. First, he finds the notion of "duty to society" as being a psychological demand for pleasure. Consequently, he asserts that the individual is so constituted that in the benefiting and preserving of his society through dutifulness to its laws the individual feels extreme pleasure and finds a condition for self-realization. Thus, despite its renunciatory demands, to perform one's duty, as the State asks it of the individual, is necessary to his ultimate happiness.

Not only do we notice here an evaluative assumption as to what men's feelings ought to be but, further, there is an unclarity of central concepts: "society," "individual," "duty." Schlick presents these concepts as if they referred to simple, given, atomic objects. Obviously, for instance, the concept of society does not; it seems more properly to connote a complex situation that is composed, among other elements, of various institutions, groups, forces and ideals—some deserving more, some less, some none of our allegiance. Schlick's approach leads to a *justificatio post festum,* i.e., that the established social institutions are the only right, useful, and possible ones.

A second instance: Schlick finds that polygamy, monogamy, and celibacy should be viewed as mere particular solutions for ordering pleasure in terms of the sexual aspect of being human. Here again Schlick's tendency to over-simplify becomes apparent; surely the solution to the ordering of physical pleasure, even if we grant the

---

9 Schlick, trans. H. L. Brose, *Space and Time in Contemporary Physics* (Oxford University Press, New York), p. 86.

assumption that pleasure itself is the only basis for such an ordering, cannot be seen in isolation from other conditions and goals. Schlick, in fact, assumes that an ideal ordering of our pleasure would be equal to an ideal ordering of our lives. This error is pointed out by Richard von Mises, "Some authors, e.g., M. Schlick, even think it necessary to assume the existence of a kind of pre-established harmony between the results of unconscious, instinctive processes and the results of reasoned thought."[10]

What Schlick depends upon for the justification of his empirical hedonism is a view of science as the investigatory agent whose task is to discover the ideal ordering of physical pleasure. However, as von Mises suggested, this assumes a "preëstablished harmony" between simple, unanalyzable feelings of pleasure and empirical conclusions about the physical nature of mankind. If we accept this dubious assumption, at best, Schlick's empirical ethics merely seems to prescribe a style of life where the various sciences provide information about pleasure in the form of generic assertions which may be taken as recommendations by the individual for his emulation.

Furthermore, Schlick, unlike Mill, does not allow for a qualitative view of these simple, unanalyzable, pleasure feelings. If Schlick chooses Socrates dissatisfied over the pig satisfied it is because he assumes that there is quantitatively more pleasure for the dissatisfied Socrates.

Obviously, such an approach to ethics restricts in a most extreme manner the function of the intellect in the normative situation: ". . . mere intellectual operations have very little influence on the feelings, the motive of proper conduct is not the result of such calculation."[11] Thus, a disjunction between feelings and intellect seems to result from the unfruitful methodology of logical positivism. A methodology which allows the intellect to have no genuine role in the normative process, except within a narrow and rather mechanistic view of the empirical.[12] Consequently, Schlick does not realize that although human behavior may often

10 Richard von Mises, *Positivism* (Braziller, New York, 1956), p. 347.

11 Schlick, *Problems of Ethics*, p. 86.

12 Martin A. Bertman, "Philosophical Notes on the Usage of 'Reality,'" *Rendezvous*, Vol. III, No. 2, Winter, 1968. Cf. remarks on Ernst Mach.

be explained by habit, instinct, or feelings of pleasure, this in itself does not preclude or contradict the possibility of the intellect's having a crucial role in normative behavior.

State University of New York College at Potsdam

11

STRAWSON AND THE NO-OWNERSHIP THEORY

by

JOHN A. DRISCOLL

In his article "Persons,"[1] which may well be the single most published piece of philosophy since Russell's "On Denoting," P. F. Strawson asks two questions: "Why are one's states of consciousness ascribed to anything at all?" and "Why are they ascribed to the very same thing as certain corporeal characteristics, a certain physical situation, etc.?" (I., 84) The answer to the second question is the fundamental thesis of Strawson's article: states of consciousness and corporeal characteristics are both ascribed to *persons* since "person" is a primitive concept, "logically prior" to whatever it is states of consciousness would necessarily be ascribed to if they were not necessarily ascribed to persons, i.e., "egos" or "pure consciousnesses." (I., pp. 97-99) It might be argued, however, that states of consciousness are not necessarily ascribed to anything, but only contingently ascribed to particular bodies—only contingently since it is quite conceivable, though in fact false, that one man should feel pain in another man's arm, for example, if their nervous systems were spliced.[2] Strawson calls this position the "no-

---

[1] First published in Volume II of *Minnesota Studies in the Philosophy of Science* (1958), "Persons" reappeared as Chapter Three of Strawson's *Individuals: An Essay in Descriptive Metaphysics* (London: Methuen, 1959; Garden City: Anchor, 1963) and has since been anthologized at least four times: in V. C. Chappell, ed., *The Philosophy of Mind* (Englewood Cliffs New Jersey: Prentice-Hall, 1962), Donald F. Gustafson, ed., *Essays in Philosophical Psychology* (Garden City: Anchor, 1964), G.N.A. Vesey, *Body and Mind* (London: Allen and Unwin, 1964), and Harold Morick, ed., *Wittgenstein and the Problem of Other Minds* (N. Y.: McGraw-Hill, 1967). References in the text of this paper will be made in the form: "I" followed by the page number of *Individuals*, Chapter Three.

[2] For other interesting examples, cf. Wittgenstein's *Blue Book* (*The Blue and Brown Books:* Preliminary Studies for the *Philosophical Investigations.*

ownership" theory and suggests that Wittgenstein and Schlick may have held it during the thirties. To secure his thesis against this possible position Strawson asks and attempts to answer his first question: "Why are one's states of consciousness [necessarily] ascribed to anything at all?"

Let us look first to Wittgenstein and Schlick for a statement of the position, then to Strawson's refutation and Ayer's reply. Finally let us examine in detail whether Strawson succeeds in answering his first question and, even if he does, whether that answer is able to bear the weight placed on it by his answer to the second question, the thesis of his article.

I

Strawson suggests that Wittgenstein seems to argue for the no-ownership position in his lectures of 1930-1933 as recorded by Moore,[3] when he says that "I" in "I have a toothache" does not "denote a possessor." (Moore, p. 123) For clarity's sake we may distinguish three steps in Wittgenstein's argument. (1) There is a strong *asymmetry*[4] between "I have a toothache" and "He has a toothache" (or "You have a toothache"). Wittgenstein expresses this asymmetry most strikingly when he says, in Moore's words, that ". . . they are not both values of a single propositional function 'x has toothache'" since it makes no sense to say "I don't know whether I have toothache" or "It seems to me that I have toothache" whereas it makes very good sense to say "I don't know whether he has toothache" or "It seems to me that he has toothache." (Moore, p. 121) However, (2) there is also a misleading similarity or symmetry between other uses of "I" and corresponding uses of "he" which tends to obscure the asymmetry in the case of "I have toothache" and "He has toothache"—e.g., "I've got a bad

---

N.Y.: Harper, 1958), pp. 52-54. References in the text will be made to "BB" followed by the page number.

    3 G. E. Moore, "Wittgenstein's Lectures in 1930-1933," *Mind* 63 (1954), especially "Section D," pp. 13-14. Reprinted in Harold Morick, ed., *Wittgenstein and the Problem of Other Minds* (N.Y.: McGraw-Hill, 1967). References in the text will be made to the Morick volume.

    4 This word, useful for understanding Wittgenstein, I have taken from S. Coval, *Scepticism and the First Person* (London: Methuen, 1966), pp. 50-61, e.g.

tooth" and "He's got a bad tooth." Wherever "I" is replaceable by "this body," Wittgenstein argues, both "I" and "he" are on the same grammatical level, whereas in the case of the toothache "the two expressions are on a different grammatical level. . . ." (Moore's words, p. 121) The expressions are used in "two utterly different ways." (Wittgenstein's words, p. 124) Finally, (3) in those cases where "I" is asymmetrical, on a different grammatical level from "he," it may be replaced by an impersonal expression: e.g., "Ich denke" may be changed to "Es denkt." In a comparison with the "visual field" reminiscent of *Tractatus* 5.633 ff., Wittgenstein says that the "I" may be extruded from "I have a toothache" since "the idea of a person doesn't enter into the description of it, just as a [physical] eye doesn't enter into the description of what is seen." (Moore, pp. 122-3)

II

If this is the no-ownership theory, it would seem disingenuous of Strawson to give the impression that Wittgenstein held the view only "at one time" and then presumably abandoned it. (I., p. 90n) In the last thirty pages of the *Blue Book,* dictated in 1933, variation after variation of the same three-part argument is presented. In the first part of the *Philosophical Investigations,* returning to the question of the visual field, Wittgenstein says:

> The "visual room" is the one that has no owner. I can as little own it as I can walk about it, or look at it, or point to it. Inasmuch as it cannot be any one else's it is not mine either. In other words, it does not belong to me *because* I want to use the same form of expression about it as about the material room in which I sit. (PI, #398)

Finally, even in the second part of the *Philosophical Investigations,* written in the late 1940s, the three-part argument reappears in Wittgenstein's analysis of Moore's paradox. (1) There is an asymmetry between first-person and third-person uses of "I believe" since "I believe this is the case" means the same as "This is the case" whereas "He believes this is the case" does not. (2) This asymmetry is obscured by the symmetry of the hypotheticals "If I believe this is the case" and "If he believes this is the case," neither of which mean the same as "This is the case," and of the pasts "I believed this was the case" and "He believed this was the case," neither of which mean "This was the case." (3) "If there were a verb meaning 'to believe falsely,' it would not have any significant first person present indicative." (PI, p. 190) Similarly there could be a language in which the form "I believe it is so" would be replaced by the tone of the assertion "It is so" and the verb corresponding to "to believe" would simply lack one inflection, the first person singular. (PI, p. 191)

III

To illustrate the argument recorded by Moore that "A has a gold tooth" and "A has a toothache" are not used analogously ("They differ in their grammar where at first sight they might not seem to differ."), Wittgenstein in the *Blue Book* proposes the interesting philosophical statements, "I may have toothache in another man's tooth, but not *his* toothache" (BB, p. 53), and "I can't feel his pain" (BB, p. 49). In his article "Meaning and Verification"[5] Moritz Schlick develops very carefully Wittgenstein's thesis that "I can't feel his pain" and the equivalent

"I can feel only my pain"   (Q)

can be interpreted *either* as the contingent experiential generalization "We can't have (haven't as a rule) pains in another person's tooth" (BB, p. 49) and the equivalent

"I feel pain only when the body M is hurt"   (P)

or as the metaphysical-grammatical dictum "I may have toothache in another man's tooth, but not *his* toothache" and the equivalent

"I *can* feel only *my* pain,"   (T)

where *"can"* means not empirical but logical possibility and *"my"* does not mean anything! (Schlick, pp. 163-166) Schlick's point is that when statement Q is interpreted to mean statement P the "my" has a function in the sentence: the "my" *could* be changed to "your" or "his" even as the "body M" could be changed to "body N." But when Q means T, the "my" does no work not already performed by the "I"—which is itself replaceable by an impersonal expression: " 'I feel pain' and 'I feel my pain' are, according to the solipsist's definition, to have identical meaning; the

5 *The Philosophical Review*, 45 (1936); reprinted in Herbert Feigl and Wilfrid Sellars, eds., *Readings in Philosophical Analysis* (N.Y.: Appleton-Century-Crofts, 1949), pp. 146-170. References in the text are to the reprint.

word 'my,' therefore, has no function in the sentence." (Schlick, p. 166) Similarly, the word "owner" makes sense "only when it is logically possible for a thing to change its owner, i.e., where the relation between the owner and the owned object is empirical, not logical. . . ." (Schlick, p. 167)

IV

The argument against the no-ownership theory is crucial to the thesis of Strawson's "Persons," for unless there is a type of ownership of experiences conceptually distinct from the contingent ownership of experiences by a particular body it will not be possible to demand persons as more primitive entities than bodies— i.e., as basic particulars capable of exercising both conceptually distinct types of ownership whereas bodies taken simply as such can exercise only contingent or logically transferable ownership (at least according to Wittgenstein, Schlick and Strawson; Ayer will challenge this point). Therefore if Strawson is to allow for "persons" as primitive, he must somehow refute the no-ownership theory.

This he attempts to do by arguing (1) that a necessary and logically non-transferable type of ownership is a condition for defining contingent and logically transferable ownership (which he will say the no-ownership theory must do in order to define its own position) and (2) that, since reference to an experience is possible only if there is ascription in some form—whether necessary ascription to some ego or person or contingent ascription to some body or person—accordingly "the theorist could maintain his position only by denying that we could ever refer to particular states or experiences at all. And this position is ridiculous." (I., p. 93) Clearly (2) is dependent on (1), for if contingent ascription is possible independently of necessary ascription, then the no-ownership theorist can "maintain his position" without "denying that we could ever refer to particular states or experiences at all." Strawson must refute the no-ownership theory if his own position is to be possible; if he is to refute the no-ownership theory Strawson must prove that stating necessary ownership is a condition for stating contingent ownership.

It is within the context of his elaboration of the no-ownership theorist's position that Strawson attempts to prove that stating necessary ownership is a condition for stating contingent ownership. He describes the theorist's argument that grammatical confusion makes us pass from contingent having or ownership by a body (valid) to necessary having or ownership by an ego (invalid):

> Suppose we call the first type of possesion, which is really a certain kind of casual dependence, "having$_1$" and the second type of possession, "having$_2$"; and call the Individual of the first type "B" and the supposed individual of the second ·type "E." Then the difference is that while it is genuinely a contingent matter that *all my experiences are had$_1$ by B,* it appears as a necessary truth that *all my experiences are had$_2$ by E.* But the belief in E and in having$_2$ is an illusion. Only those things whose ownership is logically transferable can be owned at all. (L., p. 91)

Strawson then takes the statement, "All my experiences are had$_1$ by B," which he has already shown to be the starting point of the theorist's argument (I., p. 90) and focuses on the word "my." He argues that (1) the "my" cannot be eliminated, for that would make the statement clearly false; that (2) the "my" cannot be defined in terms of a body, for that would make the statement a tautology; and that (3), for lack of any alternative, the "my" must therefore be defined by the very having$_2$ (or possession$_2$) which the theorist wants to deny. The argument is quite obviously taken from Kant, who also uses the need for a definition of "my" and a determination of what experiences are "my" experiences to arrive at a logically necessary (or, in his own terms, transcendentally necessary) sense of belonging:

> It must be possible for the "I think" to accompany all my representations. . . . The unity of this apperception I likewise entitle the transcendental unity of self-consciousness. . . . For the manifold representations, which are given in an intuition, *would not be one* and all *my* representations, if they did not all *belong* to one self-consciousness. As *my* representations (even if I am not conscious of them as such) they must conform to the condition under which alone they can stand together in one universal self-consciousness, because otherwise they would not all without exception belong to *me.*[6]

It is not surprising that the author of *The Bounds of Sense* should have brought his appreciation of Kant to bear on the issue.

6 *Critique of Pure Reason,* tr. Norman Kemp Smith (N.Y.: St. Martin's Press, 1965), B 132, p. 153 (emphasis altered). Cf. *Individuals,* p. 99.

Because a knowledge of its close reasoning will be helpful throughout the remainder of the paper, Strawson's own version of the argument will be given here in full:

> I think it must be clear that this account of the matter, though it contains some of the facts, is not coherent. It is not coherent, in that one who holds it is forced to make use of that sense of possession of which he denies the existence, in presenting his case for the denial. When he tries to state the contingent fact, which he thinks gives rise to the illusion of the "ego," he has to state it in some such form as "All *my* experiences are had₁ by (i.e., uniquely dependent on the state of) body B." For any attempt to eliminate the "my," or some other expression with a similar possessive force, would yield something that was not a contingent fact at all. The proposition that all experiences are causally dependent on the state of a single body B, for example, is just false. The theorist means to speak of all the experiences *had by a certain person* being contingently so dependent. And the theorist cannot consistently argue that *"all* the experiences of person P" *means the same thing* as "all experiences contingently dependent on a certain body B"; for then his proposition would not be contingent, as his theory requires, but analytic. He must mean to be speaking of some class of experiences of the members of which it is in fact contingently true that they are all dependent on body B. And the defining characteristic of this class is in fact that they are *"my* experiences" or "the experiences *of* some person," where the idea of possession expressed by "my" and "of" is the one he calls into question. (I., p. 92)

V

A. J. Ayer claims to "rebut" this argument of Strawson that the no-ownership theory is inconsistent because it requires that the proposition that all my experiences are causally dependent on the state of my body be both contingent and analytic.[7] Ayer says that the inconsistency may be resolved by distinguishing the sense in which the theory requires that the statement of dependence be analytic and that in which it requires that the statement be contingent:

> The contingent proposition is that if my body is in such and such a state, then an experience of such and such a kind

7 A. J. Ayer, "The Concept of a Person," in *The Concept of a Person and Other Essays* (N. Y.: St. Martin's Press, 1963), p. 116.

results; the analytic proposition is that if an experience is causally dependent in this way on the state of my body, then the experience is mine. . . ." (Ayer, pp. 116, 117)

In assessing Ayer's proposed rebuttal, it is necessary to distinguish his purpose from ours. Ayer is interested in establishing the thesis "that the fact that [one' own experiences] are one's own, or rather the fact that they are the experiences of the person that one is, depends upon their being connected with this particular body." (Ayer, p. 116) Ayer's thesis is actually quite similar to Strawson's, except that where Strawson wants to postulate a basic particular called a "person" more primitive than either the ego or the mechanical human body of the Cartesian economy, Ayer is willing to say that experiences depend directly on the body, although they are not to be physicalistically identified with the body (cf. Ayer, p. 126): "It is analytic that if the experiences are connected with his body, they are his experiences. . . ." (p. 117) "It is not a necessary fact that my body has the physical attributes that it does, but given that this is the body by which I am identified, it is a necessary fact that *this* body is *mine*. (p. 126; emphasis Ayer's; contrast I., p. 87)

In one sense Ayer is undermining Strawson on a more fundamental level than the essentially Wittgensteinian counterattack which we will present below: he questions the basic position or assumption, which Strawson shares with Wittgenstein and Schlick, that experiences cannot be *necessarily* ascribed$_2$ to a body. However in another sense, by maintaining a purely contingent relationship between experience and body (although in Wittgenstein's case, it must be stressed, *not* a purely contingent relationship between language about experience and body!) Wittgenstein, Schlick and Strawson are better able to explain the origin of Cartesianism and solipsism. It is on this level that we will confront Strawson below.

VI

In the sentence "All my experiences are had$_1$ by B," the no-ownership theorist works with "have$_1$," arguing that "have$_1$" does not allow any conclusions about "have$_2$" since their grammars are distinct; Strawson works with "my," arguing that it makes "have$_2$" a condition for the statement of "have$_1$." At this point attention might well be turned to yet another word: "experiences."

In arguing that "the proposition that *all* experiences are causally dependent on the state of a single body B is just false" (I., p. 92) Strawson clearly implies that the extension of the term "experiences" must *necessarily* be broader than the extension of what Strawson chooses to call "my experiences." He says that the theorist "must mean to be speaking of *some class of experiences* of the members of which it is in fact contingently true that they are all dependent on body B," (I., p. 92 italics added) where the entire set is defined as "experiences" and the class in question is a subset defined as "*my* experiences." But if the set of "experiences" has no other non-empty subsets besides the subset of "my experiences," then it is *not* "just false" to say that "all experiences are causally dependent on the state of a single body B." Strawson merely assumes that the term "experiences" has a broader extension than the term "my experiences." But this is no innocent assumption, since the question of other minds *is* the question whether there are any other possible non-empty subsets of the set "experiences" besides the subset "my experiences." To assume that there are is a *petitio principii* against the solipsist—and it is the solipsist, after all, that the no-ownership theorist sets out to refute. (Cf. Moore, pp. 125-26; PI, #402)

The no-ownership theorist would draw a distinction between first-person ascribed experience predicates ("experiences$_x$") and second- and third-person ascribed experience predicates ("experiences$_y$") and argue that it is perfectly correct to say "All experiences$_x$ are dependent on the state of a single body B." The extension of the term "experience" might then be restricted to either one side or the other of the distinction and a new term coined for the remaining side. Wittgenstein, for example, suggests such a possibility:

> If I were to reserve the word "pain" solely for what I had hiterto called "my pain," and others "L.W.'s pain," I should do other people no injustice, so long as a notation were provided in which the loss of the word "pain" in other connexions were somehow supplied. Other people would still be pitied, treated by doctors and so on. It would, of course, be *no* objection to this mode of expression to say: "But look here, other people have just the same as you!" (PI, #403)

This is simply another way of stating his earlier conclusion that experiences$_x$ and experiences$_y$ are not "values of the same propositional functions" simply because those functions contain the word "experience."

Strawson hangs too much argumentative weight on the extension of the term "experience" across first, second, and third persons just as the solipsist puts too much weight on first person "privileged access." Wittgenstein's example shows that the difference in use between first person pain statements and all other pain statements is such that we *could* use different words if we wanted to.

Strawson might well object that "experience$_x$" is still defined in terms of "I" and "mine." But this is not precisely true; rather, "I" and "mine" are used in the same way as "experience$_x$." As Strawson himself recognizes (I., p. 100 ff.) the set of predicates defined as ascribable in the first person partially intersects the set of predicates defined as "experiences" but also contains many subsets of predicates ascribable equally well to material bodies ("I am tall"; "The tree is tall.") In this he is merely following Wittgenstein's distinction in first-person grammar between "the use as object" ("My arm is broken") and "the use as subject" ("I try to lift my arm"). But whereas Strawson calls this distinction "a rough division" (I., p. 100) Wittgenstein suggests an explanation for the distinction when he notes that there are criteria and rules for the "use as object" but none for the "use as subject" (in the former "the possibility of error has been provided for"—BB 67). But this is the same basis as for the distinction of have$_1$ and have$_2$: having$_1$ the experience$_y$ admits the possibility of error whereas having$_2$ the experience$_x$ does not.

Thus Strawson, with the assistance of Kant, has proved his original argument against the no-ownership theory over the above objections: for if experience$_x$ is defined in the same way as having$_2$ (i.e., neither has any criteria or any possibility of error), then experience$_x$ in "all experiences$_x$ are had$_1$ by B" makes just as strong a case as "my" in "all my experiences are had$_1$ by B" for taking have$_2$ as a condition for the statement of have$_1$. The statement of necessary and logically non-transferable ownership *is* a condition for the statement of contingent and logically-transferable ownership: Strawson has satisfactorily answered his first question.

VII

But it would be a Pyrrhic victory at best, for if Strawson were to accept the escape just outlined in order to answer his first question, he would thereby invalidate his answer to the second question, the thesis of "Persons." If he were to employ the basis of the distinction of experiences$_x$ and experiences$_y$ (viz., no criteria vs. criteria) as above in answer to the no-ownership theorist's employment of the distinction of experiences$_x$ and experiences$_y$ as an objection against his (Strawson's) assumption that the extension of the term "experiences" is broader than the subset of "my experiences," Strawson would be bound by consistency to accept the disastrous consequences of the basis of the distinction for his own subsequent argument concluding to "persons" as basic particulars capable both of having$_1$ experiences$_y$ and of having$_2$ experiences$_x$. Strawson wants to argue on the basis of the meaning (i.e. the intension) of the term "have" (whatever is had$_1$ or had$_2$ has an owner$_1$ or an owner$_2$) from an owner$_1$ to an owner$_2$. This is why he must use the Kantian "my" (an owner$_2$ necessary to make statements about an owner$_1$) to counter the no-ownership theorist's denial of an owner$_2$. But the no-ownership theorist has objected that there need be no single meaning of "have" or "experience" spanning first-person experience statements and second- and third-person experience statements, to which objection Strawson has been able to reply that such an extensional restriction on the meanings of "have" and "experience" (calling for two distinct intensions in each case) is itself based upon "I" and "my" and thus upon an owner$_2$. However at this point one apparent no-ownership theorist, Wittgenstein, would reply that the basis for distinguishing two different meanings of "have" and "experience" is not intension but *use* (i.e. the presence or absence of criteria, the possibility or impossibility of error). It should be noted very carefully here that the argument does *not* presuppose that Wittgenstein is right concerning the delicate question of criteria and the so-called "criteriological connection"; it merely presses against Strawson the objection that he may not with consistency rely on a criteria-no criteria distinction to defend his answer to question one (as he has presumably been forced to do if the arguments presented above are in any way correct) and then rescind it in order to defend his answer to question two.

Here Strawson must either admit defeat because of the distinction between experiences$_x$ and experiences$_y$—the contingent relationship between experiences and a particular body *can* be expressed without any "my" or owner$_2$ simply by saying "All experiences$_x$ are had$_1$ by body B"—or else attempt to turn the *basis* of the distinction against Wittgenstein *et al.* by arguing that experiences$_x$ involve ownership$_2$ just as well as *"my* experiences" do (i.e., experiences$_x$ are had$_2$ by me without criteria, whereas experiences$_y$ are said to be had$_1$ by—ascribed to—my body or Smith or Jones, etc. according to criteria). The parallel grammars of experience$_x$ and have$_2$ thus allow Strawson to argue from "all experiences$_x$ are had$_1$ by B" to the conclusion that have$_2$ is a condition for the statement of have$_1$. But once such a grammatical or use basis, rather than an intensional or extensional basis, has been accepted for the distinction in meaning between experiences$_x$ and experiences$_y$, it is no longer possible to argue from characteristics of experience$_y$ to characteristics of experience$_x$ or from characteristics of have$_1$ to characteristics of have$_2$ without making unwarranted assumptions. Thus if Strawson is to employ the *use* of experience$_x$ and have$_2$ to prove his preparatory argument against the no-ownership theory that have$_1$ cannot be defined without have$_2$, he cannot in his principal argument contend that what is had$_2$ has an owner$_2$ simply because what is had$_1$ has an owner$_1$.

Accordingly the conclusion reached above at the end of Part VI (that the statement of necessary and logically non-transferable *ownership* is a condition for the statement of contingent and logically transferable ownership) must be modified by the removal of "ownership" or any other word that might take its place in the first clause as an illegitimate assumption about have$_2$ on the basis of have$_1$. The modified conclusion would read: "Necessity and logical non-transferability are a condition for the statement of contingent and logically transferable (ownership) ," where the parentheses around "ownership" indicate that *any* word with criteria for its use might be inserted. But this is neither more nor less than Wittgenstein's version of no ownership, whether in the *Blue Book* or in the *Investigations*. That is, necessity is built into the "depth grammar" of our language.

Thus Strawson could refute those versions of the no-ownership theory which would deny philosophical necessity and non-transferability (i.e., by denying having$_2$ *tout simple*) only by accepting in the end Wittgenstein's version (which accepts having$_2$ but not an owner$_2$) and abandoning his thesis that persons are more primitive and more basic particulars than bodies. " 'I' is not the name of a person. . . ." (PI, #410) Nor is the necessary "transcendental" unity of apperception confused by Kant with the empirical ego which is personal. By Strawson's own admission, "Kant's doctrine that the 'analytic unity of consciousness' neither requires nor entails any principle of unity is not as clear as one could wish."[8] Perhaps neither Wittgenstein nor Kant was as far from Hume as Strawson would like to think. (I., p. 99)

University of Michigan

[8] This quotation is taken from the concluding passage of "Persons" as contained in Chappell, *op. cit.*, p. 146. It is not contained in Chapter Three of *Individuals*.

Felix Alluntis, O.F.M., formerly ordinary Professor in the CUA School of Philosophy, is now devoted to research. He is the author of *Filosofía de la Propiedad* (Havana, 1960). He has contributed extensively to Spanish and English philosophical journals, symposia and encyclopedias; has translated and edited several works of Scotus into Spanish including the *Quaestiones quodlibetales* (BAC, 1968) and *De primo principio* (BAC, 1960). He is Lector Generalis in the Order.

Henri Bergson (1859-1941). While his great popularity before the 1914-1918 war lessened somewhat in later years, Bergson's position is now stabilized and his influence, perhaps not wholly in accord with his intentions, is seen in various contemporary movements.

Martin A. Bertman is a member of the philosophy faculty of State University of New York College at Potsdam. Educated at Syracuse and Columbia Universities, he is co-editor of *Agora* and has published in *Philosophy Today, Islamic Quarterly*, and elsewhere.

Gregory desJardins, M.A. is Assistant Professor in the School of Philosophy, CUA. He studied at the University of Chicago and has published in the *Journal of the History of Ideas*.

John A. Driscoll made his undergraduate studies and two years of graduate study in the School of Philosophy, CUA, and now holds a Danforth scholarship at the University of Michigan where he is a doctoral candidate in philosophy.

Angelita Myerscough, A.S.C., Ph.D., has taught in St. Louis University. She is now superior of the Ruma, Illinois, province of her community, the Adorers of the Blood of Christ.

John E. Pattantyus, Sch.P. studied in Budapest before coming to the United States. He has earned a doctorate in philosophy and an M.A. in history at CUA. His article is a revision of a chapter in his doctoral dissertation.

Thomas Prufer is Associate Professor in the School of Philosophy, CUA. He is the author of *Sein und Wort nach Thomas von Aquin* (Munich, 1959), and has published in SPHP, *International Philosophical Quarterly*, and other journals.

Mother Caroline Canfield Putnam, R.S.C.J. is engaged in social work in the Roxbury section of Boston. She has taught at Newtonville College of the Sacred Heart. Among her publications is a translation with commentary of Denis the Pseudo-Areopagite's four letters to the Monk Caius in SPHP, Volume 4.

John K. Ryan is Elizabeth Breckinridge Caldwell Professor of Philosophy Emeritus, CUA, and formerly dean of its School of Philosophy.

Allan B. Wolter, O.F.M. is a Professor in the School of Philosophy, The Catholic University of America, and has been a visiting professor at Princeton, New York, and Michigan Universities, and has published extensively on philosophy. He is the author of *The Transcendentals and Their Function in the Metaphysics of Duns Scotus* (Washington, 1946), *Duns Scotus: Philosophical Writings* (Edinburgh, 1962) and other works. An article on his work, with a bibliography of his writings, appeared in the CUA School of Philosophy *Newsletter*, Vol. 5, No. 2.

Leo J. Zonneveld, C.I.C.M. made his philosophical studies at Nijmegen, did theology in Belgium, and took his Ph.D. at CUA in 1969. He has been a lecturer in the School of Philosophy and is superior of the American province of his community.

INDEX

Aeschylus, 109

Albert of Saxony, 14

Albertus Magnus, 14, 233

Alexander of Aphrodisias, 13-14, 23

Alfarabi, 101-02n

Alluntis, F., 178

Anselm, St., 17

Aristophanes, 133

Aristotle, 1-4, 11, 13-72, 73-78, 79-135, 180-83, 189-90, 196-97, 199-200, 202-10, 213-22, 223, 341; justice in, 80-137, background of doctrine, 80-105, definition of, 106-12, division of, 113-21, general, 106-37, in general, 80-105, law, relation to, 113-18, prudence and, 99-101, psychology of, 83-105; place, his doctrine on, 20-27, criticism of other doctrines of, 13-17, definition and kinds of, 44-57, empty space impossible, 32-35, matter, form, and, 29-32, origin of doctrine, 66-71, solution of problem of, 60-66

Armstrong, A. H., 99n, 138n, 140n, 148-52, 158, 172, 177

Augustine, St., 176, 181, 187, 202, 211-12

Averroes, 14, 203, 217-18

Avicenna, 218-19

Ayer, A. J., 347, 355, 357-58

Bacon, R., 14

Barker, E., 116

Basch, V., 231

Baumgarten, A. G., 223

Bergson, H., 11-19, translated, 20-71

Bernays, J., 82

Bias, 124

Blondel, M., action, his doctrine of, 243-47; contingency and necessity, 287-97; freedom, determinants of, 272-87, problem of, 270-71; solution of, 287-97; knowledge, insufficiency of, 268-70; method, his, 248-68; philosophy and Christian revelation, 310-38

Bonaventure, St., 14

Bonhoeffer, D., 243

Bouillard, H., 289-90, 299-301, 306-09, 331-32

Brandis, C. A., 14, 20

Bréhier, E., 139, 156n

Brennan, R. E., 140, 150, 161

Brightman, E., 246

Brumbaugh, R. S., 10

Buridan, J., 14

Burke, E., 224

Burley, W., 14

Burnet, J., 96n

Burque, M., 169

Carrière, G., 143n

Cephalus, 4

Chance, R., 115n

Christ, Jesus, 247

Chroust, A.-H., 82, 83n

Cicero, 14, 51, 82

Clark, M., 82

Clinias, 8, 11

Colonna, Egidio, 14

Copleston, F., 102

Commentator, the, see Lombard, Peter

Critias, 9

De George, R. T., 109

Del Vecchio, G., 107-08

Democritus, 13, 33, 68, 71, 79, 102

Denis the Pseudo Areopagite, 232-39

Diogenes Laertius, 14

Dirlmeier, F., 87n

Dru, A., 299

Duméry, H., 254, 308

Dunham, B., 230

Duns Scotus, John, see Scotus